FIGHTING FOR PEACE
BOSNIA 1994

General Sir Michael Rose

FIGHTING FOR PEACE
BOSNIA 1994

THE HARVILL PRESS
LONDON

First published in Great Britain in 1998 by The Harvill Press,
2 Aztec Row
Berners Road
London N1 0PW

www.harvill-press.com

3 5 7 9 8 6 4 2

Copyright © The Rose Partnership 1998

Sir Michael Rose asserts the moral right to be
identified as the author of this work

A CIP catalogue record for this book
is available from the British Library

ISBN 1 86046 512 9

Designed and typeset in Miller at
Libanus Press, Marlborough, Wiltshire

Printed and bound in Great Britain by Butler & Tanner Ltd,
Frome and London

This book is dedicated to the young peacekeepers of UNPROFOR, many of whom did not return home. Although under attack and often accused of being accomplices to genocide, they never lost faith in their mission. Their true thanks can only come from the people of Bosnia who saw at first-hand their heroism and achievement.

When I wanted to be,
Then I was not . . .

INSCRIPTION ON A STECHAK,
A MEDIEVAL BOSNIAN TOMBSTONE

CONTENTS

ACKNOWLEDGEMENTS

In writing this book, I have only used UN documents, publicly available material and my own diaries kept at the time. The views expressed therefore do not in any way reflect British Government policy.

I am grateful particularly to the UN Under Secretary General for Humanitarian Affairs, Sergio Vieira de Mello, for having read the script in its entirety and for the important suggestions that he made. I am also indebted to Simon Shadbolt for having not only read the manuscript but also for his invaluable help in sorting out a mass of papers in the early stages of the book and for his subsequent useful comments. In addition I made much use of notes kept by Nick Costello and Jamie Daniell and others during their time in Bosnia, which happily reminded me of a number of significant details and stories. These were much embellished by George Waters, Jeremy Bagshaw and Goose. I am also grateful to those people who lent me photographs, especially Colour Sergeant Pearce who provided me with some excellent material.

Finally I could not have written the book without the tremendous support of my two sons Edward and James who, turning the tables of yesterday, sustained me through a drawn-out essay crisis. The person, however, to whom I owe the most is my wife Angela, who not only had to cope with a year-long absence while I was in Bosnia, but then had to live with the preoccupations of an author. Her knowledge of the publishing world and meticulous eye for detail proved invaluable.

LIST OF ACRONYMS AND TERMS

APC	Armoured Personnel Carrier
BSA	Bosnian Serb Army
CDS	Chief of Defence Staff
CONTACT GROUP	Representatives appointed by France, Germany, Russia, the United Kingdom and the United States to negotiate with the parties involved in the conflict
HDZ	Croatian Democratic Union
HVO	Bosnian Croat Army
ICRC	International Committee of the Red Cross
JNA	Federal Yugoslav Armed Forces
JC	Joint Commission
JCO	Joint Commission Officer
MOD	Ministry of Defence
NATO	North Atlantic Treaty Organisation
OBSTINA	Local-government district in Bosnia-Hercegovina
PTT	Postes, Télécommunications et Télédiffusion
RS	Bosnian Serb Republic
SA	Surface-to-air missile
SACEUR	Supreme Allied Commander Europe
SDA	Bosnian Muslim Party of Democratic Action
SDS	Serbian Democratic Party
TEZ	Total Exclusion Zone
UN	United Nations
UNHCR	United Nations High Commission for Refugees
UNMO	United Nations Military Observer
UNPROFOR	United Nations Protection Force

LIST OF MAPS

All maps drawn by Reginald Piggott

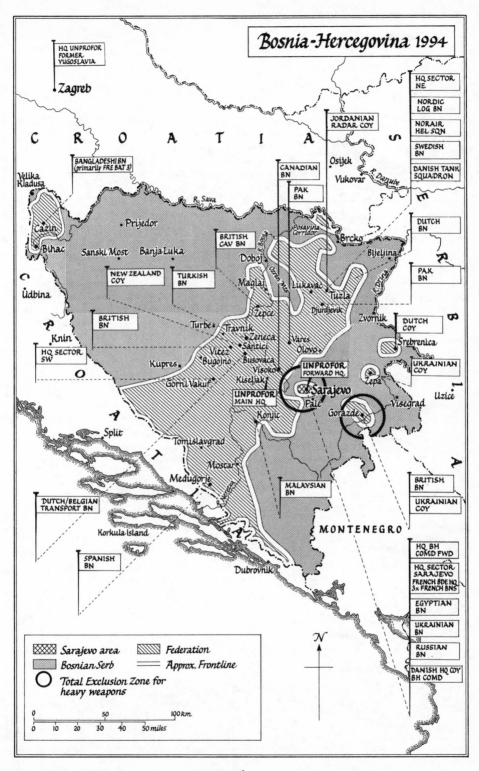

Bosnia-Hercegovina 1994

HQ UNPROFOR
FORMER
YUGOSLAVIA

Zagreb

CROATIA

HQ SECTOR
NE

NORDIC
LOG BN

JORDANIAN
RADAR COY

NORAIR
HEL SQN

SWEDISH
BN

DANISH TANK
SQUADRON

Osijek

Vukovar

R. Danube

BANGLADESHI BN
(primarily FRE BAT 3)

Velika
Kladusa

CANADIAN
BN

PAK
BN

Cazin

Prijedor

DUTCH
BN

Bihac

BRITISH
CAV BN

R. Sava

Posavina
Corridor

Brcko

Bljeljina

Sanski Most

Banja Luka

Doboj

NEW ZEALAND
COY

TURKISH
BN

Maglaj

Lukavac

Tuzla

PAK
BN

Udbina

Djurdjevik

Zvornik

BRITISH
BN

Turbe

Tepce

Vares

Olovo

DUTCH
COY

Srebrenica

Knin

Travnik

Zeneca

Santici

UKRAINIAN
COY

HQ SECTOR
SW

Vitez

Bugojno

Busovaca

Visoko

UNPROFOR
FORWARD HQ

Zepa

Uzice

Kupres

Kiseljak

Sarajevo

Gorni Vakuf

UNPROFOR
MAIN HQ

Pale

Visegrad

Konjic

Gorazde

Split

Tomislavgrad

Mostar

Medugorje

MALAYSIAN
BN

MONTENEGRO

BRITISH
BN

UKRAINIAN
COY

DUTCH/BELGIAN
TRANSPORT BN

Korkula Island

HQ BH
COMD FWD

SPANISH
BN

Dubrovnik

HQ SECTOR
SARAJEVO
FRENCH BDE HQ
3 x FRENCH BNS

EGYPTIAN
BN

UKRAINIAN
BN

RUSSIAN
BN

DANISH HQ COY
BH COMD

N

▨▨▨ Sarajevo area   ▨▨▨ Federation

▨▨▨ Bosnian Serb   ══ Approx. Frontline

◯ Total Exclusion Zone for
heavy weapons

0   50   100 km
0 10 20 30 40 50 miles

xi

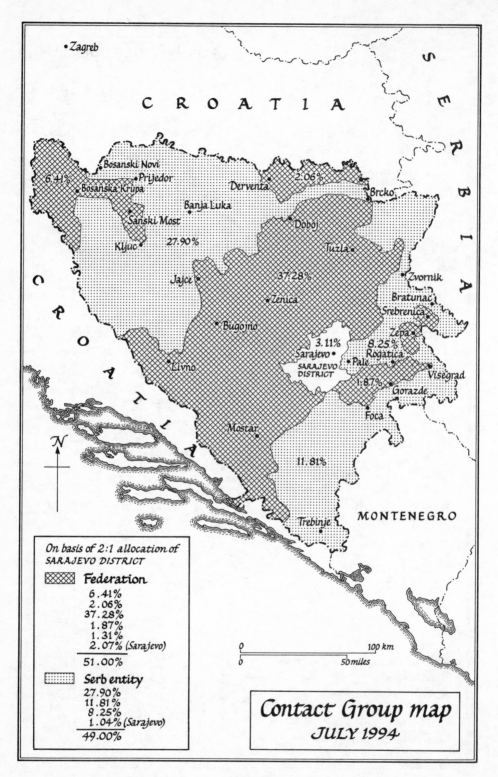

• Zagreb

C R O A T I A

S E R B I A

Bosanski Novi
Prijedor
6.41%
Bosanska Krupa
Derventa
2.06%
Brcko
Banja Luka
Sanski Most
Doboj
Ključ
27.90%
Tuzla
C R O A T I A
Jajce
37.28%
Zvornik
Zenica
Bratunac
Srebrenica
Bugojno
Žepa
3.11%
8.25%
Sarajevo
Rogatica
Livno
SARAJEVO
DISTRICT
Pale
1.87%
Višegrad
Gorazde
Foca
Mostar
11.81%
MONTENEGRO
Trebinje

N

On basis of 2:1 allocation of
SARAJEVO DISTRICT

☒ **Federation**
6.41%
2.06%
37.28%
1.87%
1.31%
2.07% (Sarajevo)
51.00%

Serb entity
27.90%
11.81%
8.25%
1.04% (Sarajevo)
49.00%

0 ——————— 100 km
0 ——————— 50 miles

Contact Group map
JULY 1994

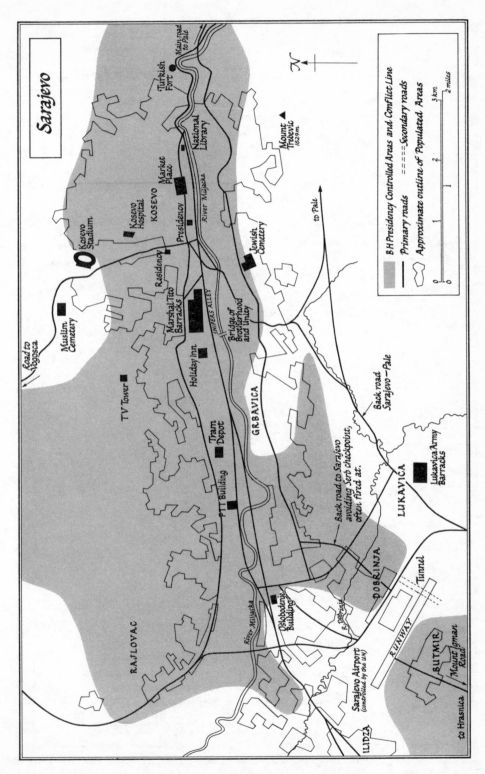

Sarajevo

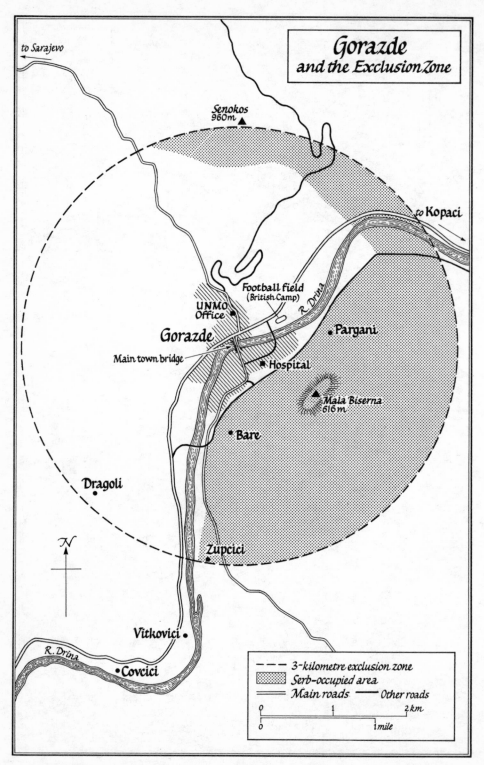

Gorazde
and the Exclusion Zone

to Sarajevo

Senokos
960m ▲

to Kopaci

R. Drina

Football field
(British Camp)

UNMO
Office

Gorazde

Pargani

Main town bridge

Hospital

Mala Biserna
616m ▲

Bare

Dragoli

Zupcici

N

Vitkovici

R. Drina

Covcici

- - - 3-kilometre exclusion zone
▨ Serb-occupied area
═══ Main roads   ━━━ Other roads

0   1   2 km
0   1 mile

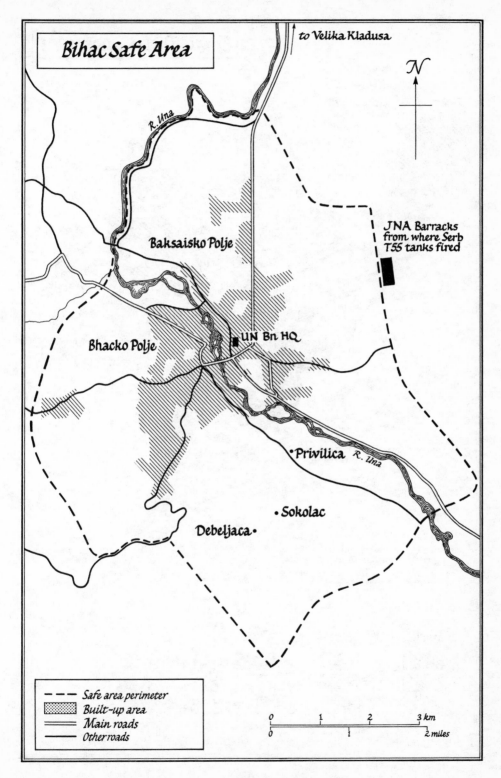

Bihac Safe Area

to Velika Kladusa

N

R. Una

Baksaisko Polje

JNA Barracks
from where Serb
T55 tanks fired

Bhacko Polje

■ UN Bn HQ

• Privilica R. Una

• Sokolac

Debeljaca •

- - - - Safe area perimeter
▨ Built-up area
═══ Main roads
─── Other roads

0   1   2   3 km
0   1   2 miles

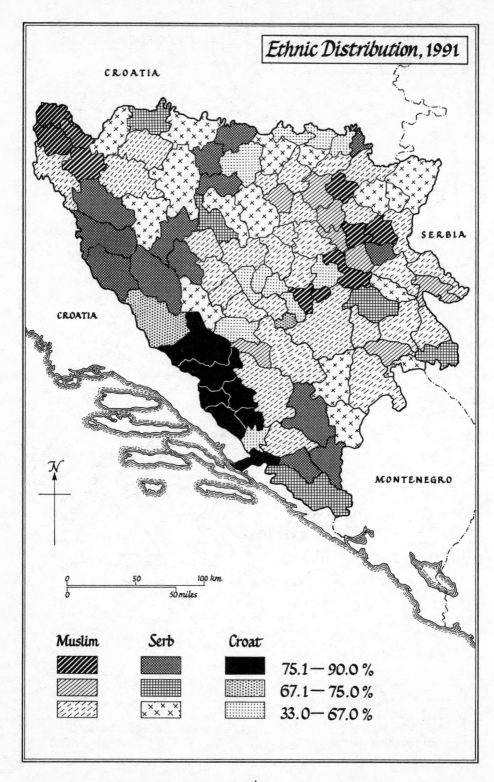

Ethnic Distribution, 1991

CROATIA

CROATIA

SERBIA

MONTENEGRO

N

| 0 | 50 | 100 km |
| 0 | 50 miles | |

Muslim	Serb	Croat	
			75.1 — 90.0 %
			67.1 — 75.0 %
			33.0 — 67.0 %

INTRODUCTION

The true searcher in life knows not the object of the search

WHEN I ARRIVED IN SARAJEVO AT NIGHTFALL ON THE 23 JANUARY 1994, it had been a city under siege for two years and seemed deserted. Amid the rubble of the shattered buildings, its 350,000 inhabitants were living like rats in cellars, only venturing out at night to search for their means of survival. Sarajevo was where the war had started but would not end.

Once a meeting place between East and West where pleasure was its inspiration, and people of different races, cultures and religions had freely mixed together, Sarajevo ("serai" in Persian means "court" or "mansion") had been reduced to a grim symbol of the savagery of man and the fragility of civilisation. Its destruction was a warning to everyone around the world of what happens when mankind does not stand up to tyranny.

In Marshal Tito's[1] time it had been a modern industrial city, an example of what could be achieved under the Yugoslav form of communism, but his policy of creating competing centres of political power was eventually responsible for turning racial and religious differences into divisions, leading to a bloody civil war. Now it was a city of hatred, deprivation and death. Since April 1992, there had been no electricity or running water, no adequate supplies of food or fuel. Each day around 1,200 shells fell on the city and its people also faced the constant threat of being killed or maimed by the seldom seen but ever watchful snipers. Since the start of the war it was estimated by the Bosnian Government that 10,000 people had been killed in Sarajevo, 3,000 of them children.

In winter, the temperature can fall to -27°C, and because the city lies beneath mountains at the end of a deep valley, the frozen air in Sarajevo does not move. Instead it forms a dense fog that stings the nostrils and penetrates the lungs. In 1994 this fog was not caused by cars, as in modern cities elsewhere, because in Sarajevo there were very few cars on the road. It was caused by the many thousands of fires that were lit for warmth and for cooking and by the burning of rubbish and excrement. In times of peace, the people of Sarajevo had been accustomed to taking the chairlift to the top of the neighbouring Trebevic mountain to escape the freezing fog, but for the past two years of the war there had been no prospect of any such relief.

When Rebecca West visited Sarajevo in 1937, she observed that the Miljacka River ran red as it flowed through the city.[2] The night I arrived it lay black and still, as did the city itself. The few flickering lights that could be seen among the wrecked buildings came from the bunkers where soldiers were preparing evening meals, or from the shaded torches of the police checkpoints set up along the road. Sarajevo was a place of total silence, except for the rumble of an exploding shell or the crack of a sniper's bullet. There was no movement, no laughter. Yet, as I came to discover, beneath the rubble and ugliness of war, Sarajevo was fiercely alive. Its people had a tough, passionate and sometimes fatalistic attitude to life. They were determined not to allow the terrible conditions to compromise their humanity or to extinguish their civilisation. They cherished the ideal of a multi-cultural, multi-religious society and wanted one day to return to a world where differences of view would be expressed in the arenas of literature, music or art, not in death and destruction.

Within a week of my arrival, I found myself in a smoke-filled, freezing cellar crammed with people who had the pale complexions and trembling hands of the condemned. Having outlived communism, they had survived by learning that the inner life is the only life. This typical group of Sarajevan intellectuals, led by a man called Adil Kulenovic, had now formed an organisation called Circle 99, in order to keep alive their ideals in the midst of war.

They vehemently rejected the propaganda statements of their own politicians, and the notion of the "victim State" of Bosnia. For them civilisation and humanity were the victims of the war. The war in Bosnia affected the entire world as well as the ordinary people of the nation. It was their children who were forced to fight in the trenches, while the politicians' children remained abroad, studying at foreign universities. For many hours at that first meeting we debated the human condition in times of adversity. They explained how dangerously simple life had become, living in the shadow of death. It absolved a person of all future social responsibility. Without money or work, there was only the need to survive for one more day. A person in these terrible conditions had to struggle with an absurd sense of complicity and guilt, as friends died or were injured. It was important to them that their Bosnian culture was not diminished by their circumstances. We talked of Plato and Hobbes and I tried to tell them what was happening in the world outside. They were engaged in a battle that was being fought not just in the blood-drenched trenches, but also in the minds of people. It was a war about the survival of civilisation and all that was decent in mankind.

It was to be many weeks before I fully understood what they were saying. It happened when I saw a sniper carrying a Simonov rifle leave his position in a ruined block of flats. He was a good-looking boy, blond with blue eyes, in his late teens. But when he looked at me, his eyes were as dead as the small child he had almost certainly killed that day in a sniping attack on a Sarajevo street. It was not my war, but as a human being I was involved. I came to understand that this sniper represented as great a threat to civilisation itself as he did to the citizens of Sarajevo. It took too long for the world outside to understand this simple fact, but at long last peacekeepers did come to the aid of the people of Sarajevo and Bosnia. By late summer of 1995 people were once again able to tend their gardens and orchards in relative peace.

In 1992 the nations of Western Europe became engaged in the Balkans, as they had in the nineteenth century; though this time mindful of the words of Bismarck, that the Balkans "were not worth the bones of a single Pomeranian grenadier". Soldiers came in their thousands wearing the distinctive blue beret and uniform of the United Nations (UN), and they brought with them people from Asia, Latin America, the Antipodes, as well as from the countries of the former Soviet Union. They were not there as imperialists to fight a war, nor to defend a people or their territory. They came as peacekeepers whose purpose was to alleviate the suffering of all the peoples of the Balkans and to try, through peaceful means, to bring about an end to the war. This demanded of them the same fighting qualities that soldiers need in battle: guile, courage, determination and endurance; but, without the clarity of purpose of a war, perhaps peacekeeping demanded more of them than fighting ever did. Peacekeeping was their mandate, and it is on this that they must be judged.

The UN was deployed in the former Yugoslavia because no nation or military alliance was prepared to fight a war to stop aggression in the Balkans or to impose by armed force a just political settlement on the conflict in Bosnia. Even the North Atlantic Treaty Organisation (NATO), which had recently emerged victorious from the cold war and was the only military alliance in the world capable of maintaining peace in the Balkans by force of arms, refused to become engaged in a combat role on the ground. This was partly because the political leaders of NATO feared that such action would bring about renewed confrontation with Russia and partly because they believed it would create schisms within its own ranks. The NATO countries could not afford to fight a war, neither politically nor economically.

America, the militarily dominant partner in NATO, and the most vocal about the plight of Bosnia, also proved to be the most reluctant to deploy its own troops into the middle of the bloody civil war. American congressmen said repeatedly that they did not see why their soldiers should lose their lives helping Europe sweep up the mess in its own backyard.

Bosnians frequently pointed out that an international coalition led by America took military action against Iraq when Kuwait was invaded, whereas the international community did nothing to help Bosnia in the face of a similar aggression. However, the situation in Bosnia was not simply that of one nation invading another. It was a civil war about territory in which the Bosnian Croats and the Bosnian Serbs sought to secede from the State and join with their compatriots in neighbouring Croatia and Serbia.

In 1991, when the conflict in the Balkans began, the post-cold war political situation made military intervention by the West unlikely. The peace dividend had been paid, NATO armies had been reduced in size and substantial portions of national defence budgets had been transferred to health, social welfare and education. No one could turn the clock back and not even Lady Thatcher at her most persuasive could have cajoled the world to rearm and fight a war in the Balkans on behalf of the Bosnian State. Such action was never on the West's political agenda.

More importantly, there was no clear political agreement in the West about the future shape of Yugoslavia. This was unsurprising given the volatility of the region, where national, religious, ethnic and social currents run deep and where the bloody history of the Balkans casts a perpetual shadow over every event and action. Every child is taught stories of the cruel deeds perpetrated against its community throughout the ages and of the heroic resistance which kept their own faith alive in difficult times.

Throughout its history the region has been one of migration and conflict. Although the Slavs, from whom the Croats and Serbs are descended, were thought to have come from the north, Bosnia's cultural inheritance is Near Eastern rather than Western European. For many centuries the region was part of the Ottoman Empire. Indeed, lying as it does between West and East, Bosnia has never flourished as a truly independent State. Rather, it derives its identity from a mix of nationalities and religions. While the Croatian element of the population looked to Rome, the Serbs remained part of the Orthodox tradition emanating from Constantinople. The Muslims of Bosnia were Slavs who had converted to Islam during the 500 years of Turkish occupation.

Although there were substantial concentrations of ethnic populations in certain areas of Bosnia (such as Muslims in Zenica, Croats in Prozor and Serbs in Banja Luka), and nearly all administrative districts or obstinas contained a predominant ethnic group, there were also many isolated Muslim, Croat and Serb communities scattered across the country. This made it impossible to partition Bosnia along religious or ethnic lines.

At the end of the Second World War, Tito had designated Bosnia as one of six republics and two autonomous regions that made up the Communist State of Yugoslavia and for over 40 years he had maintained order in the country by the use of oppressive State machinery and by the careful distribution of power between the Serbs, the Croats and the Muslims. When he died, however, the forces of nationalism that Tito had successfully held at bay were unleashed.

Of course, men like Radovan Karadzic, Slobodan Milosevic and even Franjo Tudjman, by their incitement of sectarian hatred and their use of intimidation and violence, could be held directly responsible for igniting the flames of war. Nevertheless, it is impossible to overestimate the significance of the violent history of the region that led to the emergence of a fanatical nationalism and hatred of other races. At least a million people were killed in Yugoslavia during the Second World War, and no Serb has forgotten that over half of these were Serbs who died at the hands of the Germans and their Croat collaborators, the Ustashi. I once suggested to Gen. Ratko Mladic, the Bosnian Serb Army (BSA) commander, that the solution to Serb fears of Muslim domination of Bosnia lay in the democratic process, when a Christian alliance between the Serbs and the Croats during the 1992 elections would have defeated the Muslims. His face went a mottled colour and he exploded with rage: "You understand nothing

of what the Croats did to the Serbs in the war . . . they will always be our enemies!"
The tragedy of the Balkans is that the cycle of violence goes on repeating itself.

Initially America and Europe had attempted to pursue a policy of trying to hold
Yugoslavia together in some form of pan-Yugoslav confederation. In this the Serbs,
who represented the majority group in Yugoslavia, supported them. The culture of
the Serbs stems from a dangerous mix of raw passion and religious mysticism. They
also hold to the conviction that any land on which Serb blood has been spilled
belongs forever to the Serbs. They see themselves historically as the forward defence
of Western civilisation and Christianity against Islam. The fact that the Serbs have
frequently fought on the side of their Turkish rulers against the Habsburgs over the
centuries does not diminish the fervour of their hatred for Muslims. Tito's death gave
them the opportunity to pursue their ambition to recreate the old fourteenth-century
Serbian empire in which Slovenia, Croatia, Bosnia, Montenegro, Kosovo, Macedonia
and even Albania would become part of Serbia.

In 1991 this grand design had to be radically modified when the European
Community (EC), led by Germany, officially recognised Slovenia and Croatia as independent States. Already attempts by the Serbs to maintain military control of Croatia
had resulted in the destruction of the city of Vukovar and some of the most concen-
trated artillery bombardment experienced in Europe since the battle of the Somme.
Sadly, this turned out to be a mere preamble to the main event in the Balkans: the
civil war in Bosnia.

The State of Bosnia was only recognised by the EC on 6 April 1992, by which time
the Bosnian Serbs were already firing on unarmed crowds in Sarajevo. While the
Serbs had been obliged by force of circumstances to let Slovenia and Croatia go,
they were determined to fight to the death to prevent Bosnia establishing itself as
a Muslim State in their midst. To allow this to happen would be to deny the sacrifices
their people had made over the centuries. By securing the Krajinas (the traditional
Serb areas of Croatia) and by withdrawing the Yugoslav Army (JNA) units into
Bosnia, the Serbs hoped to hold together the major portion of the former republic
of Yugoslavia and turn Bosnia into a client State.

According to the last census in 1991, before the war, the Bosnian population
contained three main religious groups: 44% Muslim, 31% Orthodox Serb and 20%
Catholic Croatian. There was also a community of Sephardic Jews in Sarajevo, who
had been there since the fifteenth century, protected by the Ottomans. They had fled
to Bosnia from Spain during the Inquisition, and the Jewish influence on current
events was to play a significant role in shaping US policy towards Bosnia. The speech
made by Ezer Weizman, the President of Israel, at the opening of the Holocaust
Memorial Museum in Washington in 1993, was to stir the American conscience
and swing the powerful American Jewish lobby into action on behalf of the
Bosnian State.[3] Not only did American Jews foresee another Holocaust taking
place in the country, they also felt a historic sense of gratitude towards the Muslims,
who had sheltered members of their race for 600 years and had allowed their
religion to flourish.

After the December 1990 elections, Bosnia was governed by a coalition representing the three main religious parties, but dominated by a Muslim–Croatian alliance
under a Muslim president, Alija Izetbegovic. In October 1991, the Muslim Party of
Democratic Action (SDA) and the Croatian Democratic Union (HDZ) voted to make
Bosnia a sovereign State, while the Serbian Democratic Party (SDS) wished to
remain part of Yugoslavia. In a chilling speech made after he had lost the vote,
Radovan Karadzic predicted that a civil war in Bosnia was now inevitable.

In the West there was a growing feeling that something should be done to halt the
slide of events towards war, but no clear political or military strategy was developed
to accomplish this end. Europe and America could not turn their backs on Bosnia,
but equally they could not agree a way forward. Although European military intervention on the ground without the involvement of the Americans was considered
impracticable, two opposing strategies emerged from discussions among leaders of
the international community. On the one hand it was passionately argued that the
solution to the civil war in Bosnia lay in an air campaign that would stop the flow
of arms to the Bosnian Serbs from the Yugoslav Army. President Bill Clinton, Lady
Thatcher and the former British Foreign Secretary, Lord Owen – appointed in 1992
to replace Lord Carrington as the European negotiator in the Balkans – were of this
opinion.

It was argued with equal passion, on the other hand, that the response of the international community should be limited to the deployment of a peacekeeping force
and the delivery of humanitarian aid. According to this argument, civil emergencies
– such as the one in Somalia, in which hundreds of thousands of refugees were at risk
– were unlikely to be solved by simple military action at a tactical level.

The use of air power was especially problematical in Bosnia. During the cold war,
Tito had installed a military infrastructure throughout Yugoslavia with many of the
communications buried deep underground and there was a sophisticated air defence
system controlled from Belgrade. Furthermore, every village and town had its own
military organisation, equipped with heavy weapons, communications and logistical
support. Any air interdiction campaign was likely to have a limited effect, as was
proved when NATO finally did launch an air bombardment against Bosnian Serb
positions in 1995, and the military effect of some 3,500 sorties was judged by many
commentators to be negligible.

The parallel was also cited with a similar air campaign mounted by the US Air
Force against Viet Cong positions in Cambodia in 1971. This had begun with limited
tactical aims, but the operation ultimately involved the deployment of so many
American ground forces in Cambodia that the US Administration lost sight of its
original purpose. As a result of this ill-conceived and hugely unpopular operation, US
foreign policy in the Far East collapsed. All this led to the general conclusion in the
West that the maximum that could be done in Bosnia was to alleviate the suffering
of the people and to try to bring about the conditions in which there could be a
peaceful solution.

However, nothing is simple in the Balkans and the way in which the UN deployed a small peacekeeping force in the former Yugoslavia was no exception. Initially the UN designated four "protected areas" along the south and eastern borders of Croatia. These were areas in which Serb communities had settled many centuries before and where they had lived continuously ever since. This limited deployment by the UN had the immediate effect of halting the sectarian fighting between the Croats and Serbs and for the next three years there was relative peace in these border regions. The deployment was supposed to be of short duration, pending the success-ful outcome of political negotiations.

This peacekeeping army was called the United Nations Protection Force (UNPROFOR).[4] In retrospect it proved to be an unfortunate title, in that it created public expectations well beyond the practical capabilities of any peacekeeping mission. Given what was to happen later on in the inappropriately named "safe areas", one of the major lessons that emerges from the UN experience in Bosnia is that language creates its own culture, and amid the propagandist distortions and brutalities of a civil war, it can also make victims of its creators. Even the expression "peacekeeping" can have little meaning when all around the peacekeepers there is slaughter and destruction.

The rhetorical question of the propagandist anxious to conceal his own responsi-bility for the carnage – "Why aren't you keeping the peace when so many innocent lives are being lost?" – can only be answered by a soldier who replies: "Why are we here as peacekeepers when there is no peace to keep?" In the clamour of war, the distinc-tion between political aspirations and military limitations becomes forever buried.

The UN's failure to use appropriate language greatly undermined the credibility of the UNPROFOR mission and put a long-term question mark in many people's minds concerning the UN's ability as a peacekeeper to respond effectively to the chal-lenges of the new world disorder. Nevertheless, the ethnic differences in Bosnia which were to result in a three-sided civil war over territory are mirrored elsewhere in the world and the story of the UN peacekeeping force in Bosnia raises important questions for the future.

Edmund Burke said: "Civil wars strike deepest of all into the manners of the people. They vitiate politics, they corrupt morals; they pervert even the natural taste and relish of equity and justice." To escape the horrors of the numerous civil wars that have broken out in the years following the end of the cold war, millions of people became displaced between 1991 and 1994, 12 million of them moving to Europe. During that period the world also witnessed the greatest movement of populations in the history of mankind, notably in the region of the Great Lakes in Africa. So far the West has seemed incapable of developing any sort of coherent response to this threat of large-scale human disaster. Nor can any nation in the world stand aside and expect that things will be resolved without its involvement. If, in the words of John Donne, "no man is an island", then equally no *nation* can isolate itself from the world's problems. Although the solutions to modern humanitarian disasters are more likely to be found in the traditional activities of peacekeeping – chiefly persuasion, persistence and pressure – in most circumstances armed soldiers, deployed as peacekeepers, will certainly have a role to play.

Peacekeeping, which the experiences of Bosnia and Somalia show to be at the tougher end of a range of military activities, deserves a better hearing than it has hitherto had. The soldier's complaint that he joined an army corps, not a peace corps, is no longer appropriate. Dag Hammarskjold[5] once said, in an earlier, simpler era of peacekeeping: "It is not a job for soldiers, but only soldiers can do it." As we come to the end of the twentieth century, armies everywhere have been obliged to review their defence strategies to be able effectively to respond to the changing nature of conflict.

Even NATO, which was founded as a war-fighting alliance, has come to accept that peacekeeping is likely to be its principal future military activity. Yet as recently as 1991, NATO was still committed in its strategic guidelines to a war-fighting doctrine, which made no mention of peacekeeping. Four years later its troops were deployed beyond the boundaries of its member States in peacekeeping roles. It was Bosnia that forced this radical change in the organisation's thinking.

Since the end of the cold war, the nature of conflict has changed from being predominantly wars between States to civil wars within States. The requirement for peacekeeping missions around the world has also increased, and the means by which these far from straightforward operations could be mounted have been insufficiently developed, both conceptually and materially. Perceptions of failure in Somalia, Rwanda and Bosnia have tarnished the reputation of the UN. Yet if people lose faith in either the concept or the undertaking of peacekeeping operations, then the world will become a more dangerous place than it is at present. It is vital that the ideals enshrined in the 1945 UN Charter in San Francisco are upheld. That charter was fashioned by men and women who had lived through two world wars and were determined to "save succeeding generations from the scourge of war".

Three clear themes emerge from the story of the UN's mission in Bosnia in 1994. The first is the extent to which some people will conspire to undermine a humanitarian or peacekeeping mission, even if that mission is mandated by the supreme intergovernmental peace and security body in the world, the UN. Nor should this be surprising, for the humane act of saving life or alleviating suffering becomes a hostile political or military action when seen through the eyes of those whose strategy it is to achieve their goals through siege and terror. All sides in the conflict are likely to try to gain the moral high ground and to win sympathy for their cause from the international community through diplomacy and propaganda, with the object of enlisting the UN peacekeeping force on their side against the enemy.

A State in danger of collapse, as Bosnia was in 1992, will initially depend on the presence of UN forces for its survival. But eventually its leaders will turn against its saviours as its military strength revives and as the need for humanitarian aid diminishes. By mid-1994 the Bosnian Government had undoubtedly ceased to support the peacekeeping efforts of the UN, believing that a ceasefire might turn into a permanent freezing of the conflict line which would then result in an unfair division of the country. It therefore ordered its army to move to offensive operations to recover territory lost in previous battles with the Serbs, thus bringing it into confrontation with the UN whose job it was to restore peace to the country.

The Bosnian Government had the additional aim of getting the US and NATO committed to the war on the ground. By harnessing the support of many members of the media circus in Sarajevo and by promoting images of war and suffering, the Bosnian Government was able to appeal directly to the emotional "something must be done" attitude of people around the world. It was a politically naïve hope that the US or NATO would come to their rescue, but it was one which increasingly obsessed the political and military leaders of Bosnia. UN peacekeeping efforts to halt the fighting were clearly an obstacle to their endeavours and by 1994 it became obvious to us in Sarajevo that the UN's primary concern to alleviate the suffering of the people was of less consequence to Bosnia's leaders than the achievement of their own political goals.

The second theme that emerged from the war in Bosnia is the significance of the role played by America in the conflict: first, in prolonging the war in pursuit of a "just" solution, and second in bringing the war to an end. Until the autumn of 1994, the US Administration believed that Bosnia should be reconstituted as a fully integrated State inside its original historic boundaries. It was felt that this objective could be achieved within the context of the peacekeeping mission, as long as UNPROFOR could be persuaded to use high levels of military force against the Bosnian Serbs. If the UN was not prepared to do this, then what became known as the "lift and strike" option should be implemented. This option envisaged lifting the 1991 arms embargo imposed on the former Yugoslavia by the UN with the assent of America, and subsequently launching air strikes against the Bosnian Serb Army. The policy had strong support in the US, particularly within the Republican Party, officials in the State Department and sections of the media. These people were determined to see the Serb aggressors punished by military force, though it was always accepted by the US Administration that the UN would have to withdraw its peacekeeping mission before any such action could take place.

In response to this pressure President Clinton developed a new policy which fell short of "lift and strike" and required the UN, while continuing with its peacekeeping mission, to authorise a sufficiently high level of force by NATO for it to be seen to punish the Serbs. The peacekeepers referred to this new policy as "stay and pray"; observing that it was, after all, *their* lives, not American lives, that were put at risk by this policy. It was a significant achievement by the UN in 1994 that this policy was resisted and that the peacekeepers were not recast as combatants in the war, as happened with tragic consequences in Somalia. By the end of 1994, with the presidential elections less than a year away, the US Administration accepted that compromises would have to be made if peace was to return to Bosnia, and its subsequent intervention at the Dayton Peace conference brought this about. More than once this century, Europe has seen that pax Americana is needed to bring conflict to an end.

The third theme is the extent to which the UN during its time in Bosnia, between 1992 and 1995, transformed the traditional concepts of peacekeeping. In its original guise peacekeeping involved the peaceful settlement of disputes under Chapter VI of the UN Charter. In these circumstances there is supposed to be complete consent from the warring parties towards the presence and activities of the peacekeepers. In the absence of such consent in Bosnia, UNPROFOR was required to use a great deal of force, under Chapter VII of the Charter, in pursuit of what was primarily a humanitarian aid mission. However, although UNPROFOR used more force in Bosnia than had hitherto been used on any comparable mission, it never crossed the line into war-fighting and important principles regarding the permissible levels of force in peacekeeping were once again reaffirmed.[6]

The UN can only become effective in its principal role of peacekeeping if there is a will in the international community to make it so. The UN represents the collective political will of all nations, and it is pointless blaming the UN as if it were some autonomous organisation. The UN represents all of us. Its peacekeepers belong to all of us. They are, in the words of Dag Hammarskjold, "The front line of a moral force which extends around the world . . . their successes can have a profound effect for good in building a new world order." This book is dedicated to the peacekeepers of UNPROFOR.

CHAPTER ONE

A Collapsing Mission

No language can describe adequately the condition of that large portion
of the Balkan peninsula – Serbia, Bosnia, Hercegovina and other
provinces – political intrigue, constant rivalries, a total absence of
all public spirit ... hatred of all races, animosities of rival religions
and absence of any controlling power ... Nothing short of an army
of 50,000 of the best troops would produce anything like order in
these parts.

Benjamin Disraeli, addressing the House of Lords, August 1878

I WAS IN MY OFFICE JUST BEFORE CHRISTMAS 1993, REFLECTING ON HOW the UK Field Army was going to cope with yet another reduction in its budget, when Lt-Gen. Willie Rous called me. He was at that time the Military Secretary and a fellow Coldstream Guards officer and he wanted to find out how I would react to my name going forward as the next UN Commander in Bosnia. Lt-Gen. Francis Briquemont, the present Belgian Commander, had unexpectedly resigned and if I took the job, I would leave for Bosnia within a month.

Willie explained that there were other names going forward, but the chances of my getting the job were good. Francis Briquemont had resigned in disgust at the conflicting political instructions he was being given and the post was universally regarded as something of a poisoned chalice. Without hesitation I said that I would accept the job if it were offered to me. I had spent the year as the Deputy Joint Force Commander overseeing the UK contribution to the UN mission in the former Yugoslavia and had visited Bosnia several times. I had also been Commandant at the Staff College in Camberley shortly after the end of the cold war, where we had begun to look in some detail at peacekeeping operations in support of the UN. A year in Bosnia would give me the opportunity to put many of the ideas that had emerged from our discussions into practice. Willie told me that I was to say nothing to anyone, not even to my wife, Angela. Typically, within eight hours she had heard about the possible appointment from a friend.

I knew from my previous visits to Bosnia that if I was appointed to command the UN troops there, my life would change radically. I would cease to live the relatively sane, routine existence of a senior British Army officer. In Bosnia, unlike Great Britain, which had not suffered the ravages of civil war for over 300 years, I would have to survive in a brutal, chaotic environment in which the corrosive effects of continuous war had destroyed all notions of justice and fairness. It was a place where decent human values had ceased to have much meaning and where the only basis for action was political or personal gain. In Bosnia, deceit and treachery had become a way of life.

Willie Rous called back within 48 hours to tell me that my name had gone forward to New York for the routine approval of the Secretary-General, and that I could assume that the job was now mine. I was to hand over command of the UK Field Army to Lt-Gen. Richard Swinburn, GOC Eastern Command, who was about to retire. He had generously agreed to give up all thought of retiring early to Exmoor to farm sheep, but warned me that I had to be back when the lambing season began in 1995.

After Christmas, I spent a busy week visiting the capital cities of the key international players involved in Bosnia. I was anxious that the nations who had contributed troops to the UN mission, as well as the UN in New York, clearly understood and approved of the strategy I was determined to pursue in Bosnia. This strategy was designed to reverse what appeared to be a collapsing mission and to restore the credibility of UNPROFOR. I would do this by concentrating on the three main elements of the mission, which were, in order of priority: the delivery of humanitarian aid, the creation of conditions for a political settlement of the war and the prevention of the conflict from spreading beyond Bosnia. By adopting a more robust approach in our dealings with the local warlords who had so paralysed the mission, and by more closely integrating the activities of the humanitarian agencies involved in Bosnia, I also hoped to improve the flow of aid. Above all, I was determined to confront the negative propaganda surrounding UNPROFOR that was damaging the image of the mission in the eyes of the world.

I was extremely fortunate in being able to select as my Military Assistant someone who had run the Yugoslav operations desk at my HQ for the previous two years. Lt-Col. Simon Shadbolt was a highly intelligent Royal Marine officer who read history at Aberystwyth. Not only did he understand the complexities of Balkan history, he had been one of the staff officers who originally set up the British component of the UN mission in the former Yugoslavia. He had strong ideas about how the UN mission in Bosnia should be restructured and many of these ideas later appeared in the campaign plan that I followed during my time as the Commander of UNPROFOR. For a level-headed Royal Marine, he was surprisingly passionate about the humanitarian goals of the mission and was determined that nothing would prevent the UN from succeeding in its primary role.

We began a round of visits in Paris with the French Chief of Defence Staff, Adm. Jacques Lanxade and his team. The French were the largest contributors to the mission in Bosnia and their support would provide the key to implementing our ideas about developing a new approach.[1] It was fortunate that I was able to conduct the discussions in French, having studied and taught in France before I joined the army. I discovered later that my Francophone attitude succeeded in defusing the considerable suspicions the French were already harbouring about the arrival of a British commander in what up until then had very much been a French-dominated mission. Adm. Lanxade strongly supported our plan, and he was particularly delighted by our intention to be tougher on the warring parties. Subsequently the close working relationship that developed between the British and French, the two most important players on the ground in Bosnia, meant that at least two of the European countries were able to present a united front. This *entente cordiale* turned out to be one of the main planks on which the UN mission in Bosnia depended.

The next day I arrived in Downing Street for an interview with the Prime Minister, John Major, armed with the latest thinking in Paris about what could be done to rescue the mission in Bosnia. We discussed the different courses of action facing Britain's military, which ranged from pulling out the troops to reluctantly becoming involved in a war. John Major mentioned the possibility of a greater use of air power and I suggested to him that, although NATO air power certainly had an important role to play in Bosnia, it could not be applied much above a tactical level without collapsing the entire mission. I made it clear to him that hostile media reports from Sarajevo were one of the main difficulties I wanted to confront. "The problem with the press," he remarked somewhat waspishly, "is that they only write about who is sleeping with whom – and whether they enjoyed it!"

"Fortunately, Prime Minister," I replied, "I don't think we are going to have that problem in Sarajevo."

I left the meeting with a firm impression that John Major believed in the humanitarian role being played by the UN in Bosnia, and that Britain had a special contribution to make. He was not about to pull out the troops. This was a great reassurance to me, and his firmness allowed me to develop many initiatives that would have been impossible had he ever wavered in his intentions. Despite the many pressures he subsequently came under from within his own government and from his allies in 1994, he never altered the peacekeeping basis upon which British troops were deployed.

Next day, Simon and I flew to New York for discussions with the UN and the ambassadors of the different countries involved in Bosnia. It was here that I first met Kofi Annan, who was at that time the head of the UN peacekeeping department, and one of his closest advisers; Shashi Tharoor. The preconceptions I had about the poor quality of UN bureaucrats were instantly dispersed, as I found myself talking to two people with an impressive knowledge of the Balkans. Their grasp of the military technicalities involved in mounting a peacekeeping operation in such difficult circumstances, their ability to overcome the political problems associated with such a large and disparate organisation, and their seemingly inexhaustible energy left me feeling very optimistic. With such capable and open-minded people in support, Simon and I were confident that whatever problems arose in Bosnia, they would always be dealt with in a rational and helpful manner by the UN HQ in New York.

During our meeting, I explained the need for a proper campaign plan and a more coherent approach, and I expressed my firm belief that much more could be achieved by the UN in Bosnia if the political, military and humanitarian aid effort could be better coordinated. I also told them that during my tenure of command in Bosnia, I would never publicly disagree on matters of policy with the UN or criticise them personally. I explained that I came from an army where the military were wholly subordinate to the political body, and that to rehearse any disagreements we might have in front of the media would be inimical to the mission and damage the UN's credibility.

Finally, I told them that I believed a more robust military approach to the peace-keeping mission would be required if it was to survive. I presented them with the outline of a campaign plan that identified the aid delivery programme as the highest priority of the mission, with the creation of conditions necessary for a peaceful resolution of the conflict as a secondary task. We agreed that the latter could only be accomplished in the right political context and that military forces alone could not deliver political solutions.

Sir David Hannay, the UK Permanent Representative to the UN, reminded me of the various hazards and pitfalls awaiting us in Bosnia, not least of which was the media. As silence in the face of the press was not an option, handling the media was going to be an important part of the mission. Images of failure would only under-mine the resolve of the troop-contributing nations to continue with the mission. We also discussed the size of the UN HQ in Bosnia, which had grown to grotesque proportions. It had ceased to resemble a military command cell and looked more like a holiday camp. I suggested to Kofi Annan that we should drastically reduce it in size. For the first time I saw him look uneasy as he explained the political problems that this would cause. Troop-contributing nations had come to regard the seniority and rank of their staff in the HQ as a status symbol, and it was something which also gave their own constituents at home some reassurance about how their peacekeeping troops would be used. This was particularly important after their experiences in Somalia, where the general view was that the US element of the mission had hijacked the command chain, which resulted in the UN taking unnecessary casualties.

Kofi Annan agreed with my analysis, but pointed out that it would be almost impos-sible to reduce the size of the national staffs in the HQ in Kiseljak. This had been tried before, but had failed for the reasons we had just discussed. Simon and I had already decided that we needed no more than 100 people in the forward HQ in Sarajevo, and that the main logistical element should be moved to a place called Split on the Croatian coast, where its administration would be easier. On the way back to England, I told Simon that we should aim to bring about the reduction of the HQ within the first month, when people were still reluctant to oppose us.

Kofi Annan then briefed us on the different positions taken over Bosnia by the various members of the Security Council, who had never spoken with anything like one voice on the subject. On the one hand, America and the Muslim States demanded that the UN mission be used to pursue war-fighting goals, while on the other, Russia and Greece wanted a more conciliatory attitude towards the Serbs. In the middle, trying to balance the debate, stood Britain and France, who had the largest number of troops on the ground. The position of Germany was somewhere between France and

America, but their influence was limited by their wartime history in Yugoslavia.

I soon realised the political complexities surrounding Bosnia, and saw the difficulties facing all those who had to live in the Byzantine world of the UN. But I also understood that I could not hope to succeed as mission commander if I allowed these conflicting factors to divert me from my primary task. UNPROFOR's humanitarian role was a simple one and could be understood by the whole world. I believed that if we succeeded in this, then no one could criticise the mission. This turned out to be a hopelessly naïve view, as I soon discovered. In a civil war situation, humanitarian aid becomes a strategic factor that the warring parties seek to exploit to their own advantage. For them, there is no such thing as neutrality or an impartial peacekeeper.

Following the meetings with the UN officials, Sir David Hannay gave a luncheon for us in his elegant house overlooking the East River, at which all the main players involved in Bosnia were present. Although, as British Ambassador to the UN, he was representing a country no longer in the first division, he possessed all the necessary wit and experience to keep Britain at the centre of the international decision-making process. On one occasion, when debating Bosnia in the Security Council, Madeleine Albright had quoted Karl von Clausewitz's remark that, "after all, war is merely an extension of politics by other means".

"Yes, Madeleine," David replied, "that is exactly what Clausewitz said. But he was a German, and the Germans listened to him. Look what happened to them, twice."

Towards the end of lunch, he asked me to describe my campaign plan for Bosnia, which I did, finishing by asking everyone present for their support for the new strategy I had outlined. Kofi Annan responded with a strong statement committing the UN to supporting my ideas. This left little room for debate among the others, so Madeleine Albright asked me what value I placed on air strikes. I explained that there was no case for mounting a strategic air campaign in Bosnia similar to the one in the Gulf War. The circumstances were entirely different. However, I had no problem with the use of close air support in self-defence or to support the mandate. Nevertheless, any use of force had to be proportionate, timely and sufficiently precise. For example, air power alone could not be used in Bosnia to defend Srebrenica or to open Tuzla airport.

Madeleine Albright listened intently to everything I said, then warned me not to be too critical of the Security Council mandates. I assured her that I would not be. Everyone in New York seemed to be referring to Gen. Jean Cot, the UN Force Commander in Zagreb, and Briquemont, who had both publicly fallen out with the UN, and this seemed to have become something of an obsession with them.

Although there appeared to be common ground between the ambassadors, I realised that it wouldn't be long before the different sides parted company and knives were drawn once again. I hoped I would survive in this dangerous world. I had learned from Lt-Gen. Tim Creasy, for whom I had worked in Northern Ireland, how important it was both to operate from a firm political base and to keep the politicians behind what you were trying to do. It had been difficult enough to achieve this in one country over the issue of Northern Ireland, but with 185 nations represented by the UN, it would be almost impossible.

I spent the fourth day of my final week before going to Bosnia in the Ministry of Defence in London, which I remember more for the general messages of goodwill than for any specific instructions or advice, let alone intelligence, about the warring parties. However, the Chief of General Staff, Gen. Sir Peter Inge, who later became Field Marshal Lord Inge, did sit me down in a corner of his office and with an air of utmost gravity, told me that I was about to become a player on the world stage. It didn't seem quite the right moment to ask whether he thought the play in which I was about to appear was a tragedy or a comedy.

Sitting, 24 hours later, in the cargo hold of a giant Ilyushin 76 UN plane flying from Zagreb to Sarajevo, I reflected on the answer to this question myself. The scene was not a happy one. The UN mission in Bosnia was in immediate danger of collapse, with the British Foreign Secretary, Douglas Hurd, and ministers of other troop-contributing nations, threatening to pull out their forces in the Spring. Using more cautious language, the Secretary-General of the UN had asked for "a thorough assessment of the entire UN operation in the Balkans". A public row had broken out between the delightfully Napoleonic Gen. Cot and the Secretary-General in New York. This quarrel resulted in Cot being relieved of his command, although he was to remain in the former Yugoslavia until March.

My predecessor, Gen. Briquemont, had resigned after only six months in the post because he thought there was a "fantastic" gap between what he was being asked to do in the constant UN Security Council resolutions and the support he was getting politically and materially. He also stated, in a long article in *Le Point*, that he could no longer withstand the psychological pressures of the job.[2] The Bosnian Government had just declared it was ready to move to an all-out offensive, and, in response, the Bosnian Serbs had mobilised their entire population for war. At the same time the UN High Commissioner for Refugees, Sadako Ogata, had reported that the quantity of aid being delivered had fallen to a dangerously low level because of renewed outbreaks of fighting and the continual hijacking of aid convoys. The US–British relationship was under severe strain as a result of the radically opposed policies being pursued over Bosnia, and the cooling of relations between the US and Russia risked bringing about a return of the cold war. NATO was concerned about its credibility, and serious differences were emerging within the organisation about its future role now that the cold war had ended.

Meanwhile, in Bosnia, six small children had been killed by a mortar bomb that weekend as they tobogganed down a slope on the outskirts of Sarajevo, and images of their torn and bloody bodies dominated the newspapers and my thoughts. The *Guardian* reported that morale in UNPROFOR was at an all-time low, and that senior officers were openly contemptuous of their political superiors. The *Spectator*, which had taken to echoing much of the Bosnian Government's propaganda, accused the UN of being "a hired gaoler – a Balkan Group Four Security – on the Serbs' behalf".[3]

No wonder Gen. Philippe Morrillon, who had preceded Briquemont as UNPRO-FOR Commander in Bosnia, had called the operation "mission impossible". Looking on the bright side, it was clear that such a disastrous situation could only get better. If the mission in Bosnia did prove impossible, then the UN would have probably given peacekeeping its last shot, and this would surely make the world a more dangerous place; for the conflict in Bosnia was the stuff from which world wars are made. It was to be my job to prevent the mission from collapsing.

On arrival at Sarajevo airport, a brief and rather French change-of-command ceremony took place, led by Gen. Cot accompanied by a great deal of saluting of national flags, handshaking and standing to attention. It was attended by the Sarajevo press corps, and this gave me my first taste of their hostility towards the UN. The meeting was held in a large hall, which in happier times had been a terminal lounge for travellers and tourists. The windows were now boarded up and it was extremely cold. At the end of the room were a few trestle tables covered in blankets and on the walls behind were draped the flags of the UN and those of nations who had deployed troops in Bosnia. In front of the tables a struggling mass of journalists and television cameramen pushed and shoved each other to obtain the best view of the proceedings. My bodyguard, known to everyone as "Goose", glared at them in disbelief and muttered, "What they need is a good drill sergeant."

Ignoring the noise and confusion, Gen. Cot began the ceremony by delivering a powerful speech in which he thanked Lt-Gen. Briquemont for advancing the cause of peace in Bosnia under such difficult circumstances. He then courageously launched into a strong attack against the iniquity of those in authority in Bosnia who were prepared to use the suffering of civilian populations for their own political ends and who did not care if their own people lived or died. At the end, he briefly wished me good fortune and invited the press to ask questions. No quarter was given or allowance made for the fact that I had only just arrived in Bosnia.

Firstly I was asked whether I had come to Sarajevo to preside over the withdrawal of the UN from Bosnia. I replied that I had not. I was then asked whether I thought that the UN had enough resources to fulfil the tasks given to me. I replied that, although no military commander would ever admit to having enough resources, I had to be realistic and accept that the UN probably did have sufficient resources to accomplish its mission, if it set about things properly. This diplomatic reply provoked howls of derision from the assembled press. I had just fallen headlong into the first trap they had set for me.

"In which case," a reporter asked, scenting an early kill, "are you saying that Gen. Briquemont was totally wrong when he repeatedly claimed throughout his tour that his resources were inadequate?" I replied, rather lamely, that the amount of resources needed would clearly depend on the level of hostilities, and that "if there was no war, then we'd have adequate resources." The questions rapidly followed each other as if the journalists were not the slightest bit interested in the replies, but only in catching me out. Once or twice I glanced at Francis Briquemont, who responded with a sympathetic look. Just before Christmas I had spent a night with him in the Residency in Sarajevo, when for many hours he told me of the difficulties he faced and his frustrations with the UN. We had worked together on a NATO exercise and

I regarded him as a good friend. At the end of the conference as we walked over to the aircraft waiting on the apron to fly him out of the country, I felt sad for him. He had worked enormously hard and displayed great courage as the Commander of UNPROFOR, yet he was leaving the mission with the bitter taste of failure in his mouth. I wondered how I would feel when I finally left Bosnia.

As I drove for the first time from the airport to Sarajevo, we swept through the main Serb roadblock, Sierra Four, without stopping. A year before, a Bosnian Government minister had been killed there, sitting in the back of a French armoured personnel carrier (APC). Along the way we passed wrecked tanks and shattered buildings. It seemed strange to see the remains of battle on the streets of a modern city, but over the next 12 months these monuments to the brutality of mankind were to become as familiar to me as Stonehenge, which I had daily passed on my way to work in England.

As we crossed the conflict line on to the Bosnian side a detachment of 120mm mortars opened fire close by the road to our left. Bosnian forces were shelling Serb positions on the hills above the city. I asked rather nervously what was happening and Viktor Andreev, the Russian UN civil adviser in Sarajevo, who had come to meet me and who was to become my inseparable friend and colleague, told me there was nothing to worry about. There was no such thing in the eyes of the Bosnian Government, he explained, as a purely military action. There was only political action. They always greeted new arrivals to Sarajevo in this way, and the Serbs always responded in kind with artillery fire on the city. Visitors were thus given a practical demonstration of the aggression being committed against the State of Bosnia. In this way, the Bosnian Government hoped to persuade the West to become involved in the war on their side. When I asked about the civilian casualties that this tactic resulted in, Viktor merely shrugged and replied that civilians mattered less to the Bosnian Government than images of suffering and war.

In New York, I had mentioned this tactic of the Bosnian Government to Madeleine Albright. She confirmed that the US Administration knew what was happening but could do little about it. Now the quiet, civilised apartment overlooking the East River where we had discussed Bosnia seemed very far from the shattered city and the noisy bombardment I was witnessing. Here, humanity and decency had been banished to another world in which the ends always justified the means. Obviously my first task would be to tell President Izetbegovic that this grim strategy of inflicting such horrors on his own people would never succeed and that I would do all in my power to prevent the UN from becoming engaged in a war in Bosnia as a combatant.

The UN HQ was located in a large rambling building in the centre of Sarajevo known as the Residency. It had been built in the distinctive style of the Austro-Hungarian Empire, and, in Tito's time, had been the Delegates Club, where senior officials of the Yugoslav Communist Party came each day for lunch. As a result the building had been extensively bugged by Tito's secret police, who wished to be kept informed of any indiscretions or infidelities. The Bosnian Government security service also wished to keep track of the deliberations of the UN, and I had been warned that they were still bugging the building. The Residency was set in its own grounds beside the US Embassy, and it looked to me, as we drove through the entrance past the Egyptian guards, rather like an Austrian ski chalet. It was to be my home for the year.

It was a mighty relief to be met at the door by the smiling faces of my own team from Britain, who had come out a few days earlier in order to set things up. They had already completely reorganised the layout in the Residency, increasing the office space at the expense of accommodation. UN officers were no longer allowed their own single rooms and offices. Capt. George Waters, my aide-de-camp, had forced them to share rooms. As the British officers were sleeping at least three to a room, it was difficult for the officers of other nations to complain. When a Spanish full colonel protested about sharing a room with someone of a lower rank, we instantly posted him to an outlying HQ in the middle of the fighting near Gornji Vakuf. We had no more complaints.

While the ground floor contained the kitchens and dining rooms, the first floor was given over to offices and a large briefing room. Viktor and I lived in our own rooms on this floor, which we shared with the Royal Signals communications team who lived and worked in what had once been a ballroom. In the far corner of the room they had built a small wooden hut in which the UK cipher machine was housed. Apart from the authorised signallers, only Maj. Willy Levak was allowed inside. After a particularly heavy night, he would disappear into the hut for hours to sleep off the effects. Above, in the old servants quarters, lived the UK officers. The UN HQ had also expanded into an annexe beside the Residency that they shared with the Bosnian Army intelligence organisation. While this arrangement eased the pressure on space, it also made the job of eavesdropping on the UN much easier.

Most of the local staff of the Residency had been working in the building since it had been the Delegates Club. They remained on the payroll of the Bosnian Government but, as they were paid only 2 DM a month, the UN supplemented their rations. We suspected that they belonged to the Bosnian intelligence services, so we were careful not to say too much in front of them, unless, of course, we wanted something passed on to the Bosnians. Inside the Residency the walls were still hung with old Communist-era paintings and drawings designed to reflect the culture and history of Bosnia. I developed a great affection for my Sarajevan home and was sad to hear that, after the war, it had been taken over as an annexe to the US Embassy.

The Residency was the location of a small forward element of the UNPROFOR HQ, while the main HQ was still situated in the small town of Kiseljak about 20 miles away on the other side of the conflict line. It was from here that the UN Chief of Staff ran all UN operations in Bosnia, leaving the UN Commander in Sarajevo to conduct negotiations at the strategic level with the warring parties. Because communications between the two sites were so bad, I discovered that, for much of the time, the UN Commander and his Chief of Staff were out of touch with each other. People seemed to get on with what they thought was best at the time, and there appeared to be little central coordination or direction of the many activities and units that comprise a peacekeeping operation.

In the Residency, next door to my own small office, was a large room that rapidly became the nerve centre of my command organisation in Bosnia. It was here that the small team I had brought with me from England worked. It was headed by Lt-Col. Simon Shadbolt, my Military Assistant, who ran the office and who, among the British elements, probably wielded more influence than anyone else on UN strategy in Bosnia. Beside him sat Capt. George Waters, who had the impossible task of running my ever-changing daily programme. He was also responsible for the domestic arrangements in the Residency, which had been left in a chaotic state when the Belgians left. Across the room Maj. Willy Levak, my intelligence officer, had a desk, though he spent most of his time out in the field or sitting in the dark cubby hole in the UK communications centre across the passage, deciphering classified telegrams. For this reason, visitors to the HQ usually established themselves at Willy's desk. Capt. Nick Costello, my liaison officer and interpreter, had a desk by the door, from which he was able to keep in touch with what was going on. Finally, Viktor Andreev's civil affairs officer also had a desk in the office. This ensured that Viktor and I were never out of step with each other.

Over the months, the outer office of the Residency developed the atmosphere of a university common room where new ideas were debated. In a radical change of policy, we allowed journalists into the Residency and outer office, where we briefed them on what was happening and repeatedly argued the logic of what the UN was attempting to do in Bosnia. We often drew on their knowledge and experience, as many of them had been in Bosnia since the outbreak of war and had a greater understanding of the causes of the conflict. By giving them access to UN communications and allowing them to talk directly to those involved in running operations, we were able to correct much of the hostile propaganda that surrounded the UN mission. On one occasion, Jim Muir, foreign correspondent for the *Daily Telegraph*, wandered into the outer office while I was talking to the Commander of the UN detachment in Bihac, which was under severe Serb attack at the time. When Jim asked me what he was saying, I simply handed the telephone over to him and replied, "Ask him yourself." His report the next day was a great deal more balanced than those in any other newspapers covering the crisis. By the end of the year, a number of journalists whose judgements we respected were almost a part of the decision-making process.

Although there were considerable risks in throwing open the doors to the press in this way, the UN undoubtedly benefited from its change of policy. By the end of 1994, the international community had come to better appreciate the dangers of constantly undermining the UN mission in Bosnia.

In addition to Simon Shadbolt, the other members of the UK team were also experienced. Indeed, one of the greatest advantages that I had over Francis Briquemont was that the UK team supporting me in Bosnia had experience of peacekeeping operations elsewhere in the world, and most of them had a detailed knowledge of the UN's mission in Bosnia. Britain had contributed troops at the start of the mission and since then throughout the British Army regular briefings had taken place, bringing people up to date on events. Early on, a number of journalists commented on the fact that the new British command component in Sarajevo had hit the ground running.

Capt. George Waters was the son of the Deputy SACEUR. This allowed him to telephone his father in moments of crisis and explain to him exactly what was happening on the ground in Bosnia, a line of communication to the top that was to be extremely useful in the coming months. Throughout his childhood he had become used to wielding authority and expected high standards of performance from everyone. He was appalled by the squalid living conditions of the Residency and had ruthlessly reorganised the entire establishment. As a symbol of his refusal to let civilised standards slip, he changed his socks every day and went for a run, ignoring the shells and the snipers who made life so difficult for everyone in Sarajevo.

His finest moment came when, at very short notice, he had to rearrange the entire programme of a visit to Sarajevo by Madeleine Albright and Gen. John Shalikashvili, the US Chairman of the Joint Chiefs of Staff. The officials of the US State Department who had flown in ahead of the visitors to make the necessary arrangements had no previous experience of organising a visit to Sarajevo, and it became clear that the programme they had agreed with the Bosnian Government was unachievable. There was insufficient transport, clearances to cross the conflict line had not been properly obtained, and inadequate time had been allowed for each event on the programme. I was at the airport to greet the visitors. Watching the growing discomfiture of the US embassy officials who were unsuccessfully trying to sort out the muddle, I decided to bundle Madeleine Albright and Gen. Shalikashvili into my Range Rover and told George to rearrange the programme while I briefed them in my office in the Residency. This he duly did, brushing aside the protests of the Bosnians and Americans. None of this escaped the notice of the two visitors and at the end of the day, as she departed, Madeleine Albright said to George, "Thank God for the Brits."

Capt. Nick Costello was the third member of our team. A British Army officer, his family were Krajina Serbs from Knin. He had previously served in Bosnia as liaison officer to Gen. Morillon, who had rightly put him up for a gallantry award after they halted the Bosnian Serb attack on Srebrenica in 1993. When the Muslim defences had collapsed, leaving the way open for Serb tanks, Nick and the General placed themselves on the road between the firing lines and remained there until Gen. Mladic arrived and agreed to cease the attack in return for a demilitarisation of the enclave. As a result of this and other incidents, Nick was well known to the leaders of all the factions in Bosnia. An extremely tough-minded officer, he was a valuable calming influence during some heated moments with the Serbs.

Goose was my driver and bodyguard for the duration of my stay in Bosnia. Built like an ox, he was a member of the Parachute Regiment and combined shrewd judgement with charm and humour. He had no thought for his own safety, but once admitted to my wife Angela that the thing he feared most was meeting her as he came down the steps of an RAF aircraft carrying my coffin. He met any obstacle or threat to life with extreme force. Soon after we arrived in Sarajevo, he saw a sniper shoot a woman on the pavement near the Holiday Inn. The sniper was foolish enough to remain exposed for a moment in a window, laughing at what he had done. Goose slammed on the brakes, grabbed his G3 rifle and shot him. He then took the woman, who survived, to hospital.

On another occasion, sitting in a bar in Pale with one of Gen. Mladic's body-guards, a Serb soldier challenged Goose to an arm-wrestling contest. Mladic's bodyguard whispered to him that he should let the Serb soldier win, as the day before this particular soldier had killed someone who had beaten him at arm-wrestling. Just as he was about to let the man win, Goose suddenly changed his mind and slammed the man's arm down on the table. The angry soldier abruptly left the room and returned soon after with his rifle. He walked to the table where Goose was still sitting. Suddenly he put down his rifle and shook Goose by the hand. When I asked Goose what he would have done if the soldier had tried to shoot him, he replied, "Don't worry, I had him covered with my pistol under the table from the moment he entered the room."

Goose had a warm smile that would slowly spread across his face as he realised the ridiculous nature of some event and he rarely became angry. When he did, he could be extremely menacing. He was adept, as only British soldiers can be, at defusing a situation with some ironic comment. He regarded the situation in Bosnia as something of an incomprehensible joke. During the year that I was there he never once left my side when I was out of the Residency.

Colour Sgt "Percy" Pearce of the Coldstream Guards, who had been with me for many years, was an urbane, cool Cornishman. By the time I had arrived in Sarajevo he had already managed to transform the chaos left by the departing Belgians into a semblance of order. He had mustered the staff of the Residency and explained to them that, even though they were paid by the Bosnian Government, he was their boss, and they were going to find things different and better now that the British had taken over. Things were going to be done the Coldstream way. Accounts would be properly run, the pilfering of food would stop, and rats and rubbish would no longer be permitted on the premises. He established a fair system of duty rosters and rewards. By the end of his time in Bosnia, the morale of the staff had risen greatly and the Residency was run like St James's Palace.

Colour Sgt Pearce was also a brilliant photographer, but not necessarily familiar with the dangers of war, and we often had to pull him out of the line of sniper fire when he was trying to take the perfect photograph. He was helped in the kitchens by Cpl Bennison who belonged to the Army Catering Corps. By the time the main UN HQ had completed its move from Kiseljak, Cpl Bennison was responsible for feeding more than 100 people a day. Food was often short in the Residency because of the Serb blockade of Sarajevo and the Residency was frequently without electricity or water. However, like all British soldiers, he was adept at improvisation and, by exchanging UN dried emergency rations for eggs and other fresh supplies available throughout the war in Sarajevo, he made certain the UN staff never starved. His crowning moment came when, in the middle of a long period without a resupply of fresh rations, he was able to obtain lobsters from the Canadians in exchange for British Army tinned sausages.

By the end of my first week in Bosnia it was plain to me that, in the absence of a forward strategy and without central direction, the UN peacekeeping effort had become unstructured and fragmented and that the UN command organisation itself was unwieldy.

The single HQ in Kiseljak directly commanded all units and controlled all operations taking place in Bosnia, including all military and aid convoys. There was no intermediate or brigade level of command, except in Sarajevo where the French had unilaterally established their own sector HQ. As a result, the UN staff seemed to work long hours and had become bogged down in a web of interrelated negotiations with the three main warring parties. The inability of the HQ to take rapid and relevant decisions in response to a fast-changing situation was undoubtedly beginning to undermine their morale and credibility of the entire UN mission. The Kiseljak HQ was comfortably established in a ski hotel in the Laskva Valley built in 1984 for the winter Olympics and was located well away from the nearest fighting.

There was centrally-heated accommodation for the 500 people living in the HQ, and a constant supply of hot water. The UN bar in the hotel was always full. The atmosphere in the HQ was inward-looking and each department seemed to spend most of its time trying to find out what the other UN departments were doing.

Every troop-contributing nation had its own national command structure within the main UN staff, and each nation had its own political agenda as well as a chief of contingent who held the national red card. This meant that if I gave an order and the chief of one of the nations considered it to be wrong, he could block it using his red card. The first time this happened, I was told by a Spanish general that I could not reassign one of his officers for "national reasons". As I had spent some time consulting with him on the matter, I replied that if he used the national red card on this occasion, I would send him off the pitch as well. This outburst caused him to shut himself in his office. After three days he emerged to announce that Madrid had given him authority to agree to the reassignment. Every attempt to reduce the size of the HQ had previously been thwarted by these national representatives. It seemed to me to be a tragedy that the efforts of so many committed, hard-working people in the UN were being frustrated by bureaucracy.

I liked the Chief of Staff of the HQ, a British officer whom I had worked with in Northern Ireland. I felt able to talk to him in a straightforward manner, so, at our first meeting, I confided to him my view that the mission was failing because of the lack of strategic vision and direction. Nor would it ever succeed with its present unwieldy command structure. A radical reorganisation of the UN force was required if we were to succeed in our peacekeeping endeavour. I explained that I was also going to order the unit commanders to adopt a more robust approach to peacekeeping. They were no longer to involve themselves in deals or trade-offs with the local warlords. Complete freedom of movement for the UN in Bosnia had been reaffirmed at a recent meeting of all the leaders of the warring parties in Geneva, and I intended that UNPROFOR should demand compliance with this agreement.

I asked the Chief of Staff to assemble the commanders of all military units in Bosnia in the HQ on the following Saturday, so that I could issue a new set of mission orders that reflected my different approach. I also suggested that he invite the heads of all the aid agencies to the meeting, in order that they could be involved in the new planning. I finally gave him a copy of the campaign plan produced by the Staff College at Camberley so that he could prepare a set of written orders based upon it.

The Chief of Staff looked horrified at my suggestions. He believed that any attempt to adopt a more robust approach to peacekeeping would upset the delicate relationships that existed between the UN and the warring parties. He also strongly advised me against issuing orders to the UN unit commanders, saying that it would be better to use a process of consultation and negotiation in getting them to accept my new strategy. He thought it was impossible to change the culture and the structure of the UN in the way I intended. When I asked him to give me a critical path analysis of the linkages and deals that he felt needed to be followed if the mission was to progress, he handed me a diagram that resembled a tangled ball of wool.

He was a deeply caring, highly intelligent person, but it seemed to me he had become a prisoner of the situation in Bosnia. I also suspected that he viewed my analysis of the failings of the UN as a personal attack against himself. Francis Briquemont had warned me that the Chief of Staff had recently written an unusually critical letter about Gen. Mladic that had fallen into the hands of the Bosnian Serbs. He was now *persona non grata* to them. This made it difficult for him to fulfil his role and Francis had suggested that I should sack him. However he was due to be replaced in the near future by a tough-minded Dutch brigadier called van Baal and I determined to get on with my existing Chief of Staff until his departure. He was an intensely loyal person and, although he disagreed with my new policies, he worked hard during his last few weeks to put them into practice.

My first meeting with the Bosnian Government took place shortly after my arrival in Sarajevo and showed me how difficult it was going to be for me to keep a sense of direction and proportion during the year to come. I had decided to walk with Sergio Vieira de Mello, the UN Head of Civil Affairs, from the Residency to the old Austro-Hungarian building that had originally served as the city hall. It was now the Presidency, the seat of the new Bosnian Government. It was a fine cold day, with a clear blue sky contrasting brilliantly with the snow lying on the hills above Sarajevo. Sergio, whom I came to admire above anyone else I worked with in Bosnia, was the son of a Brazilian diplomat. He was immensely good-looking, spoke fluent English and French as well as his own native Portuguese, and had an old-world courtesy that concealed a brilliant mind. He was as at home in the grand palaces of heads of states as he was in the squalid refugee camps in Africa. On loan to UNPROFOR from the UNHCR HQ in Geneva, he had previously worked in Cambodia with Yasushi Akashi, the Secretary-General's Special Representative in Yugoslavia, and was probably the only person Akashi completely trusted. Sergio had great courage and was to be a key player in 1994 in the search for peace in Bosnia.

On the way to the Presidency, we stopped and talked to people who seemed surprised to see us walking, like them, in the streets. They were accustomed to seeing UN peacekeepers driving by in armoured cars at high speed. One man asked me whether the UN would ever bring peace to Sarajevo.

"Only the people of Bosnia can do that," I replied. "If you want to stop this senseless killing, then it will stop. You must tell your political leaders this, and so will we."

I never ceased to be astonished by their fatalistic acceptance of the war, which, they were forever telling me, was not their war: it was their bosses' war. When I asked them why they didn't exercise their democratic right and change their government, they merely shrugged their shoulders. They had existed under a repressive regime for too long to change their ways.

They seemed pleased to talk to me, however, as they never saw their own political leaders on the streets. I determined to spend as much time as possible walking about the city like an ordinary citizen, which would allow me to identify as closely as possible with the people of the city. It would also prevent me suffering a siege mentality which I had already observed was the fate of some peacekeepers.

Goose went ahead of us, glaring at the Serb trenches in the hills above when we passed signs that read "Pazi snipr", which Nick Costello told him meant "Danger, snipers". On one occasion Nick and Simon tried to hurry me past a pleasant-looking street vendor with whom I had stopped to talk, but only because they had realised he was selling pornographic literature. Happily, Jeremy Bowen, a BBC reporter who had attached himself to us, could not read Serbo-Croat either. Apparently, when Tito was sharing out State undertakings around the six republics of Yugoslavia, Sarajevo was allocated a car manufacturing plant – and pornography.

At the Presidency, our first meeting was with the Vice-President, Ejup Ganic. We met rather formally in an elegant room decorated with French Empire-style furniture and chandeliers, but also with modern paintings of Sarajevan scenes. The meeting was accompanied by a concerto of heavy explosions as Serb artillery shelled the city. Despite the high windows, little light penetrated the building and because there was no electricity, the room where we met was dark and gloomy and the temperature well below freezing. Nobody removed their coats or hats. Waiters in white gloves carrying silver trays served orange juice and biscuits taken from UN aid supplies. From time to time the building shook as a shell landed nearby and a shower of light dust fell from the ceiling. Everyone tried not to notice, but when I looked at Sergio, although he was desperately trying to maintain an air of gravitas, I could see he was struggling hard not to giggle. The occasion was taking on the appearance of a mad hatter's tea party.

Ejup Ganic explained that the Serbs greeted first-time visitors to the Presidency with an artillery bombardment in order to demonstrate that they controlled the city of Sarajevo. A large, shambling man, Ganic spoke English with an American accent and adopted an earnest, evangelistic manner similar to religious broadcasters in the US, where he had spent many years. He was always surrounded by a group of depressed-looking officials who hung on his every word and smiled at every joke, while their eyes flickered nervously about the room.

Ruthless, without once demonstrating to me during my time in Bosnia a shred of human decency, Ganic seem to use other people to advance his own wealth and power. He had been the person in charge of the Bosnian Government during the massacre of Serb officers who were leaving Sarajevo under UN safe passage. A Sanjak Muslim, he had abandoned his name and birthright early on and thrown in his lot with Tito, who had sent him to America to study at the Massachusetts Institute of Technology in Boston. On his return, he entered politics, initially as the Yugoslav representative in the Bosnian Parliament, but before long he had once again switched allegiance and ended up heading an extreme political element within the ruling Muslim Party for Democratic Action (SDA). His oily charm and good English endeared him to the international media and as a result he acted as thechief propagandist and spokesman for the Bosnian Government. He was also in charge of military operations.

This arrangement enabled President Izetbegovic to distance himself from some of the more unacceptable things that happened under his regime. As the person in charge of the Bosnian Army, Ganic was responsible for implementing the Government's strategy designed to drag the US and NATO into the war on the side of Bosnia. He seemed to be interested neither in peace, nor in the continued suffering of the Bosnian people. Instead he fed the media the political concept of the "victim State". He once said that ultimately Muslims from Bosnia, Sanjak, Kosovo and Albania would form a single political entity. On one occasion he offered me what appeared to be a bribe, but, when he saw the look of utter contempt in my eyes, he swiftly turned the offer into what seemed to be a veiled threat against my life. By the time I left Bosnia a year later, I regarded him as a contemptible individual.

Haris Silajdzic, the Prime Minister of Bosnia, detested Ganic, and it was said that on one occasion, meeting Ganic on the steps of the Presidency, he had punched him in the face. This story endeared Silajdzic to me immediately. He was a brilliant Arabist and philosopher who had taught at the University in Tripoli. He chain-smoked small cheroots and was greatly depressed by what was happening to his country. He had the dark, brooding appearance of a hero in a Greek tragedy. He hated formality, so we used to meet in his small office at the back of the building. Once he left a UN memo that Simon had written to me the day before on his desk for all to see. Another time he told me that everything we said in the Residency was overheard by the Bosnian intelligence services. I replied that I knew this and that we found it a useful way of confusing him. Prime Minister Silajdzic was a great friend of Sergio de Mello and he was the only politician I met in Bosnia who had a genuinely European attitude or offered any hope for the future of the country. Much later he was to attack me ferociously in front of the assembled television cameras of the world. To his credit, he was probably the only leading Bosnian SDA politician who actually believed in a multi-party democracy and the values and freedoms that go with it. He later resigned from the party in protest at its sectarian policies.

He frequently discussed military strategy with me, and would complain that every time his army launched an attack, it was defeated. It was always the civilians who ended up paying for these failures with their lives. He never seemed to understand the limitations on the use of military force imposed on a peacekeeping mission and he frequently criticised the UN for not bombing its way to peace. He had a direct line from his office to the State Department in Washington and was not averse to putting in a call to the US Secretary of State Warren Christopher in my presence, as though to tell me that his guns were bigger than mine.

Early in the first week, I visited the French HQ in the ruined Postes, Télé-communications et Télédiffusion (PTT) building on the main airport road. It had the atmosphere of a besieged Foreign Legion fort in some far away place. Brig.-Gen. André Soubirou, who met me at the door, was the most senior French officer in Bosnia and commanded the French Sector Sarajevo. The French had been in Sarajevo since the start of the troubles and were now the largest contingent. They had suffered the highest casualties in the war, and yet their commitment to the mission was unwavering. They were responsible for the airport as well as for running the city.

Wherever the French Army deploys on operations, it always brings with it a part of metropolitan France, and Sarajevo had almost become a dependent territory. There was an excellent French hospital in the PTT building as well as a shop where it was possible to buy anything from Gauloise cigarettes to perfume. There was also a French bakery in Sarajevo that produced a ton of bread each day. The units from other nations deployed in Sector Sarajevo, except for the British, were only deployed on static guards or escort duties which allowed the French to get on with the more challenging roles of running the airport and patrolling the conflict line. Their HQ in Sarajevo had a direct line to Paris and on a number of occasions Paris disagreed with Soubirou about policy. This caused him some embarrassment.

Soubirou told me that he welcomed the launch of my new robust approach to peacekeeping but warned me that I would find it difficult to get the majority of nations to implement the policy on the ground. I could depend only on the French, the NATO countries and the Scandinavians. It was clear that we were going to get on well. We conducted the discussions in French learned in the streets of Paris, and his soldiers were often amused to find themselves talking to a British general who could swear like a Parisian taxi driver.

André Soubirou had a French-speaking Canadian officer on his staff Maj. David Fraser. He was skilled at explaining the respective military idiosyncrasies of the French and British contingents to each other. On the odd occasion when he was excluded from conferences by Soubirou, he always sat in the outer office, along with most of the secretarial staff, listening to what was going on behind the closed door. By this means he kept us informed of French tactical thinking. Sometimes he was unable to pick up anything of importance because of the amount of shouting that was taking place. At the end of these noisy meetings, when he asked what decisions had been taken, he was invariably told that nothing had been decided.

Some evenings I would dine with Soubirou. After dinner he would call on his officers one by one to sing legionnaire songs, which are very slow, with a sadness all their own. One evening he invited a colonel to declaim Victor Hugo's poem "Waterloo". By the end, everyone, including the British, had tears in their eyes at the images of the wavering lines of soldiers vanishing into the smoke and fire of battle. The evening was made all the more poignant by the sound of an occasional shell falling nearby.

The French officers were some of the best I have ever commanded. They remained unaffected by political correctness and preserved a proud military culture based on honour and tradition. They maintained an old-fashioned courtesy combined with elegance and style. They could sometimes be maddeningly bureaucratic in their staff procedure, but they never failed to deliver regardless of the personal cost.

During my first week in Sarajevo, I learned my second lesson of survival in the brutal, manipulative world in which I was now living. I had been visited by Fred Cuny, a strange, shadowy figure straight out of a Graham Greene novel. A tall, gangling ex-US Marine Corps officer, he was running a water project in Sarajevo for the International Rescue Committee, largely funded by the international financier George Soros. He lived in a well-maintained house behind the Residency, guarded by tough-looking people who reminded me of the US Secret Service. He also had close connections with Capitol Hill in Washington. We all assumed he was working for the CIA, though he denied this.

At our first meeting he was highly critical of the UN, which he clearly thought was manned by corrupt and weak people. He wanted to see tough military action taken against the Bosnian Serbs, and even though I explained to him that we were about to launch a new strategy based on a tougher military approach to peacekeeping, he didn't believe me. He said he would do everything he could to undermine me, unless I could demonstrate my resolve by action on the ground. At which point I threw him out. Unrepentant, he invited himself back the next evening with a group of "concerned lawyers", as he called them, from New York. The leader of the group was Aryeh Neier, a lawyer, who worked for a New York organisation called the Open Society Fund whose chairman was George Soros. Despite the bad feeling between Cuny and myself, I agreed to see this influential group, provided our conversations remained private.

I began by saying that, as I had been in the post less than a week, I would rather listen than talk, but restated my determination to deliver a tougher approach to peacekeeping. I felt that the UN troops could do more than merely count shells falling on the city, and that I would redeploy them to help with the humanitarian aid effort. As soon as I finished, Neier asked me whether I considered Sarajevo to be a city under siege. I replied that it was not a siege in the true sense of the word, as the UN had generally succeeded in maintaining a flow of supplies into the city, and this had at least kept the people alive. A look of triumph crossed his face and he launched into a tirade against me.

He said that, as a lawyer, he could prove that, under many different inter-national protocols, Sarajevo was legally in a state of siege, created by the aggressive Montenegran-Serb regime of Karadzic.

He struck me as something of a zealot, and I realised the pointlessness of any further attempt at logical debate. Once again I threw Fred Cuny out, along with his visitors. As they left, I reminded them that whatever had been discussed should remain confidential.

I might as well have saved my breath. The next morning the headlines in the local newspaper, the *Oslobodjenje*, reported that I did not consider the citizens of Sarajevo to be under siege. Neier also wrote to the Secretary-General of the UN urging him to order me to "reverse" my plan to redeploy observers from their task of counting shells, as this procedure kept the international spotlight on the attacks that were being mounted.

It was clear to me that this adverse publicity against me in my time in command could prove disastrous, so I immediately called a meeting with the Prime Minister, Haris Silajdzic, and explained to him that whoever had reported my views to the local papers had got it wildly wrong. What I had *actually* said was that I did not want to develop a siege mentality and that I wished to live in Sarajevo like any other citizen. Giving me a look which clearly said "My, my, you are learning fast", Silajdzic asked me whether I would be prepared to repeat this statement on local television. I agreed and a camera team appeared as if by magic. Silajdzic had evidently already read the transcript of my conversations with the Americans, but had chosen to sign up to the lie, probably on the grounds that he did not yet know if I would turn out to be helpful to the Bosnians or not. It had been a narrow escape and I sent Cuny a rude message, accusing him of setting a trap for me. He replied with a dinner invitation. Before a month was out, he had radically changed his position and we became good friends. Tragically, he went missing two years later in Chechnya and I never did discover whether he worked for the CIA.

During my first week in Bosnia, I spent two days in Zagreb visiting the staff in the operational UN HQ responsible for the peacekeeping mission in the whole of the former Yugoslavia. Most of the people in the Zagreb HQ were intelligent and fun to work with, though they seemed surprisingly conscious of rank within the UN organisation.

Yasushi Akashi, the head of the UN mission in the former Yugoslavia, was a diminutive Japanese lawyer who had worked in the UN for many years. He was 63, but, being of samurai stock, he rarely looked tired or complained of the punishing regime or the humiliations which the job imposed on him. He never lost his temper or showed emotion and he used an old-fashioned, somewhat pedantic form of speech which allowed him time to work out negotiating tactics as he went along. He had a love of rather quaint dirty stories which he repeated whenever he wanted to illustrate a point. He claimed that he was like a boxer in defence, always rolling with the punches and never giving up. He seemed to work instinctively without any planned agenda, which made it difficult for the warring parties to defeat him in negotiation.

As the UN Secretary-General's representative, he was accompanied wherever he went by a large group of attractive secretaries, bodyguards and advisers.

Although he could be unforgiving to those who worked for him, once he had decided that he liked you, you could do no wrong. Sergio de Mello was the only person he really listened to and who could make him change his mind. Akashi was a courageous, quixotic individual whose determination to reach a peace in Bosnia, long after the opportunities had disappeared, greatly damaged his reputation.

Life in Zagreb was very different to life in Sarajevo. We drove in large American limousines and stayed at the luxurious Intercontinental Hotel, with its swimming pools, bars, nightclubs and casino. Staying there made me uneasy, as the Intercontinental was a notorious meeting place for gun-runners, black marketeers and spies attracted by the war in Bosnia. Once when the UN administration tried to accommodate us at a lower grade, George Waters ignored the instructions and continued to book us into the Intercontinental, sending our hefty bills to the UN. He told me he had discovered that not only did members of the UN HQ in Zagreb live permanently at the hotel, but RAF aircrews also stayed there. He was incensed that people from the front line should be given lesser treatment. I later found out that George played a good hand at blackjack and each time we went to Zagreb, he returned with his pockets full of winnings. It was important for us all to have regular breaks from Sarajevo and when I raised the subject of moving from the Intercontinental Hotel with him, Akashi insisted we remain where we were.

In Zagreb I met Nicholas Morris for the first time, the head of the UNHCR mission to the former Yugoslavia. Mild-mannered, but with a core of steel, his organisational skills were responsible for the delivery of aid to nearly three million people in Bosnia. Since most of them had fled their homes, they depended almost entirely on UN aid for survival, especially during the winter when the temperature remained below freezing for many weeks. Karadzic once told Nicholas that the Muslims leaving Banja Luka were doing so of their own free will, and that the Serbs were treating those who chose to stay behind extremely well. Nicholas was the only person I ever heard call Karadzic a liar to his face. He could be equally tough on anyone else who tried to interfere with the flow of aid or the return of displaced people to their homes.

He explained to me that the mission in Bosnia was the first time that UNHCR had ever been required to deliver aid in a war situation, and they were having to learn as they went along. I told him that I regarded the delivery of aid as the main objective of UNPROFOR and I would always defer to his advice. We agreed to co-locate our respective HQs at each level of command throughout Bosnia, so as to be able to respond immediately to any problem encountered by the aid convoys. The result of this improved coordination was dramatically to increase the flow of aid to people who tended to be dispersed in remote places throughout Bosnia. UNHCR published a monthly analysis of what aid had been delivered, and this I regarded as the only true indication as to how far the UN was succeeding with its mission. By the end of 1994, the tonnages of aid that had been delivered in Bosnia had increased so much that the number of people dependent on UN aid had fallen by a half.

The night before I met Nicholas in Zagreb, Paul Goodall, a British UN aid worker, had been killed by Muslim extremists in Zenica, and Nicholas had been forced to halt all convoy runs in the area. I sent a message to Maj. Paddy Darling, one of my old students at the Staff College, who was then commanding a squadron of the Blues and Royals in Tomislavgrad in the south of Bosnia. He had previously told me that he was getting bored because nothing was happening in his area. I ordered him to move a troop of light tanks that night to Zenica to provide escorts to the UN, and although he warned me that all new deployments were supposed to be cleared by politicians in the UK, he was there by dawn the next day. This immediate action had an extremely positive effect on Nicholas, although it did cause difficulties within the UK chain of command.

The war in Bosnia was relatively static, with the continued shelling of Sarajevo remaining the greatest threat to peace. The Croats were said to be massing troops around Prozor with the intention of launching an offensive against the Muslims in central Bosnia. The French battalion in Bihac in the north-west of the country was occasionally being sniped at and shelled both by the Muslims and the Serbs. The plight of the people living in the enclaves was deteriorating because of the failure of successive UN aid convoys to reach them in the winter months. This was particularly true of the Maglaj where UNHCR reports predicted that before long people would die in great numbers. I decided to spend the next week travelling through the countryside, talking to people and seeing for myself what was happening. Before I could do this I had to meet with the Bosnian Serbs.

On 30 January 1994 I met with the Bosnian Serb political leadership for the first time in their temporary HQ in a ski hotel in Pale, which is a small town high in the mountains to the east of Sarajevo. It was a lovely day with a fresh fall of snow masking the ugliness of the war-torn countryside. The road to Pale ran through the mountains above Sarajevo, and as we looked down at the peaceful scene, it was diffi-cult to believe that more than 10,000 people had been killed in the city in the last two years. We were, however, reminded of the war by the lines of Bosnian Serb trenches that ran alongside the road that were reminiscent of the trench lines of the First World War. I stopped to talk with some of the soldiers, who were chopping wood or huddled around the woodburning stoves for warmth, but they seemed more intent on surviving the intense cold than in discussing the war. Nevertheless one of them pointed out to me the Residency clearly visible in the city below.

The Bosnian Serbs at that time controlled about two thirds of Bosnia and they intended to establish a separate State, the Republika Srpska (RS) in Bosnia, with close links to Belgrade. The Pale leadership was deeply mistrustful of the UN, even though 600,000 Serbs were dependent on international aid. They felt isolated and betrayed by America, Britain and France, on whose side the Serbs had fought in both world wars. Now they lived in a world so far removed from reality and so full of hatred for the Muslims, that their own propaganda was contributing to their state of paranoia.

Karadzic headed a ruling clique consisting of himself, Momcilo Krajisnik and

Nikola Koljevic, known collectively to us as the KKK. Karadzic had been, among other things, resident psychologist to the Sarajevo football team. He was also a poet and, perhaps as a result, was extremely plausible. He could be courteous in his dealings with the UN, but when he came under pressure he could lie through his teeth with a look of sublime innocence on his face. When accused of carrying out some terrible atrocity, such as the shelling of the market place in Sarajevo, he would always blame the action on the Muslims. He had once been in prison with Izetbegovic, but had split from him after he had been freed. His gunmen had fired the first shots in the civil war on 6 April 1992 in Sarajevo, when they gunned down unarmed civilian demonstrators. His fingernails were often raw and bleeding, and he clearly suffered extreme anxiety beneath his calm exterior. He had the haggard look of someone living in a nightmare, as though convinced he would ultimately die an unpleasant death.

Momcilo Krajisnik, the second and most balanced of the team, was also the most hard-line. He had prominent bushy eyebrows and the look and demeanour of a successful Communist Party apparatchik. The only time I ever saw him moved was following the death of his 86-year-old mother who had been killed by a Muslim sniper on the outskirts of Sarajevo.

Koljevic, the third member of the triumvirate, had taught Shakespeare at Nottingham University for a number of years and spoke fluent English. He had the typical appearance of an absent-minded academic and wore the traditional uniform of a professor, including a tweed coat with brown leather patches on the elbows. He was alleged to have been responsible for the "rape camps". I once asked him how he could live in such a chaotic, brutal world where no human values could survive. He replied with a sad smile, that sometimes it was very tiring. Two years later, after the Dayton Peace Agreement had been signed, he committed suicide.

At this first meeting we discussed the need to open the airfield at Tuzla in the north of the country, so that the UN could start a second airlift operation in Bosnia. However, the airfield was surrounded by Bosnian Serb artillery positions and it was thus vulnerable to interdiction. Karadzic stated that he had no general objection to opening the airfield as long as Serb inspectors could be part of the UN operation so as to prevent arms smuggling to the Bosnians. This arrangement existed in Sarajevo, and did not appear to present a problem. Karadzic, however, claimed that if Tuzla airfield was reopened, the Muslims would shoot down an incoming UN aircraft in order to blame this act on the Serbs, adding in a characteristically dramatic way: "The Muslims would kill Allah himself in order to discredit the Serbs!" This prediction, of course, gave him *carte blanche* to shoot down any UN aircraft himself and to subsequently blame the Muslims. When I left Bosnia a year later the airport had still not reopened, because the Bosnian Government refused to accept the presence of Serb inspectors on the airfield. Indeed, President Izetbegovic was later to state that he was prepared to see 10,000 Bosnians die of starvation rather than accept a single Serb on Bosnian territory.

The meeting continued through lunch, and as we left I felt encouraged by Karadzic's statement that he thought the continued shelling of Sarajevo was senseless and that it should stop. Typically, within two weeks of his assurances, not only had the shelling in Sarajevo greatly increased, but there occurred the terrible mortar attack on the market place that was dramatically to change the course of events in Bosnia.

Karadzic ended our first meeting in Pale by reassuring us that all the Serbs wanted was peace. In his opinion the Muslims wished to fight on until defeated in battle. Then the West would be obliged to enter the war on behalf of the Muslims and this would result in a Serb defeat. It took me some time before I began to unravel this complicated piece of logic, which clearly owed nothing to Socrates.

Mladic, the Commanding General of the Bosnian Serb Army, was in the classic Soviet mould of generals: fat, swaggering and coarse-featured. He had never known his father or grandfather, both of whom had been killed in battle. He had a reputation among his soldiers for bravery and success in the fighting that took place in 1991 in the Krajina region of Croatia. For him, the dominant mode of battle was the attack. He was revered by his soldiers for his habit of jumping into a tank and leading from the front. He was also deeply religious, and once told me that he prayed every day for the lives of his men. Nevertheless he saw nothing wrong in using terror as a weapon or civilians as targets for his artillery if this advanced his strategy. Mladic suffered rapid changes of mood and used a combination of persuasion, trickery and intimidation to win arguments. It was said that he was once challenged by one of my predecessors to chess. Having won two games and then having been challenged to a third game, Mladic had replied, "No, I will not play with you again, I am beginning to humiliate you." It was said that this UNPROFOR commander had never quite recovered from this reply, especially as he had then gone on to lose a game of ping-pong.

Gen. Rasim Delic, who was commander of the Bosnian Army and had been in the same class with Mladic in the Yugoslav Army, did not like negotiating with him face to face. He knew that at some point in the meeting he would be made to look inadequate. Mladic, though brutal and manipulative, generally kept his word if he agreed to something. Delic rarely did.

Mladic started off by making the ridiculous announcement that from now on Bosnia-Hercegovina could only be referred to as "ex-Bosnia-Hercegovina", since the State no longer existed. It took all the diplomatic charm of Sergio de Mello, who was present at the meeting, to get us off this silly idea. Once we were able to leave this topic and begin a proper discussion, Mladic surprised us by firmly rejecting the agreement that we had already made with Karadzic regarding the reopening of Tuzla airfield. He would never allow this to happen. Sergio said that it would be regrettable if the UN were compelled to reopen the airport by force, as it was entitled to. This observation threw Mladic into a terrible rage. Striking the table with his fist, he shouted that he was not afraid of the Americans or their NATO lackeys, and that he would shoot down any aircraft that attempted to land there. "It will take NATO a hundred years to find us in these woods!" he exclaimed.

Mladic softened when I said that it was the continued blocking of UN convoys by his soldiers that made the reopening of the airfield so necessary. He replied that the UN had never lost a convoy in the Serb-held areas, and that no UN soldier would ever be subject to attack by the Serbs. This was so evidently pure theatre, laid on to impress the new British general, that it would have been funny were it not for the many lives being lost in Bosnia through lack of aid.

Goose used these first two meetings to establish good relations with the body-guards belonging to Karadzic and Mladic. Over the months he was able to glean a lot of information from them regarding what they thought about the situation and what their bosses were doing. It was especially interesting to hear that Mladic regularly travelled to Belgrade on Tuesdays. From this it was clear that Mladic at least was receiving direct orders from the military HQ there.

Tuzla, which we visited the next day, was the home of the Scandinavian brigade which was commanded by Brig. Ridderstadt, a Swedish part-time officer. In civilian life he was the chairman of a group of newspapers in southern Sweden and he spent much of his time worrying about the possibility of a board take-over in his absence. The commanding officer of the Swedish battalion was Col. Hendrikson. As the Swedes have no standing army, his soldiers were all volunteers who had been recruited for the tour of duty in Bosnia through newspaper advertisements. More than 6,000 people had applied for 600 posts. As a result the Swedish soldiers were of an exceptionally high quality and were well equipped. Although Sweden has not been at war for 300 years, it was plain that they had lost nothing of the martial quality that allowed them to dominate northern Europe in the seventeenth century. They could be extremely bloody-minded and always returned fire immediately with their heavy weapons if they were fired upon.

Hendrikson had personally led their first convoy across the conflict line. At a Bosnian Serb roadblock, he was confronted by an aggressive soldier who told him he had orders not to allow him to pass. Hendrikson immediately put a loaded pistol to the soldier's head and informed him that he had just received a new set of orders. The convoy was allowed through without any further interruption. Because of their tough-minded approach, the Swedes were respected by all of the warring parties.

Ridderstadt had invited the mayor of Tuzla, Mr Beslagic, to meet me. He had come to power on a genuinely multi-ethnic ticket, and was considered a thorn in the flesh of the Bosnian Government, whose orders he frequently ignored. His one concern was the lack of supplies in central Bosnia, and he supported the idea of reopening the Tuzla airfield. However, the local Bosnian Army military commander, clearly under briefing from Sarajevo, stated that they had driven the Serbs off the airfield some months before, and not one of them would be allowed back. I told them that a precedent for such an arrangement had been set in Sarajevo, and they could not hazard the lives of so many people for so stupid a reason. He ignored me.

On the flight back to Sarajevo, we passed over mountain ranges where many of the villages that we could see had been destroyed. This ethnic cleansing had occurred the previous year when the Muslims drove the Croats out of central Bosnia. The Croatian refugees from Bosnia had settled in the Laskva Valley to the south, driving out, in their turn, the Bosnian Muslim population living there. In this way ethnic cleansing had spread to all parts of the country. During the war, the Bosnian Muslims became the main victims of a deliberate and systematic policy of ethnic cleansing and in certain areas extermination. Although all three sides were to some extent guilty of war crimes, genocide as defined by the UN Convention on Genocide, did not form part of official Bosnian Government policy in the way that it so clearly did with the Serbs. Nevertheless the Bosnian Serbs were not the sole perpetrators of atrocities, and this fact was often difficult to communicate to the members of the international community.

Delivery of aid had fallen to 40% of required levels, and a paper had been produced by UNHCR predicting that some 800,000 people might perish during the winter of 1994–95 if aid targets were not met.[4] While it was plain that this could not be allowed to happen, it was equally clear that radical changes would have to be made to the UN mission if such a disaster was to be averted. At the heart of these changes would be better coordination between the UN peacekeepers and UNHCR. Before I could achieve this, I needed to restructure my own command arrangements.

I presented these ideas at my first meeting of the assembled commanding officers and representatives from UNHCR and the other NGOs, where they were warmly received. I therefore issued orders for the reorganisation of Bosnia-Hercegovina Command into three separate sector commands. One would be in Gornji Vakuf in the south-west of the country, headed by a British brigadier, John Reith, an experienced Parachute Regiment officer in whom I had great confidence. Sector Sarajevo would remain under French command, but its boundaries would be extended to include eastern Bosnia and the two Muslim enclaves of Zepa and Gorazde. A third sector covering north-west Bosnia, including the Muslim enclave of Srebrenica, would be established on Tuzla airfield under command of Brig. Ridderstadt. At each level of command, operations centres would be established alongside the area UNHCR coordination cells. Together they would be responsible for organising all aid and military convoys in their region and for collecting data regarding the condition of the population.

The Sector Commander would present a unified plan for humanitarian assistance to the political leaders of the three communities, who would then be held responsible for any blocking or hijacking of convoys by their respective armies. If aid were prevented from getting through, the UN would not hesitate to expose the illegal actions of the warlords in the press, or to explain to the people the consequences. No longer would the UN engage in deals with these warlords to obtain the passage of convoys, which had resulted in much of the aid being held up or not delivered to the people at all. We would attempt to open up two new convoy routes, one running from the coast via Mostar and Konjic to Sarajevo, and the second going north, through Zenica and Zavidovici to Tuzla. For many months both these routes had been closed by fighting between the three factions and several bridges had been destroyed.

In order to ensure that there would be no more attacks on these convoys, I ordered a platoon of Danish Leopard tanks – known as Snow Leopards, because they were painted white – which were languishing in Split, to move immediately to Tuzla. I had already been told that the use of tanks for peacekeeping duties was a politically sensitive issue and that I would need permission from Zagreb and New York. This had not so far been forthcoming. I have always believed that the man at the front line will invariably give the best advice, so I telephoned the Danish squadron commander of the tank company and asked him if he could take on such a task. He explained that his men were fed up waiting for specific orders. They had been messed about now for nearly three months, having been moved from Zagreb to Belgrade and then on to Split, and they would, of course, welcome such an assignment. He felt that his own bosses in Denmark would support the mission, as they had already expressed some disappointment at the lack of proper employment for the unit. He confirmed that if he was given the orders to move immediately, he could be in Tuzla within 48 hours. To allow the heavy tanks to move along roads which had been destroyed, it would be better for him to move the tanks to Tuzla while the ground remained frozen, and as a thaw was forecast in a couple of days he needed to move immediately. I told him to move that night and, although there was some bureaucratic criticism from members of the Security Council about my failure to consult with New York, I detected that Kofi Annan was pleased that a long-running problem had been resolved. The firepower of the tanks was to prove indispensable in the next few months. I learned from this episode that the UN administration in New York often secretly welcomed independent action from the field, as long as it proved successful, and I was to repeat the manoeuvre many times in the coming year.

At the end of the meeting, I gave firm direction that as long as clearances had been obtained in the correct manner for the passage of a convoy, any illegal roadblocks or other obstacles to the movement of a convoy were, after due warning, to be forcibly dealt with. Shortly after, a young French lieutenant smashed down a roadblock outside Pale with his armoured cars. When asked by the enraged Serbs why he had done this, he replied that he was demonstrating the new muscular approach to peacekeeping which had been ordered by the new UN commander.

Goose, not to be outdone, then drove through the same roadblock a day later, by which time the Serbs had laid anti-tank mines in the middle of the road to prevent the same thing from happening. After sounding his horn and getting no response from the Serb soldiers who were lounging around, he accelerated his car down the road, sending the mines flying. He had suspected, correctly, that the mines had not been armed. When I asked him if he had considered the consequences had he been wrong, he thought for a moment. "It wouldn't have mattered," he said. "I was driving Briquemont's second-hand Renault."

Although I did not reveal it at my first meeting with the commanding officers, I was determined to engineer a situation in which I could legitimately employ NATO air strikes in order to demonstrate a more robust UN approach to peacekeeping. After some discussion with Viktor Andreev, who firmly supported the idea, I decided that it would be better to launch an air strike against the Croats rather than the Serbs. The Croats were not central to our main effort, and even if they reacted by closing routes, they could not afford to do this for long as the sizeable Croatian population in the Laskva Valley was wholly dependent on UN aid. Such an attack would send the right message to Mladic, who would also understand that NATO was not set on destroying the Serbs and that the use of force was impartial. After some research Willy Levak, my UK intelligence officer, identified the perfect situation for an air strike against the Croats.

Willy was the ideal person to have as intelligence officer, being a Glaswegian with an impenetrable accent that defeated even the most determined eavesdropper. He had established good relations with NATO intelligence staff in the NATO HQ in Naples and the NATO Air Commander, Gen. Joe Ashy of the US Air Force, who would sometimes send his personal plane to fly Willy to Naples so that he could personally brief him. He would never allow Willy to return to Sarajevo without first sending him and his aide into Naples for a good night out.

For the past three weeks there had been a series of attacks against a Canadian convoy on the road between Vitez and Fojnica. The purpose of the convoy was to supply a hospital for mentally handicapped children, run by a religious order. The route crossed the line of conflict about seven miles from Vitez and on the last engagement a lorry carrying coal had been destroyed by the Croats. The children in the hospital were in danger of freezing. We had a situation that encompassed the extreme suffering of mentally handicapped children and the Croats firing on the UN, which gave us the right of self-defence and some obvious targets for an air strike, as the Croatian positions were easy to spot. I told Willy not to target the firing trenches, but to go for the command structure, preferably a company HQ. I meant this action also to send a tough message to the leaders of all the factions.

Ashy was delighted with the plan. He was a tall, languid airman who often reassured me that he really did understand the complexities of peacekeeping, but invariably added under his breath, "The trouble is, all I want to do is bomb the bastards!" As the Canadian armoured vehicles had only limited protection, I invited Maj. Richard Margesson of the Coldstream Guards (my own regiment) to lead the convoy. He was to take a NATO forward air controller with him.

The day of the convoy dawned clear, with blue skies and no fresh fall of snow, which might have made target identification difficult. Four A10 tank-busting aircraft from NATO were overhead, and the trap was ready to be sprung. Annoyingly, for the first time in several months, the convoy was not fired upon, nor was it ever to be again. The UN HQ staff in Kiseljak had been resolutely opposed to the operation from the outset, advising me that many carefully built-up relationships with the Croats would be destroyed by such an action. I suspect that a member of staff, or an aid worker, who had heard of the plan in the Kiseljak HQ had decided to abort the operation by warning the Croats of the impending air strikes. This was something of a set-back for the UN. Although a tactical advantage had been gained by opening up the route, the overall strategic impact of carrying out an early air strike was lost.

On the political level things were also not looking good. Following a visit by the British Foreign Secretary Douglas Hurd, Boutros Boutros-Ghali, the Secretary-General of the UN, had issued a warning that many countries were considering withdrawing their forces from Bosnia in the Spring, although he himself favoured maintaining a UN presence. In order to shore up international confidence in the UN mission in Bosnia, he stated that the UN would be increasingly prepared to use air power in the exercise of its mandate if obstruction of its activities continued. But he drew a distinction between close air support in self-defence and the aggressive use of air strikes in pursuit of strategic goals. By also stating that he was opposed to any lifting of the arms embargo, the Secretary-General placed himself firmly on the side of the peacekeepers and in opposition to those in the US Congress who favoured a more warlike approach.

In Sarajevo Yasushi Akashi, his Special Representative in the former Yugoslavia, also issued a warning that the Government of Bosnia-Hercegovina was considering pulling out of the Geneva peace talks which had been continuing under joint UN–European arrangements since the conflict started. Having attended the meeting between President Izetbegovic and Akashi that had triggered this announcement, this statement came as a surprise to me. The meeting had started with President Izetbegovic giving an extraordinary account of the deaths of three men arrested by the Bosnians as the chief suspects in the murder of Paul Goodall, the British aid worker. It seemed that they had escaped from prison, stolen a Land Rover and attempted to flee up Mt Igman. President Izetbegovic assured us that a full inquiry was under way and the results would be made public. They never were.

President Izetbegovic had then spoken with some force about the need for a just and fair peace for Bosnia. The military situation had forced Bosnia to accept conditional partition of the country based on a federal arrangement. The Serbs wanted not only their historic territory, but also places like Zvornik, that had traditionally belonged to the Muslims. To partition the country in any way that did not conform to the population distribution defined by the census held in 1991 would be to reward aggression. President Izetbegovic delivered this homily in a quiet, undramatic manner, but in a voice full of passion.

President Izetbegovic still remains an enigma to me. Small in stature and dignified in bearing, during my dealings with him he appeared to be detached from what was happening around him. He certainly affected to be so. When he acted, however, his authority was absolute, and although he used people like Ganic to protect his reputation, it is likely he was fully aware of the policies and actions of his officials. Tito had imprisoned him for his religious and political beliefs and the experience had taken a physical toll. When under pressure he would purse his lips and fall silent for long periods before agreeing to some course of action, which was very rarely implemented. By the time in I left Bosnia, I came to believe that his talk of creating a multi-religious, multi-cultural State in Bosnia was a disguise for the extension of his own political power and the furtherance of Islam. He in his turn came to regard me as the supreme obstacle to his plan to get the US involved in a war in Bosnia.

The visit by the prime ministers of Pakistan and Turkey the next day proved to be something of a propaganda coup for the Bosnian Government. Both Benazir Bhutto and Tansu Ciller demanded air strikes and a lifting of the arms embargo so that the

Bosnians could "at least defend themselves". They also offered additional troops to the UN, an offer gratefully accepted by New York, even though it was not possible to deploy Muslim troops on 70% of Bosnia that was occupied by the Serbs.

As we left the airport *en route* for Sarajevo, we crossed the rubble-strewn line of conflict. Observing the devastation, Mrs Bhutto politely asked if my family had accompanied me on my tour of duty. Possibly the scene reminded her of Karachi after a day of rioting. She was accompanied by her husband, who contributed little to the discussions. Dressed in a helmet and flak jacket, Mrs Ciller looked remarkably like Goldie Hawn in *Private Benjamin*. I had long taken the decision not to wear a flak jacket or helmet when travelling in Bosnia, because it created a psychological barrier when talking to people who did not have such protection. I was rarely able to persuade visitors to do likewise.

I waited until the visit by the two prime ministers was over before putting into effect my new hardline tactic with regard to enforcing the passage of convoys through-out Bosnia. The Bosnian Serbs in particular were obstructing convoys at Sierra One, a Serb control point sited on the road between Kiseljak and Sarajevo. At the time it was the only usable land route along which the UN was able to deliver aid into the city. Since the Serbs knew approximately what the daily rate of consumption of food and fuel was for the 350,000 people living in Sarajevo, they were able to prevent stocks in the town from building up to beyond about 10 days' worth of supplies. When they wanted to exert pressure on the besieged city, they merely turned off the flow of aid. For the past two days, Sierra One had been closed to all traffic on orders from Gen. Manojlo Milovanovic, Chief of Staff to Mladic. I therefore issued instructions that all convoys that had proper clearances were to force their passage through this check-point if they were blocked. I was, after all, merely enforcing the Geneva agreement signed on 18 November 1993 by the leaders of all the warring parties, including Karadzic, to allow free passage of aid throughout Bosnia. Once again, my Chief of Staff advised against this action because of the possible effect it might have on the Serbs. They could react by halting all aid delivery across the territory they controlled. I pointed out that the UN was failing in its mission because the aid was not getting through, and that if we did not do something drastic to reverse the trend, then all credibility would be lost.

I ordered my old regiment to break through Sierra One. The Coldstream Guards were equipped with Warrior APCs capable of stopping the rocket-propelled grenades habitually used by the Serbs. I sent Nick Costello along to explain to the Serbs manning the roadblock what was happening. On his previous tour of duty in Bosnia he had got to know them and I thought this might prevent them opening fire on the Coldstream Guards. On arrival at the roadblock, he explained to the Serb interpreter, a woman he knew well, what was about to happen. She pleaded with him not to press ahead with the enforcement plan, saying that the Serbs liked the British, and him in particular, but that they would be forced to open fire if any attempt was made to break through the barrier. This would be a tragedy, as she didn't want to see him die.

"Well," said Nick, "You have your orders and I have mine. But before you do anything stupid, take a look above. I wouldn't want to see you die either." As he spoke, four A10 aircraft from NATO screamed overhead. Giving her a cheery wave, he closed down the hatch of the APC and Maj. Richard Margesson gave orders to his company to move forward through the flimsy barricade.

Looking through the vehicle commander's weapon sights, Richard could see the Serb soldiers dashing in a panic to their trenches and grabbing their weapons. However, as the Warrior vehicles drove down the road, with the A10s still circling menacingly overhead, the Serbs held their fire. This was a great disappointment to the guardsmen in the Warriors. Such was the fearsome reputation of the British units among the warring parties, for returning fire they were known by the title of "Shootbat", rather than by their usual UN designation, "Britbat". This action at Sierra One was well reported by the international media, and a leading article in *The Times* demanded that the "politicians match the more robust military approach".

That evening on BBC television I outlined my new policy, explaining that at present the UN was unable to run more than about 50% of the convoys required in central Bosnia. Since all parties to the conflict had agreed to allow the free flow of aid throughout Bosnia, but had subsequently obstructed the passage of such aid, the UN had a right to use force. When asked about the use of air power, I replied that I would use air power in riposte. "If they shoot at us," I said, "we will shoot back, and I will have no hesitation about that either!"

After this small victory by the Coldstream Guards, there was a distinct reduction in the stopping or hijacking of convoys, and UNHCR statistics showed that delivery of humanitarian aid began to increase from that moment. By the end of the year, all the aid that was needed for the people of Bosnia had been delivered. Furthermore, sufficient seed had been supplied to most parts of Bosnia to allow people to start planting their own crops again. This was a splendid achievement by the young men and women who ran the convoys through the battle lines, who built and maintained the roads or who operated the airlift and airdrop programmes. Of course all those in need did not receive what they should have done; there was, after all, a bloody three-sided civil war going on. Criticism for any failures would have been more logically directed at the warlords and their political leaders, not at the humanitarian aid workers or the peacekeepers. As a UNHCR official in Sarajevo once said: "Debit the dead to the warmongers. Credit the living to the UN." But it came as no surprise to me that an anonymous correspondent writing in the *Spectator* accused the UN in Bosnia of "attempting to establish a welfare state in hell" through its efforts to alleviate the suffering of the people.[5] I wonder what he would have written if the UN had pulled out, as he suggested, and as a result thousands of people had suffered and died.

The day after the opening of Sierra One (4 February) at 1100 hours, the Bosnian Serbs carried out a mortar attack on a bread queue in a Sarajevo suburb called Dobrinja. This attack killed 10 people and injured many more. News of it did not reach me through the official UN chain of command (usually last with any incident report) but through a journalist who asked me to comment on the atrocity.

I immediately went to the scene with Nick Costello and spoke to the Bosnian military commander.

He was a tall man with dark, brooding eyes who walked with a limp, having been wounded in the initial battle for Sarajevo. He had been a civil engineer before the war, and was in the defence line only 75 metres from the Presidency when the Bosnian Army finally halted the Serb attack on the city. He had subsequently taken part in the defence of Dobrinja when it was surrounded on all sides by the Serbs. The population had been forced to live for nearly three months in their cellars as the Serb gunners were only 300 metres away on a hill looking down into Dobrinja and would practice firing their 152mm artillery over open sights at stray cats and dogs. During this time it was suicide to venture outside except in very small areas screened by high-rise buildings.

The Serbs used to watch the UN aid vehicles driving into the area and would, from time to time, mortar people queuing for food. On this occasion four shells had been fired and, from analysis of the craters, it was plain that the firing position had been on the Serbian side of the conflict line. I asked the brigade commander why the people had not remained under cover in a nearby underground car park while collecting their supplies. He replied that, after so much time spent underground in cellars, people would seize any chance to be out in the open air if there appeared to be a lull in the shelling. Better to die living a normal life rather than live like rats in a cellar. I couldn't argue with this.

That evening in the Residency, Sergio de Mello gave a party to mark his departure from Sarajevo. He was moving to Zagreb to become deputy to Akashi. Although I was sad to see him go, his deputy Viktor Andreev, whom I was already getting to know and like, had been promoted to take his place. An experienced and skilled Russian diplomat, he had worked for the UN for the past 20 years and knew people in high places in the old Soviet Union. He spoke several languages fluently including Burmese, was amusing, highly intelligent and very capable. His first great test as head of civil affairs in Bosnia was to come sooner than expected.

CHAPTER TWO

The Bombing of the Market Place

*The Security Council declares that the capital city of the Republic of
Bosnia-Hercegovina, Sarajevo . . . should be free from armed attacks
and any other hostile acts.*

UN Security Council Resolution 824

I HAD BARELY BEEN IN THE COUNTRY TWO WEEKS WHEN THE TERRIBLE
events in Sarajevo on 5 February catapulted me unexpectedly onto the world
stage. It proved to be the most fateful day of the Bosnian war. The handling of this
crisis was to set the direction and pace for everything that followed that year and, as
so often in Bosnia, it occurred when I was least well placed to deal with it.

Simon and I had departed early that day to visit the UN Spanish battalion in
Mostar where I also intended to meet the local commanders of the Bosnian Croat
Army (HVO). The Spanish battalion's base was at Medjugorje, close to the Catholic
shrine, which may have given the Spanish soldiers spiritual reassurance, but their
location was too far removed from Mostar, where most of the incidents in southern
Bosnia were taking place. I had been surprised to hear that the bodies of three Italian
journalists recently killed by a mortar shell, had lain on a road near Mostar for several
days before the Spanish recovered them. As we left Medjugorje in a fleet of Spanish
APCs, we were instructed to put on helmets and flak vests and close the steel hatches
of the vehicles, as if for action. Since the streets were full of tourists and pilgrims and
there was no sign of fighting in the area, I asked the fierce-looking, bearded Spanish
platoon commander why this was necessary. He replied that battalion standing orders
were to close down all vehicles at that time of day because children, coming out of
school, threw stones at them. This was just the kind of siege mentality that I wished
to eliminate so I ignored his order. As we drove along with our heads out of the
open turret of the APC, waving at the children.

The platoon commander told me that the destruction of east Mostar, the Muslim
part of the city, was worse than any other part of Bosnia. People were still forced to
live in their cellars, there was no electricity or running water and it was difficult for
aid to reach the besieged Muslims who were living in desperately poor conditions.
The Croatian part of the town, on the other side of the Neretva River that flows
through Mostar, was very different. Here there had been little shelling and life was

relatively normal, apart from the fact that most men carried weapons. The high-performance sports cars tearing about the town had, I was informed, been stolen in nearby Austria or Germany.

I was being shown the remnants of the historic bridge built in 1566 by the Turks and destroyed by the Croats, when Simon received a call from my HQ. There had been a massacre in Sarajevo. As details of the incident started to filter through, all thoughts of the destruction of Mostar were cast aside. A single mortar bomb had been fired into the Markele market place, not far from the Presidency. Early reports stated that more than 200 people had been injured, and that at least 50 were dead. The final toll was 68. I abandoned my visit to Mostar and flew to Split, hoping to catch a flight to Sarajevo, but the airport had been closed due to bad weather and helicopters were unable to cross the mountain range which divides Bosnia from the coastal plain. We were therefore forced to spend the night in Split watching increasingly depressing news bulletins. Akashi and Gen. Cot had decided to fly to Sarajevo for emergency talks with the Bosnian Government, but had also been prevented from doing so. I was relieved to hear this, as I wanted to be in Sarajevo ahead of them. Meanwhile Soubirou and de Mello, amid the shock and anger, were handling the situation as best they could and keeping Akashi and me informed.

Early the next day I met Akashi and his team at Sarajevo airport, where a large crowd of journalists confronted us. Pushing cameras and microphones in our faces, they demanded to know what we were going to do to stop the killing, as if the UN had been guilty of the massacre. Akashi ignored them. As we forced our way through the crowd I saw Goose grab a woman holding a heavy CNN television camera in order to prevent her from going down under the mass of jostling journalists.

In the calm of the airport waiting room, a tense Akashi suggested that the outraged response to the massacre worldwide should be turned to good effect. He proposed that we call an immediate halt to the fighting and demand the withdrawal of all heavy weapons from around Sarajevo. The leaders of many nations were calling for military intervention to stop the slaughter, which he presumed meant the launching of NATO air strikes against the Serbs, even though it was too early to say with any certainty which side had fired the mortar bomb. We had to act quickly if we were to prevent this "we must do something" reaction of the international community from dragging the UN mission into war in Bosnia, as had happened in Somalia.

The Bosnian Government blamed the Serbs for the massacre. The Serbs categorically denied responsibility, accusing the Muslims of having fired on their own people with the intention of bringing NATO into the war on their side. Preliminary examination of the site by French military engineers indicated that the proximity of high buildings around the market place made it impossible for a mortar shell to have followed a low-angle trajectory and land where the explosion took place. This suggested that the bomb might not have been fired from a mortar at all, but detonated in situ. Subsequent analysis contradicted this. An international team of experts finally agreed that a mortar had probably fired the shell, but that it was not possible to identify the exact distance from the firing point, although the direction from where the mortar had been fired lay to the north-east. When I was asked by CNN which side I thought had been responsible for the attack, I replied that it was impossible to say with certainty since only one bomb had been fired. The mortar attack in Dobrinja the previous day in which four shells had been fired had undoubtedly been the work of the Bosnian Serbs. The attack had killed 10 people and injured 18 and I invited the world to draw its own conclusions as to who had fired the bomb the next day at a similar target in the Markele market place.

At the market place we were met by the mayor of Sarajevo, Mr Kresevjakovic, who looked exhausted and, despite the intense cold, wore only a thin anorak over a pullover and trousers. He was a decent man, untarnished by the corruption that affected so many Bosnian officials. He was not popular with the Bosnian Government and shortly after the Markele bombing, he was replaced by someone closer to the party. In a trembling voice he thanked us for coming so soon, and also for all that the UN had done to help the citizens of Sarajevo survive the siege. There was little that we could say in return. Standing amid the twisted market stalls on ground still slippery with blood and human tissue, he managed to retain an air of quiet dignity. I felt as though we had somehow failed him and his people. Apart from the French engineers examining the shell crater, the market stalls were deserted as if the area had become a cursed place. We returned to the Residency in sombre mood. Akashi wanted me to accompany him straightaway to Belgrade. He intended to put pressure on President Milosevic to get the Bosnian Serbs to agree to an immediate ceasefire and to withdraw their artillery from around Sarajevo. He did not want to take Cot with him and although this might have caused friction between us, Cot seemed happy for me to go.

At the Presidency everyone was in a depressed mood. Things this time had gone too far. In response to President Izetbegovic's query "what to do?", Akashi announced that he would be going to Belgrade, and would try to secure an immediate ceasefire and the demilitarisation of Sarajevo as the first step in a renewed peace process. The UN had too few troops to enforce a ceasefire or a peace plan, so a great deal depended on the willingness of each side to abide by their agreements. After the meeting, which produced no firm commitment from the Bosnian Government to respond to any Bosnian Serb ceasefire, I returned to the airport to meet Malcolm Rifkind, the British Defence Secretary.

Rifkind was on a visit, previously arranged, to discuss the consequences of a withdrawal of British troops from Bosnia. The timing of the visit was disastrous, as obviously the merest mention of a UN withdrawal in the days that followed the massacre would have been grossly inappropriate. Consequently he found himself having to make decisions about the British contribution to UNPROFOR while events were still unfolding, which is something all politicians dread having to do. He looked extremely uncomfortable as he declared to the media that "very serious consideration would be given to a military response", but that on the other hand "air strikes would carry a huge price tag and might collapse the mission." I suspected it was clear to one and all that he had not the faintest idea what to do next. Nor was he alone in this predicament.

Intense political activity was taking place at the international level in an attempt to produce a credible response to the atrocity. The Secretary-General of the UN wrote to the Secretary-General of NATO inviting him to "prepare urgently for the use of air strikes to deter further such attacks".[1] The French Prime Minister, Alain Juppé, had called for an immediate withdrawal of all Serb weapons from a 30-kilometre zone around Sarajevo without agreeing to send extra troops to monitor this vast area, and Lady Thatcher accused the West of soft words and empty threats. Employing a more practical approach, Lord Owen met Karadzic in Zvornik to obtain his agreement to a general demilitarisation of Sarajevo. Unhelpfully the US Administration aligned itself with the Bosnian Government and refused to consider the full demilitarisation of Sarajevo, although it continued to insist on a withdrawal of heavy weapons from around the city.

Full demilitarisation of Sarajevo would have required the removal of all Bosnian Army units. For the Bosnian Government this was a step too far, as it would mean that they were no longer sovereign in their own capital. Handing over the security of Sarajevo to the UN would also reduce the possibility of any financial gain that control of all movements in and out of the city generated for the party leaders. In the view of some extremists in the SDA it was better to keep the shells falling on their people in the hope that the US would one day enter the war on their side and to conceal this inhuman strategy, they continued to blame the world for allowing "slow-motion genocide" to take place in their country.

President Clinton, careful not to be drawn into committing troops on the ground, called for a wider use of air strikes, while recognising the need for the UN humanitarian action to continue. The new US Secretary of State for Defense, William Perry, was more realistic about military intervention from the air: "The question is not whether we are capable of air strikes, but of what happens afterwards. If air strikes are Act I of a new melodrama, then what will be Acts II and III?" In the end, because of a lack of agreement about what ought to be done, it was left to the beleaguered UN to continue with the peacekeeping mission as best it could, using the traditional weapons of persuasion, patience and persistence.

The decision by the international community not to take military action in Bosnia allowed propagandists around the world to condemn the West for letting the wicked go unpunished, but at least the aid programme continued and aid was still being delivered to the people. Supporters of the Muslims were particularly incensed by this refusal of the West to take direct military action. In the *Sunday Telegraph* Noel Malcolm, author of *Bosnia: A Short History*, accused Douglas Hurd of having blood on his hands.[2] But the West was not responsible for the atrocities being committed in Bosnia. Blame lay with the perpetrators of these acts, as well as with the Serb, Croat and Bosnian leaders who so often ignored the opportunities for peace.

In Belgrade it was obvious that UN sanctions were working. The airport was carpeted with weeds, the control tower had a dilapidated appearance and most of the Yugoslav civil aircraft fleet lay rusting on the disused runways. A police escort drove us at speed along a virtually deserted motorway, forcing off the road the horse-drawn carts we passed. In communist countries old habits die hard. The hotel in the centre of Belgrade, however, was surprisingly modern and well run. As in Zagreb, it had been kept going throughout the war by aid workers, journalists and black marketeers.

First, we called on Karadzic in a private villa near the centre of Belgrade. Akashi firmly told him that unless he agreed a ceasefire and pulled his big guns 20 kilometres away from Sarajevo, the UN would have to bow to mounting international pressure and agree to NATO air strikes. After repeatedly denying that the Serbs had anything to do with the market place bomb, Karadzic agreed to consider this, but only if the Muslims moved *all* their military units out of the city. When Akashi doubted if the Muslims would agree to this, Karadzic triumphantly declared that it was plain, therefore, for the world to see that the Serbs favoured peace and the Muslims wanted war. Our second meeting, only slightly more sensible, was with President Milosevic. He seemed to be enjoying the role of mediator rather than that of alleged war criminal. He agreed to put pressure on Karadzic to get him to comply with the UN proposals, but he too said that the Muslims would have to accept compromises with regards to the complete demilitarisation of Sarajevo.

Late that night I received a phone call in Belgrade from Simon Shadbolt who had remained in Sarajevo. He had received a message from the Ministry of Defence in London saying that Rifkind, under pressure from the Americans and NATO, was wobbling seriously on the issue of air strikes. Unless we could convince him otherwise he was going to support a wider use of NATO air power designed to force the Serbs to the negotiating table. At that time Rifkind was somewhere in the Adriatic on board HMS *Invincible* and I told Simon it was obvious that the NATO HQ in Naples had got at him. Only hours before in Sarajevo, with Simon present, Rifkind had agreed with my position concerning the limitations of air power in a humanitarian peace mission.

Unable to do anything from Belgrade about this unexpected volte-face by Rifkind, I asked Simon to set out our arguments once again in a signal to him. Working late into the early hours with Sergio de Mello, a "UK Eyes Only" paper was produced, reiterating the dangers of abandoning peacekeeping for war-fighting. Simon was later told by a friend in the Ministry of Defence that it was this paper that finally convinced Rifkind to stand firm against the Americans, and it always amused me that some of the most compelling arguments in the "UK Eyes Only" paper had been drafted by a Brazilian diplomat.

In Sarajevo on 8 February, President Izetbegovic stated that he would never agree to the withdrawal of his infantry from Sarajevo, or indeed to any ceasefire that was not tied to an agreed political solution to end the war. He pointed out that any temporary ceasefire based on the present conflict line would undoubtedly result in a *de facto* division of Bosnia, with the unfair result that the Serbs would have obtained their strategic goals. It was not acceptable under international law to reward the aggressor. He repeated that the Serbs would only agree to end the war when they had lost it and that NATO should help the Bosnian Army to bring about this eventuality.

Prime Minister Silajdzic was yet more damning of UN efforts, accusing Akashi of trying to arrange a compromise deal which would allow the UN to continue with its ineffective policy in Bosnia, and with some bitterness he added that "a ceasefire would merely save the Serbs from being punished by air strikes." When Silajdzic asked Akashi if he had put it to the Serbs that they had to withdraw all their weapons out of range of Sarajevo, Akashi rather primly replied that he had put many such suggestions to them. He had done his best and what was on offer was the maximum that could be achieved. I felt desperately sorry for him. He was accustomed to using a precise legalistic form of words and was unable to respond adequately to the deep sense of betrayal and anger of the Bosnians. In the logic of the Bosnian leaders you were either with them or against them. There was no place for an impartial mediator.

Before leaving for Zagreb that night, Akashi quite unexpectedly asked Viktor Andreev and me to continue the present negotiations between the Serbs and the Bosnians. We immediately arranged a meeting with Gen. Mladic later that evening in the old Yugoslav Lukavica barracks, situated at the western end of the airport runway.

It was almost dark as we arrived and snow lay on the ground. The line of conflict ran about 300 yards from the front entrance of the barracks. Behind us sporadic firing had started from the Muslim trenches. Perhaps they had seen us crossing through the lines. Mladic was not there but was represented by his Chief of Staff, Gen. Milovanovic. A small, brisk-looking officer, Milovanovic had the hollow-eyed appearance of a man who never slept. He often seemed to me to be drunk by midday, but on this occasion appeared to be sober. He began the meeting by saying that he was fully empowered to carry out negotiations on behalf of Karadzic and Mladic. We repeated to him that the Bosnian Serbs would have to stop the fighting and withdraw their heavy weapons from round Sarajevo. If they did not, the UN would ask for NATO air strikes against them. He remained concerned about the large numbers of Bosnian infantry in Sarajevo, who would be able to attack the Serb position around the town if they gave up their heavy weapons.

While we were discussing this, the boarded-up windows facing the Muslim lines rattled as the crescendo of small-arms fire outside was interrupted by the thump of heavy mortars. It was difficult to work out who was firing at whom, but the fighting seemed to be getting closer. Sensing that this was a good moment to put pressure on Milovanovic, I said that unless he agreed to all the Bosnian Government's proposals, I would ask for NATO air strikes against his positions the following day. At that moment, as if to reinforce my point, a grenade exploded nearby and a burst of machine-gun fire hit the outside of the building, causing plaster to come off the inside wall. The lights went out, but flickered on again as an emergency generator took over. A soldier ran in and said something to Milovanovic, who looked nervous. "Any minute now," I muttered to Simon, "the Bosnians will be coming through the window." Milovanovic explained that a Muslim attack had just reached the perimeter wire of the camp, and a counter-attack was being launched. Looking back at this critical moment in the meeting, it is plain that the combined pressure of the Muslim attack and the threat of NATO air strikes proved too much for Milovanovic, as without further argument he agreed to an unconditional ceasefire. He also agreed to attend a meeting of a Joint Commission at the airport the following day when details of the plan's implementation would be worked out.

After the meeting, Goose, who was outside the building with the UN vehicles, said that the Muslim assault had advanced to a point about 40 metres from the building. He had been about to order the UN team to join the Serbs in the defence of their barracks, when two Serb T55 tanks had appeared and driven off the attackers.

One thing I did notice during the battle was that Viktor Andreev did not show any concern at all at being in the midst of a battle and had continued to argue the UN position as if nothing untoward was going on. I later discovered that as a cadet he had led a mutiny at the Military Academy in Leningrad, an institution reserved for the sons of the most highly placed party officials under Soviet rule. He was expelled from the Red Army and joined the Soviet Foreign Ministry which sent him to Burma to learn the language, where he lived for four years with a Burmese family. On his return, he had become the Foreign Ministry's principal Burmese interpreter and as a result had known all the Soviet leaders from the time of Stalin.

We made our way back through the lines and went directly to the Bosnian Army HQ. It was 2030 hours. We were met by the Deputy Commander, Gen. Divjak, an elderly Serb who spoke fluent French and was fighting on the side of the Bosnian Muslims. When I asked him how his attack on Lukavica barracks had progressed, he looked surprised and pretended to know nothing about it. Brig. Hajrulahovic, also present at the meeting, merely grinned at me. Hajrulahovic was known in Sarajevo as the "Italian", because few people could pronounce his name. He was young for his rank and had earned himself a reputation for bravery in the battle for Sarajevo in 1992. He had since been instrumental in the liquidation of two corrupt Bosnian brigade commanders, one of whom had been shot in his flat. I always suspected that the "Italian" worked for Bosnian Army intelligence. His office was located in the building behind the Residency, and it was from this direction that laser beams had been directed on to the windows of my office. I always liked him, and in 1998 I was sad to hear that he had died of a heart attack.

Although the Serbs had now agreed virtually everything the Bosnians had asked for, Divjak was reluctant to sign up to a ceasefire, once again on the grounds that the UN proposal was not linked to any long-term political settlement. I told him that the people of Sarajevo would at that moment certainly settle for something short of this, just to be able to live in peace. He still would not agree. At this point I sprang a nasty surprise on him. I told him that the first UN examination of the bomb crater in the Markele market place indicated that the bomb had been fired from the Bosnian side of the battle lines. The room went deadly silent and Hajrulahovic looked anxious. He coldly asked me to explain. I told him that the angle of the trajectory of the mortar bomb suggested that it had been fired at extremely short range from their side of the lines or perhaps detonated *in situ*. It was difficult, I said, to be precise when only one bomb had been fired and also because the Bosnian Army had removed some of the important forensic evidence before the UN arrived.

However, it would not look good if, just as these facts became public knowledge, the Bosnian Government refused to agree to a ceasefire plan. Not only would the people of Sarajevo not understand, but also much of the international support they currently enjoyed would disappear. I was not trying to put pressure on them, I said, I was merely explaining the consequences of rejecting the UN proposals that, of course, had already been agreed by the Serbs.

There was another long silence in which I saw Hajrulahovic and Divjak exchange glances. Finally Divjak asked me to repeat the four proposals that would be laid on the table at the airport the next day. I repeated that the plan consisted of an immediate ceasefire, a withdrawal of all heavy weapons from a 20-kilometre circle round Sarajevo, the positioning of UN peacekeeping troops between the lines of conflict, and the establishment of a Joint Commission, which I would chair. Another long silence ensued and I could hear an old-fashioned clock ticking on the wall. This was a critical moment in the war. Somewhat unexpectedly Divjak said that, as long as the discussions went no further than that, he could agree to the proposals and would turn up at the airport the next day in order to discuss their implementation with the Serbs. He looked strangely relieved as we toasted the continuing success of the peace process before returning to the Residency after midnight.

I was at the airport at 1100 hours the next morning to ensure that arrangements for the first meeting of the Joint Commission were in place. Our hopes were high and our spirits lifted when we saw that the Serbs had already arrived. At about 1130 hours I took a call from Divjak. Certain "political difficulties" had arisen and he could no longer attend the airport meeting. I asked him what he meant by this, as he had assured me that he had full political as well as military negotiating powers. He hung up without replying.

I sent Nick Costello to the Army HQ to find out what was happening. It was already midday and the Serbs were beginning to complain that the whole thing had been a trick by the Bosnian Government. Milovanovic said that they had often done this before, and he warned me that the Serb delegation would not remain at the airport for long. I told them I was sure there had only been some procedural problem between the Army HQ and the Presidency, and that I was confident it would be resolved.

I was conscious that most of the world's press had gathered at the airport to see what was about to happen. I had already been warned by a number of journalists that I had been strung along by the Bosnians, who would never agree to a ceasefire. It was clear to me that the credibility of the UN and of myself as the new Commander hung in the balance. At about 1230 hours Nick telephoned from the Army HQ saying that the Bosnians would not come because the Serbs had agreed nothing on paper. He had told them this was *muda* (bollocks), and that the world would judge them accordingly if they failed to turn up.

I was beginning to get angry. I told the Serbs to stay put and drove at high speed back to Sarajevo, stopping only to pick up Viktor Andreev as he hurried to the airport to find out what was causing the delay. I told him I intended to take Divjak to the

Presidency, if necessary by force, and confront President Izetbegovic. By the time I reached the Army HQ I had worked myself into a considerable fury at the duplicity of the Bosnians. Taking the stairs three at a time, I ran past the startled sentries and burst into Divjak's office to find Nick Costello still there, trying to prevent Divjak from leaving.

Seizing hold of Divjak's arm, I asked him what the hell he thought he was playing at. When he did not reply I said that I was taking him to see the President. He resisted, saying that a senior officer of the Bosnian Army should not be treated like this. Putting my face close to his, I shouted at him that I represented the Secretary-General of the UN and I would not be lied to or given the run-around by the Bosnian Government. I had the support of the entire international community for what I was trying to achieve. This angry exchange took place in French. Not even allowing him to get his coat, I bundled him into the Range Rover behind a grinning Goose who raced us round to the Presidency. Goose was clearly enjoying this unexpected shift from Chapter VI to Chapter VII of the UN Charter – from the peaceful settlement of disputes to enforcement.

At the Presidency I demanded to see President Izetbegovic and was told that the President was giving an interview to Christiane Ammanpour of CNN. All the better, I thought, and hurried the reluctant Divjak up the stairs and into President Izetbegovic's outer office. After a short wait, the door opened and Ammanpour emerged with her television team. I told her that important developments were taking place and she should stay in the building. Izetbegovic, no doubt already *au fait*, listened carefully as I repeated that the Serbs had signed up to everything he had asked for at the meeting with Akashi and were no longer demanding any preconditions. The world would not understand why the President would not agree to the UN proposals to halt the fighting round Sarajevo. Without much conviction Izetbegovic said that he could not agree to a ceasefire unless it was linked to a political settlement. I told him that we had to approach the problem sequentially and that such a settlement would surely emerge. In the meantime, the Bosnian Government had to retain the support of the international community. If this was lost, as it surely would be if he did not agree to the meeting at the airport, all hopes of a just political settlement would vanish. I added that the world's media was already waiting at the airport. They had seen the Serbs arrive and they would draw their own conclusions if the Bosnian side did not appear.

Sitting on a low sofa in a dark corner of the freezing room, Izetbegovic looked a lonely figure, staring silently at the table in front of him. I almost felt sorry for him, for I was asking him to abandon a central component of his strategy and there were probably great political risks for him in doing so. However I was not about to relent. After a long pause, carefully choosing his words, he said: "If you are prepared to restrict the discussion at the airport to the four proposals you have outlined, and you will say as much publicly before the meeting, then I will give my authority for Gen. Divjak to attend the meeting." I thanked him for his wise decision, and on leaving the room I made the required statement to a local television camera team that was waiting for me. CNN had been asked to leave. We then all made our way back to the airport in a better mood, although Divjak sat gloomily in the back of the car. As we drove along, Viktor said to me, "I like this British form of diplomacy; it reminds me of the way we used to do things in the Soviet Union."

The Serbs still sat patiently in their own little waiting room back at the airport, enjoying an excellent lunch that had been prepared by the French battalion. These lunches were an invaluable part of any negotiation, as they allowed the representatives of the warring factions to forget their differences for a moment, and useful discussions often took place between them. It is certain that on this occasion, but for the lunch, the Serbs would have departed.

Arriving at the airport I briefed the Serbs and the Muslims in separate rooms on how I would run the first meeting of the Joint Commission. I would start by reading in front of them the UN proposals to which they had both agreed. Then I would ask each of them to agree the proposals publicly in front of the opposing party. No other statement would be allowed. I had already been warned that, given half a chance, each side would launch into a diatribe against the other. I told them that this was a historic moment, a time for reconciliation and not a time to rehearse past grievances. I explained to them that once both parties had agreed the proposals, I would then invite the media into the room and read a statement explaining what had been agreed and what steps were being taken by the UN to implement the agreement. Both sides assented to this procedure, and we entered the main hall where the French had strategically placed chairs and tables so that the UN separated the two sides who sat opposite each other. I read out the UN proposals, and asked the Serbs for their assent.

Milovanovic stood up and began an emotional oration about the Serbs being the victims of NATO aggression. I rapped on the table and told him to stop. The only words that I required from him were either "Yes, I agree", or "No, I don't agree." Giving me a reproachful look for having denied him his moment of rhetorical glory, he said tersely, "Yes, I agree." Divjak then followed suit. The press was called in, a statement read and the deal was done. History had been made in less than three minutes.

It can be said that the 9 February Airport Agreement was the beginning of the end of the civil war in Bosnia. From that moment on the rules of the game changed. Most important of all, the Americans began to understand that negotiation could work. That afternoon, Akashi sent a signal congratulating us on what had been achieved.

Earlier in the day Angela, my wife, having seen press statements emerging from Brussels speculating on the impending NATO response to the bombing in the market place, had warned me that NATO might be trying to impose their own demands on the UN-brokered agreement. Determined not to allow the UN peace process in Bosnia to be hijacked by NATO, I phoned an old friend who was involved in the discussions in Brussels, Lt-Gen. Rupert Smith, and told him it was crucial that the UN and NATO demands regarding the ceasefire and withdrawal of heavy weapons be completely aligned.

I had known Rupert when he commanded a company of the Parachute Regiment in South Armagh, Northern Ireland, and his military career subsequently had led him to command the UK armoured division in the Gulf War. By chance, he was now working in the operations branch of the Ministry of Defence that dealt with Bosnia. When we had met in London we had agreed that it would be impossible for Britain to follow two conflicting strategies in Bosnia. Either the UN should be supported in its efforts to negotiate a peaceful end to the war, or NATO should replace the UN and attempt to impose a political solution by force of arms. For as long as Britain had peace-keeping troops on the ground it was vital that our approach did not differ from that of the UN, whatever difficulties this might create for NATO. It was particularly important that the text of the NATO ultimatum being drafted that afternoon accurately reflected the wording of the negotiated agreement that had just been obtained in Sarajevo, and that the threat of NATO air strikes would be directed against *any* party that reneged on the Airport Agreement. Fortunately, Rupert was able to introduce the necessary clauses into the document and when the NATO ultimatum was published later that day its wording conformed precisely with the Airport Agreement.

In the NATO ultimatum, both the Bosnian Government and the Serbs were warned that any heavy weapons that remained in the "exclusion zone" round Sarajevo after 20 February would be subject to NATO air strikes.[3] This proved to be the only occasion during 1994 that the mandates of the UN and NATO were properly aligned.

NATO was in Bosnia at the request of the UN Secretary-General to support the peacekeeping mission. Consequently it was subject to the same rules governing the use of force as the UN. However, the need for NATO to "maintain its credibility", in the words of its commander, Gen. George Joulwan, meant that it frequently forgot this basic fact, and NATO often seemed to advocate taking disproportionate action against the Serbs, while ignoring violations on the side of the Muslims. This made it difficult for the UN to conform to the prime requirement of peacekeeping: impartiality. In a way NATO's concerns were understandable. It was a war-fighting alliance designed to deter an attack by the Warsaw Pact against Europe; whereas the UN had been formed to bring about, by peaceful means, the settlement of international disputes. The respective cultures of the two organisations were poles apart.[4]

The following day (10 February) Gen. Sir John Wilsey, Joint Commander of British Forces in the former Republic of Yugoslavia, made a visit to Sarajevo from his HQ in Wilton. We had been at Staff College together 20 years before and had remained good friends. He was someone who cared passionately about the predicament of other human beings, whether soldiers or civilians. He was a soldier with a conscience, something that did not always make him a comfortable bedfellow to his more politically minded colleagues on the Service Boards. We spoke almost daily throughout my time in Bosnia as I felt it was important that there was someone in Britain who would defend, at the strategic and political level, what I was trying to do at the tactical level. I had seen for myself how British lives had been unnecessarily lost in the Falklands because of political interference and John had suffered the same experience commanding in Northern Ireland. In John Wilsey I was fortunate to have someone who instinctively understood and supported the peace process. I often placed him in exceedingly awkward situations politically, but he never appeared to lose faith in what we were doing. It was also perhaps convenient for us both that as I was serving in a UN post, he could not directly give me orders.

On this particular visit, I presented him with a request for British reinforcements, including a battalion of infantry and a radar-locating unit. Until the latter arrived in Bosnia, the UN had no means of being certain who was firing at whom. Even though Malcolm Rifkind had been considering withdrawing troops from Bosnia at the start of that fateful week, the British reinforcements I asked for arrived within two months. As a result the UN was able greatly to increase its coverage on the ground in the more difficult areas around Sarajevo and Gorazde.

It was now 24 hours after the ceasefire, and I wanted to judge its effectiveness. I went with my team to a notorious flashpoint in Sarajevo, a bridge over the Miljacka River inappropriately named the Bridge of Brotherhood and Unity (Bratsvo-Jedinstvo). The river separated the battle lines and some of the fiercest fighting in Sarajevo had taken place in this vicinity. As we arrived, we could see a mass of press and local people who had clearly had the same idea. French engineers supported by infantry were carefully checking for booby traps and mines, watched by the Serb snipers on the other side of the bridge less than 100 metres away. No one had yet crossed the bridge, so I suggested to the French Sector commander who was directing operations, Brig.-Gen. André Soubirou, that we make a public demonstration of our confidence in the ceasefire by doing so ourselves. As we crossed the bridge we followed the centre line of the road where we hoped there were no mines.

The Serbs on the other side were delighted to see us, and even though they refused to come out of the buildings because of the threat from Muslim snipers, we were able to talk to some of the soldiers. They said they intended to abide by the agreement, but did not trust the Muslims to do the same. On the way back to the Muslim side of the river, we were nearly crushed by the assembled press who fought each other to get pictures of us. One of the cameramen had blood streaming down his face and someone else was trampled under the seething mass of people. At the back of the crowd, John Simpson of the BBC had sensibly placed himself in a position from which he could see everything without getting involved in the fracas. Once again Goose had to step forward and get them into some semblance of order. He held the media in the same contempt as he did the warring factions.

Since there is no such thing as a tidy end to fighting, a certain amount of shelling in Sarajevo continued throughout the day, mostly from the Muslim side. When I sent a note of protest to Divjak, he replied that he would no longer talk to me because of the way I had treated him the day before. I also received an abrupt message from Gen. Milovanovic, complaining that many of the UN military observers whom we had sent to monitor the ceasefire were from Muslim countries and would therefore not be tolerated on Serb territory. He also pointed out that the Serbs "will never accept anybody's ultimatum, even at a price of being wiped off the face of the planet." I soon learned to ignore such messages, although Simon Shadbolt used to pin the more idiotic ones to a notice board.

About that time, I watched a dramatic report by Peter Arnett of CNN, filmed from the roof of the Holiday Inn, implying that the UN ceasefire had already broken down and that Sarajevo was under heavy attack by the Serbs, although from his footage, it seemed to us that the rounds were outgoing and had been fired by the Muslims, not by the Serbs. Someone commented that he appeared to be confusing Sarajevo with Baghdad. I immediately complained to CNN, and I was not sorry to see Arnett leave Bosnia. In total, the UN had detected only six mortar and 17 small arms violations in the first 24 hours of the ceasefire, which I found encouraging given the previous disregard for ceasefires. Not everyone agreed with me, and it was amusing to see how the resident BBC reporter, as the days went by, was reluctantly forced to accept that the ceasefire was there to stay. He, too, disappeared from Bosnia at the end of February. It was not only military reputations that were lost in the Balkans.

I was beginning to be able to distinguish between those journalists who unquestioningly used material provided by the Bosnian Government propaganda machine, and those who were interested in presenting a more objective view of the war. Much seemed to depend on individual personalities and what sort of relationship the reporters had developed with the female interpreters attached to all foreign news teams by the Bosnian Government. Not all the journalists in Sarajevo were biased, and I worked with many courageous reporters who often put their own lives at risk in order to discover the truth. Kurt Schork, an American who had been at Oxford with President Clinton and worked for Reuters, and Remy Ourdan, a Breton who reported for Le Monde, were two such people. A television news clip once showed Kurt running out from under cover under heavy mortar fire to pull a wounded woman to safety. He was often highly critical of the West's response to Bosnia, but I always felt he was at least prepared to give the UN a hearing. Remy Ourdan, who made himself unpopular by writing about (among other things) the Islamisation of Bosnia, was finally forced out of Sarajevo at gunpoint. From time to time I also enjoyed sensible debates about what was happening in Bosnia with visitors like Misha Glenny, whose book The Fall of Yugoslavia had contributed so much to my understanding of the Balkans.

However, I found that the best way to keep a sense of perspective was to talk to the ordinary people of Bosnia. After a day spent negotiating with their leaders – who rarely showed an interest in peace and often accused the UN of being responsible for the suffering of the Bosnian people – it gave me a renewed sense of purpose and rekindled my faith in humanity to be told by people in the streets how grateful they were for what the UN was doing for them. I began to spend more and more time walking the streets, taking the tram and visiting the trenches so that I could meet not only civilians but soldiers as well who were also victims of the war.

The day after the ceasefire came into effect I was asked by Sue McGregor on the BBC Today programme to reply to a statement made earlier by Mohammed Sacirbey, the Bosnian Government representative to the UN. Speaking from Miami where he had a law practice, he said that the UN-brokered ceasefire was a sham and that Serb shells were still falling on the besieged city of Sarajevo. Nothing, he said, had changed. As he spoke, I looked out of the window. I could see in the streets the people of Sarajevo walking peacefully in the sunshine with their children, something they had been unable to do for many months. I described to Sue McGregor the view from my window and suggested that it was the people of Sarajevo, rather than I, who should reply to Mohammed Sacirbey, who was, or so I understood, "speaking from a sunbed in Miami". Every time I met him thereafter, he would try to convince me that he had actually been in his office at the time, not on the beach, and complained that my comment had done him much damage. It was curious that so consummate an advocate for the Muslim cause did not appreciate how propaganda can work both ways.

Now that a semblance of peace had returned to Sarajevo, my main objective was to keep pressure on both sides to comply with the agreement. NATO clearly believed that the Serbs would not, and they were already issuing press releases to this effect. Madeleine Albright, speaking in the UN Security Council in New York, stressed the need for clarity in advance regarding arrangements for the use of NATO air power following any expiry of the ultimatum. She did not want to hear arguments about "the vulnerability of UN troops on the ground". It seemed to us in Sarajevo that there was a growing belief in Washington that all peacekeeping goals should be ignored and that NATO should carry out air strikes without reference to UNPROFOR. It was vital to ensure that this never happened and that the UN controlled what was happening in Bosnia both from the air as well as on the ground.

On 13 February, as a result of this growing fear that a NATO air campaign might be launched regardless of the UN mission, Akashi convened a meeting in Zagreb with the Commander of Allied Forces South, Adm. Mike Boorda, which I and Gen. Cot attended. This meeting coincided with a three-day brainstorming session that Akashi had already organised for that week. I had invited Angela to Zagreb. Apart from missing her, I was keen for her to learn as much as possible about the situation at first-hand. She was proving to be invaluable in keeping me informed about possible shifts in UK policy with regards to Bosnia. She had acquired a network of supporters and informants all of whom were keen to pass things on to me. Angela was particularly good at reading the mood of the press, who she warned would soon start attacking me, although at that time they seemed to be giving me the benefit of the doubt.

Adm. Mike Boorda brought a full team with him from Naples and at the start of the meeting, in a very American way, he delivered a Staff College-style lecture on the use of air power. This obviously irritated Cot, who had commanded the 1st French Army and was quite unused to being addressed in such a way. However, Boorda made sense. He accepted that a successful resolution of the war in Bosnia could not be arrived at by bombing and that he would act only at the request of the UN. In effect, he was sensibly acknowledging the fact that the UN had in effect a veto on the use of air power in Bosnia. This was a brave thing for him to say, given that the US Administration believed the NATO ultimatum should not be subject to interpretation by the UN and that all that was required was a "coordination of any air strike with the UN".

Having resolved this issue, I then made my position clear on the subject of control of heavy weapons in the UN collection sites. I said that if anyone tried to remove a weapon from one of these sites, they would have to fight for it. I kept my fingers crossed as I said this, for I could not guarantee that all the UN troops under my command in Bosnia would be as good as my word. Nevertheless, the idea seemed to please Boorda. Next we discussed in great detail the form that monitoring of the total exclusion zone (TEZ) and verification of possible targets would take. We agreed that NATO aircraft could not be relied upon to verify potential violations of the ultimatum. For much of the time between October and May there was low cloud and poor visibility in central Bosnia, and the terrain was wooded and mountainous. Also, many wrecked vehicles littered the countryside round Sarajevo following two years of fighting. Comprehensive verification could only be achieved on the ground.

UN observers and forward air controller teams would visit all the sites in the TEZs suspected of containing heavy weapons. If they were satisfied that violations of the 9 February Airport Agreement and the NATO ultimatum had taken place, they could then direct NATO aircraft to attack suitable targets. Boorda looked uncertain when I asked him whether these arrangements would be applied as firmly to the Muslims as to the Serbs. In the end he had to agree that they would, but his hesitation made me realise how reluctant America would be to carry out air strikes against the Bosnians. It was also agreed that a special US satellite communications team would be assigned to my HQ in Sarajevo, so that Boorda and I could be in permanent touch wherever I was in Bosnia.

On my return to Sarajevo I found a surprising note from the British Chief of Defence Staff, Peter Harding, telling me that UNPROFOR did not have the right to veto NATO air strikes in Bosnia, adding that "it *will* happen if conditions are not met". When I told him that Boorda had agreed that UNPROFOR did have a veto, he said that I had to understand that the credibility of NATO was more important than peace in Bosnia. I told him somewhat drily that I thought the purpose of the NATO alliance was to preserve peace not to provoke a war. Shortly after this conversation he was forced to resign for personal reasons. Gen. Peter Inge, who had briefed me in the MOD before I had left England for Bosnia, took his place. Being a soldier, I was confident that Gen. Inge would be less in favour of the use of air power than his airman predecessor.

On 15 February Cot returned to Sarajevo for a meeting with Gen. Mladic. We sat through the usual tough-guy act from Mladic who, at the mention of NATO, flew into a rage. "No one", he shouted, "can threaten a Serb and live!" This cut no ice with Cot, and we finally got down to discussing many important matters: the withdrawal of Serb heavy weapons from the exclusion zone, the verification process which required complete freedom of movement for UN observers, and the location and size of the weapons collection points. It would have been simpler if there had been no weapons remaining in the TEZ. However neither side trusted the other to respect the ceasefire, and they both wished to retain a number of weapons within the zone for self-defence. It was agreed that eight Serb weapon collection sites under UN control should be established on the outskirts of the city, with one in the former JNA barracks in Sarajevo for the Bosnians. The UN would only release weapons from these sites to the warring parties as a last resort.

In the event the Serbs produced a far greater number of weapons than did the Bosnians, perhaps reflecting the unequal military balance between the two sides. However, both sides concealed a substantial number of weapons within the TEZ, but as long as they did not use them, this hardly mattered. If anyone employed heavy weapons within the exclusion zone, I intended to call for air strikes against them. There was also the additional benefit that, by keeping their weapons in the Sarajevo TEZ, the warring parties could not use them elsewhere in Bosnia.

The verification process would be critical to the success of the ceasefire. The United Nations Military Observers (UNMOs) had originally been established at the start of the first UN mission in Palestine in 1948. They comprised an unlikely group of people, purportedly from the sea, air and land forces of the UN member states. It was not unusual to see a naval or airforce officer from a small Third World State trying to make sense of a confused land battle in Bosnia. It was obvious that some UNMOs used the job to profit from black-market deals and their sizeable UN allowances. They were frequently billeted with local military commanders and as a result I did not feel able to rely on the impartiality of their reports. Fortunately, among the UNMOs there were some highly professional officers serving in Bosnia.

One such officer was Roy Thomas, a hard-working Canadian who headed the Sarajevo team of UNMOs. His role proved crucial in the next few days as he was responsible for the verification process in the TEZ. He was later awarded a well-deserved medal for his vital work. Another stroke of good fortune had occurred when my wife spotted an old friend, Col. Rupert Prichard, dining in a restaurant in Zagreb. A Green Jacket officer, he was at that time working as deputy head of the UNMO organisation, and he had told Angela that he was frustrated by UN bureaucracy and felt cut off from the main action in Bosnia. He was an extremely experienced officer who had previously worked for me, so I asked him to come to Sarajevo to help Roy Thomas set up the verification programme. Ignoring an unhelpful boss who refused to let him go, Rupert arrived in Sarajevo the next day and with Roy set to work. There was no time to waste.

By then I had already decided to raise a new group of military liaison officers and observers called the Joint Commission Officers (JCOs). Their job would be to provide me with reliable reports from the field and also to liaise on my behalf with the military commanders of the warring parties. In principle the UN has no intelligence gathering capability and, though this may not matter in traditional peacekeeping operations, in Bosnia it was essential that I had a better knowledge of what was happening across the country than the patchy information provided by the UNMOs. I could only take timely and relevant decisions if I was able to see through the mass of disinformation that poured out from the propaganda machines of the combatants. The role of the JCOs was to act as my eyes and ears. They were selected for their personal qualities and language skills and were drawn from across the UN contingents under my command in Bosnia, and included French, Danish, British and Dutch soldiers, as well as one Russian officer.

The JCOs were equipped with long-range communications and reported directly to me. Without doubt, during 1994 they provided me with the most reliable information about what was happening in all the crisis areas of Bosnia and their work also proved of vital importance to the UN internationally. Kofi Annan would sometimes telephone from New York about a developing situation and the JCOs' eyewitness accounts from the front line usually allowed him to head off trouble in the Security Council. The JCO HQ was located in the Residency, next to the NATO air cell and I could talk to both the NATO air cell and the JCO HQ through my open office window. It was by this means that I used to direct some of the air strikes.

The media in Sarajevo was already predicting a collapse of the ceasefire and the launch of an air war against the Bosnian Serbs. The *Daily Telegraph* commented that NATO was on the verge of its first military action since it was founded in 1949.[5] In the same newspaper, Wg Cdr LeHardy, a Spitfire pilot in Yugoslavia during the Second World War, predicted that "one or two RAF air strikes today would have the same salutary effects as they did then". A headline in *The Times* reported that 180 aircraft had been put on alert for Sarajevo bombing runs,[6] and the *Irish Times* published a cartoon of a survivor standing amid the ruins of Sarajevo shouting: "The rhetoric is coming! The rhetoric is coming!" In Belgrade, the families of diplomats were reported to be packing their bags and leaving.

In spite of this, the tally of weapons being placed under UN control or withdrawn altogether from the TEZ was slowly rising. It had also been the quietest week in Sarajevo since the war started, with no reports of casualties. None of this was widely reported by the Sarajevo media circus, yet it was my job to convince people in Bosnia and abroad that the ceasefire was going to hold.

Much of the week I spent visiting the battle lines around Sarajevo talking to Bosnian and Serb soldiers who were sometimes only metres apart in their trenches. As the midnight deadline for full compliance approached (Sunday 20 February), I began to sound more confident and the media less certain. I repeated my belief that Monday, the day following the expiry of the NATO ultimatum, "would be just another day", and Simon pinned a notice to this effect on the wall of his office. When a journalist asked me where I would be at midnight as the NATO ultimatum expired, I replied, "Asleep, in bed".

All this was in sharp contrast to the ominous noises coming from Washington and Paris, where sabres were still being rattled. "On the evening of the 20 February, everyone should know what can be expected to happen," warned France's Defence Minister, François Leotard. "No one should doubt our determination. Europe's future is being played out here."

Behind the scenes, things did not always look so promising. There were too few troops to monitor the ceasefire along the 70-kilometre conflict line round Sarajevo, so after getting the necessary authority from John Wilsey in Britain, I redeployed two companies of the Coldstream Guards, under command of the French in

Sarajevo. Their Commanding Officer, Col. Peter Williams, had already told me that his battalion was underemployed in central Bosnia and that the Guards would be delighted at the prospect of renewed action.

Because of the difficult terrain, as well as the blizzards and obstruction by the Bosnian Serbs, the work of ensuring the TEZ was clear of heavy weapons was proceeding extremely slowly. By 18 February, only a handful of the 99 locations where NATO suspected there were weapons had been visited, yet they would all have to be inspected to satisfy NATO that the TEZ was clear. Fortunately many of the sites identified by NATO as containing Serb weapons turned out not to. One potential target, for example, identified by NATO air photography as heavy mortars aimed at Sarajevo, proved to be a line of haystacks. In Bosnia haystacks are built around poles in circular patterns and from the air they look exactly like mortar base plates. Another embarrassment was avoided when a positive NATO identification of a Serb T55 tank turned out to be a French APC, deployed to monitor the ceasefire. To prevent NATO from dragging the West into a war by attacking such false targets, the UNMOs had to complete their work on time, and they still had a long way to go.

At the international level, some helpful diplomatic action was taking place. On a visit to Moscow, John Major had persuaded President Boris Yeltsin to send a Russian battalion to Sarajevo to help the UN monitor the ceasefire. They would serve as a buffer between the Bosnian infantry and the Serbs. Their deployment would give enormous confidence to the Serbs and encourage them to comply fully with the UN agreement and NATO ultimatum. Yeltsin immediately dispatched a special envoy to Sarajevo, Vitaly Churkin, to put pressure on the Serbs. He was an old friend of Viktor Andreev and the two of them spent the few days remaining before the expiry of the ultimatum travelling between Sarajevo and Pale. Their work proved to be the single most important factor in persuading the Serbs to respect the ceasefire and to withdraw their heavy weapons from Sarajevo.

Not to be outdone, Ambassador Charles Redman, President Clinton's special envoy on Bosnia, also flew in. Chuck Redman, as he was known to all, was a calm, assured diplomat, who looked a little out of place in the chaos and destruction of Sarajevo. He was protected by a posse of nervous-looking US Secret Service bodyguards. Redman was up to date with much of what was happening and at our first meeting he told me that at all costs we had to stop the Serbs from playing cat-and-mouse with us. I explained that the Serbs had shown themselves to be more than happy to stop the fighting while they were ahead, and that it had been the Muslims who had tried to renege on the meeting at the airport.

Redman replied that the Serbs could not be allowed to benefit from their aggression, and that nothing would stop America from pursuing its goal of re-establishing a unitary State in Bosnia. It was obvious he had been sent to Sarajevo with a specific agenda, influenced by the need for Clinton to be seen to get tough on the Bosnian Serbs in the run up to the congressional elections. It was left to John Major to point out that the President's "get-tough" policy would have had more credibility if the US had been prepared to put their own troops on the ground in Bosnia and expose them to the risks this policy entailed.[7] Without such a commitment, President Clinton was, in effect, playing with the lives of soldiers from other nations.

I refrained from saying this to Redman, whom I instinctively liked. He was a skilled negotiator, tactically astute and determined to get his way. He reminded me of the saying, "like serpent, like dove". He certainly shared my appreciation of the need to maintain momentum following the Airport Agreement, and he now planned to bring to an end the fighting between the Muslims and the Croats. Simon Shadbolt did not altogether trust Redman. He reminded me that, after all, it had been the Americans who had pulled the plug on the Vance–Owen deal at the end of May 1993. They had also probably been behind the scuppering of the talks held on HMS *Invincible* in September later that year, when Izetbegovic had unexpectedly gone back on a position that he had agreed 24 hours earlier.[8]

Within three days of the announcement by President Yeltsin that he would move a battalion from Croatia to Sarajevo, the Russians started to arrive in Sarajevo and were warmly received by their brother Slavs, the Bosnian Serbs. Their arrival was a diplomatic coup for Yeltsin. He was able to demonstrate to the world that Russia still had a central role to play on the world stage, and also in the international effort to end the war in Bosnia. His spokesman even claimed that the arrival of 400 Russian troops in Sarajevo had prevented a world war. In fact, they arrived without rations or much idea about what they were supposed to do, and spent much of their first week scattered around Grbavica asleep in their APCs and being fed by the French.

On 20 February Viktor Andreev arranged for Vitaly Churkin and two Russian generals to see me in order to discuss the detailed deployment of their troops. I told them that the battalion had been placed under command of Brig.-Gen. André Soubirou, who had allocated the Russians a number of staff posts in his HQ. Their main job would be to establish secure bases in Grbavica and provide observation posts on the conflict line in the southern part of the city. If necessary I might call on them to guard UN weapons collection sites. As the discussion widened and we talked about the situation the UN was facing in Bosnia, I realised that our common determination not to allow air strikes placed me in some kind of unholy alliance with the Russians against NATO. Indeed, over the next year the Russians proved invaluable in putting pressure on Washington and Brussels to prevent the UN peacekeeping mission being hijacked by the logic of war.

Their arrival in Sarajevo was ill-received by the Bosnians. Ganic had already told me he would not accept Russian troops on his territory, as they were "no better than the Serbs". He pointed to a photograph that had appeared in local newspapers of the Russians driving through Pale on their way to Sarajevo, giving the Serbian three-fingered salute, which was, indeed, a most unfortunate fact. I told him that he should not prejudge them, and that it was not his responsibility to decide the locations of UN troops. He then said that he would have any Russian who ventured into the Bosnian part of the city follow by the Bosnian police. I accepted that he had the right to do so. "After all," I added, "your police follow me wherever I go!"

The next day Mark Almond in the *Daily Mail* echoed the hostility of the Bosnians

when he warned against the dangers of allowing the Russians into Europe's backyard.[9] Perhaps no one had told him that the cold war was over.

The Serbs, in their characteristically chaotic way, had left things until the last
possible moment, and actually meeting the NATO deadline at midnight on 20
February turned out to be a close-run thing. It had begun to snow heavily that
morning and many of the Serb tanks and other vehicles towing guns had become
stuck. On a visit to Grbavica, we found two Serb Army tanks whose drivers claimed
they were bogged down in the snow. I warned them that neither the UN nor NATO
would accept any such excuse for non-compliance and that if they were still there
at midnight, they would be killed. With a miraculous roar of engines their tanks
started and disappeared at lightning speed up the hill towards Pale, pumping clouds
of black exhaust in their wake. As a result of the chaos, Akashi, Sergio and Viktor,
who were returning from Pale, were forced to spend the night in their cars in the
snow, on the narrow mountain road between Pale and Sarajevo, which was jammed
with Bosnian Serb tanks and guns all trying to leave the TEZ before the NATO
ultimatum expired.

To add to the complications of my life, I was unexpectedly asked by Chuck Redman
to chair a meeting on 20 February – the day the NATO deadline expired – between
Gen. Anto Roso and Gen. Rasim Delic, the commanders of the Croatian and Bosnian
forces respectively. The meeting was to be held in my HQ in Kiseljak about 45
minutes' drive from Sarajevo. I was reluctant to go, as my help was needed in resolv-
ing some of the problems that had arisen with the verification process. Chuck urged
me to attend, as he believed there was a good chance the Bosnians and Croats would
be prepared to agree a ceasefire. I reluctantly agreed.

Gen. Rasim Delic turned up wearing blue ankle-length Chelsea boots and looking
more obese than ever. I often wondered how he could put on so much weight, with
people starving all around him in Sarajevo. In contrast, Roso, a former French
Legionnaire, looked trim and fit. Neither side showed the slightest interest in talking
about peace, refusing even to look at each other and spending most of their allotted
time accusing the other side of atrocities. Halfway through the meeting I received a
message asking me to return to Sarajevo, so I left, handing over the meeting to John
Reith, the UK brigade commander of the sector. He made no more progress than I
had, though he did manage to negotiate an important exchange of prisoners between
the two sides.

On my return to Sarajevo, I went to the French HQ where the monitoring of the
withdrawal of heavy weapons was taking place. The atmosphere in the operations
room was highly charged as messages flooded in from around the exclusion zone. The
news was not good. A total of 183 weapons had been handed in by the Serbs and nine
by the Bosnians. The Serbs appeared to be making belated efforts to clear their
weapons, but many of the suspected weapons sites in the surrounding country had
still not been inspected by the UNMOs. I kept Boorda informed about the difficulties
we were experiencing, but he warned me NATO would not want to hear about the
difficulties encountered by UN observers or by the Serbs. He had been on the ground

in Bosnia and he had seen how chaotic the command and control arrangements could be in the different armies. Although he could appreciate my dilemma, it was unlikely that any request for extending the deadline would be agreed by NATO.

Boorda told me that there was to be a meeting of NATO ambassadors and military chiefs in Naples at 1200 hours on the following day, Monday 21 February, to decide whether there had been compliance with the ultimatum. He would keep everyone talking for as long as possible, but he guessed that if it were not possible to demonstrate full compliance by 1300 hours, a decision would be taken at the meeting to launch air strikes. He warned me that, even as he spoke, throughout the Eastern Mediterranean aircraft were being "bombed-up" and pilots were being briefed on which targets to attack. I told Rupert Prichard that he had 18 hours to cover the remaining 42 sites. He said that he thought it could be done. I hoped so. I went to bed that night not knowing whether the next day would bring peace or war.

Monday at 1200 hours the NATO meeting began in Naples and I passed the message to Boorda that of the 42 remaining sites suspected by NATO of containing Serb heavy weapons, 32 had been inspected and found to be clear. Ten sites remained unvisited. At 1300 hours only five sites remained unvisited. Still no weapons had been found. In Naples, Boorda had to use every device he could think of to delay the NATO ambassadors from making a decision. They had finally decided to launch air strikes against the remaining unverified sites when, at 1315 hours, I sent a last message to Boorda that all sites had been visited and no weapons found. There had been full compliance by both sides. A few minutes further delay and it would have been too late to prevent the aircraft taking off.

There was, I suspect, bitter disappointment among the hawks in NATO. If their wishes had prevailed and air strikes had taken place, the UNHCR aid programme would have been severely disrupted and the future of the UN mission in Bosnia would have been placed in doubt. I remembered Gen. Milovanovic's words: "In case of air strikes, all foreigners who find themselves on our territory will become hostages. These include International Red Cross and UN relief workers." I sent a message to the UNMOs and JCOs congratulating them on their historic achievement. Monday 21 February had, only just, turned out to be just another day.

That afternoon I made a visit to the suburb of Dobrinja, the scene of so much fighting in the past. All the buildings were damaged and the debris of war lay all about. In places exposed to direct Serb observation and fire, wrecked cars had been piled up and trenches dug so that people could move about the area without being killed. The brigade commander once again seemed pleased to see me. I told him I would like to talk to some of his soldiers in the front line to see how confident they were of the ceasefire.

An elderly man was summoned, who said that he had fought in Dobrinja throughout the siege but was now too old to be in the front line. As we approached an open patch of ground between the wrecked buildings I observed that the local people were still using a trench that ran round the edge of the area to reach the other side. Our guide jumped into the trench and beckoned to Goose and me to follow. He explained that we were close to the line of conflict and that Serb snipers were less than 100 metres away and would not hesitate to open fire. I told him that we all had to have confidence in the ceasefire, and to demonstrate this I invited him to accompany us in our walk across the open ground. To reassure him, I unbuttoned my coat to show that, like him, none of the UN party wore flak jackets. This did not reassure him, but he finally agreed.

We set off with Goose hanging back, staring hard in the direction of the Serb trenches, as if challenging them to open fire. No one said anything until we reached the other side, at which point I shook the old man's hand and congratulated him. He replied with a smile that it was the first time in two years that anyone had walked on that ground – and lived.

Some children nearby were playing hopscotch and the old man pointed out the curious patterns they set for themselves as they played. He explained that the children knew almost instinctively the precise limits of the Serb field of fire, and they had programmed themselves never to cross certain invisible lines on the ground, for to do so meant instant death. Some of them were not even four years old, yet everyone obeyed the rules of this macabre game. The children's paintings covered the walls of their schoolroom, which was hidden at the back of a building. Many depicted dead people on the ground, with crimson pools of blood painted around them.

I later heard that the old man had walked across the same piece of ground the next day and had been shot in the neck and seriously wounded. At the hospital he was asked why he had been so stupid. He replied that unless people demonstrated confidence in the peace process, the country would be permanently at war. He would do it again when he recovered.

The afternoon of our visit to Dobrinja we also visited the Serb positions immediately opposite. I wanted to see for myself what sort of people the Serb snipers were. The young Serb company commander who showed us round was a professional soldier from the former Yugoslav Army. In stark contrast, his men wore a motley collection of uniforms and seemed old enough to have fought in the Second World War, though the trenches were more reminiscent of the First World War. We were led through an intricate system of trenches and bunkers, some of them several levels below ground. Water ran everywhere and we walked cautiously in the dark on broken duckboards. Candles in old biscuit tins flickered on the wall, throwing the soldiers' faces into sinister relief. At the end of the trench line we were told to be quiet, since the Muslims were only yards away. Standing on an ammunition box and peering through a periscope I could see, about 200 metres away, the open patch of grass we had walked across earlier that day.

I asked the soldier manning the position if he had seen us. He boasted that he had tracked Goose all the way across the exposed area with the cross hair of his telescopic sight held steady on the middle of his back. He had not pulled the trigger as he had heard there was a ceasefire. Otherwise we would all be dead. It made no difference that we were UN personnel. During the war, no one walked across that space. Goose stared thoughtfully at him but said nothing.

The soldier then pointed out a number of bullet marks at the back of the trench, behind the narrow firing aperture. When I remarked that the Muslim snipers must be good, he scornfully replied that at such close range it was difficult to miss. After some confusing directions, looking through the periscope, I finally identified the Bosnian trench. It was less than 10 metres away. The two sides had been fighting like this for nearly two years. When I asked him if he had ever opened fire at children, he told me that he had never seen any, but that he would undoubtedly shoot them. After all, they would grow up to be Muslims and it was better to kill them now. He had been a teacher before the war, and his reply was a grim indication to me of the fragility of civilisation.

On 24 February our first month in Bosnia came to an end. The pace of life had been hectic and in the last four weeks none of us had slept for more than a few hours a day. Simon Shadbolt in particular had performed heroically. Apart from keeping up with daily events, he had planned the reorganisation of the UN staff, which included moving key elements of the HQ in Kiseljak to the Residency in Sarajevo. He had also drafted the initial set of operations orders for the UN, reflecting the campaign plan we had developed in England. George Waters, the aide-de-camp, had had to keep ahead of the hectic programme that changed daily, while Nick Costello had spent many hours translating during the lengthy negotiations. Apart from the practical aspects of commanding UNPROFOR, I had been heavily involved with Akashi and Cot in trying to steer NATO and the Americans away from their determination to end the war in Bosnia by bombing the Serbs.

While all of this was going on, the UNPROFOR HQ continued to facilitate the flow of aid across the battle lines to nearly three million people in Bosnia. Clearance for convoys had to be obtained, bridges had to be built and roads had to be cleared of snow and mines. None of this had been straightforward for the men and women in the UN and the difficulties of their jobs had been compounded by the poor weather and the renewed fighting between the Muslims and Croats in the south of the country. Despite their heroic efforts, only half the aid required in Bosnia was delivered during the month of February.

We also had to contend with increased media hostility. I was particularly annoyed by a TV reporter who accused me during a news report of being "economical with the truth" when, at a press conference, I had described the progress being made by the UN in establishing weapon collecting sites. He was in effect calling me a liar. The day after his report, I met him on a visit to a weapons site manned by the Coldstream Guards. With an ingratiating smile he asked me for an interview and to his surprise and horror I responded by dragging him bodily away from his camera team where I challenged him to repeat his accusation. He was in such a state of shock he couldn't speak, no doubt because he believed that anyone who has served with the SAS was probably a mad killer. I told him that if he ever called me a liar again I would tear out his tongue. This was especially well received by the Guardsmen sitting on top of a nearby APC who started to offer me words of encouragement such as "Why don't you break his leg as well?" They too felt frustrated at the constant criticism levelled against the UN. The reporter failed to see the funny side of the incident and he went on to file some extremely negative reports on the UN's efforts to bring peace to Bosnia.

Later that day we visited the Jewish Cemetery in Grbavica. For me it was the most dramatic reminder so far of the inhumanity, violence and chaos of the war in Bosnia. The cemetery was one of the most bitterly contested areas of the conflict line round Sarajevo, because from there it was possible to shoot directly down into the city centre only a few hundred metres away. On the Serb side, part of the line was held by a group of extremists calling themselves the "Heroes", a dangerous bunch of mercenaries who had volunteered their services to the Bosnian Serbs. They were apparently not much interested in money or ideology, only in killing people. Most of the sniping at civilians in the area round the Holiday Inn came from this area of the Jewish Cemetery. It was even said that the "Heroes" hired out their best sniping positions to wealthy big game hunters from abroad who wanted to add a human being to their bag. Among the ranks of the "Heroes" were Japanese, Russians and even an American. Following the ceasefire, when Soubirou and the local Serb commander had tried to enter their part of the line in order to establish a French observation post between the lines, the "Heroes" simply fired over their heads and told them to go away.

We approached along a road running above the cemetery and found our way blocked by a makeshift barricade that we removed without difficulty, despite the proximity of some Serb soldiers, who peered at us from fortified houses beside the road. They asked us if we were the reinforcements they had been promised. When we told them who we were they looked disappointed. Clearly they had never seen the UN before. We drove into no man's land, carefully skirting the suspicious-looking mounds that lay just beneath the snow. From their geometrical pattern we guessed they were mines. After travelling about 100 metres, we spotted a group of French soldiers on their hands and knees at the edge of the road probing for mines. The lieutenant in charge looked extremely surprised to see us coming from the Serb side of the minefield and told us that we could not go any further, adding somewhat unnecessarily that we were in a minefield and were "standing in the most dangerous place in the western hemisphere!" Goose asked me to translate, but I didn't think it would be particularly helpful to repeat this to a man whose job it was to ensure my safe return to Britain.

The French lieutenant went on to explain that the Bosnian Army had begun to take advantage of the ceasefire to extend their trenches towards the Serbs, who had frequently fired on them to prevent this happening. I made a mental note to report this to Delic, as both sides had agreed not to advance their trenches. Meanwhile we still had the problem of whether to go forward or back. In the end, with the help of the French soldiers we cautiously made a three-point turn and returned the way we had come. As a result I never met the "Heroes" and the Serbs forcibly removed them from their positions some weeks later.

The next day I was summoned by Cot to attend yet another conference in Zagreb.

He had been asked by Chuck Redman to try to obtain a peace accord between the Bosnians and the Croats. The latter were fighting to carve out for themselves a piece of southern Bosnia, which they called Hercog-Bosna, and in doing so, they had committed some of the worst atrocities of the war. These included the destruction of east Mostar and the massacre in 1993 of over 100 women and children in a small village called Ahmici in the Laskva Valley. At the start of the civil war in Bosnia, the Croats had been prepared to form alliances with anyone who would help them. In some sectors they sided with the Bosnians, in others with the Serbs. In Sarajevo, surprisingly, a Croatian Brigade still formed part of the defences of the city. The Bosnian Croat Army (HVO) had been reinforced with up to 5,000 regular soldiers from Croatia. Black-market fuel for the Bosnian Serbs flowed through Croatia, as well as weapons and ammunition for the Bosnians, in defiance of the UN arms embargo and despite the fact that in some sectors the arms were used against the Bosnian Croatians. All attempts to impose sanctions on Croatia had failed because of the opposition of Germany. The UN was forced to turn a blind eye to this breaking of their arms embargo by the Croats as many of the UN HQs and logistical bases were situated on Croatian territory. It was all a bit of a muddle.

Gen. Roso had only recently been appointed head of the Bosnian Croat Army. As a former French Legionnaire he had served under the command of several French officers now serving in Bosnia and liked to salute his former officers in the style of the French Army. He called Cot "mon Général". He was highly amusing and once tried to persuade me to accept a plan that he had developed to use the UN and NATO to launch a joint attack with the Bosnian Croat Army against the Serbs. I had laughed, saying that if we eliminated the Serbs for him, the way would be open for him to overrun the rest of Bosnia.

The peace conference took place in a room devoid of furniture except for three chairs and a table. Cot began by making an elegant welcoming speech to Delic and Roso, who sat opposite each other looking uncomfortable. When Cot had finished, he quite unexpectedly got up and left the room, telling me that he wanted me to run the remainder of the negotiations. Normally it would take a whole day for me to prepare for such a meeting and with such short notice I had no strategy for breaking the deadlock between the two sides that had been so evident in Kiseljak three days before.

Using the old Staff College adage that if you have nothing to say at least say it with confidence, I gave them once again the opening speech that I had made in Kiseljak. To my astonishment, Delic and Roso suddenly came to life and, as if rehearsing a play, they agreed that the fighting between them had to stop, that the real enemy to peace in Bosnia was the aggressor Serb. In fact, they would sign a complete cessation of hostilities there and then. Trying to conceal my astonishment, I switched on my computer and started drafting the details of the agreement including troop withdrawals, the establishment of weapons collection sites and the interpositioning of UN troops. In places where the Bosnian and Croatian armies faced the Serbs, I agreed that each side would be permitted to retain mortars and artillery, so that they could continue to fire upon the Serbs. However they could not fire against each other and in order to ensure that this didn't happen, I insisted that UN officers should be located in each fire base. For the first time in history, peacekeeping duties now included the direction of artillery and mortar fire. Five hours later the details of the implementation of the peace deal had been settled, typed on the computer, and signed by both sides. As the discussions proceeded, it became clear to me that Delic and Roso had both been briefed by their respective political masters before the meeting arranged by Redman. The phrases they used were identical and even the sequence in which they discussed the details of the plan was the same. When Delic, not a bright officer, muffed his words, Roso had prompted him and there was no sign of the personal animosity which had clouded our previous meeting. At the end of the conference Cot returned, photographs were taken and we all went our separate ways. The two generals had simply followed the instructions of the politicians, who remained in total control throughout the war. In Bosnia, it was undoubtedly the politicians who called the shots, including those fired by their snipers at children in the street.

As I climbed the rickety step ladder of the Ilyushin 76 on my way back to Sarajevo that evening, the Ukrainian captain of the aircraft shook me by the hand and said that he had seen me on television. I scarcely responded. I was so tired that I fell asleep in the bunk behind the pilots and slept throughout the flight. As we approached Sarajevo, I was pleased to see that the aircrew no longer put on their flak vests before landing. At the Residency, Brig. John Reith was waiting with a complete plan for implementing what became known as the Washington Accord, which created the federation between the Croats and the Bosnians. He was required to take control of some 560 kilometres of battle line, roughly half the distance of the line that NATO forces subsequently had to manage under the Dayton Agreement. Nevertheless John had to accomplish this task with a tenth of the troops and of course he still had the war between the Serbs and the new federation to cope with. He was also responsible for establishing the Joint Commission set up to resolve any disputes between the two sides. He wrote many of the rules of procedure for implementing the peace agreement, which were subsequently adopted by the NATO peacekeepers serving in the Implementation Force in 1995. He was a tough-minded officer, greatly respected by the military commanders of both sides. On one occasion, in a delaying tactic, the commanders of the warring factions told him they wanted their personal representatives to walk along the entire line of conflict, in order to determine its precise location. John duly dispatched them with a team of extremely fit British liaison officers and on the first day they covered more than 30 miles. Since the conflict line ran through mountainous country, the Bosnians and Croatians were reduced to physical wrecks and at the next Joint Commission meeting their commanders signed up to John's map without further question.

Looking back on the month, I believe that, had Chuck Redman arrived with a different brief – one which accepted the need for compromise – then the signing of the Dayton Agreement in 1995 could well have been achieved a year earlier. The momentum generated by the ceasefire, the withdrawal of heavy weapons round

Sarajevo and the cessation of hostilities between the Bosnians and the Croats had undoubtedly created a window of opportunity for a permanent peace in Bosnia. That hard-won opportunity was tragically wasted. Nevertheless it was in the spring of 1994 that the US Administration began to grasp the realities of the situation and that compromises would have to be made. The catalyst for this process was the visit by Gen. John Galvin, former Supreme Allied Commander Europe (SACEUR), who was sent to Bosnia by President Clinton to advise on the structure of the new Federal Army. He was to see for himself the danger for the USA in pursuing a foreign policy in Bosnia shaped by the propaganda machine of a clever, ruthless government.

CHAPTER THREE

A New Direction

We know the purpose of the journey and we have an idea of the final destination. However, the road is not defined, and there are many obstacles and detours. Indeed, our car may be requisitioned at any time.

Shashi Tharoor Under-Secretary, United Nations,
Lecture on "Peacekeeping" to Royal College of Defence Studies.

THE PACE OF EVENTS DURING OUR FIRST MONTH IN BOSNIA HAD LEFT us breathless but exhilarated. The Washington Accord,[1] the political agreement between the Muslims and Croats to establish a new Bosnian Federation, the 9 February Sarajevo Airport Agreement and the NATO ultimatum, had transformed the strategic situation in Bosnia. We had demonstrated to the world that it was possible to bring about peace through negotiation. Now our job was to maintain the momentum of the peace process, something that I believed could only be done by the deployment of an additional 10,000 peacekeeping troops in Bosnia. These reinforcements were urgently needed, partly to garrison the remaining safe areas of Gorazde and Zepa where no troops had yet been deployed, and partly to monitor the ceasefire between the Bosnians and the Croats in central Bosnia. Additional resources would also allow the UN to help rebuild the shattered infrastructure of the country. Only by doing these things could the newly found sense of confidence among the people of Bosnia be sustained.

I knew that the opponents of the peace process would be working against us, people who felt that Serb aggression should not go unpunished and that the West should take military action to reimpose a unitary State in Bosnia. These included people in the US Congress with an eye on the forthcoming elections, such as Senator Bob Dole, as well as hawks in the State Department and NATO who felt that bombing the Serbs would quickly end the war. Within our own Foreign Office and Ministry of Defence, opinions were evenly divided between those who wished to support that line and those who saw the dangers of pursuing a war policy. It was not clear to me which way the debate in the UK would go. Many journalists in Sarajevo also supported the war option, either because they believed that it was morally right to engage in some form of holy war against the Serbs or else because images of war sell better than those of peace. A journalist working for a leading London newspaper summed up this view when he told Simon Shadbolt that he did not care about the facts or the UN argument in favour of peace, his object was to get the West involved in a war in Bosnia.

Nevertheless, I remained confident that if the UN was able to demonstrate practical progress on the ground and a sufficient number of ordinary people in Bosnia saw that there was a credible alternative to war, then it should be possible to isolate the hawks.

My chief ally in the Foreign Office was the Head of the UN Department, Glynne Evans. She had taught international affairs at the University of Wales for several years and, since joining the Foreign Office, had worked in the UN in New York, where she had first met Sergio de Mello and Viktor Andreev. During her frequent visits to my HQ, she would disappear into the worst-hit areas of Sarajevo on her own and talk to the local people and to aid workers. These solitary excursions had given her a uniquely different perspective on Bosnia from her colleagues, who usually regarded the preservation of Britain's "special relationship" with America and the credibility of NATO as more important than peace in Bosnia. The day before the NATO deadline was due to expire, when the rest of the world seemed concerned with the impending air campaign against the Serbs, Glynne Evans had typically spent the afternoon visiting the isolated community of Hrasnica, at the foot of Mt Igman. Hrasnica had seen some of the worst fighting around Sarajevo and because it was so difficult to get aid through to its inhabitants they were among the most deprived of Sarajevo's population. At the end of her visit, she had sent a letter home called "Bombs or Bread?" It began elegantly: "The people of Sarajevo have taken to the streets. It is no longer just a hunt for food or water. The Sarajevans are rediscovering their city ... "

Even the UN peacekeepers benefited from the relative peace that had descended on Sarajevo. Since the ceasefire had come into effect, living conditions had noticeably improved: there were more cars on the streets, the traffic lights and tramlines were being repaired, the boarding on windows was being taken down and cafes were opening up for business. The new mood of optimism had affected even VicePresident Ganic, who, though not famed for his courage, had taken down the sandbags from his office, giving the lie to his repeated assertion that he could still see Serb artillery pointing down at the city from the hills.

UNPROFOR still faced many difficulties in changing the situation in Bosnia from war to peace. Although the big guns had gone and the ceasefire was holding, Sarajevo was still technically under siege and the UN remained the main source of provisions for its inhabitants. Clearances for aid convoys had to be obtained and these were frequently held up for trivial reasons. When the Serbs decided to co-operate, the Bosnian Government would often become obstructive. This happened in early March when Ganic refused to allow coal to be delivered by the UNHCR over the Brotherhood and Unity bridge from the Serb-held suburb of Grbavica into the Muslim part of the city. On another occasion in Sarajevo, when Fred Cuny switched on a water-purification plant built with money from the George Soros Foundation, the

Bosnian Government ordered the water to be diverted back into the river, stating that it had failed an unspecified test for purity. Since the people of Sarajevo had until then been drinking water straight from the river, it is more likely that the Government was reluctant to lose the money it made from licensing water carriers.

Away from Sarajevo, the fighting between the Serbs and the Bosnians continued unabated. On 28 February, four Serb Galeb jets bombed a munitions factory in Novi Travnik in central Bosnia, and were shot down by NATO fighters. The Galeb aircraft were in violation of the NATO ultimatum, "Operation Deny Flight", that forbade the use of aircraft by all combatants. Karadzic flatly denied that the aircraft were Serb, though this denial was somewhat undermined by the subsequent funeral of the pilots in Belgrade. It was becoming plain to me that in the Balkans a lie is not supposed to be for ever.

The shooting down of the Serb aircraft had been a useful demonstration of the military effectiveness of NATO and it was many months before the Serbs attempted a similar raid. Unfortunately NATO air power proved less effective against helicopters, to which "Operation Deny Flight" equally applied. It was difficult for the fast NATO jets to identify and destroy slow-moving helicopters flying close to the ground. NATO was also reluctant to engage helicopters, fearing that they might be carrying injured soldiers or civilians. As a result the warring sides used their helicopters with impunity throughout the war.

In Sarajevo evidence was emerging that both the Bosnians and the Serbs were ignoring the Airport Agreement. On most nights we could hear the Bosnian Army tanks or mortars, which they kept in a tunnel behind the Residency, firing at the Serbs in the area of the Jewish Cemetery, and the Serbs firing back. Despite protests from the Serbs and the UN, Delic's soldiers continued to advance their trenches towards Serb lines in the area of the Jewish Cemetery. When I confronted him, Delic simply denied that these encroachments were happening, even though I had taken Karavelic, his deputy, to point out the violations on the ground.

The Serbs were subtler in the way they broke the rules. By night they moved T55 tanks to and from their main repair workshop, located inconveniently for them in Hadzici, just within the 20-kilometre exclusion zone. The day NATO had shot down the Serb jets, an UNMO reported seeing a large number of Serb tanks moving through the TEZ to the west of Sarajevo. If this were true, I knew that such a violation would soon prompt calls from New York for the UN to take punitive action against the Serbs. There was fresh snow on the ground and it would be relatively easy to tell if tanks had moved through the area, so I set off to see for myself. In fact no tank tracks were discernible but as it grew dark Goose spotted a T55 tank, partially hidden, with its gun pointing directly at us from a range of 10 metres. Fortunately, the tank was unmanned and had obviously not been moved for several days, probably not since the NATO ultimatum had expired.

As Goose attempted to start it, we were surrounded by men carrying automatic weapons. They claimed to belong to a paramilitary organisation not answerable to Mladic and therefore not subject to the rules of the NATO ultimatum. Nick Costello told them that there could be no exceptions to the ultimatum and that if the tank was not placed in a UN weapons collection site by dawn the next day it would be destroyed by NATO. They responded to this threat by taking up firing positions around us, and I heard Goose behind me quietly cock his weapon. It was probable that they were trying to take us hostage against the possibility of an air strike. Just as it looked as though we were going to be involved in an armed stand-off, two Coldstream Guards Warrior APCs came clattering noisily down the track and a young ensign, Christopher St George, popped his head out of a turret and cheerily asked if he could be of help. George Waters had happened to be in the UN operations room in Sarajevo when we reported our discovery, and he had called St George to the scene. At the sight of the APCs, the Serb soldiers backed off and, after I had repeated my warning, they departed at speed down the track towards Ilizda where a Serb brigade HQ was located. I suggested to St George that he should park his APC in front of the tank, and shoot anyone who tried to move it. He looked delighted at the prospect but later told me that, after a tense night, a civilian driver had arrived early next day and had meekly driven the tank under escort to the nearby UN weapons collection site at Osijek.

Life in the Residency was now settling into a fairly pleasant routine. Despite the fact that the number of people living in the building had increased (when most of the Kiseljak HQ moved to Sarajevo), Colour Sgt Pearce and Cpl Bennison had managed to transform the living arrangements within the Residency. I lived in a room beside my office on the first floor. Viktor was lodged across the landing in a bedroom that doubled as his office. This arrangement had its drawbacks because of the enormous size of the double bed. It was not unusual to find a clutch of Russian generals sitting on the bed, surrounded by UN officials, while Viktor sat crouched over a tiny desk in the corner. From here he could put telephone calls directly through to Moscow or Belgrade.

When the main HQ had moved from Kiseljak to the Residency, a complex of Portakabins was built in the garden beside our offices. From Simon's office, we could walk directly across a bridge to the Chief of Staff's office, from where all day-to-day operations in Bosnia were directed. As the UN officially can have no secrets, peace-keeping operations are "transparent". No classified documents relating to the mission were held in any of our offices. In the evening Simon's office often became a public meeting place in which journalists, UNHCR personnel, visitors from abroad and anyone else who was interested would be invited to sit around and discuss the situation.

At 0800 each day a general briefing would be held, attended by about 30 military officers, aid workers and civil affairs representatives. At this meeting the events of the past 24 hours would be reviewed, new tactics discussed and fresh orders given. In this way it was possible to coordinate all the different political, civil and military agencies. Following this meeting there was a separate briefing of the press held some-times in the French HQ in the PTT building and on other occasions in the Holiday Inn. However, every day around 1100 hours, an anonymous typewritten account of our meeting would be slipped under the doors of the journalists' rooms located in the Holiday Inn. I suspected that it was probably the Bosnian intelligence service that was circulating these reports, as the briefing room in the Residency, like most other rooms, was bugged.

After the main meeting, Viktor and I would retire to my office with the Chief of Staff where we could talk on a less restricted basis. Despite the rule that there can be no secrets in a UN mission, it would have been impossible to run a military operation without keeping some things from the world at large. This was especially necessary because UNPROFOR had been deployed into the middle of a civil war in which there was only limited co-operation from the warring parties, who were supposedly our partners. My office had been swept by British and American technical teams and officially declared free of all electronic listening devices. However, I was later told that the Americans had installed their own device in my office and that what we said was apparently being reported to the US Commander in Chief in Naples. The telephone system in Simon's office was also tapped, this time by the Bosnian intelligence service and often what we said on the phone was leaked within hours to the media.

On the whole these eavesdropping operations in the Residency were of little consequence. In fact, they helped to demonstrate that the UN had no hidden agenda other than its publicly declared commitment to peace. We were usually careful about what we said in the Residency, although in moments of irritation or excitement things sometimes slipped out with unexpected results. Shortly after calling the Bosnians "savages" during dinner one evening, I was summoned to the Prime Minister's office and asked why I had done so, when the Bosnians were Europeans like myself. I refrained from replying that, in my view, after the way they had slaughtered each other it would take them at least 500 years to achieve that status.

As the ceasefire became more established, members of my HQ in Sarajevo were able to adopt a more relaxed lifestyle. Once the routine morning meetings were over, unless I was involved in negotiations in Pale or Sarajevo, I would spend the remainder of the day visiting my command elsewhere in Bosnia with Goose and anyone else who wanted to come. As a matter of policy I liked to see all UN battalions at least three times in their six-month tour of duty, and since there were 16 battalions under command in UNPROFOR this took up much of my time. I would also visit local UNHCR aid distribution depots and call on the local military commanders of the warring parties. When we crossed the conflict line leaving Sarajevo we would have to pass through both Bosnian and Serb checkpoints, and I insisted that we got out of our vehicles and spent time talking to the soldiers manning them. It was far better to sit with them in their bunkers drinking coffee and discussing the current situation, than to stare at them from behind armoured glass. When we first started to tour the countryside, we got mixed reactions from the soldiers we met; sometimes they were threatening, sometimes welcoming. By the end of the year we had got to know some of the soldiers manning the checkpoints so well that even when their bosses had ordered them to block our movements, they would let us pass.

Occasionally a local commander would decide to play games with us. On the way to Vitez one day, as if telling us to turn back, the Croats began firing shells at 100 metre intervals beside us as we drove along the valley. We ignored them. Once, when I saw a Bosnian soldier shooting in our direction from a bunker, I turned to point him out to Simon, only to find my military assistant crouching on the floor in the back of the Land Rover. I asked why he was doing this when we were in an armoured vehicle and Simon confessed that, as our own vehicle was being serviced, we had been issued for the day with an unarmoured one. On another occasion we were confronted by a renegade Croat called Vlasko, who was working as a mercenary for the Serbs. Vlasko was a notorious killer. He had a long black beard, wore a necklace of human teeth and drove round Bosnia in a black Toyota Land Cruiser with a child's skull on the bonnet. The week before he had threatened to kill a UN brigadier. As we left a Serb HQ near Ilijas, he was waiting for us, surrounded by his heavily armed, black-suited henchmen. I walked by without comment, but Goose stopped in front of Vlasko and stood for some time staring down at him. Vlasko suddenly turned around, clambered into his vehicle and drove away. Goose had heard from one of Mladic's bodyguards that Vlasko had been boasting that he was going to kill my bodyguard. It appeared that, on meeting him, he had changed his mind.

If we were in Sarajevo in the afternoon we would often go running, something which demonstrated to the local people our confidence in the peace process and also allowed us to get away from the office for a couple of hours. Our runs created confusion among the Bosnian secret police, who had orders from Ganic to follow us everywhere. As the routes we chose took us close to the conflict line, they were unable to run themselves, nor could they loiter slowly behind in their cars. In the end they gave up trying to follow us, though we noticed that the Bosnian soldiers in the trenches along the route would sometimes fire at the Serbs as we passed by, presumably in the hope that the returning Serb fire would force us to abandon our run. I was once running and panting alongside L/Sgt Daly when a sniper's bullet cracked close by. When I asked him whether he had heard it too, he smartly replied, "Got it, sir", leaving me wondering for the rest of the run where on earth British soldiers learn these smart sounding but completely meaningless phrases.

One of the charms of Sarajevo is that most of the ugly, high-rise flats are confined to the bottom of the main valley, so by climbing the hills behind, it is possible to reach the countryside in a few minutes. Here people live in small farming communities among orchards and meadows. Each house is built around a courtyard and many of the villages seemed untouched by the war. Where Serb trenches overlooked the villagers as they tilled their fields or tended their goats, they had constructed walls of corrugated iron to protect themselves. They seemed determined to maintain their traditional way of life.

Throughout the year we were able to follow the passing seasons. From the long, dark, freezing winter afternoons when smog filled our lungs and our running shoes slipped on the ice, we progressed quickly through the short Bosnian spring in April, when the shutters of the houses were thrown open and bedding was hung out to air. In the summer, dust lay deep in the streets and behind the closed shutters as we passed we could hear the quiet murmur of voices or the sound of water splashing in the fountains. In the autumn, we saw people preparing for the winter by chopping wood and building neat log stacks beside their houses. These pastoral images of Sarajevo have endured in my memory far more than those of the war.

The evenings in Sarajevo were usually spent discussing strategy and exchanging ideas with whoever was visiting the Residency at the time. Gen. Briquemont, my predecessor, had banned all journalists from the Residency and preferred to dine alone with selected members of his personal staff. By throwing open our door to journalists and others we were actually implementing one of the main elements in our campaign plan. We firmly believed that the media was part of the solution in Bosnia rather than an impediment to what the UN was trying to do. It was true that the biased reporting of some journalists often made our job harder. But if we only met journalists during formal, sometimes confrontational press conferences, and if we did not allow them to travel with us to experience at first-hand the difficulties facing the UN, then we only had ourselves to blame if media reports were over-simplistic or too critical of us.

Most of the team who had come out with me from England had served in Northern Ireland, where the British Army had learned painful lessons about handling the media. It was our job to introduce these lessons to the UN. Dealing with the press in a peacekeeping mission is always going to be more complex than in wartime. In a war environment, journalists cannot travel freely about the battlefield or talk to the enemy, and they are often obliged to depend on the military structure for their information as well as for their survival. In a UN mission, however, journalists owe peacekeepers nothing. Many of them had been in Bosnia since the start of the war and had already formed fixed views about the situation. As a result of our evening debates, we learned as much from them as they did from us, though I doubt if we changed many minds.

When we arrived in Bosnia, the most commonly expressed view was that the UN had lost its way and that by delivering humanitarian aid it was in fact prolonging the war. In response we argued that some UN aid would obviously be used by the warring parties to feed their soldiers, but that it was morally and politically unacceptable to subject many millions of people to further slaughter, dispersion and death by not trying to help them. The argument that the UN should not have intervened in Bosnia was most often expressed by commentators living in safety and comfort abroad. It was not a view that found favour with the common people of Bosnia, who understood that they depended on the UN for their survival.

Another prevailing view was that the UN mission was badly run, overstaffed and that when UN soldiers were required to risk their lives to help others they frequently did not do so. Endless stories were recounted of injured people being abandoned under fire while UN soldiers cowered in their armoured vehicles. The media had been particularly incensed by the murder of a Bosnian Vice-President under French armed escort at a Serb roadblock the year before. I was determined not to allow such things to happen again, but, like every other commander on a peacekeeping mission,

I had to accept that, in the final analysis, it was up to the individual soldier to make the right decision. I could not order them to act in a particular way, I could only create the conditions that would encourage a more robust approach in the execution of the mission.

Firstly, the young peacekeepers needed to be confident that I would support them if they used force. Secondly, I had to demonstrate to them that the UN mission in Bosnia could succeed and that, despite the negative propaganda against it, the mission in Bosnia had been successful in alleviating suffering and creating opportunities for peace. Peacekeepers had to believe that any risks they took or sacrifices they made would be justified by results. No one is prepared to sacrifice himself or his comrades for a failed mission. The perception created by the media in Bosnia and abroad was that the UN mission was in danger of collapse. This perception had to change. As part of our attempt to improve the mission's profile, we had to make the media understand what we were trying to do and why we had reacted in certain ways to events. I gave selected journalists the campaign plan to read and spent many hours with them explaining the short-term difficulties and setbacks we faced and the eventual benefits of the long-term strategy we were following.

By the end of March, even the most hostile members of the press in Sarajevo had started to admit that extraordinary progress had been made in Bosnia during the first three months of the year and that there was a new mood of confidence in UNPROFOR. Indeed, there was a danger that people were beginning to expect too much from the UN. The humanitarian situation in central Bosnia had been transformed by the creation of the federation and aid now moved freely from the UN depots on the coast through central Bosnia to Tuzla. Civilian casualties from the fighting had fallen dramatically and there was growing evidence of military co-operation between the Bosnians and the Croats.

In Sarajevo the absence of political will among the Serbs and the Bosnians to bring the war to an end made progress extremely difficult. Their representatives on the Joint Commission – whose task it was to improve freedom of movement in and out of Sarajevo, to restore the utilities, to stop the sniping and to bring about an exchange of prisoners – barely met. Relations between the two parties remained openly hostile, with Delic refusing to meet Mladic and Mladic agreeing to nothing unless he met Delic face to face. The restoration of electricity was postponed because the Bosnian Government refused to accept electricity along "Serb" power lines, and arguments about civil contracts for the repair of the Sarajevo water system prevented people from enjoying running water for many months.

A Royal Navy officer on my staff eventually solved this last problem by driving a Serb engineer and a Bosnian engineer separately in two Danish APCs to a critically damaged part of the pumping system that lay between the opposing lines of trenches. Placing the two vehicles back to back, he opened the doors and the two engineers stepped out. To everyone's surprise they had been at school together. The water pumps were repaired in less than an hour and most of Sarajevo was instantly supplied with running water. Elsewhere in Sarajevo the tram system was undergoing

repairs and the shops were fast filling up with commercial goods. It was hard sometimes to believe that the bloody civil war was still going on.

On 3 March I visited my old regiment, the Coldstream Guards, located in Vitez.
I had served with them 30 years ago in Aden when I had been engaged, for the first
time, in peacekeeping duties. I hoped to get an opportunity to see how the
Washington Accord between the Croats and Muslims was faring in the Laskva Valley,
an area that had seen some of the fiercest fighting of the war. On the way to Vitez, we
nearly found out the hard way that all was not going quite as well as we hoped. We
had had a long day and I had fallen asleep in the front of the Range Rover. Suddenly
we started to lurch violently from side to side. Waking with a start, I asked Goose
what the hell he was doing. "Just trying to avoid the mines," he replied. In the headlights I could see the anti-tank mines, which Goose was skilfully avoiding, laid across
the road. When we got to Vitez, I asked the operations officer why he had sent us a
report saying that the road between Kiseljak and Vitez was clear of mines. "Ah well,"
he said with a disarming smile, "I meant that the road was only clear by day. At night
both sides place mines on the road, as they still don't trust each other. We didn't think
anyone would be so stupid as to drive here at night!"

In the intense fighting the previous year in the Laskva Valley many towns, among
them Gornji Vakuf, Novi Travnik and Vitez, had been destroyed and some of the
worst massacres of the civil war had occurred in the region. Although the Croats
controlled the high ground above the valley, the lower slopes of the hills and the floor
of the valley had been successfully held by the Bosnians. In Stari Vitez, in the middle
of the valley, a small Croat enclave measuring less than a square kilometre had
resisted all Muslim attempts to capture it and people who had previously lived as
neighbours savagely fought each other from trenches only metres apart. Because of
the bitterness caused by fighting in such a small community, neither side had left
their trenches and they were still pointing their weapons at each other.

Walking through the Croat enclave in Stari Vitez with the local Croat commander,
the intensity of the fighting was immediately apparent. Few houses had been left
standing and empty cartridge cases, shrapnel and the tail fins of exploded rockets lay
everywhere. As we approached the end of the Croat trench system the Croat
commander became nervous and, putting his finger to his lips, whispered to us that
we should keep very quiet. By now, we were only separated from the Bosnian
trenches by a small lane. Crouching behind the ruins of a stone wall that separated
the garden of the house from the road, I decided personally to test the effectiveness
of the Washington Accord. If it was not working here, then Chuck Redman's efforts
and my own had been wasted. Without warning, I sprang into the middle of the
lane and shouted in the direction of the Bosnians that I was from the UN and that
I wished to talk to them. Behind me the Croats dived for cover, though Nick and
Goose followed me.

Not 10 metres away in the shell of a house across the road, I could see heads
bobbing up and down amid the rubble. I also noticed weapons being trained on us.
With Nick shouting words of encouragement, I kept talking and moved across the

road to where I could look directly down into the Bosnian position. A group of rather sheepish-looking soldiers huddled round a machine-gun looked back at me. They told Nick that they had been startled by our sudden appearance and, although they had heard about the ceasefire, they still feared a Croat attack. I invited them to come out of their trenches and meet the Croats on the other side of the road but they refused saying that they did not trust them. I told them that this was exactly what the Croat commander had said about them.

The Bosnian commander soon appeared and I told him that I would get the Croat commander to come out on to the road to meet him, if he would agree to do the same. He said that he knew him well, as he had been the English teacher in Stari Vitez before the war and had taught his children. He had not seen him for nearly two years, but he agreed that if the Croat would come out, then he would do the same. Within five minutes, not only were the two opposing commanders standing in the road talking to each other, but a number of their soldiers were doing the same. After about 10 minutes, I said that I intended to return to the Croat HQ by walking down the middle of the lane, and I invited the Croat commander to come with me, rather than return via the muddy trenches. To my surprise he agreed and on the way back I noticed that he never once looked over his shoulder. Building confidence in a peace process can sometimes take a remarkably short time and similar scenes were taking place elsewhere in central Bosnia. When I visited the town about two weeks later the Joint Commission was in full swing and there was no sign of soldiers manning the trenches.

Before returning to Sarajevo I also visited the HQ of the newly established UN sector command in the south west of Bosnia in Gornji Vakuf, where John Reith told me that the Washington Accord implementation was generally going well. He had developed good relationships with Delic and Roso, as well as with their subordinate commanders. He had installed Joint Commission liaison officers from both sides in his operations cell at his HQ in Gornji Vakuf, and problems regarding the implementation of the Washington Accord were solved directly across a table. On the other hand, the 9 February Airport Agreement between the Serbs and the Bosnians was not making any progress because of the lack of political support for the deal. It was clear that a fresh, internationally backed political initiative was urgently needed.

Taking a southern route on the way back to Sarajevo, we drove through the Serb town of Hadzici where a group of women had for many months been blocking the road. They were campaigning for the return of 120 of their menfolk who had been taken away early in the war by Muslim forces and were being held in appalling conditions in a grain silo not far distant in Tarcin. The Bosnian Government had taken them hostage in exchange for the return of missing Muslims captured or killed by the Serbs at the beginning of the war. Karadzic had always denied knowing their whereabouts, saying that neither side at the start of the war had kept records and that it was probable these men had been killed in action. On the Bosnian side, it was believed that the missing men were being used as forced labour. Even the International Committee of the Red Cross had failed to trace them.

The women of Hadzici were a militant lot and would allow nobody through their roadblock. They had once held Gen. Briquemont hostage for an entire day. Because we arrived late in the day, when it was sleeting and a bitter wind was blowing up the valley, we managed to pass through the block before the women had time to rush out of their hut and stop us. I halted the vehicles 100 yards past their position and Simon, Nick, Goose and I walked slowly back to where the women were standing in the road shouting at us. Through Nick, I introduced myself and asked them if they were the famous women of Hadzici. They seemed rather pleased by this and replied, "No, we are the *infamous* women of Hadzici," before proceeding to recount the sad story of their missing husbands and sons. I said that I would do everything I could to raise the matter again with the Bosnian Government and also with the media, as their story was little known. They looked desperately cold and undernourished, so I told them I would send them some soup and bread. When Nick and Goose turned up several hours later with a container full of soup, they burst into tears. As result we never had trouble passing through Hadzici, though later on they held up a French military convoy for five weeks. Sadly, we were never able to get the men released, although the Red Cross did manage to visit them on one occasion. What was baffling was the unwillingness of the international media to take up their cause. Maybe the incarceration of Serbs in inhuman conditions was not news. As we arrived back in Sarajevo, the clouds cleared away and a full moon shone down on a peaceful city lying beneath the snow-covered mountains. It had been an eventful day.

So far political action at the international level to follow up the successes achieved by UNPROFOR had proven woefully inadequate. On 4 March, the Security Council passed a new resolution calling for the consolidation of the ceasefire in Sarajevo and the establishment of complete freedom of movement for the civilian population and humanitarian aid agencies in Bosnia.[2] This resolution also urged the Secretary-General to appoint a civilian official who would develop a plan for the restoration of public services in Sarajevo.

The Secretary-General also called for reinforcements for Bosnia. Good intentions come cheap and sadly no nation responded to his call by offering to send the sorely needed additional troops that were vital to progress. Consequently, much of our time during the first week in March was taken up with Izetbegovic and Karadzic, when Akashi tried unsuccessfully to get them to comply with the conditions of this UN resolution.

In Washington at the end of February Prime Minister Silajdzic had agreed to the opening of Tuzla airfield, but at our meeting on 6 March with the Bosnian Government, Izetbegovic went back on this agreement. At the same meeting Ganic reneged on the agreement he had made with me to open the Brotherhood and Unity bridge, between the Bosnian-held areas of the city and the Serb suburb of Grbavica, to allow the passage of civilians and UN aid. Silajdzic had never been a dominant figure in the ruling Muslim Party for Democratic Action, and by 1994 it was apparent even to occasional visitors to Sarajevo that his power had started to wane.[3] Ganic, on the other hand, who was responsible for the Bosnian Armed Forces and the para-military police, had become ever more powerful. He remained close to President Izetbegovic and by the end of 1994 he was the main point of contact between the UN and the Bosnian Government. As a member of the inner cabinet he also controlled the Bosnian press, radio and television. He was detested by his own people who called him the "Silk Man".

Despite fresh assurances given to me by Delic, Ganic continued to prevent the opening of the bridge by stationing two lorry-loads of armed police on the Bosnian side. When French engineers set about removing the wrecked buses and cars that blocked the bridge, Ganic's policemen threatened to open fire on them and Soubirou, the French commander, came round to my HQ in a fury demanding action should be taken against the Bosnians. At the subsequent meeting in the Presidency with Ganic, Delic, Karavelic and Muratovic (the inappropriately named Minister for Co-operation with UNPROFOR), were also present. I told Ganic that I would order Soubirou to open fire on his thugs if the French troops were threatened again. I reminded him that the day before I had dispatched NATO aircraft to the enclave of Maglaj at the request of Delic to support the Bosnian Army. It was intolerable that the UN was being treated in this way. I accused Ganic of forcing the people of Sarajevo to suffer unnecessarily and told him that I would lodge a record of what he had done with the Secretary-General in New York. I ended by asking him whether he was aware that the press had discovered he had personally ordered the water from the IRC plant to be directed into the river. The next day the bridge was unblocked and civilian traffic started to move across it for the first time in two years.

In practice only the old or infirm were able to use the bridge and those wishing to cross it had first to obtain permission from their respective governments. As a result complete freedom of movement for the people of Sarajevo was never fully achieved. This reluctance to open up the city to civilian movement was not just a military instinct, it was also due to a sense of insecurity and desire to control everything that so characterised the political leaders in Bosnia. When electricity had been restored to Sarajevo, the traffic lights were among the first things to be repaired and a radar speed trap was erected in the centre of town, though there was still scarcely any traffic on the roads. The Bosnian police also set up roadblocks in all the main thoroughfares, where they flagged down vehicles and asked their occupants for details. I once asked a policeman at a checkpoint what he was doing, pointing out that his activity was contrary to the spirit of the UN resolution regarding freedom of movement. He replied that it was for reasons of control. I asked him what was the purpose of the control. He said it was to find out where people were going and why they were travelling. I asked him why he needed this information. He repeated that it was for control. I never did discover the true reason, but I suspect it had something to do with the fact that the officials responsible had lived under Tito's totalitarian rule in the former Yugoslavia and the habit of regulating all aspects of life had not left them.

After 42 days without a break, on 7 March George Waters suggested that we should attempt to ski down the Olympic downhill run on Mt Igman. A fanatical skier, he was

Walkabout in Sarajevo, *en route* to my first meeting with President Izetbegovic I stop and talk to an elderly man who wishes me good luck. Jeremy Bowen of the BBC looks on (26 January 1994).

The visit of Tansu Ciller, Prime Minister of Turkey, and Benazir Bhutto, Prime Minister of Pakistan on 1 February 1994 proved to be a propaganda coup for the Bosnian Government as the two prime ministers publicly called for air strikes and a lifting of the arms embargo. They also offered additional troops to the UN. (*Anthony Burridge*)

Brig.-Gen. Soubirou, French Commander of Sector Sarajevo and I demonstrate our confidence in the 9 February Airport Agreement by crossing the ill-named Bridge of Brotherhood and Unity (21 February 1994).

Gen. Sir John Wilsey was Commander-in-Chief UK Land Forces and Joint Commander of all British elements deployed in the former Yugoslavia. We spoke almost every day and I was lucky to have support in Britain from someone who instinctively understood the peace process.

French UN troops engaged in mine clearance behind the Jewish Cemetery in Sarajevo following the 9 February Airport Agreement.

Yasushi Akashi, the UN Secretary-General's Special Representative and Gen. Jean Cot, Commander-in-Chief of UNPROFOR, explain to the press the requirement for troop reinforcements in order to support the "safe areas" (3 March 1994).
(*Popperfoto/Reuters*)

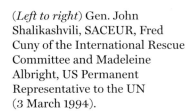

(*Left to right*) Gen. John Shalikashvili, SACEUR, Fred Cuny of the International Rescue Committee and Madeleine Albright, US Permanent Representative to the UN (3 March 1994).

A visit to Lukavica barracks, the Serb HQ in Sarajevo, for talks with Gen. Mladic, Commander-in-Chief of the Bosnian Serb Army, about weapon-collecting sites in the total exclusion zone (TEZ).

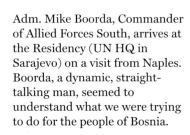

Adm. Mike Boorda, Commander of Allied Forces South, arrives at the Residency (UN HQ in Sarajevo) on a visit from Naples. Boorda, a dynamic, straight-talking man, seemed to understand what we were trying to do for the people of Bosnia.

Aid being unloaded at Sarajevo Airport from a RAF C130. Aircraft were turned round in less than 10 minutes and the Sarajevo airlift was the longest running in history. Many of the flights were flown by the US National Air Guard.

An important part of my job was keeping in touch with the Commander-in-Chief in Naples, who commanded all Allied Forces in the southern region of NATO. I am here using the US satellite communications system that accompanied me wherever I went.

The people of Sarajevo used every available space in the city to cultivate vegetables as a supplement to the UN rations on which they depended for their survival.

(*From left*) Gen. de Lapresle, Baroness Chalker, Lt-Gen. Rupert Smith, Malcolm Rifkind, Secretary of State for Defence, and Prime Minister John Major in Sarajevo on 18 March 1994. John Major was delighted by what British troops were doing to help keep alive hopes of peace. Gen. Rupert Smith was to succeed me as Commander of UNPROFOR in January 1995.

Capt. George Waters and others explain to me the fighting qualities of the Warrior armoured personal carrier (APC) on a visit to the Coldstream Guards.

With Eyup Ganic, the Bosnian Vice-President, at the football match at the Kosovo stadium on 20 March 1994 between a UN team and the Red Stars of Sarajevo.
(*Gubelic/Independent*)

The band of the Coldstream Guards, led by their Director of Music, Major David Marshal, after their performance at the football match.

I visit a Danish Leopard tank and its crew in position guarding Route Duck near Zavidovici in March 1994. I had moved the platoon of Danish tanks from Split to Tuzla where they later took part in the biggest UN tank battle of the war. The unit fired almost 100 rounds of main armament, destroying five Serb tanks.

Vitaly Churkin (*right*), President Yeltsin's Special Representative to Bosnia, on a visit to the Russian battalion.

(*From left*) Charles Redman, US Special Envoy to the Former Republic of Yugoslavia and Viktor Andreev (April 1994).

The outer office in the Sarajevo Residency was always crowded with people and was the nerve centre of UNPROFOR in Bosnia. Here, Nick Costello is talking to Gen. Mladic. After an angry exchange Nick slammed down the receiver and was applauded by everyone present. We had all had enough of Mladic for one day (April 1994).

On the phone discussing the use of NATO air strikes against the Serbs with Akashi, who was lunching with Karadzic in Pale at the time. (*Left to right*) Brig. Van Baal, Gen. de Lapresle, me and Viktor Andreev.

Ukrainian soldiers carry out casualty evacuation from Gorazde in April 1994. The undamaged buildings in the background refute the propaganda that the town had been largely destroyed.

Under an apple tree I meet the Serb commander Colonel Masal (*seated, bearded*) who led the assault on Gorazde. I told him I had personally ordered air strikes against the Serb units and that I would order more if he violated the town's TEZ or fired at my soldiers.

Haris Silajdzic (*right*), the Prime Minister of Bosnia-Hercegovina, often denounced the UN for not punishing the Serbs with air strikes. To his credit, he was probably the only leading Bosnian SDA politician who actually believed in multi-party democracy. He later resigned from the party in protest. (*EPA Photo*)

Sir Fitzroy MacLean, who led the UN mission to Yugoslavia in 1944, met me in Sarajevo. We concluded that our missions were very different. He had been waging a war against the Nazis, while I was fighting for peace (27 April 1994).

General George Joulwan, who succeeded General Shalikashvili as SACEUR, speaking to a French UN soldier inside a French observation post near the Jewish Cemetery in Sarajevo (5 May 1994). (*Popperfoto/Reuters*)

very frustrated by the fact that he was missing the ski season in the Alps. We started our ascent of the mountain from a Swedish Army camp located at the bottom of the ski run in a hotel destroyed by the Serbs when they withdrew from Mt Igman. The Serbs had smashed the ski lifts and it was rumoured that they had also put mines on the ski runs. No one had attempted the Olympic run before, but the Swedish company commander was keen to make the descent and equipped us with skis and skins. It was a brilliant day with a clear blue sky although below us Sarajevo was languishing under a layer of smog.

The climb took nearly two hours. By the time we had reached the top, our party had grown to include a group of French *Chasseurs Alpins*, an American Special Forces soldier from the US communications team, Jim Lenski, who was carrying my satellite radio on his back, Goose, George and myself. As we approached the summit it became plain that, however much we had assured ourselves that we were only out for a leisurely afternoon, we were in fact about to repeat the 1984 Olympics! With a shout – " 'Ware mines!" – we launched ourselves down the near-vertical start to the course. Normally the descent would have taken less than three minutes, but because the snow was soft and the *piste* unmarked, it took us about 10 minutes to complete.

When I arrived at the bottom I looked round to see that most of the French and Swedes were already there. Predictably, the winner of the race was Capt. George Waters. There was no sign of Goose. High on the hill above us we could just make out a small figure trudging down through the snow. When he finally arrived carrying a broken ski, I jokingly asked him whether he had hit a mine. "Nothing like that," he said, grinning, "but this skiing is definitely harder than it looks." It turned out that he had launched himself down the Olympic course without ever having skied before, on the grounds that it was his duty to stay with me at all times.

On 9 March Gen. John Galvin, special adviser to President Clinton, arrived in Sarajevo tasked with bringing the Croat and Bosnian Armies into a new Federal defence structure. Probably it was the most important visit that occurred during my year in Bosnia, as for the first time a senior US general was able to see for himself the situation on the ground and the dangers inherent in the policies apparently being advocated in the USA by the State Department.

I had first met Galvin on a NATO exercise in Germany three years previously when he had been SACEUR. He was a small, silver-haired man with a courteous, scholarly manner, a brilliant intellect and a reputation for open-mindedness, though he could be impatient with fools. I told him that while I realised that it was politically impossible for President Clinton to deploy troops to Bosnia before a peace deal had been agreed, it was also true that without them, there could be no permanent peace. We also discussed the desire of the State Department to enforce a "just" solution on Bosnia and the consequences of the "lift and strike" option so favoured by Congress. As a military man, Galvin understood perfectly that the fighting ability of the Bosnian Army was not merely determined by the size of its armoury. It would take years for the Bosnians to receive sufficient training and to acquire the necessary command disciplines for them to fight successfully at the strategic level. By its very presence the UN mission had prevented military defeat and preserved the State of Bosnia. To withdraw it would be to drag America into war in support of the Bosnians.

At dinner that night in the Residency, I suggested to Galvin that his programme should include a visit to Mladic, since it would be difficult for him to advise President Clinton on the situation in Bosnia without meeting the Serbs. He thought that this would be an excellent idea and I agreed to arrange a meeting with Mladic at short notice. Before I could send a message to Mladic, one arrived from him saying how delighted he would be to see Galvin and suggesting that we meet at the Lukavica barracks near the airport when the General's programme ended. Obviously someone had been listening in to our conversation in the dining room via an electronic device, or perhaps Mladic had a spy planted within the Bosnian Government's own eaves-dropping organisation.

The next day I took Galvin to see the commander of the 2nd Bosnian Corps near Tuzla, Gen. Hazim Sadic. We were escorted by a woman from the US embassy , who was in my view the most hostile American that I met during all my time in Bosnia. In every discussion she insisted on referring to the Serbs as "the criminal and illegal regime of the Karadzic Montenegran Serbs" and protested strongly if I referred to them simply as "Serbs". This wasted a great deal of time during meetings.

On a fine winter morning as we flew north towards Tuzla, our US embassy escort repeatedly pointed down at destroyed villages high in the Zvijezda mountains, and exclaimed excitedly to Galvin, "Look at what the criminal Serbs have done!" Each time Simon Shadbolt had to point out to Galvin that, as the mosques in the area were still standing while the churches in the neighbouring villages had been destroyed, it was obvious that Muslim forces had been responsible for most of the ethnic cleansing in this region of Bosnia. The conflict had occurred in 1993 in the fighting for the copper mines around Vares. It became obvious to Galvin that the woman from the State Department was simply not prepared to accept the notion that the Bosnians had been involved in any form of ethnic cleansing.

At the end of the day, as we stood in Mostar amid some of the worst devastation of the war, she planted her hands on her hips and triumphantly exclaimed, "Well, at least *this* was done by the criminal Serbs!"

Simon could not resist replying, "Wrong again, lady, this was done by the other half of your federation, the Croats." At this point she burst into tears. The fact was not lost on Galvin.

At the 2nd Corps HQ of the Bosnian Army, Sadic, dressed in crisp US-style fatigues, gave Galvin a briefing that would have gained top marks at the Camberley Staff College for presentation and nothing whatsoever for substance. Galvin, who had evidently been briefed in this fashion many times at NATO, quickly realised that most of what Sadic was saying was complete rubbish. He politely brought the briefing to a close after about 10 minutes and quietly told me that he would like to visit a section of the front line, without Sadic. Making excuses about not being allowed to carry members of the Bosnian forces in the UN helicopter, I flew Galvin to a position to the north of Tuzla, high above the Posavina corridor from where it was possible to see Brcko and the Serb positions on the plain below.

At that time there was much concern being expressed in the UN about reports that Serb Army tank brigades were massing in the area of Brcko with the intention of overrunning the safe area of Tuzla to the south. In response the Bosnian Army was threatening to attack across the Posavina corridor and cut off the eastern-held Serb areas from their western territories. The subject had been raised in the Security Council and the UN was called upon to prevent the Serbs from launching their offensive. The Serbs, however, consistently denied that they had any such plan, nor could NATO see any signs of such activity from the air.

The Posavina corridor runs through one of the most fertile plains in Bosnia and it is the main source of wheat for the country. It was a lovely spring day and the only sounds were the singing of larks in the sky above and the noise of the tractors in the valley below. There was no sign of fighting and we could not even make out the line of the trenches below. People seemed to have abandoned the war as they prepared the ground for the sowing of crops. We met an old man resting under a tree and I introduced him to Galvin. He was a Muslim and two of his sons were fighting in the Bosnian Army. He had no idea who we were but, suspecting that Galvin was someone of importance, he called another of his sons away from his work minding some cattle nearby. The son told Galvin that there had been no movement in the battle lines since the start of the war two years before and that the Bosnian Army had so few weapons, whenever platoons changed over, the weapons stayed in the trenches. There was only a makeshift chain of command and his platoon commander had absolutely no idea what was going on elsewhere in Bosnia.

It became obvious to Galvin that most of the assumptions that would justify "lift and strike" were false and that international policy was based on propaganda rather than reality. He could see that the Bosnian Army was in no military position to defeat the Serbs in battle, no matter how many weapons were parachuted into Bosnia. The Bosnian Army was a gallant, though *ad hoc* group of fighters capable only of skirmishing at company level and conducting old-fashioned trench warfare. It was probably this single conversation between the one-time commander of NATO and a young, part-time soldier in Bosnia that began a major shift in US policy. As we left the position, Galvin asked the old man whom he had fought for in the Second World War. With a brisk Nazi salute, he replied that he had fought for Hitler and had seen Moscow in flames. He then proudly showed us his war wounds.

Some time after at a later meeting in Belgrade, chaired by Milosevic, it was agreed that Sergio should travel to Brcko and that a number of UNMOs should be permanently positioned in the area. Within days of the deployment of the UNMOs, the Brcko crisis was totally defused and was never again mentioned by either side. Quiet diplomacy and the traditional weapons of peacekeeping had triumphed over force.

On our return to Sarajevo I took Galvin to meet Gen. Mladic, who tried his usual aggressive opening gambit of attacking America for helping the Islamic extremists establish a State in the heart of Europe. Galvin listened politely the first time, but as Mladic started on a second round of invective, Galvin sharply rapped the table and said, "General Mladic, you are beginning to repeat yourself. If this meeting is to have any value, move on." Mladic reacted like a startled rabbit and lamely outlined his ideas for the division of territory between the Serbs and the Federation in the future State of Bosnia. It was the only time I ever saw Mladic put in his place.

By the end of the visit, I believe that Galvin had come to understand that the establishment of a single, unitary, multi-national State in Bosnia was an unrealisable ideal and that compromises would have to be made. He also recognised that continued humanitarian support from the UN would be necessary for the people of Bosnia and that no short-term solutions such as "lift and strike" were possible. His report to President Clinton stated that it was essential for the international community to make another sustained effort at peacekeeping and that the US Administration should continue to back the UN, with NATO support. I suspect that Galvin also privately informed the President about the great damage being caused to US foreign policy by the biased reports emanating from the State Department, as shortly afterwards Clinton brought in Richard Holbrooke, US Assistant Secretary of State, to redefine US policy on Bosnia.

Similar battles were being fought on the European side of the Atlantic. John Wilsey arrived the day after Galvin had departed with the depressing news that no clear decision had yet been taken regarding the sending of the extra British troops to Bosnia. Nevertheless, there was some support for this in the British press. On 3 March Max Hastings had written a lead article in the *Daily Telegraph* pointing out in no uncertain terms that unless additional troops were sent to Bosnia an important opportunity for peace would be lost. Without more men, he argued, it would be impossible for UNPROFOR to implement, let alone extend, the fragile ceasefire. John Wilsey told me that John Major and Douglas Hurd were strongly in favour of sending reinforcements, but that there was strong opposition in the Cabinet led by Kenneth Clarke.

To cheer him up, we flew Sea King helicopters into the Kosevo stadium in Sarajevo, right under the noses of the Serb guns, to demonstrate once again to the people of the city our confidence in the ceasefire. It was the first time this had been done, as our route took us along the battle line for five miles, where we were within range for small arms fire from both sides. However the Royal Navy pilots of 845 Squadron, with whom I had last operated in the Falklands War, showing their usual disregard for their own safety, had agreed to go. We had an excellent view of Sarajevo as we roared down the main street of the city, level with the tops of the tower blocks and the Serb trenches on the hills behind. The Serbs did not react and the stadium subsequently became a UN designated helicopter-landing zone.

By the end of the day John Wilsey had become more optimistic, as he was able to see for himself what had already been achieved by the work of the young peacekeepers, including many from the British Army, since the 9 February Airport Agreement. The city was starting to regain an appearance of normality as shops opened, houses were repaired and children once again played in the streets. At the airport a tall, leathery-looking Texan who worked for an American charity, shook us both warmly by the hand and congratulated us on what had been achieved by the UN. With tears in his eyes and almost speechless, he punched me on the shoulder and turned away. I looked at John, who also had tears in his eyes. A great burden seemed to have been lifted from his shoulders. The massive effort that he and many others had made in Britain to maintain support for the UN suddenly seemed worthwhile. As he climbed up the steps to the aircraft I felt unexpectedly sad for him, knowing that he had to return to a world of political infighting and intrigue in the Ministry of Defence, while all I had to do was try and keep the peace. Within a week of his visit, a decision was taken by John Major to send the 1st Battalion of the Duke of Wellington's Regiment and a radar-locating detachment to reinforce the UK contingent in Bosnia.

On 12 March, Nicholas Morris, head of the UNHCR in the former Yugoslavia, had arranged a farewell dinner in Zagreb for Cot, which was also attended by Akashi, his replacement Gen. de Lapresle, Sergio de Mello, Simon and me. Midway through dinner, Cot received a call from Col. Legrier, the officer commanding the French battalion in Bihac, asking for an immediate air strike against a Serb T55 tank that was firing at the HQ of the Bosnian Army 5th Corps in the centre of the town. A number of rounds had landed inside the French base. I was a bit surprised that Legrier had bypassed the UN chain of command by telephoning Cot direct, but I said nothing as it was his final day in office. Cot, however, politely asked me if I would consent to Legrier's request for air support. I said that I would, as only two days before I had told Mladic that I would call in air strikes if his troops continued to fire into Bihac. Akashi would first have to obtain authority from New York and he left the restaurant immediately to make the necessary call to Boutros-Ghali. Cot left for the UN HQ in Zagreb to warn Naples that a request for air strikes was imminent, using a predetermined procedure code-named "Blue Sword". Like the Guards before the battle of Waterloo, the rest of us continued with our dinner party.

At 2200 hours we arrived at the UN HQ to see how the air strikes were proceeding and found utter pandemonium. Cot was in a corner fuming at the delay in obtaining authority for the air strikes from Akashi. A second problem had also arisen: NATO aircraft could not identify the target because the ground was obscured by cloud. Whenever the clouds covered the area, the T55 tank emerged from its concealed position like a spider from a hole and started firing. When the sky started to clear it scuttled back under cover. This had been going on for more than two hours.

Akashi's voice was being relayed into the room, and he warned Cot that he was having difficulty making contact with Karadzic and that he needed an extra 10 minutes to give the Serbs a final warning. Cot lost his temper and told Akashi that he had already had an extra 10 minutes. He told Akashi that the time for negotiation was over and he wanted either a yes or a no from him, warning him that if he said no, then he would bear all responsibility for the decision. Akashi ignored this and asked about the likely extent of collateral damage caused by any air strikes. Cot repeated that he wanted either a yes or a no, adding that if Akashi said no, then the press would hear about it the next day. This was too much for Akashi. In an icy voice he replied that he would not be put under pressure in this way and rang off.

Silence descended in the operations room and everyone looked at the floor. I glanced at Adm. de Lapresle, who looked rather thoughtful but said nothing. Sergio offered to speak to Akashi and within five minutes Akashi had given him the necessary authority for NATO aircraft to be used against the Serb T55. It was all to no avail. After a further three hours playing cat-and-mouse with the Serb tank, the NATO aircraft returned to Italy and the air strike was called off. I had long since gone to bed. Later, de Lapresle told me that he thought Akashi had been looking for reassurance rather than confrontation. It also transpired that the reason Akashi had not been able to get through to Karadzic was that my new Chief of Staff, Brig. van Baal, had been on the phone to him for an hour introducing himself.

There were more serious developments elsewhere in Bosnia. Reports were coming in from the mainly Muslim enclave of Maglaj, 50 miles north of Sarajevo, that the condition of the 19,000 people living there had seriously worsened. No convoys had been able to reach the region since October, partly because of a Serb offensive in the area and partly because the Croats, who were in alliance with the Serbs in Maglaj, had refused to allow them to reach the enclave. Because most of the town of Maglaj was directly overlooked by Serb artillery, people were forced to live in their cellars and the limited food supplies that had reached them in the last few months had been from air drops. Larry Hollingworth, who had been in the British Army and was now head of UNHCR in central Bosnia, spoke to me about the situation and on 31 March the UN Security Council in New York passed a resolution demanding that the siege of Maglaj be lifted.[4]

I decided to obtain an accurate assessment of what was happening on the ground and within 48 hours two JCO teams were reporting from the enclave. One team had walked into Maglaj under cover of darkness and the other had been flown there in Norwegian helicopters. Using the poor weather conditions in the mountains around Maglaj, the Norwegian pilots had made an approach at high altitude and then spiralled down into the enclave to avoid Serb air defences. Although the pilots were used to flying in similar poor weather conditions in Norway, they were not used to having surface-to-air missiles fired at them. Unperturbed by this, the Norwegian pilots flew in reinforcements the next night.

By 20 March the Serbs had entirely withdrawn their forces from the enclave. Seizing this unexpected opportunity, an aid convoy was taken directly into the town by Larry Hollingworth and Richard Margesson with his Coldstream Guard company. The area was later reinforced by a regiment of the Light Dragoons to prevent any new attempt by the Serbs to establish a stranglehold on the town. I later received a mild rebuke from New York for using peacekeeping troops in what to them appeared to be a clandestine military operation.

In Bosnia, when one problem was solved, another always took its place and in Sarajevo the Russians were becoming an increasing problem. Although their com-manding officer, Col. Vorobiev, a tough-looking parachutist, was evidently a professional soldier, his deputy commander was cast in the mould of a Soviet political commissar. The deputy cared nothing about the subtleties of peacekeeping and drove at high speed in his Gaz jeep round Sarajevo, scattering the townspeople in his path. On one occasion he so annoyed Goose by overtaking us in a dangerous manner that Goose, using the full power and speed of the four-ton armoured Range Rover, forced him into a ditch.

As a result of this deputy commander's policy, the Russian positions between the Serb and Bosnian trenches in Sarajevo began to resemble the fortified border between East and West Berlin. This did nothing for freedom of movement. When I ordered them to clear Serb artillery from a position near Sarajevo, the deputy commander refused, saying that the Russians received their orders from Moscow, not from me, and intimating that they would never do anything hostile towards their Serb brothers. He must have complained about me personally, as on 16 March the Russian Ambassador in New York, Mr Sidorov, raised concerns about my handling of the Russian contingent with the Secretary-General. Things finally came to a head during a meeting I held of UN contingent commanders, when the deputy commander embarked on a long diatribe against the Muslims and accused the French of being their running dogs. I cut him short, to applause from the other commanding officers, and reminded him that he was attending peacekeeping conference of the UN, not a meeting of the Soviet Praesidium.

Vitaly Churkin, President Yeltsin's special adviser on Bosnia, was staying with us in Sarajevo at the time. When I told him about the problems I had been having with this man, Churkin had him removed and from that moment on relations with the Russians began to improve. However they never did take action against the Serb guns and justified their refusal by saying that accomplishing such a task would jeopardise Russian lives.

The Russians arrived in Sarajevo with little understanding of Western peace-keeping doctrine or indeed with any logistic support, and for a while the French soldiers in neighbouring positions supplied them with food in return for vodka. In their first week in Sarajevo they spent much of their time sleeping in their APCs with only one man on sentry duty. As they became accustomed to the style of command of the UN, they started to perform more like the other UN soldiers and at a political level their presence gave the Serbs great confidence.

We had noticed for some time that the outside of the Presidency was being smartened up in preparation for the forthcoming visit of Crown Prince Hassan of Jordan and his brother. The soldiers guarding the Presidency had cleaned their rifles and wore new, highly-starched uniforms. The carriageway of the main road from the airport was cleared of rubbish and trams were seen making trial runs around Sarajevo. It was obvious the Bosnian Government was determined to make a positive impression on the heir to the Hashemite Kingdom. I was due to meet the royal party at 1030 hours at the airport.

At 0850 hours on the day of the visit, a messenger arrived from the city council inviting me to attend the opening of the tram system at 0900 hours. There was to be a speech by the mayor and a band. I realised this was an occasion not to be missed and dashed from the office, telling my staff that I would go directly from the event to the airport to meet the crown prince. With only 10 minutes notice we drove at speed through Sarajevo towards the tram depot. When we arrived there was an enormous crowd of people milling around an ancient tram decorated with flags and bunting. In former years it had been Tito's personal conveyance in Sarajevo and at the start of the war it was hidden away in a shelter where it had survived without evident damage. It had been recently varnished, and its brass ornaments gleamed in the sunshine.

Like most of the trams in Sarajevo it had been built before the Second World War and epitomised the style and elegance of a past age. Trams had been running in Sarajevo since 1895 and were revered by the citizens as objects of beauty and enjoyment. They were particularly popular with small boys, who would test their nerve and strength by clinging to the outside of the trams as they clattered along. At the start of the fighting, when the electricity supply had failed, many trams were abandoned where they halted. Festooned with fallen power lines and riddled with shell holes they symbolised a quieter, more peaceful age and a lifestyle that the people of Sarajevo had now lost.

As we moved through the crowds, it was difficult to distinguish the official party from the spectators amid the swirling mass of good-humoured people surrounding the tram. A band played national folk songs and Sarajevo tram system officials dressed in blue-and-gold uniforms struggled unsuccessfully with the street urchins to prevent them from climbing into the main exhibit.

After we had made our way to the front of Tito's tram, which was by now crammed with people, the mayor of Sarajevo, whom I had last seen on the day of the market place bombing, proceeded to read a lengthy speech. Occasionally he would say "Gospodina Generali Majkl Rouz!" and the crowd would cheer reassuringly. Nick told me that the mayor was recounting a highly exaggerated story of how I had brought peace to Sarajevo. At the close of his speech, I was presented with a garish painting of the event (obviously copied from some heroic battle scene), and the official party was invited to board the tram. In order to allow this to happen, those already on board had first to be removed. This took some time, for as soon as one of the urchins was ejected, he immediately ran round to the other side and climbed aboard again. After much effort we were all safely installed, but I was starting to get anxious about my appointment at the airport.

We sat crushed together on wooden benches while gnarled waiters (evidently conscripts from the Pioneer Corps, incongruously dressed in black jackets and white gloves), handed out canapés and drinks to the guests. The succession of toasts came to an end and with an ear-splitting blast from the bullhorn at the front, a crescendo of martial music from the band and a great cheer from the crowd, the tram lurched off for about 20 metres before coming to an abrupt halt. Some VIPs had been spotted in the crowd and room was immediately made for them on board. The horn sounded, the band struck up, the crowd cheered but this time the tram shot back-wards amid cries of alarm. By now all of the passengers had been spattered with food and drink by the inexperienced waiters. No one seemed to mind and after a final blast on the horn we set off down the main street towards the Presidency. As we clattered along, small boys ran alongside or clung to the outside of the tram. Everyone waved and cheered as we sped by. A yellow carpet had been rolled out in front of the Presidency on which a guard of honour and a band were drawn up. No doubt thinking that the Crown Prince of Jordan was aboard, the band struck up the Jordanian national anthem and the guard of honour presented arms as the tram rattled past, coming to a halt 100 metres further on. Here I gratefully abandoned the tram for the Range Rover.

I arrived at the airport just as the Yak 40 carrying the Jordanian visitors touched down. First out of the aircraft was a bulky-looking Crown Prince dressed in a loden coat that did little to conceal a flak vest. For some obscure reason he was carrying a shepherd's crook. Behind him came Prince Abdullah, commander of the Jordanian Special Forces. He was holding a cocked Heckler & Kock machine pistol and looked ready for battle. He was followed by an array of ambassadors, generals, military staff, royal servants and baggage carriers.

We had been told there would be nine people in the royal party, but on a quick count we estimated there must be more than 30. We had only arranged transport for about half that number. With a quick word to George Waters to find more transport, I invited the two royal princes into my vehicle and, led by a French APC, we drove off towards Sarajevo through the Serb lines. Once through the Serb checkpoint, we stopped to allow George to catch up. He had requisitioned some construction vehicles from a building site in the airport and, after a brief delay, a convoy of open pick-up trucks and lorries arrived carrying the rest of the royal party, battling to retain their hats in the slipstream.

We set off in procession down the main road towards Sarajevo to find it still lined with people waiting for the return of Tito's tram. The Crown Prince was obviously used to seeing crowds lining the streets in Amman, for he made no comment on what was, in Sarajevo, an extremely rare sight. About halfway into town, coming from the opposite direction, I spotted Tito's tram making a triumphal return journey. Halted in the middle of the road was the French Chief of Staff, who stood with his head out of the top of the APC watching the tram approach. His timing could not have been worse. At the very moment that we drew level with him, Tito's tram passed him in the opposite direction. Our vehicle contained the Crown Prince: the tram, the mayor. With an anguished expression, he solved the problem by saluting with both arms and desperately trying to look both ways simultaneously. Goose and I burst out laughing and later George declared it to have been a great Balkan day.

The next day Cot left his command in the former Yugoslavia. He was a highly amusing person with enormous charm and a short fuse. I had enjoyed working with him and was sorry to see him go. It was typical of his thoughtfulness that in his final moments he found time to send to me a signal saying: *Bravo, Michel, vous avez bien mérité de gagner.*

Cot's successor, de Lapresle, was a very different sort of man. When he was 11 years of age he spent a year at an English boarding school and as a result he had none of the suspicions about the British common to many of his countrymen. In Sarajevo his son was commanding the cavalry squadron he himself had once commanded. We got on extremely well. I spoke English to him and he spoke French to me. He was entirely *au fait* with the limits of peacekeeping and, although he was sometimes under pressure from NATO to use more force in Bosnia than we thought appropriate, he never compromised on his principles. He often looked exhausted and I know that he worried a great deal about the extraordinary risks being taken by soldiers and aid workers alike, scattered as they were in small groups across the most remote and dangerous parts of Bosnia. Like all senior French officers, he travelled with a large staff when he was in Sarajevo but usually stayed with Soubirou in the PTT building which housed the French Sector HQ . De Lapresle was determined never to allow differences in policy to arise between the civil and military elements in the UN, and relations between him and Akashi always remained good throughout our time together in Bosnia.

Success breeds success and the possibility that the UN peace process might produce an end to the war had encouraged a flood of visitors to Sarajevo during the month of March. The Americans came in force, led by Ambassador Robert Frasure and Joe Kreuzel, a Rhodes scholar and contemporary of President Clinton at Oxford. They brought fresh thinking to American policy on Bosnia, but both were to die tragically in a road accident on Mt Igman a year later.

Adm. Mike Boorda also made his first visit to Bosnia from Naples. He was a dynamic, straight-talking individual who was keen to see on the ground what the UN was achieving. I took him on a whirlwind tour of Sarajevo where he met both Bosnian and Serb soldiers. On arrival at the Jewish Cemetery, Boorda announced that he was going to inspect the line of conflict for himself and, climbing over a wall, he disappeared into the Bosnian trenches in full view of the Serbs. He spent some minutes there talking to the soldiers who told him that the atmosphere in Sarajevo had dramatically improved since the 9 February Airport Agreement and that the Bosnian Army had greatly reduced troop strengths in their forward positions. I next took him to meet the Serb HQ on the far side of the bridge of Brotherhood and Unity. Here Boorda gave an impromptu interview to Serb television during which he was asked what the Serbs should do to stop any further NATO attacks against them. Looking directly into the camera, he replied, "Just stop flying your jets in Bosnian airspace." It had been less than three weeks since his jets had shot down four Serb aeroplanes, killing the pilots.

Shortly after Boorda's plane had departed, Prime Minister John Major, Baroness Linda Chalker, the Minister for Overseas Development and Malcolm Rifkind arrived at the airport. As I ushered the Prime Minister from the aircraft into the Range Rover, a mortar shell – fired by the Bosnian forces across the airfield in Butmir – landed nearby. With a moan of terror, a civil servant accompanying Simon Shadbolt dived into his Land Rover and demanded protection. It was probably fortunate for him that by then the Prime Minister had already departed.

John Major had arrived looking tired and preoccupied, but his spirits seemed much revived by what he saw during the day. As we drove through the streets he could see for himself that Sarajevo was a very different place from the one described in many news reports. After a brief but unproductive call on Ganic who, being on his best behaviour, said nothing, John Major was presented with a dreadful painting of Sarajevo to commemorate his visit. The Prime Minister then toured a British-funded water project in the centre of Sarajevo with Baroness Chalker. Next we drove out of Sarajevo to Vogosca where the Coldstream Guards had established an observation post in a highly exposed position between the lines of trenches. A few days before, there had been a furious gun battle between the Guards and the Serbs when the Coldstream APCs, opening fire with their main 30mm Rarden cannon, had destroyed several Serb trenches from which snipers had been shooting at them. Since then the area had been remarkably quiet. The Prime Minister, who could see some Serb soldiers looking at him from less than 50 metres away, commented on how close together the opposing trenches were.

On our way back to the airport, a French sentry stopped the Range Rover in which the Prime Minister and I were travelling and asked to see our UN passes. Goose and I showed ours but the Prime Minister and his aide had not been issued with any. The sentry asked me why the other occupants of the vehicle did not have UN passes. I told the French sentry that I was accompanying the Prime Minister of Great Britain. The soldier looked unimpressed and replied that he did not care a fig who was in the vehicle, no one could enter the airport without a UN pass. These were his orders. I congratulated him on his determination to follow orders, then told Goose to drive on. In the rear-view mirror I saw the sentry laughing. He had obviously just won a bet.

The following day, a Sunday, Nick, Goose and I were invited to a service in St Joseph's Catholic Church to mark the Sarajevo ceasefire. Because the church was on the front line, it was the first time a service had been held there for two years. It was packed so we stood at the back, but a priest invited us to sit in a pew at the front where I tried to offer my seat to a frail elderly woman, though she refused to allow me to do so. It was an intensely moving occasion and the presence of God in the church was almost palpable. There was a passion and sincerity in the music and the prayers that seemed to extend beyond the church as people remembered friends and relations who had been killed and prayed for peace. As the sun shone through the cracked and dusty stained-glass windows on to the heads of the people below, my eyes welled with tears, for I stood among people who had lived through the horror and the deprivation but had never lost their faith or hope. Archbishop Pulic delivered the sermon and at one point he made a reference to the UN that caused the congregation to burst into applause. At the end of the service, people shook our hands or tried to hug us and one woman said to me: "As long as you stay with us, we feel safe." I told her I hoped to stay until the guns fell silent for ever.

During the sermon, Archbishop Pulic joked that, now peace had returned to Sarajevo, all that remained for the UN to do was to provide potatoes for the people. That night Nick delivered a hundredweight sack of potatoes to the door of the church. Although not a Catholic, I continued to attend the church services in Sarajevo.

The simple faith of the people was a source of great inspiration, in direct contrast to the cynicism and venality of their leaders with whom I had to do daily business.

For some days prior to the visit of John Major, Nick had been negotiating with Muratovic, the Minister for Co-operation with UNPROFOR, about holding a football match in the Kosevo stadium in Sarajevo between the UN and what remained of the Sarajevo football team. Football came second only to religion in the amount of passion it inspired among the people of Sarajevo. A football match in a city still under siege would provide a wonderful signal to the people of Bosnia and to the world that there was an alternative to war.

Unfortunately the stadium was close to the front line and Serb snipers and mortars were able to fire directly at the pitch. There was obviously some considerable risk in holding the match. If lives were lost, the image of the UN would be irrevocably destroyed. I decided nevertheless that the match should go ahead, but not before raising the subject with Karadzic. I told him that the match was going to be the first of many and that in the next match the UN would play the Serbs in Grbavica. I told him that eventually I hoped to arrange regular matches between the Serbs and the Bosnians. As Karadzic had been the resident motivational psychologist in the Sarajevo football team before the war, he could not resist the idea and gave an undertaking that the match would be allowed to go ahead without interruption.

The day chosen for the football match was 20 March. There had been many complications in making the arrangements, but Simon and Nick had managed to sort most of these out. One of them was the withdrawal at the last moment of the French military band and parachute display team. In desperation I telephoned John Wilsey and asked if the band of the Coldstream Guards was available. Within a few hours he called back to tell me that not only were they available, he had arranged with the RAF to fly them directly to Sarajevo.

The day before the football match the band had taken part in the changing of the guard ceremony in the forecourt of Buckingham Palace, London, and the scene of devastation that greeted them on their arrival in Sarajevo must have been overwhelming. Like good soldiers they said nothing as they were loaded into a collection of old buses and jeeps and driven through the Serb lines to the Kosevo stadium. One of the buses wouldn't start, so the BBC correspondent Kate Adie, who had been filming the arrival of the band, crammed as many Coldstreamers as she could into her Land Rover. Off went the convoy with a variety of musical instruments and trunks containing bearskins and tunics tied to the roofs of the vehicles. As they started down the main road into Sarajevo, Sgt Cannon, a member of my protection team who was driving one of the buses, mischievously told the Guardsmen that key members of the band should sit on the right side of the bus as Serb snipers tended to fire from the left.

When I arrived in the stadium, Nick told me that the Balkan factor had struck again. The security guards at the stadium entrances were only allowing a select few into the ground and the rest of the people who wanted to see the match were ready to riot. I told Ganic that I would call the whole thing off if he did not open the gates to everyone. He agreed to do this and the crowds started to flow in.

The programme started with several speeches by Bosnian Government officials that were of such length that the crowd started to get restless. Norwegian helicopters circled overhead carrying the parachutists for the freefall display that was to open the match. In the middle of the speeches, I received a warning that the helicopters were running out of fuel. Unless the pitch could be cleared of the crowds of officials, television crews and spectators who were milling about the field, the parachute display would have to be abandoned. I told Nick to grab a microphone from the official making a speech and announce the immediate start of the freefall display. A great cheer went up from the crowd as he made his announcement and everyone craned their necks, searching the sky, then the parachutists landed in the centre of the arena to deafening applause. A newspaper reporter, who had been briefed that the parachute display was being undertaken by Norwegian soldiers, went up to one of the parachutists and asked him where he came from. In a broad Geordie accent the soldier replied, "Aldershot – but don't tell the wife, she doesn't know I'm here!"

Around us in the stands there was a carnival atmosphere as people chanted slogans, clapped and waved to their friends. Just before midday as the clouds cleared and the sun broke through, the band of the Coldstream Guards, wearing bearskins and tunics, marched out of the ruins of the stadium into the sunshine playing "The Peacemaker", led by their Director of Music David Marshall. Another vast cheer went up from the crowd that must even have been heard by the Serbs sitting in their trenches. I kept my fingers crossed that they would not open fire. As the band marched and countermarched across the pitch, I was reminded of the many times I had marched to the same stirring music.

The next day newspapers and television screens around the world were filled with pictures of the Coldstream Guards band in Sarajevo. The appearance of the band had been a reminder to the people of Bosnia of the existence of a civilised and orderly world that had once been theirs. The match itself was a triumph of diplomacy: Sarajevo won by three goals to one.

The UK team that had flown out with me from England in January had been working without a break for more than two months. I knew that the continual pressure on everyone was taking its toll, but I didn't appreciate quite how tired we all were until I awoke briefly from a deep sleep during the flight back to England, where we were going for a week's leave. The whole team was slumped round me in their seats, totally exhausted. I resolved to give them one day off a week when we returned to Bosnia.

I was never able to do this.

CHAPTER FOUR

Gorazde

Travnik was astir. As every spring, under standing orders from the capital, an army was being raised against Serbia. The hubbub and clamour as usual greatly exceeded the results.

Ivo Andric, Bosnian Chronicle (1945)

I RETURNED TO BOSNIA ON 30 MARCH AFTER A WEEK'S ABSENCE TO find that spring had arrived and the countryside was beginning to stir. The snows had melted and flowers were appearing in the mountain meadows, which were filled with the sound of birdsong. The scent of apple blossom was carried on the breeze and, as if in response to some secret signal, window shutters that had been closed all winter were suddenly flung open and bedding was draped across window sills to air. Sometimes the noise of children playing or the gentle sound of music could be heard coming from within the shaded courtyards behind the houses.

My week away from Bosnia had allowed me time for reflection. While in Paris I discussed the war once again with Adm. Lanxade, the French Defence Chief, and met his minister, M. Leotard, who apologised profusely for having wrongly accused me of unnecessarily putting at risk the lives of French soldiers. I had not been due to see their opposite numbers in London until news reached the Ministry of Defence that I had seen Lanxade and Leotard in Paris; this had resulted in a last-minute upgrading of my programme. Gen. Peter Inge and Malcolm Rifkind were interested to hear there were signs that the Serbs were beginning to realise that all-out military victory against the Bosnians was no longer possible and were seeking a political settlement. I told them, however, that the Bosnians would be unlikely to agree to any political agreement unless it was backed by the Americans.

While in England I discovered that the media attention I had attracted in Bosnia was causing adverse comment. The news came as something of a surprise. Although I felt that it was part of my job, as Commander of UNPROFOR, to defend the peace-keeping mission in front of the television cameras, I had always refused interviews of a personal nature. Indeed, Angela and I had already commented on the fact that journalists usually write more column inches knocking people off a pedestal than they do when putting them on it. I was determined not to give the journalists an easy target, since any disinformation about me was bound to affect the UN mission.

When I returned to Bosnia the peace process was still looking good, at least on the surface. Sarajevo remained relatively peaceful and the Bridge of Brotherhood and

Unity had, at last, been opened to civilians, allowing husbands and wives, mothers and sons to meet for the first time in two years. Commercial traffic was now running without hindrance into central Bosnia and Maglaj was no longer an enclave.

Following the success of the 9 February Airport Agreement, Sergio had managed to open routes into Sarajevo for commercial traffic, at a marathon meeting on 17 March between Krajisnik and Muratovic. This made it possible for hundreds of trucks, buses and cars to move freely in and out of the city, which led to a sharp fall in prices for commodities and the restoration of some degree of normality for the citizens. On several occasions during the meeting, Muratovic fondly referred to Krajisnik by his nickname, "Momo". If these good relations had been maintained, the agreement might well have led to a complete cessation of hostilities, but sadly their political bosses were not similarly disposed.

A weekly bus service had been started between Sarajevo and Zenica. The first humanitarian aid flight had flown into Tuzla with Akashi and de Lapresle on board, and in Croatia a peace deal had been struck between the Croats and the Krajina Serbs. Even the media picked up on the UN's cautious optimism and Akashi's remark that "the dark days are almost over" was widely quoted.[1]

Even Prime Minister Haris Silajdzic shared my confidence in the peace process. He was, for the moment, backing current UN thinking on how to build on the recent success of the Sarajevo Airport Agreement and the Washington Accord. Our ideas included extending the concept of TEZs to other sectors in Bosnia, brokering an anti-sniper agreement for Sarajevo, and improving freedom of movement throughout Bosnia.

Silajdzic had long been concerned about the behaviour of Croat thugs in Mostar who had been responsible for much of the destruction of the Muslim part of the city and were now obstructing any efforts to restore freedom of movement to the town. East Mostar was still in a virtual state of siege, notwithstanding the Washington Accord. He also warned me that 7,000 Croats were still camped around Kiseljak in the Laskva Valley. They had been driven from their homes in the mining area of Vares by the Bosnian Army and could not return there because Muslim refugees were now living in their houses. He believed that the problem of the many displaced people in Bosnia might well reignite the conflict.

Of immediate concern was the fighting around the enclaves of Zepa and Gorazde, where Silajdzic told me 18 people had recently been killed. For some time the UN had received Bosnian Army reports of a build-up of Serb artillery south of the Gorazde enclave. NATO could see nothing from the air and I suggested to Silajdzic that the activity was very likely an attempt by the Serbs to put pressure on the Bosnians. I wondered whether these reports were a means of concealing the fact that the Bosnian Army was also attacking Serb villages in the area. Meanwhile Karadzic, as if to divert attention from the ethnic cleansing of Muslims and Croats from around Prijedor, was warning the UN that a new spring offensive was about to be launched by the Bosnian Army.

My continuing belief that peace could be achieved before the year's end was founded on an analysis of the changed strategic factors that underpinned the war in Bosnia. The Bosnian Serb Army was beginning to lose its military superiority as the Croat–Muslim Federation became more effective. Sanctions were seriously affecting President Milosevic and it was difficult to find support for the war even among the Bosnian Serbs in the trenches. In one Serb position on Mt Igman that we visited, the oldest soldier was 17. They told us that they did not believe in the war any more. There were also grounds for believing that the Bosnian Government could be persuaded to accept a political settlement to end the war that did not meet all their aspirations. It was not clear what political form the State would finally take, but the idea of a federal structure seemed to be most acceptable. The most difficult task remaining, in my view, was to convince President Clinton that his support for the UN peace process was needed if the war was to be brought to an end. Recent signals from his Administration were encouraging.

Madeleine Albright and Gen. Shalikashvili visited Sarajevo at the end of March and their reaction to the progress made by the UN reinforced my sense of optimism. I took them across the Bridge of Brotherhood and Unity under the watchful eyes of the Serb snipers, and they spoke to officers in the Bosnian Serb Army as well as some elderly civilians who were waiting to cross over to the Bosnian side. Shalikashvili well understood that there was a limit to what air power could contribute to a mission when its main objective is the delivery of humanitarian aid. I told him that, having an American mother, I could appreciate the pressures in Congress against the deployment of American ground troops in Bosnia while the war continued. It was clear to me, nevertheless, that once the foundations of peace had been firmly laid, it would be better for Bosnia, and for America, if US troops arrived before the actual end of the war. Shalikashvili asked me about the military capability of both sides and whether there was a likelihood of a spring offensive. I told him that no side was capable of mounting an offensive campaign that would have any strategic significance. Whenever we visited the front line, all we found were soldiers asleep in their bunkers or playing cards. Indeed, the UN had started referring to the predicted offensive as "The Great Bedspring Offensive". As we walked back across the Bridge of Brotherhood and Unity, Madeleine Albright unexpectedly said to me, "Well, General Rose, you really are a gift from God." Perhaps to prevent me from becoming big-headed, Goose asked me with a look of innocence why the Secretary of State of the United States of America had just called me a "Git from God".

On 1 April the Bosnian Croat Army commander in the town of Zepce, on the southern side of the recently liberated enclave of Maglaj, told me that he thought the notice he had received of my visit was an April Fool's joke. Not even his Army commander had visited the region. This was surprising, as Maglaj had been in the thick of the fighting and was also set in some of the most beautiful countryside in Bosnia. During my visit to the region, I was briefed by the operations officer of the Light Dragoons, who had recently arrived from Germany, using a formal briefing procedure more suited to NATO exercises in Germany than a UN peacekeeping mission. When I asked who had composed the lengthy mission statement, with a straight face he replied that I had. The local people welcomed the arrival of the British troops but the Bosnian Army was not quite so gracious. At one point we passed a small armoured column concealed under a cliff. Their weapons looked relatively modern but the soldiers wore rubber sandals. When I asked their commander if they were part of the "Great Spring Offensive", he told me rather sharply to go away. They were still there when we passed by a week later.

The town of Maglaj had suffered little damage in comparison to Sarajevo, though the people looked drawn and undernourished. Most of their food during the previous year had come from American airdrops and this had enabled them to survive. Their fuel came from timber cut from the surrounding forests and small water turbines made from bicycle parts had been placed in the river to generate electricity. As we arrived, people were collecting rations from a line of UNHCR lorries parked in the main square. They seemed unconcerned by the presence of the Serbs on a hill about a kilometre away. For an area that had been under siege for so long, the citizens of Maglaj seemed remarkably normal.

We drove north from the town, through countryside that resembled the Bavarian Alps. Oxen drawing old-fashioned wooden ploughs were being used to sow seeds on the terraced hillsides and there was a profusion of green-winged orchids, wild irises and gentians. We stopped for a picnic on top of a hill from which we could admire the tranquil countryside. Apart from the wrecked farmhouse nearby, it was hard to imagine that somewhere in the hills that stretched to the horizon, men were still fighting each other in a bitter civil war.

Later in the day we met Maj. Richard Margesson, who had led his Coldstream Guards company in the initial relief of Maglaj. He was now keen to push the frontiers of peace a little further by opening the main road from Maglaj to Duboj. This important route had not been used since the start of the war because for much of its length it ran beneath the Serb guns on the hills on the other side. I asked him about the risks but he laughingly replied that when he had been a student of mine at the Staff College he had been taught to be militant and he was trying to keep in practice. In spite of many attempts to open up this route, he never succeeded as the Serbs fired at anything that moved on the road. Nevertheless, relations between the local people and the British contingent remained extremely good and some Coldstreamers became so involved in local community projects they refused to go on leave. The Guardsmen had opened a café so that funds could be provided for other reconstruction projects and with the help of the UNHCR schools were re-built and medical supplies were given to the hospital.

Dealing with the political and military leaders of the warring parties presented a much greater challenge. On our return from Maglaj, Ganic asked me, not for the first time, if I would take him with me to Bihac. There was some risk in doing this, as the Serbs of the Krajina would not hesitate to shoot down a UN helicopter if they thought that Ganic was on board. Ganic insisted that he needed to be there to give political direction to his followers, "to help advance the peace process". In the end I agreed, although it was my strong suspicion that, since Ganic was the minister responsible for the army, it was more likely that he was going to Bihac to plan a new phase of fighting. He brought with him the Bosnian Foreign Minister, Dr Irfan Ljubjanik, a young, softly-spoken man who had been a surgeon in Bihac before the war. Ljubjanik had played a major part in moderating extremist factions within the SDA, but sadly he died in a helicopter crash a few months after visiting Bihac. Ganic was also accompanied by a posse of thugs. Strangely, he ordered them all to travel in a second UN helicopter, saying that he preferred to travel with me as the Serbs would be less likely to shoot down a helicopter carrying the British General.

As we flew across the Sava River into the Serb-held Krajina region of Croatia, we could see that every house and village had been destroyed by the retreating Croatian Army's scorched-earth policy, a tactic employed by the Croat collabora-tors of the Nazis, the Ustashi, during the Second World War. Looking down at the devastated countryside, I wondered how the Balkan people, who considered themselves modern Europeans, could behave with such savagery.

On arrival in Bihac I was met by Col. Legrier, the commanding officer of the French battalion known as Frebat 3. He epitomised all that was good about the French Army: distinguished, courageous and evidently eccentric, as he never went on opera-tions without taking his cellar of fine wines with him. On arrival I was relieved to see a large Mercedes limousine waiting for Ganic. Without saying farewell, he and his posse swept away, escorted by a troop of presidential outriders. So much, I thought, for the beleaguered enclave of Bihac. For months the Bosnian Government had been painting a picture of extreme deprivation.

There were surprisingly few signs of the war as we drove south. Legrier told me that an uneasy *status quo* existed between the three different armies fighting each other in the enclave, with only an occasional shell being lobbed across the lines. At night, arms resupply flights took place from Croatia to the Bosnian Army, despite NATO's "Operation Deny Flight". In the south of the enclave the Bosnians were fighting the Bosnian and Krajina Serbs while in the north the Bosnians fought Fikret Abdic, a Muslim. Abdic was seeking to establish an autonomous State in Bihac, and he was therefore supported by the Serbs and (until the Washington Accord) the Croats. Abdic had won more votes than President Izetbegovic in the 1992 election and regarded himself as the rightful President of Bosnia. He had done very well out of the war financially and lived in a magnificent hilltop castle near Velika Kladusa, while many of his soldiers went into battle barefoot.

Col. Legrier explained that some sort of trade arrangement still operated across the line of conflict and commercial supplies routinely came into Bihac. There was little shortage of food and petrol was available at the same price as in Croatia. He thought that things would get harder next winter because the spring planting had been interrupted by bad weather. With all three armies in the enclave each fighting a different combination of enemies, the message from Col. Legrier was that this was going to be a difficult place in which to bring about peace.

In Bihac, Legrier introduced me to the commander of the 5th Corps, Gen. Dudakovic. I was beginning to suspect that somewhere in Tito's Yugoslavia there had been a school producing standard army generals on the Soviet model: short, fat, arrogant and brutal. Dudakovic was no exception. With the help of maps and a ludicrous video (which depicted Dudakovic heroically directing a single tank into what appeared to be a failed attack), he announced that he intended to capture Banja Luka and to drive the "criminal" Montenegran Serbs out of western Bosnia. Given that he was surrounded on all sides by three different enemies, his objective was as realistic as the sweeping red arrows on his map pushing deep into Bosnian Serb territory.

His underlying strategy was familiar to me, as it was the one followed elsewhere by the Bosnian Army: (1) Attack on all fronts. (2) Retreat into the enclave amid scenes of appalling suffering. (3) Call on the UN and NATO to bomb the Serbs. I found him an unpleasant man who demonstrated his total disregard for the safety of his people by placing his HQ in the middle of the town to protect himself from Serb mortar and artillery fire. Legrier told me that he was 100% certain it had been one of Dudakovic's snipers who had killed a French peacekeeper not long before. As with all Bosnian generals, Dudakovic was surrounded by party officials and he was quite unmoved when I pointed out to him that his behaviour defied the UN's appeal to his government not to mount attacks from safe areas.[2] He seemed to believe, rightly as it turned out, that the Bosnian Army could do little wrong in the eyes of the international community.

Ganic was waiting for us at the helicopter landing zone, accompanied by the sorry-looking wife and children of a Bosnian general called Drekovic. Ganic wanted us to smuggle them into Sarajevo. By then we were used to smuggling people out of Sarajevo, so this was a new challenge. Somehow we crammed Drekovic's wife and children into the helicopter and flew to Zagreb, where Ganic abandoned us without warning saying that he was going on holiday in Turkey and that he held us responsible for getting the family safely to Sarajevo. We finally dropped them off on the steps of the Presidency in Sarajevo and Ganic never mentioned the episode again. Political survival in Bosnia, it seemed, meant never acknowledging a debt.

At the Residency there was a message waiting for me from Gen. Delic saying he wished to see me urgently about dangerous developments in Gorazde. I had already been awoken that morning at 0230 hours by President Izetbegovic telling me that there were tanks in the streets of Gorazde, the town was in flames and the people were fleeing for the hills. He wanted me to order NATO planes into action immediately to prevent a disaster on an unimaginable scale, adding that I would be held personally responsible if nothing was done to prevent the slaughter. Previous experience told me that there was an element of exaggeration in most military reports coming from the Bosnians, but I nevertheless woke Maj. Willy Levak in Sarajevo for the latest intelligence. He told me that military pressure on the Bosnian forces around Gorazde was undoubtedly continuing but that nothing like a breakthrough had occurred. I was therefore extremely reluctant to hear Delic repeating the same message later that evening. Nevertheless I went to his office where I was given yet another inaccurate account of the situation in Gorazde.

I told him that I had already received many untrue reports from the Bosnian Army and I did not believe that the Bosnian Serbs were about to overrun the enclave. It would represent a major change of strategy on their part and bring them into confrontation with the West. In my opinion, the renewed military activity was designed to gain improved terms in the UN peace talks which began in March. In response to his call for NATO air strikes against the Serbs, I pointed out that William Perry, the US Defence Secretary, had recently said that America would not use force to prevent Gorazde from falling. His spokesman had added that air power would only be used to advance the peace process. When I told Delic that I planned to visit Gorazde the next day to obtain an accurate view of the military situation, he revealed that he already knew this. He wanted me to smuggle in a new satellite communication system, acquired, no doubt, from the Americans. I refused point-blank.

I left the building marvelling at the brass neck of people who felt they could insult you one minute and ask such a favour the next, and returned to the Residency in a thoroughly bad mood. Nick told me that the only time Delic had looked surprised during the meeting was when I used the expression "crying wolf", since there were thought to be no wolves around Gorazde! Finding Sergio de Mello and Haris Silajdzic at the Residency restored my good humour. I joined them for dinner and spent a pleasant evening talking about philosophy, the history of Bosnia and American politics. Never once was Gorazde mentioned.

The next day (6 April) was fine and sunny and we set out for Gorazde in high spirits accompanied by a group of JCOs, forward air controllers and UNMOs. Sergio had also decided to come with us. We had been asked by the Serbs to stop in Pale on the way so that they could agree the route. As we drove through Grbavica we passed a group of smartly dressed soldiers in Kevlar flak jackets carrying Dragunov rifles and standing by two modern Soviet-designed APCs. Nick Costello said they were regular Yugoslav Army soldiers. It turned out later that they had been sent by Belgrade to sort out the "Heroes" in the Jewish Cemetery, who were getting increasingly out of control. In the ensuing battle a few nights later only one Russian "Hero" survived, by taking refuge in a French observation post. It was the biggest battle to take place in Sarajevo in the first half of 1994.

The road climbed the hills behind Sarajevo and for a while ran along a line of Bosnian Serb trenches. Below us a late fall of snow had disguised some of the ugliness of war and transformed the city into an enchanted winter landscape. Amid the smoke of early morning fires rising from the Serb trenches we saw an Orthodox priest in black robes moving about among the soldiers giving communion. We stopped and talked to some of these soldiers who told us cheerfully that the war was coming to an end.

In Pale we saw a CNN armoured Land Rover outside Karadzic's HQ. Whenever the Serbs invited the media to Pale it was usually an indication that they were about to spring an unwelcome surprise on us, although Akashi was due to meet the Bosnian Serb leadership later in the day. Our suspicions deepened when we saw not only Karadzic in the conference room but also Mladic, wearing a black armband, accompanied by his friend and comrade-in-arms Brig.-Gen. Tolimir. Mladic had been absent from Bosnia for over a month and it was rumoured that he was either suffering from a nervous breakdown following the suicide of his daughter or drying-out in a clinic for alcoholics. It soon became evident that he was now back in command and at his most dangerous.

Relaxed and full of charm, he explained that it was regrettably no longer possible for me to go to Gorazde. Our visit would send all the wrong signals to the Serbs about UNPROFOR being on the side of the Muslims. Anyway it was too dangerous at the moment and he could not guarantee our security. I told him that my reason for going to Gorazde was to assess the military situation in the enclave and thereby put a proper perspective on the media reports about what was happening there. Sergio emphasised to Karadzic that if the Bosnian Serb Army prevented us from going, this would only confirm suspicions that it was planning to launch an offensive. Karadzic replied that such a plan formed no part of their strategy. He claimed that the military activity in the area had been caused by the Muslims attacking out of the enclave in violation of the UN Security Council Resolution, which demanded the demilitarisation of all safe areas. The Bosnian Serbs had no intention of capturing the town itself, they merely wanted to retake the villages on the right bank of the river Drina from where they had been expelled two years before.

Karadzic always quoted UN resolutions when it suited him, yet he still refused to recognise the authority of the UN. This was perhaps understandable, given the fact that the UN refused to recognise the Republika Srpska. Mladic then revealed that he wanted me to return to Sarajevo to arrange a meeting between himself and Delic. The Serbs had new proposals to make for an immediate ceasefire throughout Bosnia, to be followed by a global peace plan along the lines that Viktor had been negotiating.

Naturally there was every possibility that this was a ruse to divert my attention from what was happening in Gorazde, but I had a duty to explore all opportunities for obtaining a lasting peace. I reluctantly agreed to return to Sarajevo, on the condition that the group that was travelling with me be allowed to continue its journey to Gorazde. Mladic agreed to this, although he asked to meet the soldiers in the group. They were still waiting patiently on the road outside the HQ building. Mladic was fascinated by their array of weapons and radios and he spent some time talking to them and examining their equipment, though he failed to identify the ground-to-air radios that were to prove so valuable in the coming days.

Mladic observed that the men I was with did not seem to be UNMOs. I explained that the JCOs were volunteers drawn from contingents within UNPROFOR and that they were more experienced than the UNMOs, some of whom were airmen or sailors. He then asked me for the map coordinates of their intended positions around Gorazde so that he could give orders to his commanders to avoid firing on these locations. I gave him these, knowing that they would become outdated within a few hours. I also told the JCOs what I had done. When I did finally call down air strikes against the Bosnian Serb artillery positions five days later, Mladic immediately ordered all the positions that I had given to him to be heavily shelled. The shells fell on vacant ground. But all that lay in the future.

As I left the Bosnian Serb HQ for Sarajevo I was attacked by an angry mob of journalists who suggested that by turning back from the planned trip to Gorazde I had spinelessly given in to the Bosnian Serbs. They asked if this was representative of the new robust approach to peacekeeping. If so, the new UN policy was not worth a damn. Presumably they had wanted to see me leading the convoy in an attempt to force a passage to Gorazde, 40 miles away, complete no doubt with NATO air strikes and the 82nd Airborne Division coming to our rescue!

On my return to Sarajevo it was clear that Mladic's newly discovered desire for peace was not shared by Delic. President Izetbegovic welcomed the proposed talks, but also called for an extension of the Sarajevo exclusion zone for heavy weapons to the whole of Bosnia. Izetbegovic was eventually prevailed upon to give Delic authority to attend the talks but – in a depressing replay of what had happened during the 9 February Sarajevo ceasefire talks – Delic still refused to meet Mladic at the airport.

The next day (7 April) was spent in a whirl of diplomatic activity, as Viktor Andreev and I shuttled between Mladic in the Lukavica barracks on the Serb side of Sarajevo airport and Delic in his HQ in Sarajevo. Delic now demanded that a full political settlement be agreed before any talk of a ceasefire could take place. Even he could see that this was an unrealistic precondition. The war had begun in the first place because of a lack of political agreement and Lord Carrington, Cyrus Vance, Lord Owen and Thorvald Stoltenberg had all failed to obtain any settlement during the past two years. Delic obviously intended this new line to be a spoiling action. He had been in the same class as Mladic in the Yugoslav Army, but had reputedly been at the bottom, while Mladic had been at the top. I think Delic was physically afraid of him.

I went to the Bosnian Army HQ to see if I could use the same strong-arm tactics I had successfully used on Gen. Divjak in February. Delic, however, had pre-empted my move and fled from his office, so I sat patiently outside the HQ in my Range Rover. Within minutes, President Izetbegovic raced past in a black Toyota Land Cruiser on the way to the Presidency, followed by Delic who drove into the Army HQ. Hard on his heels, I entered the building and caught up with him before he could take off his coat. I insisted that we go to the Presidency so that President Izetbegovic could hear the UN proposals in person. Once again the approach succeeded and we headed off to see the President.

Izetbegovic and Silajdzic looked tired and uneasy and our discussion was bad-tempered. Silajdzic claimed that by pressing the Bosnians to agree to talks and by taking a neutral position, I was in effect blackmailing them. If the Bosnians agreed to a cessation of hostilities, then the existing conflict line would become permanent and the aggressor Serb would have won. I replied that soldiers were dying in Bosnia as we spoke and that we had to bring the fighting to an end to save lives. I said that although there were political risks in stopping the fighting, no political options were foreclosed by doing this. I asked them to agree to a 24-hour halt in the fighting to permit talks to take place in a less hostile atmosphere. After some argument they finally agreed to stop the fighting at 1800 hours that evening. I said I would return the next day (8 April) at 1400 hours to hear their response to my two-part plan. This plan envisaged, firstly, a halt in the fighting around Gorazde and the withdrawal of Serb troops from the enclave, and secondly, a cessation of hostilities for a four-month period to allow a final political solution for Bosnia to be developed.

We drove straight to the Lukavica barracks where Mladic was waiting for us. He agreed to a cessation of hostilities throughout Bosnia, but would not consider a withdrawal of troops from around Gorazde unless this formed part of an overall cessation of hostilities. He restated that any talks had to be global from the start without any preconditions regarding Gorazde. After further argument, Viktor finally persuaded him to accept a truce along the entire line of conflict for the next 24 hours.

By the end of the day we had achieved a brief truce and had reached an agreement, in principle, for a cessation of hostilities. All that remained was to reconcile the differences between the Bosnian Government, who wanted a withdrawal of Serb troops to be a precondition to a cessation of hostilities, and the Serbs, who wanted Gorazde to be dealt with as part of the global solution. As this seemed merely a question of establishing the order in which things should be done, I felt that we had taken an important step towards peace.

It was annoying therefore to read a report leaked to the press from the UNMOs in Goradze:

> From the BBC World Service news of 5 April, we heard an UNPROFOR assessment that the attack into Gorazde was a minor affair into a limited area. We do not concur with that position. It is a grave situation . . . Saying it is a minor attack into a limited area is a bad assessment, incorrect and shows absolutely no understanding of what is going on here.

The statement read as if it had been dictated to the UNMOs by the Bosnian authorities in Gorazde and did not accord in the slightest way with what the official UN spokesman in Sarajevo had actually been saying. We had many times repeated that the UN was taking the situation seriously, but that we could not base our strategy on the many exaggerated reports that were emerging from Gorazde. The JCOs' reports showed that although there had been some incursions into the enclave, no serious attempt had been made by the Serbs to overrun it or to capture the town. Nor did the Serbs ever try to achieve these goals.

True to form, at the airport the next day (8 April) Delic refused to meet Mladic in person and Mladic refused to talk unless he met Delic. However, I was expecting President Clinton's special envoy to Bosnia, Ambassador Charles Redman, to return to Sarajevo the next morning and I hoped that his presence would persuade the two opposing generals to attend the peace talks.

Redman arrived the next morning on the scheduled UN Ilyushin 76 from Zagreb. We quickly briefed him on the situation in Gorazde and the difficulties we had encountered in the latest round of peace talks. I explained that I had already asked Akashi to pass a strong message to the Serbs warning them against further advances into the Gorazde enclave and there had been no more shelling of the town. I told Redman that the JCOs were providing the only accurate and reliable reports from Gorazde. The other reports, though they received enormous media coverage, came from unreliable UNMOs and local civil and military authorities, who repeated whatever line was fed to them by their government. The anguished and sensational reports coming from the ubiquitous "radio ham", whose voice always seemed to be broadcast on Bosnian television and radio from wherever there was trouble in the country, did not provide a reliable basis on which to make an assessment. Although I agreed with Redman that the situation in Gorazde at that time was undeniably extremely serious, in the context of a war that was being fought along a line of conflict 1,000 kilometres long, the fighting around Gorazde was little worse than elsewhere in Bosnia. The state of peace and normality in Sarajevo seemed to have caused people to forget that there was a protracted civil war taking place throughout Bosnia, in which no side had yet made any determined effort to find a way to peace.

Frequent commando-style raids by the Bosnian Army out of the enclave of Gorazde and the burning of a number of Serb villages to the east of the Drina had infuriated Mladic. He accused the UN of not reacting, despite the fact that it had called on the Muslims not to use safe areas for military operations.

Redman and I then went together to the Presidency to brief President Izetbegovic. Delic was in attendance and the meeting started with a highly professional briefing given by a JCO, who described in meticulous detail what was happening on the ground in Gorazde. At intervals Delic would sigh and roll his eyes to the ceiling in protest at the points being made, which clearly contradicted much of what he had told Izetbegovic. This began to annoy Izetbegovic, but Delic persisted until Izetbegovic told him to shut up. Redman then took the lead in discussing what strategy to pursue regarding the negotiations at the airport. It seemed to me that he was still keen to follow up the success of the 9 February Sarajevo Airport Agreement and the signing of the Washington Accord that had brought to an end the fighting between the Muslims and the Croats.

The next day, after several late objections from Delic about the order of arrival at the airport, both military delegations finally turned up. The meeting was held in the hangar where we had held the Sarajevo ceasefire negotiations in February. Tables and chairs were set out in a hollow square on one side of a partition, while on the other side an array of food and wine awaited the successful outcome of the talks. Before the plenary session, the two delegations were put into separate rooms while Redman tried to identify any last-minute changes to their negotiating positions. Mladic stated that, although he was prepared to listen to anything from the UN or the Muslim side, he intended to introduce a new proposal for a cessation of hostilities. This sounded ominous. It appeared that he intended to ambush Delic with proposals that had not been made known to the Bosnian side or to the UN. That Mladic wanted to intimidate Delic was clear, but it was too late now to halt the proceedings.

With Redman present, I opened the meeting by reminding everyone that the UN was only in Bosnia as an impartial mediator, that it could not force a peace on anyone but that a historic opportunity for peace now presented itself. Repeating the phrase that I had used at the talks two months before, I reminded the combatants that the people of Bosnia would judge us all harshly if we failed to take the necessary steps towards peace.

My appeal was completely wasted as both sides simultaneously launched into fierce attacks against each other. After we had calmed them down, Redman briefed them in detail on the latest UN two-phase proposal for a complete cessation of hostilities, starting with a 14-day ceasefire in Gorazde in phase one. After a lengthy lecture on Serb history, Mladic then produced his own proposals, which were surprisingly coherent and not too far removed from our own. I became cautiously optimistic, as the sole remaining sticking point was the sequence of events. The Bosnians, after agreeing to move the Gorazde issue to an annexe of the agreement, thought that there should be a preliminary 14-day ceasefire, during which time political and constitutional arrangements could be worked out before a cessation of hostilities agreement was signed. The Serbs, on the other hand, thought that a long-term cessation of hostilities should be agreed upon immediately before any discussions took place on political or constitutional matters. We seemed to be close to a global solution, so Redman returned to the Presidency to see what compromise Izetbegovic might agree to regarding the sequence of events. He returned with a much tougher set of demands from Izetbegovic, who now said that there could be no further talks until the Bosnian Serbs had returned to the positions they had held on 30 March, prior to the attack on Gorazde. Suddenly we were back to square one.

Someone in Izetbegovic's office later told Simon that Redman had secretly advised Izetbegovic to change his position, on the grounds that if the war was halted when the Serbs still held 70% of the territory, it would be impossible to obtain a fair settlement. The political risks were simply too great. It is impossible to say whether this intelligence was correct, but by suddenly demanding a total Serb withdrawal from the enclave as a precondition to any further talks, Izetbegovic brought the negotiations at the airport to an abrupt end. The Bosnian Government thereby rejected a major chance of peace, in the hope that, later on, they would be able to wring greater concessions from the Serbs. This never happened.

It was a tragedy for the people of Bosnia that the political and territorial solution that was finally imposed on the country in 1995 by the Dayton Agreement was remarkably similar to the one that had been on the table 18 months earlier.[3] The meeting ended with both sides agreeing a 48-hour cooling-off period to review their positions. As we left, Delic and Mladic accused me of bringing them to the airport under false pretences, saying that they would not be so easily tricked again.

The next day (10 April) I was due to fly to Brussels to brief the North Atlantic Council. The 48-hour cooling-off period that had been agreed by both sides made it likely that things would remain relatively calm, so I decided to go. However, as I was boarding an RAF plane in Split on my way to Brussels, a message came from Zagreb saying that I should speak urgently to de Lapresle. He told me the Serbs had attacked in heavy numbers into the enclave and that the Bosnian forces had thrown down their arms and were fleeing into the town. Clearly my visit to Brussels was off. I flew back to Sarajevo, where the Chief of Staff Brig. van Baal told me that tanks were now on the outskirts of Gorazde and were firing directly at buildings in the town from the other side of the river. The nearby villages of Uhotici, Potici and Kodzace were in flames. The Bosnian Army had collapsed and was in total retreat. The soldiers appeared to have given up all armed resistance and the Bosnian Government was calling on the UN for help. Furthermore, American intelligence had intercepted a message from Mladic to one of his commanders saying that he did not want "a single lavatory left standing in the town".

The time for diplomacy or negotiation was over and a great weight was lifted from my shoulders as I found myself back in the familiar business of war-fighting. It did not cross my mind for a moment that the UN should refrain from using force. The lives of my soldiers and the civilians in Gorazde were being directly threatened. Before leaving Split, I warned NATO that I was about to request air support and that I wanted strike aircraft over Gorazde by the time I returned to Sarajevo.

Arriving at my HQ, I went directly to the NATO tactical air coordination cell and asked Wg Cdr Des Dezonie, the chief NATO liaison officer in Sarajevo, how soon it would be before the aircraft were in a position to carry out air strikes. He told me that the official request had not yet been made by the Chief of Staff who, apparently, had been waiting for my return. Cursing under my breath, I signed the relevant air request forms and the "Blue Sword" procedure began. This procedure was needed to obtain political clearance for NATO air strikes, first from Akashi, who was in Paris, and then from New York. The clearance procedure took over an hour, and it was not until 1655 hours that the necessary authority was finally received in Sarajevo for NATO to carry out its first ever bombing mission.

Because the weather in the region was poor, with clouds covering the tops of the mountains, the attack aircraft had to descend through cloud over Sarajevo airport, about 50 kilometres distant, and fly at low-level from there to Gorazde. Being only able to fly along the floor of the valleys made it extremely difficult for the pilots to identify suitable targets in the few seconds that passed as they overflew Gorazde. Flying low also made the aircraft extremely vulnerable to Serb ground fire and shoul-der-launched ground-to-air missiles. It was a very different battle from the one fought in the Gulf, where laser-guided bombs could be delivered against static targets in the desert from high altitude without risk to the aircraft. Despite the risks and the marginal weather conditions, the pilots were desperately keen to continue with the mission, particularly as they knew that the forward air controllers on the ground would help them.

At 1450 hours I had asked Simon Shadbolt to send a message to Mladic via Pale, warning him that unless the attacks into Gorazde stopped, I would call down air strikes against his forces in accordance with UN Security Council Resolution 836.[4] I doubted if this would have any effect, but at least it would prevent Mladic from claiming I had attacked without due warning. We received no reply but Viktor Andreev, in a final effort to prevent NATO air power being used against the Serbs, had gone to Pale to try and get Karadzic to halt the Bosnian Serb Army advance. Without much hope, I told him what I had done so far and asked him to persuade Karadzic to order the Bosnian Serb Army to withdraw from Gorazde. At 1500 hours, the JCOs on the ground in Gorazde were reporting that Mladic's forces were attacking strongly to the south-east of the town and tanks had also taken up positions two kilometres to the south-west. At 1600 hours Serb artillery started to shell the town. The situation in Gorazde was worsening by the minute and we still had no clearance from New York.

At 1615 hours I received a reply from Mladic:

> The President and Commander-in-Chief of the Republika Srpska, Dr Karadzic, has ordered that no round must impact on Gorazde ... according to our observer reports, we can reliably inform you that Serb Army mortar and artillery rounds are not falling on Gorazde.

At that very moment the JCOs reported that heavy artillery and tank fire was being directed into the town. Mladic was either quite mad, a liar, or completely out of touch with his army. I ruled out the latter possibility.

At 1700 hours I spoke to Adm. Leighton Smith in Naples confirming that I had finally received the necessary authority to use NATO aircraft to attack targets around Gorazde. After a brief discussion we agreed that the aircraft should initially strike at tanks. After further delay, the pilots reported that they were unable to identify suitable targets owing to the poor light, the bad weather and the fact that the tanks were moving in and out of cover. As the minutes ticked by and repeated passes were made by the aircraft without finding a target, Simon observed drily that it was just as well the Warsaw Pact had not attacked Western Europe in the rain.

By 1800 hours the pilots were still having difficulty engaging the tanks, so I told Des Dezonie to go for static artillery positions. However, rather than attack the guns themselves, I decided to strike at artillery command posts, believing it was better to cut the head off the octopus rather than merely a tentacle. Just as we agreed this, the two A-10 aircraft over Gorazde at the time ran out of fuel. Two F-16s had been stationed nearby and at 1826 hours they finally carried out a successful attack, destroying an artillery command post. Later intelligence indicated that nine officers, including friends of Mladic, had been killed in the attack. It was shortly after this that Mladic shelled the locations of the JCOs that I had given him. By 1845 hours all firing had stopped. NATO had achieved its first success and it had done so in support of a UN peacekeeping mission, something never foreseen by the original members of the Alliance nearly 50 years before.

Redman had stayed in my office throughout the afternoon, listening closely to what was going on, but occasionally going to the US embassy next door to talk to Washington. This proved extremely useful, as we were able to send accurate reports directly back to the US Administration, rather than the biased reports they had previously been getting from the Bosnian Government. At 2215 hours a signal was received from Mladic signed by Milovanovic, his deputy: "NATO air forces carried out attacks on RS Army positions in the area of Gorazde today. Your representatives have announced further NATO forces attacks. We demand that you immediately inform us on whose order and decision NATO air forces attacked the RS Army positions." I had no difficulty in sending him a message saying that I was the culprit. In a later telephone call, he warned us that no UN personnel would be left alive in Bosnia. At long last it seemed that we were finally getting through to the Serbs. Within three hours of the attack, the Pentagon gave a detailed briefing to the media, complete with maps and video footage, on the air strikes that had been carried out by their pilots. There was surprisingly little reference to the UN, which upset all of us. When the UN was mentioned, the report's angle was inaccurate and unwelcome from a political perspective.

In the midst of all this, Akashi and de Lapresle, accompanied by a large staff known to us as the "Zagreb Flying Circus", arrived in Sarajevo. Although it was helpful having them there to deal with the political and media aftermath of the air strike, the Residency was becoming a little crowded. Russians, French, Americans, Bulgarians, Dutch, British, Danes, civilians and military, all milled about the building trying to find out what was going on, while Simon Shadbolt desperately tried to keep everyone not directly involved in the running of the operation out of my office. Old Yugoslav retainers, who provided domestic help in the Residency, and who were doubtless in the pay of the Bosnian intelligence service, busied themselves carrying coffee and sandwiches to wherever they considered the most important discussions were taking place.

Viktor arrived back late from Pale, accompanied by President Yeltsin's special representative to Bosnia, Vitaly Churkin. Churkin had had a frustrating day that had concluded in a furious shouting match with Karadzic when Churkin had accused him of lying. Churkin and Andreev were intensely depressed at their failure to prevent the bombing, and Churkin was bleeding from a cut on his head where he had banged it on the hatch of the Russian APC in which they had travelled from Pale. Their sorry state invoked the usual cure of iced vodka and caviar, the latter having been thoughtfully presented by the Iranian military attaché in Sarajevo, whose real job, I always suspected, was running guns into Bosnia. "The Staff College never trained us for this," I said to Simon as I retired to bed well after midnight.

11 April started quietly but by midday shells were falling once again on Gorazde. The weather was still bad and French Mirage jets in the area were unable to descend below the cloud cover. By 1236 hours the shelling had increased, only slackening when an American F-8 jet made a supersonic pass along the valley of the Drina causing a sonic boom. At 1315 hours Viktor, who had been speaking to Belgrade, reported that President Milosevic had personally intervened to get Karadzic to stop the shelling.

Tanks appeared at 1407 hours, heading towards the town from the west. It was obvious Mladic was taking no notice of President Milosevic. I therefore gave the order to attack the tanks. Three bombs were dropped and one tank and two APCs were reported destroyed. I asked Nick Costello to warn Mladic to halt his advance on Gorazde and to remind him that UN soldiers were non-combatants in the war, but that we had the right of self-defence and we would not hesitate to exercise that right again.

"One more attack," replied Mladic, "and I will shoot the aircraft down. I cannot guarantee the safety of UNPROFOR personnel and I will also attack your HQ." Looking out of the window at the Serb positions on the hill behind the Kosevo hospital, all seemed quiet and I decided he was bluffing. He could not take on the West in a war, unless he wanted the Bosnian Serbs to commit collective suicide. I told him he had 10 minutes to withdraw the tanks approaching Gorazde from Kopaci. Shortly before the deadline expired, the JCOs reported that the tanks had turned round and sped off in the direction of Visegrad. They never returned, although sporadic shelling continued. The Bosnian Army had positioned mortars behind a building from where the JCOs were observing the fighting and one salvo fired at the mortar nearly killed the JCO commander, forcing him to move his location. By 1630 hours things had quietened down.

Maintaining telephone contact with Mladic during the past two days had been easier than we had expected. Whatever number we dialled, whether it was Karadzic, Milovanovic, or even one of his junior staff officers, Mladic always took the call, even though he was known to be directing the battle in the hills above Gorazde. He spoke calmly, but with barely concealed fury, mixing outright denials that he was attacking Gorazde with threats of reprisals. On one occasion he said to Nick, "Tell your general not to ring my subordinates, we have a job to do." Once, after a final brisk exchange of Serbo-Croat insults, Nick lost his temper with Mladic and slammed down the telephone. Everyone in the room, including Redman and Churkin, applauded. Nick looked highly embarrassed, but we had all had enough of Mladic for one day.

The Serbs later claimed that the NATO air strikes on 11 April had destroyed not just tanks and APCs but an armoured ambulance. As ambulances are protected from attack by the Geneva Convention, I told Des Desoni that this was unlikely to go down in history as one of the Great Firsts. I suspected that the Serb report was probably propaganda, but I nevertheless kept a framed photograph of the wrecked ambulance on the wall of my office for all to see with the inscription, "Nice One Nato!" writ large upon it.

For much of the day Akashi and de Lapresle were with me in my office trying to analyse what was going on in the minds of the protagonists. We needed to know whether the Serb assault on Gorazde was a signal that the Serbs were going for all-out victory, or whether it was a tactical exercise to put pressure on the Bosnians. Our reactions to each possibility would have to be very different.

I maintained that the Bosnian Serbs had no intention of capturing Gorazde as they could have done so by now. The Bosnian forces were incapable of stopping them. Instead of fighting in the countryside away from the civilian population, where the mountains and forests provided the best defensive terrain for their infantry, the Bosnian Army had fallen back into the town and involved civilians in the battle. Now that NATO had also become involved, the Bosnian Government apparently felt it was on the road to victory. Local radio in Sarajevo was endlessly playing a pop song written to celebrate the air strikes and the UN peacekeepers were once again being hailed as their saviours. I had an uneasy feeling that this adulation was not going to last.

Throughout the day, numerous briefings took place with my own staff, in the presence of Akashi, de Lapresle, Redman and Churkin, though no one interfered with my decisions or tried to counter the orders I gave. Together, we were able to assess the tactical situation on the ground and to relate it directly to the political and strategic objectives we were pursuing. This served to shorten the long chain of command from Sarajevo back to the Security Council and pre-empted much of the ongoing debate in New York. When report of some new development in the battle was received, invariably bad news, everyone would fall silent and wait for me to react before offering advice.

We were in general agreement that an appropriate level of force was being applied against the Serbs in accordance with the UN mandate and that any attempt to raise significantly the level of bombing would risk changing the nature of the mission from peacekeeping to war-fighting. This would risk the collapse of the entire mission and result in greater suffering for the people of Bosnia. I privately decided that if we were wrong in our assessments and the Serbs *did* overrun Gorazde, then I would have no choice but to call down massive air strikes against them, though this action would spell the end of the peacekeeping mission. But as long as the level of force used by NATO remained within the limits set by the UN mandate, there remained a chance that we could revert to the peace process. Defending a safe area was a war-fighting task for which the UN was neither mandated, equipped nor trained. Sadly, the Bosnian Government believed that the NATO air strikes in Gorazde had launched the UN on a Gulf War-style air campaign against the Bosnian Serbs.

Wednesday 13 April saw more visitors to Sarajevo in the shape of Lord Owen and Thorvald Stoltenberg, who were both given an up-to-date account of the battle by the chief JCO. His view was that the fighting was centred on the high ground around the town and on the main routes in and out of the valley. Contrary to the propaganda reports, the Serbs were not targeting the civilian population but were engaging the Bosnian Army positions in the town. During the discussion that followed this briefing, Vitaly Churkin told Owen and Stoltenberg that the tactical situation had fundamentally altered and that the Serbs could not be expected to withdraw their troops from the enclave and give up their military gains. Chuck Redman insisted that there could be no peace deal until their act of aggression had been punished and the *status quo ante* restored. Churkin and Redman remained on excellent terms with each other, although they had firmly opposed points of view. They both agreed, however, that calling in another air strike was the only rational response to a particular Serb attack. It must have been something of an education for the politicians and diplomats to see a military HQ at work in the middle of a battle.

At 1200 hours the next day (14 April) the position of the UN in Bosnia was dramatically threatened. The Serbs took 150 UN soldiers and aid workers hostage and at the same time we received news of a Serb artillery attack on Tuzla, a designated safe area. There was pressure on me to call in further air strikes, but I told Brig. van Baal to see if the Danish Leopard tanks that I had deployed to Tuzla could stop the Serbs from firing. As our tanks moved towards the Serb guns, the shelling ceased, demonstrating that the UN was not completely reliant on NATO for its deterrence capability.

I spent the remainder of the day reassuring defence ministries of the troop-contributing nations that their soldiers who had been taken hostage would come to no harm as long as the UN was not drawn into the war. Although things were not looking good, I firmly believed that the difficulties we faced were not insurmountable. Meanwhile I was also trying to find out where all the hostages were being held. In war, a military commander will always attempt to retain the initiative, in peace-keeping this is rarely possible. Command of a peacekeeping mission is infinitely more challenging.

Friday 15 April proved to be the most difficult day of the entire mission. As usual it began quietly enough. Akashi departed with Nick Costello to Pale to get Karadzic to call off his attack on Gorazde, release the hostages and return to the conference table. Akashi was a tenacious individual with considerable courage. Despite the fact that the Serbs had refused all attempts at mediation, including one from President Milosevic, and that the UN was now responsible for killing a considerable number of Serb soldiers, the diminutive Akashi was still prepared to venture into a hostile camp occupied by unstable politicians, gunmen and alleged war criminals.

In Pale, Karadzic said that the Bosnian Serbs would no longer speak to military personnel in UNPROFOR, obviously regarding Nick as an honorary civilian, since he remained the chief interpreter for the talks. Although Karadzic accepted that the decision to use air strikes was the result of an internationally coordinated policy, he would never forgive UNPROFOR for what they had done. He remained intractable on the subject of the hostages, whose release he now linked to the release of Serb prisoners held by the Bosnians in Tarcin. Shortly after lunch that day, the JCO commander in Gorazde reported a strong attack by the Serbs from the north of the town.

I was also informed that a team of JCOs had been asked by the local Muslim commander to deploy forward to see what was happening. They were driving in a Land Rover up a mountain some three kilometres north of Gorazde when it was hit by a burst of machine-gun fire. The driver and front-seat passenger had been wounded, one critically. Mortar and shellfire were coming down around them and the Land Rover had gone off the track. The survivors were at that moment taking cover in a ditch, on a forward slope in front of the advancing Serbs. Unless they were rescued, there would be more casualties.

I immediately asked NATO to prepare for air strikes on the advancing Serbs. At the same time I put a call through to Nick in Pale who told me that Akashi was still having lunch with Karadzic. Meanwhile Simon had asked the French in Sarajevo to prepare two Puma helicopters for an urgent medical casualty evacuation. Even for the Balkans this was an unusual turn of events, as I needed Akashi's consent to call down an air strike on the military forces of the man with whom he was having lunch. My only means of communication with Pale was an insecure radio that I knew would be listened to by the Bosnians and the press. The following excerpts are taken from a tape that was available the next day on the streets in New York:

> ROSE: Nick, can you get hold of Mr Akashi? They are firing on our guys who are on a forward slope. They cannot get to the injured parties. We are going to have to use "Blue Sword" straightaway. Can you get permission from Mr Akashi? Say we've got casualties on a forward slope under heavy fire and we have got to use "Blue Sword" to get them out or they will all be killed.
>
> NICK: Roger, wait out. I'm going to get Mr Akashi on to this in the next 10 seconds.
>
> AKASHI: Hello Michael.
>
> ROSE: Hello, Mr Akashi?
>
> AKASHI: Yes I'm here.
>
> ROSE: The situation has deteriorated very rapidly whilst you've been in the meeting. The BiH Army [Bosnian forces] has pulled back. They've collapsed and pulled back in the north, not the south where we expected. We have Bosnian Serb Army forces directly firing on our positions. We have one, we think, fatally injured, one injured. They're all on a forward slope. They cannot extricate themselves without air support. We need air support now.
>
> AKASHI: (*after some interference with the communications*) What about Dr Karadzic ordering an immediate ceasefire allowing immediate evacuation of our people?
>
> ROSE: Sir, I think that by the time the message gets through to the units on the ground, they will all be dead or captured (*more interference*).
>
> NICK: Are you therefore willing to carry out the helicopter evacuation first?
>
> ROSE: No, the situation is critical, Nick. They're under heavy fire. They're on a forward slope. They need an air strike now. Otherwise there will be more casualties, and they'll probably be overrun themselves. They cannot move. They have injured people and cannot get down to them.
>
> AKASHI: Michael, just one question. Does this mean that you are withdrawing the request for helicopter evacuation? This has been conveyed to Dr Karadzic who is acting on it right now. Do you want him not to do that as the two are obviously incompatible.
>
> ROSE: No. The two are not incompatible. We need to stop the present people being killed, and then there will have to be a withdrawal and then they will have to be evacuated by helicopter. We have to stop the fighting as it is at the moment, and then we will have to evacuate.

In the end, owing to Akashi's intervention with Karadzic the fighting stopped before the air strikes were needed, and the evacuation of the two injured soldiers from the mountainside took place without hindrance. Whether this was by chance or because Mladic had ordered it because of the threat of an air strike, it was never possible to say.

We nevertheless kept the A-10 aircraft in the sky over Gorazde as the French Puma helicopters flew to Gorazde to evacuate the most critically injured of the two soldiers to the French military hospital in Sarajevo. Despite the speed of the evacuation and the excellence of the military surgeons, he was sadly beyond saving. A bullet had entered his head at the back just above his collar and had exited between his eyes. The next day I learned that a younger brother of the chief JCO was among the soldiers in Gorazde. Until the medical evacuation had taken place, he had not known whether either of the injured men was his brother. He had not allowed this private anxiety to surface while he carried out his duties.

That night, in sombre mood, Akashi, de Lapresle and I went to see Izetbegovic and Silajdzic, who both expressed their anger about developments in Gorazde. Izetbegovic anticipated that thousands of people would die if the UN did nothing. He accused me of minimising the threat to the civilian population and neglecting my responsibility, under UN Security Council Resolution 836, to defend the safe areas. He went on to demand that the UN lift all restrictions on the use of NATO air power.

At one point Silajdzic suddenly left the room, apparently in annoyance at the refusal by Akashi to accept that the UN should be doing more than it had already done. However, it transpired that he had simply run out of cigarettes. On his return, he told us that two shells had just landed in Gorazde and he accused Akashi of dereliction of duty and of presiding over the total discrediting of the UN. What was the purpose of UNPROFOR if it was not to defend the safe areas? Akashi, who had remained polite and inscrutable, replied that the UN was doing everything that its mandate allowed it to do. This greatly annoyed Silajdzic.

Stepping into the fray, I told the Bosnian leaders that UNPROFOR could not fight other people's wars. It was a peacekeeping force that could use only a limited degree of military force to deter attacks against the safe areas. Only the Security Council in New York could make the necessary changes to the UN mandate to allow strategic-level air strikes to take place. The Americans had already said that they were not prepared to see NATO used to defend Gorazde, nor could the UN transform itself into a war-fighting force, so there was little chance of such a decision being made. Neither Izetbegovic nor Silajdzic accepted this. Gorazde was now at the mercy of the Serbs and there was little we could do about it.

A horde of journalists and TV cameras awaited us as we left the meeting. A pent-up American journalist hurled a stream of verbal abuse at Akashi, who started to reply but I steered him firmly away. I had discovered on the streets in Northern Ireland that it was no use trying to reason with extremists. I vaguely wondered if Silajdzic, Izetbegovic and their supporters in the international press actually believed that the UN, which was doing the most in Bosnia to bring about peace, was responsible for the slaughter. I concluded, sadly, that they probably did.

The next afternoon a tank assault was launched on the remaining Bosnian forces to the east of the town. Once again I called for air strikes in response, warning Mladic that I had done so. This was becoming a familiar pattern. The cloud was extremely low and the Sea Harrier aircraft, ill-equipped for this type of warfare, had to make several passes in order to identify the tanks that had moved into the cover of some trees. Churkin was in Pale talking to Karadzic, so I sent a message asking him to get Karadzic to stop the attack. It was just possible that Karadzic would accede to a request from President Yeltsin's special representative. However, Karadzic told Churkin that the tanks were actually Bosnian Army tanks, which had mysteriously appeared in Gorazde and were firing on their own people. On his return Churkin told me that in his entire career, he had never been lied to so blatantly as he had been by the Bosnian Serbs.

On the fourth pass over Gorazde the lone Sea Harrier was shot down. The incident happened within sight of a forward air controller who was at the time talking to the HQ in Sarajevo. Suddenly we heard him say:

"A21, Fortune 5 is tracking the tank along the road. We now have communications with the aircraft and we are directing it on to the tank. The aircraft can now see the tank . . . he's got it visual. The aircraft has been hit and is on fire! Its going down . . . I think the pilot has ejected. I can see a parachute."

The operations room fell silent as this message was received. No one could believe that the relatively primitive Bosnian Serb Army had destroyed a NATO aircraft. At that moment a call arrived from Adm. Leighton Smith in Naples. He explained that he was halting the air missions over Gorazde to allow a search-and-rescue mission for the pilot. I told him that the pilot had probably landed safely on the Bosnian side of the line and we would try get to him. We then discussed the way ahead.

Smith said that he would no longer agree to requests for air strikes on tactical-level targets. It was too risky. In future he would only accept strategic-level targets such as major HQs, communications sites or logistic installations such as ammunition bunkers. I told him that neither NATO nor the UN had authority to escalate the use of air power in this manner. It was unfortunate that an aircraft had been shot down, but the incident should be considered a routine hazard of peacekeeping. UNPROFOR had suffered many casualties during the mission but we had never abandoned it. In the end he agreed to consider further requests, but no air strikes over Gorazde subsequently took place.

Following this conversation, Akashi, de Lapresle and I convened a council of war in my office. We agreed that the shooting down of the NATO aircraft had probably altered the political and military situation in Bosnia. We would be under extreme pressure to escalate the air campaign, but this in itself would spell disaster. While we contemplated our next move, Churkin called from Pale with the news that the Serbs were prepared to halt the fighting, withdraw to a distance of three kilometres from the centre of town, establish a 20-kilometre TEZ around Gorazde and release all the hostages. They also wished to return to the conference table and restart the peace process. This was extraordinary news, coming as it did at the moment of complete collapse by their adversaries. We still had to obtain agreement to a ceasefire from the Bosnian Government but, given the circumstances, there was no other course open to them but to accept.

When we conveyed the news of the Serb offer to the Presidency, Izetbegovic and Silajdzic accused Akashi of having failed in his mission. He had been indifferent to the plight of thousands of people. The UN Secretary-General himself would be called upon to resign. Akashi fended off these increasingly personal attacks in his usual moderate language. Silajdzic then said that the previous two days had been the worst of his life. For the first time since I had known him, I saw Akashi show emotion. Looking Silajdzic straight in the eyes, he said, "They have also been the worst two days of my life."

Calming down, Silajdzic asked if it was only Karadzic's words that were stopping Gorazde from being overrun. Akashi replied that this was so. In the large room, where the light never penetrated and the temperature even in summer always seemed to hover around freezing point, we sat in stunned silence. At last the truth had been spoken. Delic blew out his cheeks and rolled his eyes to the ceiling. He was a general who had been defeated.

The next night, after some discussion, I decided to withdraw the JCO team from Gorazde. There was little point in keeping them there now that the fighting was dying down. The injured JCO needed urgent attention and their radio batteries had become exhausted. Their presence no longer served a useful purpose. They flew out the next night in the French Puma aircraft with the downed Sea Harrier pilot. I did not tell anyone beforehand about the withdrawal. Not only would the Bosnian Army have tried to stop them leaving, but the Serbs might well have tried to shoot the aircraft down. The JCOs dismantled their HQ just before midnight and, leaving behind their remaining Land Rover for the UNMOs, they walked 1,500 feet up into the mountains, skirting Serb and Bosnian positions, to the helicopter pick-up point. The rescue mission was performed without difficulty by the superb French pilots, who flew through the mountains at night in bad weather, across the Serb lines, using image-intensification goggles.

The next morning I interviewed the Sea Harrier pilot in my office, giving him credit for having tried so hard to find the target. I told him that I was, however, greatly disappointed we had lost a £10 million aircraft without dropping a single bomb. He insisted he had dropped a bomb. "The only problem being," he replied with a smile, "it was still tied to the aircraft when I dropped it."

CHAPTER FIVE

A Phoney Peace

Hope has taken the place of despair.
John Major, Prime Minister, 1994

B Y 19 APRIL THE FIGHTING IN GORAZDE HAD STILL NOT COME TO AN end. The Serbs, while talking peace, continued to put military pressure on the Bosnian Army without actually entering the town. The situation had become chaotic as Gorazde filled with refugees and the food ran out. It was a similar problem elsewhere in Bosnia, since all UN movement across Serb-held territory had been halted and no aid was getting through to any of the enclaves. Stocks in Sarajevo were falling to critically low levels and even in my own HQ we had been on emergency rations for some time.

The international response to the crisis was fragmented and in Sarajevo it seemed to us that Bosnia was sliding uncontrollably towards war. Boutros-Ghali, surprisingly without consulting UNPROFOR, had asked NATO to support the UN with the wider use of air strikes and news of this request sent the Serbs into a frenzy. They had seized anti-aircraft weapons from UN weapon collecting sites against the possibility of NATO air strikes and had taken hostage 250 UN personnel.

Some members of UNPROFOR became equally frenzied. News of Boutros-Ghali's request caused the commanding officer of the Canadian contingent to order the immediate withdrawal of a unit guarding the UN weapon collecting site at Cifluk. This caused further panic among the Serbs, who had mined the exits from the site, regarding the continuing presence of Canadian troops as their best form of air defence. When the Canadians attempted to withdraw through Bosnian territory instead, the Bosnian Army blocked them, this time because they in turn needed the Canadians to defend them from the Serbs. Failing to learn a lesson from this incident, and without consulting me, the Chief UNMO in Zagreb ordered all the UNMOs in Bosnia to withdraw from Serb-held territory. The Serbs responded by taking most of them hostage as well.

Fearing that French soldiers would be taken hostage, the French President had countermanded an order by Soubirou to send a French relief convoy to Gorazde, and I had been asked by London whether I had any plans to rescue British soldiers blocked at Rogatica, deep in Serb territory. When I replied that I did not have any such plans, it was suggested I might consider a raid by Special Forces. As I already had 250 UN peacekeepers taken hostage by the Serbs and scattered across the country, this was the last thing I was about to do. I was confident they would come to no harm as long as the UN did not overreact to events. The traditional peacekeeping weapons of patience, persuasion and persistence were, in such circumstances, more appropriate than bullets. Three days later all the hostages were released unharmed following successful negotiations between Akashi and President Milosevic in Belgrade.

Meanwhile the Bosnian Army in Sarajevo had not helped the situation by firing heavy weapons at Serb positions in the Jewish Cemetery. The Serbs had retaliated and there was a serious danger that the Sarajevo ceasefire would unravel. The relationship between UNPROFOR and the Bosnians had not been improved by the killing of a Royal Marine working for the UNHCR in Sarajevo by the Bosnian police, who claimed he had tried to resist arrest. In the midst of all this, Viktor Andreev walked round the Residency offices gloomily predicting the start of a Third World War. He had some grounds for saying this, as President Yeltsin, following NATO air strikes against the Serbs in Gorazde, had refused to sign the "Partnership for Peace" deal with NATO, and had even threatened "war for ever" if the West intervened in Bosnia.

Outside the gates of the Residency, a disciplined crowd of demonstrators chanted slogans demanding the removal of the UN. Their cries were echoed by a TROOPS OUT headline in the *Daily Express*.[1] Even Goose's patience began to wear thin. When a civilian parked his car in front of the Residency and refused to move it, after twice being asked politely to do so, Goose dragged him out of his car and knocked him unconscious. It took all of my UN mediating and peacekeeping ability to prevent Goose being brought before the War Crimes Tribunal in The Hague by the aggrieved man.

Nor did I remain entirely unaffected by the tension surrounding events in Bosnia. I had not left the Residency for over a week and each day seemed to bring another nightmarish development in Gorazde, despite the tireless efforts of Churkin, Akashi and Lord Owen. However, in the same way that a surgeon cannot allow his personal feelings for a patient to affect his technical performance, I felt that I could not permit the horror and chaos of Bosnia to affect my professional judgement. According to Angela I was looking very tired and had started to sound testy during radio interviews.

For some time, I had been watching two magpies building a nest in a tree opposite my office window. They had survived a bitter winter in the midst of the war and were now setting about rebuilding their home. We would have to do the same and many people around the world were keen to help us. Angela had recently started a relief fund in Britain for the hospital in Gorazde. A friend in the Territorial Army, Mark Hatt-Cook, had already called me to say he was sending £1,000. Throughout this time, I remained convinced that the Serbs would not overrun Gorazde and that at some point both sides would stop fighting and try to resolve their differences through negotiation.

On 21 April I was told by Gen. Shalikashvili, the Chairman of the Joint Chiefs of

Staff, that the US was considering launching a campaign of punitive air strikes against the Serbs. I replied that before this could happen the UN peacekeeping mission would first have to be withdrawn from Bosnia. NATO would require at least 100,000 men, including a US armoured division, to accomplish this complex task and the deployment of such a large force on the ground in Bosnia would probably also allow a political settlement to be imposed on the warring parties. But because America could not send troops to Bosnia prior to a permanent ceasefire, and NATO would not deploy without them, it was left to the UN to bring an end to the war by peaceful means. I knew that Shalikashvili well understood this argument. He had merely needed a voice from Bosnia to help argue his case in the debate taking place within the US Administration.

The next day the North Atlantic Council in Brussels issued an ultimatum to the Bosnian Serbs, ignoring the negotiations that Akashi and de Lapresle were at that time conducting with President Milosevic and the entire Bosnian Serb leadership in Belgrade. At that time the UN team led by Akashi was still trying to persuade Karadzic and Mladic to halt their attack on Gorazde. As an agreement began to emerge, the NATO ultimatum became a problem rather than the supportive measure it was intended to be.

NATO stated that unless the Bosnian Serbs ceased their attacks immediately and pulled back three kilometres from the centre of the city by 0001 hours GMT, 24 April, and also allowed unimpeded access of relief convoys to Gorazde, then the Commander-in-Chief of Allied Forces Southern Command NATO was authorised to carry out air strikes against Bosnian Serb heavy weapons and other targets within a 20-kilometre zone around Gorazde. Although it was possible for Akashi to change the final draft of the Belgrade agreement to reflect some of the wording of the NATO ultimatum, it was impossible to alter the later UN deadline for the withdrawal of the Bosnian Serb Army from Gorazde. NATO had seriously underestimated the complicated arrangements needed to separate the Serb and Bosnian forces in the aftermath of the battle that had been raging round Gorazde for the past two weeks. Neither army would break contact until UN troops arrived in Gorazde and no nation had yet consented to send troops there.

From our perspective in Sarajevo, this intervention by Brussels seemed to be a tactic by the hawks in NATO to push the peacekeeping operation towards war rather than "bringing about a negotiated settlement of the conflict", which the preamble to the ultimatum claimed it to be. In the end, everyone, including Adm. Leighton Smith in Naples, simply ignored the NATO ultimatum and stuck with the Belgrade agreement.

In the short term, the NATO ultimatum on Gorazde undoubtedly put some additional pressure on the Serbs, but the lasting impression given was that the international community could not get its act together. Even Britain was apparently speaking with two voices. While the British ambassador to the UN, Sir David Hannay, was signing Resolution 913 of the Security Council in New York, emphasising the need for a peaceful settlement of the conflict in Bosnia, British defence staff in Brussels were committing Britain to a strategy of war. Capt. George Waters, my aide-de-camp, told me that his father, Gen. Sir John Waters, Deputy SACEUR, had attempted to argue the UN case but received no support from his colleagues.

In London, Glynne Evans, head of the UN Department in the Foreign Office, remained resolute in her support for the peace process. She reassured me that there was a growing awareness among the Europeans of how brilliantly the Bosnian Muslims had been playing the Americans and that a widening of the air campaign by NATO would be tantamount to a declaration of war. She believed that the only feasible option was to support the UN peace effort. In the US Administration there was still confusion about which policy to follow, with Warren Christopher telling Congress that the US had a "strategic and humanitarian interest" in the war in Bosnia, while the Pentagon cautioned against the increased use of air power. President Clinton, having previously conceded that there was little that the international community could do to save Gorazde, was now apparently supporting the more hawkish NATO line.

On 23 April an agreement was finally reached between Akashi and Karadzic. The Serbs agreed to halt the fighting in Gorazde and to withdraw all forces to a distance of three kilometres from the centre of the town and to remove all of their heavy weapons from a 20-kilometre exclusion zone by 26 April. It was also agreed that there should be an immediate medical evacuation of all wounded personnel and complete freedom of movement given to UNPROFOR and humanitarian aid organisations.

Before UNPROFOR could get a convoy through to Gorazde to evacuate the most seriously injured civilians, I had to persuade UN nations to allow their troops to be sent there. This proved exceptionally difficult, given the concern most governments had expressed that their soldiers in Gorazde would become *de facto* hostages of the Serbs. But in peacekeeping, as in war, risks have to be taken and it probably requires more courage for peacekeepers to venture into hostile territory armed only with a conviction that they are morally right, than it does for armed soldiers to do the same. The reward for taking such risks is likely to be great, as the people of Gorazde were to discover; for the arrival of the first UN convoys into their town not only brought food and other medical supplies but also gave them hope of survival.

As Gorazde was in the French area of responsibility, the sector commander, Brig.-Gen. André Soubirou, decided personally to lead the relief force to the enclave. Akashi wanted to go with him, but I dissuaded him on the grounds that his presence would confuse the chain of command and add considerably to the security and logistical problems of the relief operation. I had also discovered over the years how irritating it is for a commander to have his superior officer appear too early at the scene of an operation. Sergio de Mello, who had attended the negotiations in Belgrade and knew the details of what had been agreed, took Akashi's place. This delighted me, as Sergio spoke our sort of language and travelled light; so light, indeed, that I had to lend him a sleeping bag and a pair of boots to replace the Gucci shoes he was wearing. I sent with him Nick Costello to act as his interpreter and liaison officer, and also Rupert Prichard, the deputy chief UNMO who had been so invaluable in organising the clearance of Serb heavy weapons from the TEZ around Sarajevo. When Sergio asked for volunteers from the Civil Affairs and the UN Civil Police to accompany him, he warned them that they might be trapped in Gorazde. Everyone he spoke to volunteered and later they all played an important role in helping to restore some semblance of order and normality in the enclave.

As the convoy was being assembled at Sarajevo airport, Soubirou received a message that President François Mitterrand still refused to allow a French battalion to deploy to Gorazde. I therefore immediately asked John Wilsey to allow us to send the Duke of Wellington's Regiment in their place. Without hesitation he agreed, but as it would take 24 hours for the British troops to prepare themselves for this commitment, I ordered the first convoy consisting of the French HQ, a Ukranian company, a Norwegian medical team and some engineers, to leave for Gorazde without delay. Before setting out, Sergio first went to the Presidency to inform Prime Minister Silajdzic of the purpose of the mission. Silajdzic was disappointed that the presence of the UN would make further use of NATO air strikes unlikely, but he understood that the UN could not do otherwise. UNPROFOR's task was to preserve the safe areas, not to engage in war with the Serbs. He wished Sergio good luck and warned him to be careful.

Relief convoys arrived in Gorazde on the successive nights of 23 and 24 April. When the first one arrived shortly after midnight, desultory firing sounded in the distance and a number of houses were still burning. In the dark, the roads were jammed with Serb armoured vehicles and ambulances that were evacuating the Serb casualties to a makeshift hospital in a factory beside the road at Kopaci. Here Sergio and André Soubirou met Nikola Koljevic, Karadzic's representative, and Gen. Milan Gvero, one of Mladic's staff officers. Having agreed with them the details of the large-scale casualty evacuation that was to take place the next day, Sergio and Nick drove on through the eerie darkness into Gorazde.

It seemed to be deserted, apart from the carcasses of several dead animals lying on the streets. Most of the refugees who had been driven out of the villages on the west bank of the Drina had found shelter in the ruined houses around the town that had been abandoned by the Serbs two years before. There Sergio and Nick met the UNMOs who had been in Gorazde during the fighting, looking tired and unshaven. The chief UNMO, a Canadian, told them that the only food in the town was a dwindling supply of UNHCR rations and the only fuel was firewood taken from the surrounding forests. He told them that the Serb trenches, less than a mile distant and on the surrounding high ground, enabled them to fire directly into the town.

It was obvious to Nick that the UNMO team was completely demoralised. He him- self had been through a similar, if not worse, experience in Srebrenica with Gen. Morrillon two years before, so he was surprised to see the UNMOs in such a poor state. In Sarajevo I had suspected from the emotional tone of their reporting that they had ceased to function as a disciplined military unit. A subsequent investi-gation into their performance revealed that the UNMOs had spent much of their time in the cellars of a bank building, obtaining much of their information from local sources. They had also allowed the Bosnian Army to use their vehicles.

The next morning Soubirou deployed patrols and observation points between the Serb and Bosnian forces. These patrols were able to confirm that the Serbs were withdrawing their heavy weapons. As they withdrew, they blew up the water-pumping station that served the town. Sergio and Nick returned to Kopaci to protest about this and also about the burning of houses by the Serbs. The Serbs replied that they were setting on fire only those houses that had belonged to Serbs, in order to prevent their occupation by Muslims. They also said that Bosnian soldiers were firing on them as they withdrew and that at one point they had been forced to bring six tanks back into the exclusion zone to cover the withdrawal of their infantry. Sergio explained that the UN had only one Ukrainian infantry company deployed in Gorazde at present, but as more troops arrived the UN would be better able to monitor their withdrawal. Sergio later told me that he had found it exhilarating fulfilling once again the traditional role of a UN mediator in the field.

The mass evacuation of wounded civilians scheduled for that afternoon failed to take place as the expected high number of casualties from the fighting, an estimated 2,000 people, simply failed to materialise. The first patient to board a helicopter was a routine case of cancer and that day a total of only 86 people were evacuated from Gorazde. During the next two days, although there were a number of children and other injured civilians among the 200 or so people flown to Sarajevo, many of the casualties seemed to be young men of military age grabbing a lift back to Sarajevo. On one occasion Goose saw two soldiers hop off their stretchers as they were lifted from a helicopter and run off into the town. The UNHCR liaison officer in the Kosevo hospital in Sarajevo reported that the extra surgical teams placed on standby that day had not been needed.

Fortunately for the people in the enclave, the accusations of the Bosnian Government that the UN had been an accomplice of genocide in Gorazde proved to be unfounded. The Serbs had indeed launched a terrible and inhuman attack on Gorazde and had been unconcerned about the plight of civilians caught up in the fighting. They had undoubtedly directed artillery and tank fire at the Bosnian Army in the town and, during the most intensive period of fighting, it was reported that one shell a minute was hitting the small town crammed with tens of thousands of refugees. Yet neither the final casualty list, heavy though it was, nor the relatively undamaged state of the buildings in the town suggested that the Serbs had systematically targetted civilians. There was no comparison between what happened in Gorazde and what the Serbs had done in Vukovar in 1991 when they destroyed the town by bombardment and massacred many of its occupants. In UNPROFOR we had taken the situation extremely seriously. What we had not done was to allow ourselves to be deceived by a campaign of propaganda and lies designed to involve the West in a war in Bosnia.

That night Sergio and Nick were called back to Kopaci at midnight to supervise the second UN convoy into Gorazde. As they approached the village, which was famous for having one of the oldest Orthodox Serb churches in Yugoslavia, they noticed a long UNHCR convoy at a standstill beside the road. Some of the houses in the surrounding hills were still burning. As their Land Rover stopped next to the lead truck in the convoy, the unmistakable figure of Mladic appeared in the headlights. He had been angered by the desecration of the church by the Muslims and he was determined to show Sergio and Nick the damage. He took them into the graveyard and, using Nick's torch, pointed out the smashed headstones, as well as the graves of Serb soldiers killed in the recent fighting. Sergio suddenly noticed that Mladic was weeping. The man responsible for some of the worst slaughter of the war had been reduced to tears by the sight of the graves of his young soldiers. Sergio told me that he found the whole episode extremely frightening. After the macabre visit, Mladic walked Sergio and Nick back to the main road, and asked them not to forget what they had just seen. He told Sergio that the convoy now had permission to proceed, shook his hand, and disappeared into the darkness. It was 0200 hours.

The arrival in Gorazde of the Duke of Wellington's Regiment under command of Lt-Col. David Santa Ollala had an almost miraculous effect on the situation. From the moment they arrived, the Dukes made it plain they were not going to be deterred by either side from carrying out their task. Their job was to help the people of Gorazde and to restore peace. These tough, always cheerful soldiers, recruited mainly from West Yorkshire, have a natural ability for this sort of soldiering, where the humanitarian aspect of the peacekeeping mission has to be matched by firm military action.

The night they arrived, Santa Ollala sent patrols into the surrounding hills to ensure that the Serbs were withdrawing from the TEZ and also to prevent the Bosnian forces from shooting at them as they went. However it was not long before the Serbs tested the battalion's mettle.

In an obvious attempt to achieve psychological domination over the Yorkshiremen in the valley below, a Serb unit opened fire from a hilltop on a Dukes patrol led by Cpl Mills. Although Mills initially tried to break contact, as the UN rules required, it became apparent that the Serbs were outflanking him, with the intention of taking prisoners or killing British soldiers. Mills launched a counter-attack up the hill against the Serbs in which he inflicted several casualties with no losses to his patrol. In the end it was the Serbs who broke contact. The next day the commanding officer of the Serb unit called on Santa Ollala to ask whether he would be prepared to teach the successful British tactics – demonstrated the day before by Cpl Mills – to the Serb soldiers. The tables had been firmly turned on them. By the end of summer, the Duke of Wellington's Regiment was supervising the harvesting of crops that straddled the line of conflict and medical clinics in no man's land for both the Serbs and the Bosnians.

On 26 April de Lapresle and I flew to Brussels for discussions with NATO. After a polite introduction from Balanzino, acting Secretary-General, Gen. Joulwan, SACEUR, spoke on the current state of the UN peacekeeping mission in Bosnia. Unlike Galvin and Shalikashvili, who both had reputations for being men of powerful intellect and charm, Gen. Joulwan came across as a bully. His contribution to any discussion on peacekeeping appeared to be limited to repeated demands for improved "credibility, clarity and unity of command" in UNPROFOR. These admirable military requirements had no great relevance to a peacekeeping mission in Bosnia, particularly where NATO had insisted on following a different mandate from the UN. Joulwan seemed to have difficulty accepting that NATO was in a supporting role to UNPROFOR in Bosnia and that both were engaged in a mission in which there were no enemies or victories.

During the briefing, Joulwan frequently referred to the increase in violations taking place in the Sarajevo TEZ. He felt the UN was not taking them seriously and that this failure was undermining the credibility of NATO. The day before the briefing, Simon Shadbolt had managed to obtain copies of the slides Joulwan used to illustrate his point. I was able to show that these slides were based on out-dated information and that his assessment was wrong. On one occasion, when Joulwan put up a slide of a T55 tank that he claimed was menacing Sarajevo, I was able to point out that the vehicle was actually an old abandoned hulk with no gun. De Lapresle also delivered a quietly spoken but powerfully argued rebuttal, explaining in great detail the strategy being pursued by the UN in Bosnia. Joulwan made no effort to conceal his dislike for the UN approach, and sighed whenever something was said with which he disagreed. At the conclusion of the meeting the UN and NATO positions had still not been reconciled and it was decided that the North Atlantic Council should visit Sarajevo.

At 0001 hours the next day, I was woken by an alarmed looking de Lapresle. Dressed in pyjamas and white bedsocks, he told me he had just received information that the Serbs were going to take hostage all the UNMOs I had tasked to deploy the next day to ensure that the 20-kilometre exclusion zone around Gorazde was clear of Serb heavy weapons. They were due to leave for Gorazde the next day. He told me that I should rescind my order and we would have to rely on NATO to carry out the verification programme. I told him that I would talk immediately to Sarajevo. Following our experience in Sarajevo, I felt the UN could not rely on air reconnaissance to make accurate observations, nor, given NATO's apparent wish to find an excuse to bomb the Serbs, did I altogether trust the organisation.

When I spoke to Simon and Maj. Willy Levak in Sarajevo they had already heard a rumour about the possibility of the Serbs taking the UN observers hostage. In their view no such threat existed. Simon also told me that an infuriated Soubirou had received an order from President Mitterrand forbidding him to send any French UNMOs to Gorazde. He thought that the blanket ban on UNMOs by de Lapresle might be an attempt by the French to conceal their embarrassment at Mitterrand's interference.

I did not know whether this was true or not, but I agreed with Simon that the Serbs were unlikely to take hostages. They would understand, as we all did, that their best hope of avoiding NATO air strikes was to allow the UNMOs to carry out the verification procedures in the TEZ unhindered. Nor did I think the Serbs wanted to embark on a war with the West. I therefore decided to ignore de Lapresle and told

Simon to deploy the UNMOs as planned. Although I was risking other people's lives in taking this decision, I was not about to allow the fate of the UN mission in Bosnia to be determined by hawks in NATO.

Under Rupert Prichard's superb management, the UN observers, who by then were becoming extremely skilled in verification procedures, went to work. Within the next 24 hours they had visited 28 sites in the Gorazde TEZ and found them to be clear of weapons. Because of poor weather, NATO managed to verify only six out of the total of 34 sites. In this way, the Gorazde TEZ was declared clear of all Serb heavy weapons and de Lapresle sensibly did not mention the subject again.

The same day I visited Gorazde, taking with me a small television camera from the Sarajevo press pool who were desperate to obtain footage of Gorazde. Flying by helicopter, I was met on the football ground by Soubirou, Sergio de Mello, Santa Ollala and Nick, to whom I entrusted the camera. In the short time it had been in Gorazde, the UN had transformed the situation. The Serbs had withdrawn from their positions surrounding the town to a distance of three kilometres as required by the Belgrade agreement, the UN had established positions between the two opposing forces and most of the wounded had been evacuated by helicopter. A UNHCR aid convoy had also arrived in the town. The Duke of Wellington's Regiment camp on the small football pitch in the centre of town was already starting to take on the appearance of a British Army base in Belfast, where most of the soldiers had recently been.

Gorazde had an almost carnival atmosphere and everyone seemed pleased to see us. The mayor, Ezad Ohranovic, spoke warmly of the courage of the JCOs and told me how sad he had been when one of them was killed. He remained grateful to the UN for its asssistance. Later, whenever he visited Sarajevo, he always took the opportunity of visiting us. Gorazde was, after all, still a safe area, mainly because of the UN's efforts. The military commander, Col. Bulibasic, on the other hand, was extremely hostile. He barely replied to my questions and accused the UN of doing nothing to help him. He also complained that Serb soldiers were still within the TEZ but he could not say exactly where. He was a hard-liner trying to lay the blame for his own inadequacies on someone else. As we walked around the town talking to the townspeople, a number of his soldiers tried to block our way and shortly afterwards they fired a heavy calibre machine-gun at an Anglo-French patrol. However Sergio and Nick told me of the extreme relief of the civilian population that the UN had managed to prevent the town being overrun by the Serbs. They widely supported the UN course of action, rather than the use of massive air strikes by NATO, which they realised would have done nothing to save the town.

I also met the chief UNMO in the bank building who had been responsible for some of the inaccurate reporting from Gorazde. I told him that his misleading reports had done great damage to the credibility of the UN mission. I pointed out to him that one report he had sent clearly stated that a shell had hit the front of the bank building, yet I could see for myself there was no such damage, even to the glass-plated front door.

The inaccuracy of the UNMO reports was further demonstrated when I visited the hospital in Gorazde, which was in an exposed position on the west bank of the Drina, about 100 metres from where the Serb advance had been finally halted. The UNMOs had specifically stated that the hospital had "been targeted throughout the day with tanks, wire-guided missiles and indirect fire with the aim of destroying it". Yet the director of the hospital, Dr Begovic, told me that although a shell had landed in a house nearby, killing a number of patients sheltering there, the hospital itself had only been hit twice: once in a stairwell and once in an empty room on the top floor. The operating theatre had continued working in the cellars throughout the battle, and Dr Begovic agreed with me that the civilian casualties had been far fewer than original estimates suggested. A UNHCR liaison officer who later examined the medical records in the hospital in Gorazde found that 130 operations had taken place in the hospital during the 26 days of fighting in April, many on young men. In that same period there had been 65 deaths. If the soldiers were discounted, she regarded the figures as being not unusual for a population of 60,000 inhabitants.

I was greatly relieved to see that the hospital had not been destroyed and merely needed to be cleaned up after the fighting ended. Dr Begovic told me that his most urgent medical need was incubators, for the lack of which babies were dying. He looked desperately tired, but his calm description of what had happened made a great contrast to the grossly innaccurate reports of the UNMOs. It had been fortunate that throughout the battle I had been receiving reports from the JCOs based on personal observation.

After leaving the hospital I walked across the main bridge over the Drina. Although the Bosnian forces had mined it, the bridge was remarkably undamaged. On the other side of the three-kilometre exclusion zone (its centre being in the middle of the bridge), I met the local Serb commander, Col. Masal, sitting with his staff under an apple tree. He angrily attacked me for having carried out air strikes against his men. I told him that I would have no hesitation in doing the same again if his forces violated the Gorazde TEZ or fired at UN soldiers. He smiled and said that he thought this was fair. We drank coffee together in the sunshine while he explained that it had never been the intention of the Serbs to capture Gorazde. Their objective had been to retake the villages they had been driven from during fighting in the area two years previously. The limited resistance of the Bosnian forces had surprised him when the Serbs finally attacked, but he had been equally surprised by the UN's robust response. I was reminded of the fact that Mladic had once boasted to Sergio that, because of the Muslim attacks on the Serbs in the region, he would never again allow a Muslim to "dip his fingers in my Drina". It was the UN that had prevented him from achieving this aim.

On the way back to the battalion HQ, I spoke to some Dukes who asked me how it was that the Serbs had been able to move their tanks so rapidly through mountainous terrain so ideally suited to defence. I told them that I thought the Bosnian Army had probably retreated in order to get the UN and NATO embroiled in the war. In the narrow passes and ravines anyone could have stopped the tanks with a crowbar. In my opinion the Bosnians had turned and run, leaving the UN to pick up the pieces. Unknown to me, Nick filmed this conversation.

In Sarajevo I told the press pool that they could use any part of the film except for the last clip, which showed my conversation with the Duke of Wellington's soldiers. This part of the film was embargoed, as it would plainly be embarrassing to me if what I had said was made public, although I felt it to be true. As I had taken a considerable risk in smuggling the television camera into Gorazde and Nick had taken some excellent footage, I trusted the reporters to respect my embargo.

Everyone did, except for Martin Bell of the BBC, who included the embargoed section in his evening report. This seriously damaged my relations with the Bosnian Government. When I challenged Martin Bell afterwards, he told me that he had been given the film without any mention of an embargo. When I asked him whether he thought that he was helping the UN peace process or me by showing the film, he did not reply. The next day I was summoned to the Presidency by a furious Silajdzic, who had seen a transcript of what I had said. After Sergio de Mello explained what had happened, he agreed to treat the affair as a storm in a teacup and not to pursue the matter further. Sergio told me he didn't think I would get away so lightly again.

Although the Gorazde crisis was over, we would never be able to rid ourselves of the consequences. The credibility of UNPROFOR had suffered lasting damage by the failure of the international community to respond to the crisis in a coherent way. The general wish to stop Serb aggression was never backed by the West putting an army into Bosnia to fight the Serbs. Furthermore, the failure of the international community to reinforce UNPROFOR, which would have allowed the enclaves to be properly garrisoned, had made the chances of a Serb attack on places like Gorazde more likely. Finally, the subsequent efforts by NATO to extend its bombing campaign, to compensate for its own reluctance to put troops on the ground, soured its relations with the UN.

The fragmented response of the international community to the Serb attack on Gorazde gave the Bosnian Government a new opportunity to blame the UN for not using more force, regardless of the fact that the use of force had been taken further than ever before in a peacekeeping mission. The hostile propaganda that dominated most of the media coverage around the world obscured the arguments justifying the UN's actions during the Gorazde crisis. The propagandists, of course, did not have to take into account the need to sustain the humanitarian aspects of the mission, or the fact that the pursuit of war-fighting objectives by UNPROFOR would take the mission across the "Mogadishu Line", with potentially the same catastrophic results as had occurred in Somalia in 1993. As Goose once said, having listened to a discussion about the use of force in a peacekeeping mission, "If you want to go to war, you do not do so in white-painted vehicles." I was to use the remark many times in the next few months. On 27 April, too late to save Gorazde, the international community decided to send 6,500 troops as reinforcements to Bosnia.

Two days later I was delighted to hear that a major battle had taken place between the UN and the Serbs near Tuzla. Five Serb T55s had been destroyed by the Danish tank company that I had dispatched there two months before. Nearly 100 rounds had been fired by the Danes during the engagement, which was greater than any battle the unit had been involved in during the Second World War. Once again, UNPRO-FOR had demonstrated to the Serbs and to the world that the UN was prepared to use extreme levels of force, so long as that use remained within the constraints of peacekeeping.

Sadly, after the Danish effort had strengthened the credibility of the UN it was immediately weakened again when the next day during a meeting in Pale, Akashi agreed with Karadzic, without seeking Sergio's or my advice, to allow seven Serb tanks through the Sarajevo TEZ. Technically, this may have been a correct decision, as the UN remained neutral in the war, but the political consequences so soon after the conflict in Gorazde were extremely unfortunate. Izetbegovic and Silajdzic condemned the decision and said that they would never again speak to Akashi. Silajdzic claimed that the decision showed that the UN was "actively participating in the aggression in Bosnia–Hercegovina" and, not to be outdone, Ganic called Akashi a "traitor to the international community". Indeed, for several months in Zagreb, Sergio became the only senior UN official in UNPROFOR that the Bosnian Government would deal with. The international media accused Akashi of being too soft on the Serbs and said that the UN had been humiliated, and even Kofi Annan expressed his dismay at the decision. The problem was exacerbated when Akashi told Karadzic that their agreement to move the tanks no longer stood, as the Serbs had not, as agreed, moved the first three tanks under UN control. For the next few nights the French, playing cat-and-mouse with the Serbs, attempted to block the path of the remaining four tanks with APCs, but they were unsuccessful and the tanks passed though the TEZ to fight elsewhere in Bosnia. In retrospect, I believe that this was the moment when Akashi's influence as the chief mediator in Bosnia started to decline. My heart sank when Izetbegovic issued a statement saying that forthwith Ganic would be the only point of contact between UNPROFOR and the Bosnian Government. Fortunately the President and the Prime Minister continued to recieve Sergio and me and several times took the initiative in consulting us, most notably when Sergio received a request from them to organise a visit by the Muslims of Sarajevo to Mecca.

On 5 May the North Atlantic Council made a return visit to Zagreb. After a polite exchange between Ambassador Balanzino and Akashi, Gen. Joulwan bluntly demanded to know why five Serb guns remained within the Sarajevo TEZ. A violation was a violation. As he spoke, he reinforced each point by angrily rapping an ornate gold ring on the table. I explained that these particular guns were less than 100 metres inside the zone. If the Serbs moved their guns any further away from Sarajevo they would be exposed to direct fire from the Bosnians on the hills beyond. The Serb guns were engaged in a battle unrelated to Sarajevo, and it was doubtful if their range extended as far as Sarajevo. I told him that no one believed these ancient artillery pieces could threaten the credibility of NATO.

My reply did nothing to improve Joulwan's humour. He stated that the UN had not done a mission analysis and that we had no idea of Serb intentions or even any system for tracking Serb weapons within the TEZ. NATO had authorised UNPROFOR to request a much wider use of air power, but it had not done so. At this point Nick Morris, the head of the UNHCR, intervened. He explained to Joulwan that it was impossible to run a humanitarian operation with military force and that all humanitarian action would cease if force was used at the levels Joulwan was suggesting. Concluding this ill-tempered exchange, Balanzino said that NATO could not to be used as a "menu" by UNPROFOR, that Joulwan had explained his position and it was for us to understand it.

That night at dinner in the Writers' Club in Zagreb, Joulwan continued to be openly hostile to the UN, ignoring the fact that he was Akashi's guest. The next morning a senior American general, who had been at the dinner the night before, unexpectedly turned to me and said, "I've got to work with that man every day of my life." I shook my head in sympathy. It is the only time I have ever heard an American officer being disloyal about a senior.

I decided on revenge. When we flew to Sarajevo the next day, I invited Joulwan to sit on the starboard side of the Yak 40 aircraft. This was the side that was most fired at when UN aircraft landed at Sarajevo. As we approached Sarajevo, Joulwan asked me how often aircraft were shot at while landing.

"Practically every day," I replied. "If you look to your right, you will see a metal patch beside you where a bullet hit the aircraft yesterday."

On the road from the airport towards Sarajevo, as we crossed no man's land between the lines of trenches, a Serb soldier in a bunker to our left fired a rocket at the convoy. It hit the road just behind the Range Rover and in the rear-view mirror I could see Joulwan's bodyguards in the vehicle behind looking wildly around to see who had fired the rocket. By the time we had arrived at the Residency, I suspect that Joulwan had begun to understand that being the commander of the most powerful military force in the world meant nothing to a Serb soldier. Later that day, I invited Joulwan to join me and Simon on top of a French observation post overlooking the Jewish Cemetery to take a look at what the French officer commanding the position had called "the most dangerous place in the world". He declined the offer, saying that he preferred to talk with the French soldiers in the bunker. It was a distinctly subdued NATO party that left Sarajevo at the end of the day. I half believed that André Soubirou had arranged for the Serb gunman to fire at Joulwan, although he always smilingly denied having done so.

Shortly after Joulwan departed, I left Sarajevo for a holiday in England. Without telling anyone except Simon Shadbolt where we were going, Angela and I escaped to our empty house in Herefordshire where the telephone did not ring once. We spent the time working in the garden and going out for meals to the local pubs. Each morning we awoke to the sound of a cuckoo calling from the same branch of a tree that its forebears had sat on for the past 18 years. When I drew the curtains, I could see in the distance the tranquil Welsh moutains stretching from horizon to horizon, bearing no evidence that in the fifteenth century, the slaughter and devastation in the valley below had been worse than anything we had seen so far in Bosnia.

When I returned to Sarajevo a few days later it was a relief to find that the situation had not deteriorated. Viktor Andreev's face lit up as he met me at the airport and he gave me a traditional Russian bear-hug. I always regarded him as the best litmus test as to whether things were going well or not. If they were, he went about exuding a cheerful confidence, thumping people on the back and saying, "We are getting there! I think we are getting there!" He once said this in the middle of an air strike and reduced the nearby staff officers to fits of helpless laughter. In the mornings he would go for runs before breakfast, and in the evenings he gave wild parties in a flat he had recently acquired in Sarajevo. If things were not going well, he would clap his hand to his forehead and murmur, "Horrible, horrible!" During such periods, he would retire to his room in the Residency where he would spend long hours talking on the telephone to Moscow, Belgrade or Pale.

In the early summer, Viktor was full of confidence and working hard on a plan to finally end the war. His discussions with the Serbs suggested that they would settle for less than 50% of the territory of Bosnia-Hercegovina, as long as the Republica Srpska was politically recognised, either as a federal part of Bosnia or an autonomous State. He had even discussed a map with Karadzic and the Bosnians, showing which parts of Bosnia the Serbs were prepared to give up. He believed that the Serbs had accepted that they could not win military victory, as sanctions were having a disastrous effect on the Serb economy and support for the war among the populace was falling away. The Bosnian Serb Army was over-extended and finding it difficult to operate without fuel. They currently had to pay up to 16 times the normal cost of fuel, which they were still able to get from the Croats. Now was the time to persuade the Bosnians to return to the negotiating table.

Andrei Kozyrev, the Russian Foreign Minister, and Vitaly Churkin, President Yeltsin's special envoy, supported Viktor in his efforts. He had advocated setting up a troika composed of the Russians, the Americans and the EC to act as mediators to end the war. I knew his facts were accurate. I had often spoken with the Serb soldiers in their trenches, and I had seen many fuel tankers at night winding their way through the mountains on their way from Croatia. One spring morning I had sat under a tree on Mt Borasnica, south of Sarajevo, having lunch with the local Serb and Muslim commanders. They met every day and refused to fight. Every now and then they would fire a few shells across the front line to keep Delic or Mladic happy, but for them the war was effectively over.

Unfortunately, in the summer of 1994, Viktor's peace plan and his proposed territorial division of Bosnia (almost identical to what was finally agreed at Dayton), did not find favour with the international community. The Contact Group had recently been formed and they were thought to offer a better chance of success. Viktor also suspected that Akashi did not argue for his idea more forcefully because the troika did not include the UN.

Although a political opportunity had been ignored, the military and humanitarian situation in Bosnia was visibly improving. By the end of May Glynne Evans wrote, after a visit to Sarajevo:

The war has tamped down in Bosnia. The current friction points can be counted on the fingers of one hand. In some areas the commanders of opposing sides are all but colluding. In Sarajevo municipal trams and UN helicopters run down the main street, formerly Sniper's Alley. Cafés are flourishing in every part of the city and goats are patrolling the streets. Commercial traffic is flooding into the city over Mt Igman and through the Serb checkpoints. Fresh fruit, potatoes, etc. are in the market place and prices are steadily falling. Gen. Rose's drastically pruned HQ is now located in Portakabins in the garden of the Residency. He can and does issue orders out of the window.

For everyone in UNPROFOR life was slowly returning to normal as we renewed our efforts to build peace. If it was not immediately possible to obtain a cessation of hostilities for the whole of Bosnia, our best strategy now was to extend the number of areas from which heavy weapons were excluded and to demilitarise Sarajevo. A new approach was also being developed abroad following an initiative by Lord Owen, who had been responsible for establishing a Contact Group. This group, consisting of Russia, America, France, Britain and Germany, was formed in mid-April and was designed to coordinate the political efforts of the international community to bring an end to the war in Bosnia. Sadly for the first six months of its existence the Contact Group failed to live up to its name and remained conspicuously at arms length from UNPROFOR, as though we would in some way contaminate them, thus depriving themselves of essential first-hand knowledge of actions and realities on the ground. In 1994, there were therefore two separate international organisations trying to bring the war in Bosnia to an end, with the result that neither succeeded in this aim.

At this time Akashi was trying to arrange a meeting with all the belligerents in Geneva with a view to restarting the peace process that had come to an abrupt halt on 10 April when Mladic launched his attack on Gorazde. Akashi had written to Izetbegovic and Karadzic on 20 May proposing an immediate cessation of all hostilities, a disengagement of forces, a withdrawal of heavy weapons and the establishment of a Joint Commission to implement the agreed measures throughout the country. The next step would be a peace settlement defining the future political and territorial arrangements for Bosnia.

Meanwhile, on the ground, I was travelling about the country talking up the prospects of peace. Gorazde seemed to have been forgotten, except by Mladic, who refused to speak to me. Freedom of movement was rarely a problem for me and I continued my practice of never driving through any checkpoint, whether it was Bosnian or Serb, without stopping and talking to the soldiers manning it. I would always discuss the war with them and the role of the UN in bringing about peace. This did not always work in the soldiers' favour. On one occasion, at a checkpoint near Sarajevo, a Muslim sniper fired at the policeman I was talking to and the bullet passed between us. The Serb dived for cover and asked me why I had not followed suit. I told him that no one would dare shoot the Commander of UNPROFOR and we all had to demonstrate our faith in the peace process. Sadly, he was killed standing on the same spot the next day.

On 14 May I visited Travnik. I made the visit partly because I had read about the town in Ivo Andric's *Bosnian Chronicle*, but also because I needed to find out whether the rumours of an impending Bosnian Army offensive against the Serbs were true. Travnik is set deep in a narrow part of the Laskva Valley and lies astride a traditional trading route between Asia and Europe. The Romans had established a garrison in the town and it had also been the seat of government of the Turkish rulers of Bosnia. A large fort dominated the entrance to the town, which was surrounded by terraced orchards on the hills above. The Bosnian 3rd Corps commander responsible for this part of the front line was Gen. Mehemet Alagic. His long white hair, prominent buck-teeth and ill-fitting uniform gave him a comical appearance. Apparently he had been the mayor of Prijedor before the war. He spoke expansively of recapturing all the territory that had been lost to the Serbs and waved his hands excitedly across the map in his office, stating that he would drive the Serbs into the sea. I wondered how this tallied with the rest of the world's hope of returning Bosnia to a multi-cultural state. Since his soldiers had not been able to take the high ground five miles west of Travnik, from which the Serbs daily shelled the town, he clearly had a long way to go.

Despite Alagic's threat, the countryside around seemed blissfully peaceful as we climbed up through a pine forest in the spring sunshine. After half an hour we arrived in a small platoon position on the front line overlooking the town of Turbe in the valley below, which was held by the Serbs. Some desultory mortar fire was being exchanged between the two sides. However, it was clear that no great offensive was taking place. The elderly platoon commander invited his men out of the trenches to meet me and we all sat on the hillside sipping orange juice, discussing what they had all been doing before the war. They were adamant that this was not their war and they longed for it to end so that they could go back to their families.

We had flown to Travnik that day from the Kosevo football stadium after a meeting with Minister Muratovic, who was waiting for another UN helicopter for Gorazde. The UN had encountered some difficulty in negotiating his visit as, on a previous occasion, the Serbs had discovered Muratovic smuggling weapons and money to the Bosnian Army in Gorazde. They had of course confiscated it all before turning him back. I had been furious with Muratovic at the time as he had betrayed the trust of the UN and given credence to the Serb claim that the UN was helping the Bosnian Army. I had rearranged this second visit on the understanding that this time there would be no clandestine business. I was, as a result, surprised to find him waiting with a long line of sports bags on the ground beside him. I accused him point blank of reneging on his undertaking but he swore he was carrying only humanitarian items.

After we had left, L/Sgt Daly of the Coldstream Guards drove his Range Rover over the entire line of sports bags. Seeing Muratovic dancing up and down, waving his arms and banging on the armour-plated windows, L/Sgt Daly began to suspect that something was wrong. Giving Muratovic a charming but wholly uncomprehending smile, he put the Range Rover into reverse and drove over the bags a second time. This had guaranteed the destruction of, it transpired, a $250,000 Motorola satellite communications system and a bag full of blank ID cards. The Bosnian secret service thereafter treated L/Sgt Daly with great respect and caution, convinced that he had got wind of the contents of the bags and had destroyed them deliberately. It had actually been an accident, but, as George Waters later said, "Sergeant Daly is a typical Guardsman. He does everything in straight lines."

In the north-east the Bosnian forces were continuing to launch minor attacks into the Posavina corridor and the Serbs responded by occasionally shelling Tuzla, but there was still no sign of a major Bosnian Serb Army offensive. One day we made a surprise visit to a Bosnian Army HQ in Olovo, south of Tuzla. Although it was not yet midday, we found the local commander asleep in the basement of a school, having obviously had too much plum brandy for breakfast. He told us that all was quiet in the area, although the town had been badly battered by Serb shelling in the past. As we left the town, all was indeed quiet and people sat outside their houses in the sunshine. Across the river a young boy was fishing for trout using a worm for bait.

From Olovo we travelled to Tuzla through some of the most beautiful mountains in Yugoslavia, before emerging onto the wide plain on which Tuzla sits. We had stopped for a picnic in a meadow full of wild flowers and could see snow-covered mountains in the distance. Although we were still close to the front line there was complete silence, apart from the birdsong and a muezzin calling the faithful to prayer from a mosque in the valley below. A farmer left his farmhouse nearby and asked us to share coffee with him. In the fields, strong-faced women with intelligent eyes, dressed in loose, flowery dresses, their hair tied in colourful headscarves, worked with their husbands and children. Centuries of peasant-based, rural agriculture in Yugoslavia had created strong family ties. Even the smallest children accompanied their parents and although they were too young to work, they played barefoot among the butter-cups and daisies. Each village was built around a church or mosque and surrounded by terraces of alpine pastures on the steep hillsides. As we dozed after lunch, the war seemed very far away.

When we arrived in Tuzla a local military commander of the region admitted that he had started the rumours about a build-up of forces by the Bosnian Serbs. He had done this to focus world attention on Tuzla and to prevent the sort of attack that had occurred in Gorazde. At that time the Serbs would still not allow the UN to visit Brcko, their main garrison in northern Bosnia, so it had been impossible to discount these rumours, though NATO air reconnaissance had not been able to find any evidence of such an offensive.

In the south of the country, relations between the Muslims and the Croats had not significantly improved as a result of the Washington Accord. Nowhere was the situation worse than in Mostar, which provided a living example of why the Balkans will forever be a region of unresolved conflict and hatred. The European Union had unwisely decided that Mostar should be the setting for its first foreign policy action and had voted for a $24m European-style administration within the town, including a European police force. When the European administrator finally left Mostar three years later little had changed.

Certainly the return of peace had in no way diminished the hatred of the Croats for the Muslims or their wish to drive the Muslims from the town. Despite an agreement to allow complete freedom of movement, and the construction of a temporary bridge by the Royal Engineers to allow people to cross the river that divided the two communities, the Croats allowed only 50 Muslims a day to cross to their side. Even then, they could go no further than a tent set up a few yards from the end of the bridge, where they could meet their friends under the supervision of Croat policemen. No effort had been made to restore the utilities or to repair the buildings on the Muslim side of the river. The young mayor of East Mostar was bitter about the way the Muslims were being treated. They were virtually prisoners in the ruins of their own town, yet across the river they could see people living as though they were in Frankfurt.

Worse still, the UN seemed to have accepted non-compliance with the Washington Accord as a *fait accompli*. The colonel commanding the Spanish battalion responsible for Mostar told me that this was the result of a "local agreement". I told him that the UN should be working to implement the Washington Accord and that it should not accept local obstruction. I took him to see the Croat administration on the west bank of the river. We met in a cellar and after a formal welcome from Kresimir Zubak, the political boss of the Bosnian Croats, I accused the Croats of flouting the Washington Accord and of prolonging the misery of the Muslim people on the east bank. I told them that I would ensure that no money came to Mostar until there was full compliance. None of this had the slightest effect, which was hardly surprising. Mostar was firmly in the grip of the war criminals and gangsters responsible for the ethnic cleansing of Muslims from the Croat part of Bosnia. Croatia, whose army had on occasions been deployed into Bosnia in support of the Bosnian Croat Army, supported them, and as long as the international community found it necessary to deal with Croatia, nothing would change.

On 21 May I was woken early by the sound of intensive gunfire. Mercifully, it turned out to be the Muslims celebrating the festival of Bairam. The Sarajevo cease-fire had been running for 100 days, so it was a double celebration. It is traditional for Muslims to visit the graves of their ancestors on that day and I had arranged with Karadzic to give safe passage to the Muslims visiting their main cemetery on the front line. It was the first time in two years that they had been allowed to do so and the day marked yet another small milestone on the road to peace.

Earlier in the month, the UN had flown 350 Muslim pilgrims, Izetbegovic among them, to Zagreb so that they could make the pilgrimage to Mecca. Viktor and I went to see Izetbegovic on his return to welcome him back from the *hadj* and to brief him on developments. The Bosnians were still refusing to negotiate with the Serbs because, Izetbegovic claimed, there were armed Serb police within the three-kilometre TEZ in Gorazde. We urged him not to allow a detail like that to upset the peace process, even if it were true. It was obvious to me that there were five strategic imperatives that would persuade the Serbs to sign up to the present proposals: (1) The Serbs could no longer rely on support from the Russians. (2) Their economy was suffering because of international sanctions. (3) President Milosevic no longer supported the Bosnian Serbs in the war in Bosnia. (4) The Bosnian Serb Army was finding it difficult to recruit soldiers from an exhausted Serb population. (5) The military balance had now tilted in favour of Bosnia with the formation of the Croat–Muslim Federation and the growing strength of the Bosnian Army.

Izetbegovic, who had caught a cold from the air-conditioning in Saudi Arabia, told us that he was becoming more confident about the prospects for peace, but he would talk to his military leaders before making any policy changes. Despite our acrimonious arguments over Gorazde, he could not have been more friendly and shook my hand warmly as I departed. A few days later de Lapresle called me from Zagreb to tell me that the Bosnians had agreed to discuss a four-month cessation of hostilities, plus a long-term peace settlement in Geneva.

Before we left for Geneva, Viktor and I visited Gorazde to see how things had developed in the past month. It was clear from the moment we arrived that David Santa Ollala and his soldiers had taken control of the situation. The Duke of Wellington's Regiment patrolled the area continuously and had established excellent relations with both sides. As a result, the number of ceasefire violations had fallen dramatically. Stocks of food and medical supplies were now at high levels and a plan was being developed to restore running water and electricity to the town. The hospital was working almost normally again and even schools were reopening.

Some dangerously ill patients required treatment in Sarajevo, but the Serbs had linked their move to the release of 140 Serb civilians who had been held by the Muslims in Gorazde for almost two years. One of the prisoners was related to Mladic who never failed to raise the subject of the appalling conditions in which they were held by the Bosnians. When I visited one of the detention centres, a broken-down house where 42 elderly and sick people were being held, I saw what he meant. An old woman clung to my hand, pleading with me through her tears to be allowed to leave. She said that she had cancer and would shortly die unless she received medical treatment. They were pitiable pawns in a political bargaining process that was cruelly stalled.

The UN civil adviser in Gorazde was a highly politicised Israeli, whose arrival in the town seemed to have caused a degree of disaffection among the Bosnians against the UN. I had once thrown him out of my office in Sarajevo when he had begun to rant at me in a way that reminded me of Ganic. Since his arrival in Gorazde, he had tried to lead a march of the citizens of Gorazde across the Drina to confront the Serbs in the trenches on the other side. Only the fact that he was grossly overweight and needed two sticks to walk had prevented him from succeeding in his purpose. David Santa Ollala thought the UN civil adviser was anti-British, for he had been constantly unhelpful in any negotiations between the Serbs and the Bosnians. Viktor was the UN civil adviser's superior officer and I urged him to sack the man immediately. Although UN rules apparently prevented him from doing this, Viktor lured him back to Sarajevo on the pretext of a conference, took his vehicle from him, and had him subsequently transferred elsewhere. His successor, a Canadian, was a very different person and deeply committed to helping the people of Gorazde.

I flew to Geneva with Nick Costello and Simon Shadbolt on 1 June. We were booked into the Intercontinental Hotel on the floor above the Bosnian Serbs. The entire Pale leadership, including Karadzic, Krajisnik, Koljevic, Mladic, Tolimir and Aleksa Buha, the Foreign Minister, were present and several of them brought their wives as well. Ganic, representing the Bosnian Government, was staying with his team in one of the most expensive hotels in the world, the Richmond, from where they were chauffeured hither and thither in a fleet of limousines. I doubt if Ganic was at all concerned that the vast amounts of money being spent on supporting him in this way might have been better spent relieving the desperate plight of his people.

The UN party was made up of Akashi, Sergio, de Lapresle and me. Each day we walked down the hill in the sunshine to the UN building above the lake. Also in Geneva were Lord Owen and members of the Contact Group, who were in separate, parallel discussions with the Bosnians and Serbs about ending the war in Bosnia. Within the Contact Group, Churkin was hopeful of a positive outcome to the peace talks, while Redman did not feel that the Bosnians were ready to accept a division of Bosnia along the lines presented on the Contact Group map, which offered the Serbs 49% of the territory. Initially, Lord Owen felt that the chances of a peace deal were good, as long as it was backed by a package of incentives and disincentives. The UN and the contact Group, however, had still not sufficiently aligned their efforts. As a result both the Bosnians and the Serbs were able to manoeuvre between the two international proposals whenever they wished and ultimately both negotiations were reduced to a level of farce.

The talks almost ended before they began. On his arrival in Geneva, Ganic sent a message to Akashi telling him that he would not attend the talks until every last Serb policeman was withdrawn from Gorazde. Nor did it appear at our first meetings with the Serbs that they were going to be any more co-operative than the Bosnians. Mladic refused to talk to anyone from the UN or even to look at us, despite the fact we were sitting at a round conference table. Tolimir was given the task of relaying his remarks to the UN personnel. When Costello asked him the reason for this crass behaviour, Mladic replied darkly, "You know why." Nevertheless, by the end of the day, Karadzic had agreed to order the withdrawal of the Serb policemen from the three-kilometre TEZ, albeit in the face of objections from Mladic.

I telephoned David Santa Ollala the next morning to find out what had happened. He told me that all of the armed policemen were still in place and the Serbs in Gorazde had received no orders to withdraw. Akashi, Costello and I immediately went down one floor in the Intercontinental Hotel. Karadzic was still in bed, even though it was nearly midday. We hammered on his door for several minutes and he finally emerged in a maroon dressing-gown. It was not a pretty sight. Mrs Karadzic, her hair in rollers, poked her head round the bedroom door to find out what was going on. Judging from their appearance they had both been drinking heavily the night before.

Karadzic, his face crumpled and his eyes sunken, looked and spoke like a madman. First he denied agreeing to give orders to the policemen to move from the three-kilometre zone. Then he said he had given the orders but they had not yet got through and he had no authority to give orders to civilians, armed or otherwise. I told him that we knew that the "armed policemen" were in fact Serb soldiers who had merely changed their uniforms.

"Well, now they have been demobilised," replied Karadzic triumphantly. At this point, Akashi told him that there could be no meeting until all the weapons had left Gorazde. Akashi gave him 24 hours to accomplish this. Over the next two days, the Serbs continued to prevaricate over the presence of the armed men within the TEZ and it seemed to us that the talks would never get started. We had not allowed for the Duke of Wellington's Regiment, however, as on 4 June David Santa Ollala and a platoon of Duke of Wellington's soldiers drove to each of the Serb locations in the three-kilometre TEZ and physically removed the remaining Serb weapons.

When we went back to the UN building to break the news to the Serb delegation, we found Karadzic, Koljevic and Mladic slumped in deep chairs in a haze of smoke and alcohol fumes, playing cards. They jumped up like naughty schoolboys to greet us, except for Mladic. He was puffy in the face and was bulging out of his blue suit. He might have been a bookmaker after a bad day at the races. I deliberately avoided him but was pointedly cordial to Tolimir, whom I congratulated on his promotion to brigadier-general. Tolimir told me that if I apologised to Gen. Mladic for the air strikes in Gorazde – in which a number of his friends had died – he would resume friendly relations with me; but I was determined to keep Mladic at his charade. It made him look ridiculous and it would have been dishonest of me to apologise for doing something I was quite prepared to do again. The Serbs had not yet heard about the confiscation of Serb weapons in Gorazde by Santa Ollala, but meekly accepted the news. It looked as though we could now get down to the main purpose of the negotiations.

The next day we persuaded Ganic to attend the talks. As soon as Akashi had confirmed that all the armed Serbs had now left the TEZ, Ganic, looking immaculate in an expensive suit, silk tie and spotted green handkerchief, replied with a smirk that there was an entire Serb position still 200 metres inside the TEZ, located on a hill to the north of the town called the Senokus feature. He told us that if these soldiers were not removed, there would be no further meetings. For good measure, he declared that he was unhappy to have been lured from his hotel under false pretences. He had done everything he could to advance the peace process and his goodwill was now being taken advantage of. He explained to Akashi that life was like mathematics: there was an absolute position and this had not been achieved. Then he swept from the building back to the Richmond Hotel. Akashi showed no emotion while Ganic was talking to him in this way, but Sergio was furious.

David Santa Ollala reported that the Serb position was indeed there, but that the local Muslim commander had said nothing to him about it. If the Serbs pulled further back out of the TEZ, they would be overlooked by a Bosnian Army position on their flank. It was unlikely they would withdraw voluntarily.

Returning to the conference room, Akashi explained to Karadzic that there had to be total compliance with the withdrawal of troops and that the presence of Serb soldiers 200 metres inside the zone could not be accepted. Mladic objected that the Senokus feature was outside the town. I produced a map and, ignoring Mladic, told Karadzic that the centre of the three-kilometre circle defining the TEZ was the centre of the main bridge in the town. I showed him that the Serb position on the Senokus hill was in fact 200 metres *inside* the circle. After looking at the map for some time, Mladic finally said that the centre of the three-kilometre circle should have been taken from the other bridge in Gorazde, not the main one.

Turning to Tolimir, I said, "Your General must have got his map upside down. If he insists on using the second bridge as the centre, that puts his soldiers on the Senokus feature even further into the circle. He'd be better off with the main bridge."

Everyone laughed, including Mladic. Nevertheless he remained adamant that the Serbs would not move from their position. Later that day he told me that he would no longer allow my action in Gorazde to cloud our relations. I replied that, as a peacekeeper, I regretted any use of force. Mladic suddenly shook my hand and at this unexpected sign of a cessation of hostilities between the two generals, his bodyguards broke into spontaneous applause. However we still had this new and apparently insuperable obstacle to overcome before the peace talks could begin.

Once again it was David Santa Ollala who came to the rescue. That night, with a company of Dukes, he marched up the Senokus feature in driving rain and, without a shot being fired, captured the position from the surprised Serbs. The next morning he obtained a signed statement from the local military commander in Gorazde, Bulibasic, that the TEZ was now clear of all armed Serbs. I immediately went to the Richmond Hotel and told Ganic that I now had a signed statement from his own commander on the ground that the area was clear of all armed Serbs. At first he looked surprised, then annoyed, but finally he agreed to attend the talks.

Some four months before, Ganic had been a trembling wreck of a man desperately clinging to the coat-tails of UNPROFOR for his very survival. Now he was prepared to treat the UN like dirt. During the discussions in Geneva, he began to lecture us in his high nasal voice, his soft white hands fluttering theatrically for rhetorical effect. When unable to think of a logical reply to an argument, he would simply utter a string of meaningless phrases, often repeating himself. Although Akashi was duty-bound to treat him in a correct diplomatic manner, I had no such constraint and his bad manners annoyed me intensely. I soon discovered that, if I stared at him long enough, he would lose the thread of what he was saying and nervously fumble for words. Occasionally I could reduce him to total silence.

During one meeting, while I was typing on my portable computer, Ganic said over my shoulder that he would not accept the phrase "zone of separation" in a paragraph in which I referred to the drawing apart of the two opposing forces. When I asked him why, he replied that such an expression indicated that a part of Bosnian territory would cease to be Bosnian sovereign territory and become no man's land. On further questioning, he agreed that there had to be a separation of forces and that the logical consequence of this was that there had to be a zone of separation between the two opposing sides. I asked him to find another more acceptable form of words. He tried everything, including "ground zero". He seemed unable to accept that there would have to be some definition of the area of ground between the opposing forces.

After nearly an hour of futile discussion, I ignored Ganic's increasingly meaningless interventions and typed in the words "area of separation" at which point he started screaming in my ear, "No area of separation! No area of separation!"

"Fuck off, Ganic!" I said in exasperation. "I'm doing the drafting not you." The room fell silent, but Ganic retreated to his seat and made no further protests. Obviously he had been told by Izetbegovic not to give an inch in the negotiations. It would have been difficult enough if Ganic had been logical in his arguments, but having to deal with such an unstructured mind made the negotiations double torture. On one occasion Sergio had telephoned Silajdzic in Sarajevo to try to enlist his help. He had replied, with a note of regret, that Ganic had been given full authorisation to negotiate and that there was nothing he could do to kick-start the talks.

Some light relief was provided for us on the day that Akashi took the Serb delegation to a Japanese restaurant where we were obliged to sit on low benches and eat with chopsticks. The spectacle of Mladic cross-legged on the floor, his podgy fingers manipulating his chopsticks, reduced Simon and me to helpless laughter.

By 8 June it was apparent that the Geneva talks would produce no substantial agreement. Although the Serbs would have settled for a four-month cessation of hostilities, they would only do this if it was linked to a political deal. The Bosnians would only agree to it if the return to the *status quo ante* in Gorazde remained a pre-condition. In the end, to save everyone's face, Akashi cobbled together a four-week ceasefire; but the day after Ganic signed this agreement, the Bosnian Army, under his direction, launched a major attack against the Serbs in the Ozren mountains, north-west of Tuzla.

Akashi had done his best to get people talking, but neither side was genuinely interested in peace. His willingness to stay in the ring until he succeeded and his belief that, like a boxer, he could always roll with the punches, ultimately allowed those who wished to destroy him ample opportunity to do so. If there was any one single feature that characterised Akashi, it was a very Japanese quality of perseverance or *gamen*. In the impatient world of international politics, this was also to prove his undoing.

CHAPTER SIX

The Day the General Smiled

*In the first 10 days of June, 200 shells a day fell on our village. We could
not stay.*

Bosnian Serb from the village of Vozuca

I T WAS A RELIEF TO RETURN TO SARAJEVO. BEFORE WE LEFT GENEVA,
Boutros Boutros-Ghali had arrived to discuss the way forward for the UN in
the light of the virtual failure of the talks. After Akashi had given a gloomy account of
the events of the past two weeks, the Secretary-General asked what the consequences
would be of a French withdrawal from Bosnia. De Lapresle replied that the French
would only leave the mission if the UK and other NATO nations represented in
UNPROFOR also departed. For the UN to be left with only the Russians and
Ukrainians on one side, and the Muslim nations on the other, would be a recipe
for disaster. I added that we should not discount the possibility of a complete UN
withdrawal if the two sides continued to use the presence of UN troops in their
country to perpetuate their war. The consequences of such a withdrawal for the
people of Bosnia would be serious, but as they were now less dependent on UN aid,
the withdrawal of the mission would not be catastrophic. Mladic had told us he
believed it was inevitable that the war would escalate, given the strategy of the
Bosnians. In spite of this, he believed that the sensible course of action for the UN
was to remain in Bosnia in order to buy time for the political process. We should not
allow the war agenda of the Bosnian Government to succeed. Boutros-Ghali listened
carefully to this, but commented that the UN would not stay in Bosnia if the situation
further deteriorated. We would have to await events.

The contrast between the depressing atmosphere of Geneva and the situation that
we found in Sarajevo on our return on 9 June, cheered us enormously. The city was
still calm, with only occasional sniping or exchanges of small arms fire, and people
were out on the streets in the sunshine looking well-dressed and relaxed. We were
often complimented by those we spoke to, for what the UN had done in stopping
the fighting and reopening Sarajevo to commercial traffic. Sometimes I pointed out
to visitors that training shoes cost fewer DM in the market place in Sarajevo than
they did in the NAAFI in Germany.

In central Bosnia the situation was also improving. On a visit to Bugojno in
western Bosnia with the new British sector commander, Brig. Andrew Ridgeway, we
met by chance the local Bosnian Army commander. He told us that he had just
returned from a meeting in Kupres, on the Serb side of the conflict line, with his

opposite number in the Bosnian Serb Army. They had discussed the Geneva peace negotiations and what they could do to lower the tension along their sector of the line. They cared little about the new political structures in Yugoslavia that had only brought them misery.

As Andrew had not yet had a chance to meet the Serb commander in Kupres, we decided to visit him ourselves. Kupres was situated on a plateau about 15 kilometres west of Bugojno. It was an important town as the main road from the Dalmatian coast to Sarajevo and Tuzla passed through it. It had long been an objective of the UN to reopen this road. Having driven cautiously over a partially blown bridge, which Goose first checked for mines, we began to climb up on the other side of a wide valley through the beech forests towards the Kupres plateau.

Suddenly a shot rang out, then another. Someone was trying to tell us something. I stopped the car and slowly got out. Instantly, I found myself surrounded by wild-looking men carrying a motley collection of weapons. They were soldiers from a forward Serb position overlooking the road, and they demanded to know why we were driving through the middle of a battlefield. I introduced myself and explained that I wanted to talk to their brigade commander. They would not let us go any further, but said that they would ask him to come and meet us. We all sat down in the middle of the road to wait and shared our lunch with them. Some of the soldiers had seen me on television and they wanted to know how the talks in Geneva had progressed. They looked greatly disappointed when I told them that we had succeeded in getting the Bosnian Government to agree only to a one-month ceasefire.

During lunch we were joined by the unit medical officer who wanted to know about the treatment of casualties in the Falklands War. He had read Rick Jolly's book, *The Red and Green Life Machine,* and had been fascinated to discover that British soldiers were taught to stabilise the condition of wounded comrades using drips. He then asked me why I had decided that Mt Kent had been the key to recapturing the Falkland Islands. The arrival of the brigade commander cut our discussion short, and we started to talk about the war in Bosnia. By then the lunch party was becoming quite noisy as the Serbs had produced some plum brandy. No one seemed to bother about the Bosnians on the other side of the valley, although occasionally shots could be heard in the forest.

A recent arrival in Bosnia, Andrew Ridgeway looked bemused at this strange encounter. However he managed to raise with the brigade commander a recent incident when the Serbs had shelled a disused factory in Bugojno, in which a company of the Duke of Wellington's Regiment was located. The Serb commander explained that UNMOs' radio reports, transmitted from Bugojno, had been passing the map coordinates of Serb locations. These reports were being intercepted by the Muslims, who then called down artillery fire on these positions. Andrew told him he would ensure that no further reports relating to the positions of either side would be sent over the radio in future.

Before we left, the Serb commander told us that he had been the commander in Bihac in March when NATO aircraft had tried to carry out an air strike against one of his tanks. Because he was intercepting the radio transmissions between the UN and NATO, he had simply hidden his tank in a shed every time a pilot reported he could see the ground, ordering it to emerge whenever clouds obscured the pilots' view. In this way he had played cat-and-mouse with NATO aircraft for more than an hour, until the pilots had abandoned the mission and returned to Italy. The tank had not deliberately aimed at the French HQ in Bihac, but had fired at a Muslim mortar position nearby.

On the Bosnian side, the Government had gone public with its view that it should pursue a war strategy, justifying this position by saying that the UN peace process would result in an unfair political settlement. While we had been in Geneva talking peace with Ganic, Delic, the commander of the Bosnian Army, had given an interview to *Le Monde* in which he had said the only way to reach a just solution in Bosnia was through all-out war. I also knew from a source within the Federation that the Bosnian Army was being supplied with about 2,000 new infantry weapons each month, and that their tank factory in Zenica was about to start production.

A meeting with Haris Silajdzic, the Prime Minister, confirmed that the Bosnian Government had decided to abandon the peace process. He assured me the Bosnian Serbs would never accept a federal structure or a unitary State in Bosnia, and that war was the only feasible option for the Bosnians. I told him firmly that war in the present circumstances was not an option that his government could pursue. While the increasing supply of arms to Bosnia, along with the possibility that the US could lift the arms embargo, might encourage his commanders to think that military victory over the Serbs was possible, it would take many years before the Bosnian Army would be in a position to conduct offensive operations on a scale capable of delivering their political aims. If his army attempted an all-out military victory at present, it would be defeated and unnecessary suffering would be visited upon the people of Bosnia. It would be better for Bosnia if his government supported the UN in its attempts to find a peaceful solution to the war. At least this would buy time for his rearmament programme. "I am not optimistic about peace," he said.

Viktor Andreev and I often discussed the obstacles put in our way by the Bosnian Government, who believed that they were in a "no-lose" situation. If the Bosnian Army attacked and lost, the resulting images of war and suffering guaranteed support in the West for the "victim State". If they won, then the Bosnian Government would be able to dictate the terms of any future political settlement. It was the task of their propaganda machine to conceal the true nature of this policy by blaming the UN for the war.

Nor was a visit by Chuck Redman able to dispel our gloom about the chances of the Serbs signing up to the Contact Group's map. Although the UN had not been permitted to see the Contact Group's plan, from what we knew, the proposed loss of the Posavina corridor and the Ozren salient would make the map totally unacceptable to the Serbs. Viktor Andreev, at his most Russian, launched into an elaborate justification of the UN's position in an attempt to get some idea from Redman about what was being proposed at the political level, but Redman was determined only to give him those elements in the plan that he wanted the

Serbs to know, and we ended up none the wiser.

After our meeting, Redman departed for Pale, where he got no more sense out of the Bosnian Serb leadership than we had done. Since the end of the Geneva talks, they had lapsed into a state of lunacy and self-destruction, blocking convoys and cutting off communications with the world. Milovanovic had taken to sending increasingly long, rambling signals in the middle of the night to our HQ in Sarajevo, in which he threatened UNPROFOR, their only conduit to the West, with extinction.

Throughout the remaining days of June, we helplessly watched the military position in Bosnia gradually deteriorate. The Bosnian Army offensive in the Ozren region of central Bosnia had caused 3,000 Serb civilians to flee north to the city of Doboj and in the Serb village of Vozuca, 200 shells a day had fallen during the first 10 days of the month. In the far north-west of the country, Dudakovic, who commanded the 5th Corps of the Bosnian Army in Bihac, had shattered the relative calm of the area by attacking the forces of the breakaway Muslim leader, Fikret Abdic. Abdic had been forced by this assault to retreat northwards to his stronghold in Velika Kladusa, and this had created a tide of refugees who had to be looked after by an over-stretched UNHCR. The action had also resulted in the Krajina Serbs in Croatia shelling Dudakovic's positions across the frontier in Bihac, in support of the hard-pressed Abdic. Suddenly the civil war was taking on an international dimension.

The Serbs responded to the assaults of the Bosnian Army by cutting off the electricity and gas and halting the flow of commercial goods and aid convoys to Sarajevo. They also stepped up their campaign of ethnic cleansing, particularly around Banja Luka in western Bosnia. People from the minority ethnic groups were beaten and forced to dig trenches in the front line, and there were many reports of rape by men in uniform. Privately organised convoys were bringing hundreds of Croats and Muslims out of Serb-held areas every week, and the Serb authorities were preventing UNHCR officers from visiting the area to see what was going on.

As the UN struggled to keep its mission alive and aid flowing, casualties among the UN began to mount. On 27 June, a particularly serious incident occurred when a British soldier – Pte Taylor of the Duke of Wellington's Regiment – was killed by a Serb sniper in Gorazde. The next day marked the eightieth anniversary of the murder of Archduke Franz Ferdinand of Austria and his consort in Sarajevo, the event that heralded the start of the First World War. I began to wonder whether the gradual slide into war that was taking place in Bosnia in the summer of 1994 might not also end in a world war.

On a visit from England, John Wilsey warned me that NATO politicians and generals were beginning to openly criticise the performance of UNPROFOR in its handling of events in Bosnia. Even the British Head of the Military Committee, Gen. Vincent, was reported as saying there were grounds for believing that UNPROFOR had "gone soft" in Bosnia and that it was tolerating situations unacceptable to the international community. This greatly irritated me, and I pointed out to John Wilsey that UNPROFOR, far from being soft, had probably used more force than in any peacekeeping mission in the history of the UN.

I recounted an incident that had happened the previous week, when the Serbs had threatened to destroy by artillery bombardment a UN convoy north-east of Tuzla. Milovanovic had called my Chief of Staff in Sarajevo, Brig. van Baal, and informed him that the Serbs had evidence the UN were using this convoy to resupply the Bosnian Army. Van Baal had told him that this was not so. Milovanovic persisted with his threat to shell the convoy. Van Baal replied that the UN would not allow itself to be intimidated and that the convoy would run. He warned Milovanovic that he would call in NATO air support to protect the convoy, and that if it was shelled by Serb artillery, we would respond by destroying all Serb gun positions in the area. Milovanovic then shouted at van Baal that he was not frightened of NATO air power, and that he would unleash his artillery in 10 minutes if the convoy was not turned back. Van Baal ended by saying that the UN would not be diverted from doing its duty. After a short discussion with me, we both decided to continue running the convoy, as the UN mission would suffer a serious loss of credibility if it did not. The Serbs would also be given a psychological victory from which it would be difficult to recover. In making this decision, we took a considerable risk with the lives of the people in the convoy, which included a column of unarmoured lorries driven by civilians. At that time the convoy was on a plain surrounded by Serb guns. It would be impossible for the Swedish APCs accompanying the convoy to defend it.

I immediately called Adm. Leighton Smith in Naples and asked him to put NATO aircraft overhead the convoy, which he did within five minutes. Since 1993 NATO had been present in the skies over Bosnia for virtually 24 hours a day, and it usually took only a matter of minutes for an aircraft to arrive at the scene of an incident. The quick arrival of four NATO aircraft permitted the convoy to complete its task without trouble, although the Serbs did drop a few shells in the distance to save face.

I told John Wilsey that this sort of high-risk decision was being taken daily in Bosnia by the UN in order to keep aid flowing and the peace process alive. Somewhat unfairly, I asked him how many of the generals and politicians sitting in Brussels had ever had to make this sort of life-and-death decision in the politically confused and risky situations in which peacekeepers found themselves. It was one thing for a military commander to take decisions when he held all the military cards, as Norman Schwartzkopf had been able to do during the Gulf War. It was another thing to succeed as a peacekeeper when you did not hold the initiative. John listened quietly and I guessed that he agreed with much of what I was saying.

In Naples, at the operational level, Adm. Leighton Smith remained supportive of the stand taken by UNPROFOR against the use of force to pursue political objec-tives, although I suspected that Joulwan in Brussels was putting him under great pressure to use air power more forcibly. Joulwan apparently believed that UN control over heavy weapons in the UN collecting points was inadequate and that the siege of Sarajevo had returned. This was simply not the case. Although the Serbs occasionally took weapons from the UN weapon collecting sites, this action had not adversely affected the situation around Sarajevo. It was impossible for there to be absolute security of all the sites. Some UN contingents, such as the French, were prepared to stand and fight if an attempt was made to take weapons illegally from the sites, while others would turn a blind eye to the actions of the Serbs. On one occasion a young French lieutenant had stood all night in front of a Serb T55 tank, refusing to give up the weapons in the site and telling the Serbs that they would not only have to kill him, but the whole of his platoon to gain access to the weapons. At dawn the Serbs had left empty-handed and had not returned. At another site guarded by a Ukrainian platoon, they had been able to take a tank out without any resistance. My preferred tactic was to use NATO air strikes to destroy any weapons taken illegally from sites. This was not always possible if a weapon was rapidly moved into a built-up area where the use of air power was clearly not an option. It was important to me that the population of Sarajevo was not subjected to the same high level of artillery bombardment that had killed 10,000 people in the first two years of the war. It had not been since the 9 February Airport Agreement, and I wanted to keep it that way.

In an attempt to impose a political settlement in Bosnia, the Contact Group had adopted a "take it or leave it" approach. If either side did not accept the proposed plan, then "disincentives", including military force, would be used to compel them to accept the proposals. Both sides had until 19 July to comply. In the UN we were amazed that the Contact Group map was not accompanied by an overall plan in which the Serbs would accept a reduction in territory in return for political acceptance. Boutros Boutros-Ghali had responded to this initiative by saying that UNPROFOR was a peacekeeping force and could not use military force to compel acceptance of the Contact Group plan. If a greater level of military force was required, NATO forces should replace the UN in Bosnia. They would have the mandate and the military capability to perform the enforcement role. This declaration mirrored precisely the discussions that we had had in Geneva, but it caused grave unease in Brussels. NATO could not deploy without the Americans and President Clinton had already said that he would not put American troops on the ground until a peace agreement had been signed. How, then, was NATO going to compel compliance from the Serbs in order to obtain the necessary peace? This was not directly the UN's problem, but one result of the Contact Group's "take it or leave it" approach was to increase Serb hostility towards the UN. The Contact Group's declaration merely confirmed their belief that the West had taken sides against them.

As a newly-joined young officer in Aden in the mid-1960s, I had once been attacked and spat upon by crowds in the middle of Sheikh Othman. An experienced sergeant, who understood the peacekeeping principle of proportionality when using force, had prevented me from opening fire on the crowd with my automatic rifle. Thirty years later, I was trying to explain the same principle of proportionality to NATO generals, international politicians and the media. I was a long way from succeeding.

Life had to go on, nevertheless, and our existence in Sarajevo was not wholly unpleasant. Although we had been surviving on combat rations for some time because of the Serb blockage of Sarajevo, we tried not to allow the deteriorating military situation to undermine our determination to stay optimistic and live as normally as possible. We went for runs every day, and whenever it became too dangerous to venture out on certain routes, we switched to others less exposed to sniper fire. When the trams were fired upon, we deliberately travelled on the trams to give an appearance of normality. In between our endless meetings in Pale and with the Bosnian Presidency, we tried to spend time with the ordinary people of Bosnia and with the soldiers in the trenches. In this way, we were not only able to stay in touch with what was truly going on in the country but were encouraged by the resilience of the Bosnians and their own determination not to let the war destroy their civilisation or humanity. Our reception in the streets and in the trenches was always a far remove from the obstructive and hostile way in which the military and political leaders of the warring parties treated us.

Viktor Andreev had also been pressing for me to visit the Russian battalion stationed on the Serb side of the conflict line in Sarajevo. I was reluctant to go, as he had warned me that the visit was sure to include a session in the sauna where we would apparently be expected to beat each other with birch twigs. Since the Russian commanding officer weighed 19 stone, and had once defeated Goose in a weightlifting contest, I didn't relish the idea of being beaten by him, even with birch twigs. However, I needed to visit the Russian battalion and could procrastinate no longer.

The Russians lived in an old Yugoslav Army barracks on the Serb side of the conflict line and we toured the location before lunch. The soldiers came from a Russian airborne division and the barracks had few recreational amenities or comforts for them. Each time I spoke to a soldier, he would give his reply through a non-commissioned officer. They were well disciplined, but spent most of their time either sleeping or on sentry duty. I rarely saw them patrolling. Their equipment was out of date, although their communications looked modern. They maintained a permanent radio link with Moscow, to which they referred all decisions. It was difficult to get them to show any initiative of their own.

Lunch was a typically Russian affair with endless vodka and raw herrings. Viktor was in his element. He kept repeating new toasts – starting with the "airborne forces", which I could hardly refuse – and throughout lunch worked his way from "peace" to what, by the end of the four-hour lunch, sounded like the names of numerous girlfriends. As the day drew to a close I began to understand why the British and Russian soldiers had got on so well during the war. Fortunately lunch was such an extended affair and we drank so much vodka that a visit to the sauna could no longer be contemplated.

One day in the middle of June, Nick, Goose and I were invited to visit the Athos clothing and textile factory in the middle of Sarajevo by its director Mr Kemal, who had been a wealthy businessman before the war. He was also the President of the Sarajevo Football Club. In Tito's time, he had employed 5,000 people in his factories throughout Yugoslavia, supplying major department stores in Europe with suits. His business was now destroyed, but as he spoke to us in his modern office he remained optimistic about the future, saying that within one month of the roads being opened into Sarajevo, he would be able to restart his business. He had money and investors abroad, but there was little left of his factory in Sarajevo. Shelling had destroyed the top two floors of the building and only a few elderly workers remained on the ground floor, making suits by hand. His Audi, a burnt-out wreck outside his office window, was a poignant reminder of the good times that he had enjoyed before the war. The walls of the administration building were lined with photographs and fashion designs from the 1950s. Before we left, Mr Kemal insisted on giving each of us a suit as well as something for our wives. Without a currency, he explained, it was impossible to sell anything, so he always gave his suits away. The choice was limited to midnight blue or purple, complete with padded shoulders and wide lapels. I went for purple and Goose chose midnight blue. This confirmed my suspicion that Goose really wanted to be a bouncer in a Las Vegas gambling joint.

The next evening, my purple suit made its first public appearance at a performance of Mozart's *Requiem* in the ruins of the national library in the oldest part of Sarajevo. Before the war, Sarajevo had a world-class orchestra as well as its own opera and ballet companies. After two years of fighting, only a few elderly members of the orchestra survived or still lived in Sarajevo. The performance was intended to celebrate the partial return of peace to the city and to honour the dead.

It was a beautiful, calm summer evening. As we drove up to the ruins of the national library, I could see small groups of people, some in dinner-jackets, standing on the steps of the building, bathed in the golden light of the setting sun or sitting on the banks of the river. It could have been an English summer evening at Glyndebourne, if it were not for the Serb trenches dug into the hillside just across the river. The orchestra and choir were seated on a wooden stage erected on the rubble of the collapsed roof and the audience sat on chairs amid the debris surrounding the stage. Above was the open sky. The conductor was Zubin Mehta and José Carreras sang in the choir.

As the sublime music filled the library and drifted into the old city outside, I realised that the performance was not merely for the many victims of the fighting in Sarajevo. It was an expression of hope and faith for those who remained in this world. It was a protest against the futility of the war. The choir and orchestra were playing as much for themselves as for us. I had never encountered such inspired passion in any piece of music before and never will again. Across the river, in their trenches, the Serb soldiers kept their guns silent and listened to the music. After the performance, President Izetbegovic thanked us for making the event possible. I wondered if he understood the Christian sentiment behind the words and music.

By midsummer it was easy to believe that peace had begun to return as the fighting lessened and the transition from war to peace in central Bosnia continued. Andrew Ridgeway had kept up the momentum of the peace process through the mechanism of the Joint Commission. At meetings between local civic and military commanders he insisted on strict adherence to the terms of the Washington Accord, and he was ruthless with anyone who strayed. He had liaison officers from the Croats and Bosnians working in his HQ, and was able to closely monitor events around central Bosnia, although the Serbs still refused to allow a permanent UN presence in their HQs. He was responsible for an intensive UN road- and bridge-building programme that allowed the UN to open a new supply route from the Dalmatian coast to Tuzla, via Mostar and Sarajevo. Along this route thousands of vehicles were now travelling each day, 90% of which were commercial trucks carrying consumer goods. In addition to this traffic, by the end of June the Sarajevo airlift had become the longest sustained airlift in history and had succeeded in moving 120,000 metric tons of aid into Sarajevo from depots in Italy and Germany.[1]

As a result of these achievements central Bosnia was becoming independent of the UN aid programme, and the UNHCR reported that there had been a 48% decrease in the number of refugees receiving aid since September 1993.[2] Petrol stations had been opened in Sarajevo at the start of June and the price of petrol and goods in the markets had fallen to peacetime levels. Bill Eagleton, a UN civil administrator and retired US diplomat, had been appointed to help in the reconstruction of Sarajevo, and international donors had already contributed $68 million towards the reconstruction fund.

A new Federal Government headed by a Croat, Kresimir Zubak, had been elected on 23 June. The Bosnian Federation had been formed following the March 1994 Washington Accord which had brought about an end to the fighting between the Croats and the Muslims. The Federation's purpose was to give the Bosnian Croats a political voice and to create a number of federal structures, including a federal ministry of defence. Although the Bosnian Federation lacked any real authority and the Bosnian Muslim party under Izetbegovic continued to hold the reins of power in Bosnia, it demonstrated that political progress in Bosnia was possible and made a return to war less likely.

By the end of July, it looked as though we had also succeeded in breathing new life into the peace negotiations between the Serbs and the Bosnians. The Bosnian Army offensive in the Ozren mountains had petered out and the attack on Abdic's forces in Bihac had ended in stalemate. Alagic, in spite of his brave words, had still not gained any ground in his advance on Sanski Most. Although ceasefire violations were still a daily occurrence on the confrontation line around Sarajevo, we dismissed them as being of limited tactical significance as no serious attempt was made by either side to gain territory, and the casualty rate remained low.

The most serious incident to take place in Sarajevo during the months of June and July was a fierce battle between the French and the Serbs near the Oslobejene building. During the battle, the French Sector Commander, Brig. André Soubirou, had ordered his tanks to return fire with their main 90mm cannon. This had brought the fighting to a close without loss of life and the next day Soubirou was able to resume his routine meetings with his opposite number in the Bosnian Serb Army without difficulty.

Unfortunately our relations with US State Department officials in the newly opened embassy, next door to the Residency, had not improved. In mid-July I invited the US Ambassador to Sarajevo, Victor Jackovitch, to my office where I told him that his speech at the opening of the embassy, in the presence of Madeleine Albright, had been a great disappointment to the UN. He had failed to mention the young men and women of UNPROFOR, without whose tireless work it would not have been possible for the Americans to have an embassy in Sarajevo. Indeed, without the presence of the UN, it was doubtful if the State of Bosnia could have survived. I pointed out that the UN had been unfailingly helpful to his staff and to US visitors. Nevertheless he had continually treated the UN in a hostile fashion.

Jackovitch was a cool man with a thin black moustache and a secretive manner. He said little but when he did so he reminded me of Ganic. On this occasion, he grudgingly accepted that he should have acknowledged the contribution made by the UN in Bosnia and quickly left, no doubt to file yet another report back to Washington about the UN.

One day in late May, I decided that the team that had been with me in Bosnia since January needed a break from peacekeeping and that we would climb the highest mountain in Bosnia, Nadkrstac, whose summit was at 2,110 metres. We approached the mountain through the town of Foinica, 50 kilometres west of Sarajevo, where some of the fiercest battles between the Croats and the Muslims had taken place earlier in the war. As we ascended through the beech and pine forests there was no sign of the war and, emerging from the forest onto a bare plateau at about 1,300 metres, we could see a lake in the distance beneath the summit. Around the lake were clustered shepherds' huts with shingle roofs. Some had been recently renovated and smoke rose from the chimneys as the air was cold and the temperature at night often fell below freezing at this altitude. In the surrounding mountains there were bears, wolves and mountain lions. A man was fishing in the lake and sheep and cattle were being taken back to their enclosures for the night.

The scenery was reminiscent of the high Himalayas. When I asked one of the shepherds why some of the huts had been destroyed, he replied that they belonged to the Ustashi. If the owners returned to the village they would be killed. I told them about the Washington Accord and that peace had now been agreed between the Muslims and the Croats. He spat on the ground and said darkly that he didn't care what happened elsewhere. If any Ustashi ever came to the village they would be killed.

The next day we climbed to the summit of Nadkrstac, leaving behind L/Sgt Daly to guard the tents and equipment, including my fishing rod, assembled on a nearby rock. It took about two hours to reach the summit, from which we could see mountains and forests stretching to the horizon. In the distance we heard the unmistakable noise of shelling, some 20 kilometres to the west, in the direction of the Duke of Wellington's Regiment's base in Bugojno. Even here we could not escape the war. On our return, L/Sgt Daly had fallen asleep under a rock, but sprang smartly to his feet when I asked, "Sergeant Daly, where is my Grey Wolf?" I had immediately noticed that someone had removed my favourite fly from the fishing line. L/Sgt Daly looked confused.

"There haven't been any wolves round here, sir," he replied. "I've been watching out all the time." His response reduced us all to helpless laughter, and for the rest of L/Sgt Daly's time in Bosnia, if his friends found him asleep, they would wake him with cries of "Grey Wolf!"

Visiting the local commander of the Bosnian Army in Zavidovici at the southern end of the Maglaj enclave, I had another chance to go fishing, this time in the Bosna River that rises on Mt Igman and runs into the Black Sea. I found the commander in a smoke-filled cellar under an abandoned school in the middle of the town. He was a fat, half-shaven, swarthy man who broke into high-pitched giggles whenever I said something he found unusual. He was well versed in the politics of the war and we discussed the latest Contact Group plan and map. He felt that the West was unnecessarily scared of the Serbs, and that NATO should enter the war on behalf of the Muslims. I explained, once again, that even if this was politically and morally desirable, there was absolutely no chance of it happening because NATO simply did not have the political will to fight a war in Bosnia. He replied that if a coalition of forces were established between NATO and the newly-formed Federation, the Serbs would be defeated. I pointed out that the military pressures on the Serbs were mounting and that they would ultimately be forced to sign up to a peace deal. The former Commander of NATO, Gen. Galvin, had pointed this out to Mladic who had not refuted his logic. It was important that the Bosnians supported the UN peace effort until this happened.

We then moved on to the important subject of fishing. He said that he would send a young officer to take us to the best local fishing spot a couple of miles away, on a stretch of river that divided the Bosnians from the Serbs. Here the water crashed over large boulders into deep pools. The river was about 300 yards wide at this point. On the Muslim side of the river, some men were fishing from the bank or lounging beside small fires on which were smoking the fish they had caught. They laughed when they saw I intended to fish with a dry fly and told me I would never catch anything that way. They only fished with grenades, grasshoppers or small bread pellets. They did not seem to be bothered by the war.

Putting on waders, I carefully made my way to some rocks in the middle of the river and cast my line into the pools below the rocks. Goose sat on the bank watching me. All seemed peaceful. Suddenly there was a loud and prolonged burst of machine-gun fire nearby. Being in an exposed position, I looked back to see what Goose was doing. He sat motionless, so I continued to fish and to my delight caught two small fish. The other fishermen, who turned out to be doctors on leave from the front line, offered to cook them for us. It was a delicious meal. They said that the firing had been to celebrate a wedding that was taking place in a nearby village, and that the Serbs did not usually fire on people fishing in the river. On the way back, I asked Goose what he had been thinking when the machine-gun had opened fire. He told me he was considering which of two options to adopt if I had disappeared, riddled with bullets, beneath the water. One had been to try and rescue me, the other had been to pull out his pistol and shoot himself. He did not tell me which was his preferred option.

On my return to Sarajevo I had an encouraging meeting with Redman, who for the first time admitted that the US Government might have to support a territorial division of Bosnia that was less than what the Bosnian Government wanted. He believed that there were basically four options that could be pursued by the international community.

The first was to manage and control the mess. The situation was dynamic and, as more and more arms were smuggled into the country, it was likely that the war option would be pursued by the Bosnians. Peacekeeping in these circumstances would be useless. This was not a viable option.

The second option would be to enforce the TEZs and safe areas more vigorously in order to maximise pressure on the Serbs. Enforcement would require a wider use of NATO air power and involve punitive action. Such action would constitute war-fighting, and would necessitate the withdrawal of UNPROFOR. NATO air power could not, by itself, guarantee the security of the TEZs or the safe areas. As NATO troops were unlikely to be deployed on the ground in Bosnia, this was equally unworkable.

The third option was to lift the arms embargo. This might put pressure on the Serbs to agree to the Contact Group plan and map; for as time went by the military balance would tilt against them. This would force them to sign up to the plan earlier rather than later. However, once again UNPROFOR would have to be withdrawn, as the Serbs would regard the lifting of the arms embargo as a hostile act by the international community.

The final option was to withdraw the UN from Bosnia and allow the West to fight a war against the Serbs. No one would support this option. Redman concluded that the UN would have to remain in Bosnia while efforts were made by the international community to quickly bring the war to an end.

This meeting with Redman signalled the first public acknowledgement by the Clinton administration that it was no longer possible to pursue their original ideal of restoring a unitary, multi-ethnic State of Bosnia, and that the US would have to start supporting the UN peacekeeping mission. It appeared that our effort to explain the realities in Bosnia to the Americans was at last succeeding.

The Bosnian Government, naturally, was not pleased with our efforts. Kurt Schork, in a Reuters dispatch, quoted the words of a Bosnian Government official: "Because the shelling has stopped and so have the casualties, people want to believe the war is over. Persuading them to start fighting again will be difficult if it means going without water and electricity and basic necessities. Sarajevo is no longer under attack and people want to live." Kurt had then commented that the Bosnian Government was worried that I might be right when I had said recently on television: "We have helped to create the conditions for peace here and the people are ready."

A visit to Sarajevo earlier that year by Sir Fitzroy MacLean and his wife Veronica had demonstrated to me just how paranoid the Bosnian Government could be where I was concerned. I had known Sir Fitzroy Maclean for some years as we had both served in the same regiment. It was entirely natural that he should want to see me when he visited Bosnia. He happened to be accompanied by a Dutch television company that was making a film about his wartime experiences. We spent a couple of hours between filming, talking together and comparing the circumstances facing his mission to Yugoslavia in 1944 with those I was facing exactly half a century later. We reflected on the harsh nature of the countryside, the obduracy of the Bosnian people and the brutal complexity of their history. We also agreed that, apart from similar frustrations caused by these aspects of the Balkans, our two missions were very different in nature. He had been waging a war against the Nazis and the Ustashi and I was fighting for peace.

I later discovered that, as a result of his close wartime relationship with Tito, Sir Fitzroy MacLean was regarded by the Bosnians as a fellow traveller of the Slavs and a Stalinist. The Bosnian Government was convinced Fitzroy had come to Sarajevo to bring me new instructions from London, and this suspicion had been confirmed because we had talked outside the Residency building, where we could not be bugged. When I saw Silajdzic the next day and innocently asked him whether he had read *Eastern Approaches,* a book about Fitzroy's wartime experiences, I was surprised by the strength of his condemnation of Tito and Fitzroy and it was obvious I was guilty by association.

The Bosnian Government, however, had more important things on their minds than Fitzroy MacLean. This was the approaching deadline for their agreement to the Contact Group plan and the territorial division of their country. Silajdzic had called the plan the "legitimising of genocide", but the week before the deadline expired, Izetbegovic suddenly accepted it in its entirety. Although he thought that it was "morally wrong", the State of Bosnia had been recognised in the plan as a unitary State and he believed that, with time, the ethnic communities could be reintegrated. He was later quoted as saying that he only agreed to accept the plan because he knew that the Serbs would not accept it. By accepting the Contact Group plan he would be seen to support the international community without actually putting at risk his ultimate objectives.

A visit to Pale by Douglas Hurd and Alain Juppé on 13 July did little to advance the likelihood of acceptance of the Contact Group plan by the Serbs. Karadzic told the Foreign Secretaries of Britain and France that the Serbs would never accept the international community's attempt to put them in the same State as their enemies, and that it was absolutely necessary for the Republika Srpska to have some form of international recognition. Nor would the Serbs tolerate the presence of NATO troops on their land and they would, if necessary, mobilise half a million men to prevent it. Hurd told Karadzic that what he was saying was tantamount to a declaration of war against the international community. Not even Russia or Belgrade agreed with the Bosnian Serb position. Karadzic ended the meeting by saying that he would put the Contact Group proposal to the Bosnian Serb Assembly, without recommendation. This was his usual way of saying, "I reject what you propose, but you will not be able to blame me." Milosevic later told Sergio and Akashi that, because Karadzic had betrayed him by speaking against the Contact Group map in the Bosnian Assembly, the President was now "dead politically".

The next day Noel Malcolm, who often seemed to be attacking Douglas Hurd, accused him in the *Daily Telegraph* of conducting the sort of diplomacy in which it is hard to tell the difference between "a firefighter and an arsonist". He repeated once again the militarily unwise assertion that it would be better if the international community "let the Bosnians defend themselves".[3] If the international community had abandoned the peacekeeping mission, as he had so often suggested, then it might well have become necessary for Noel Malcolm himself, who once signed a letter in *The Times* under the banner of the "Alliance to Defend Bosnia", to take up a rifle rather than a pen. The next day, to emphasise the point that, at least in Britain, no one was thinking of fighting a war in Bosnia or anywhere else, the British Defence Secretary, Malcolm Rifkind, announced a programme of massive defence cuts.

Going public for the first time on this issue on 18 July, I spelt out the consequences for the international community if the Serbs chose to "leave" rather than to accept the Contact Group plan. "There is a limit to how much enforcement a peacekeeping force can undertake," I explained to Tim Butcher, defence correspondent of the *Daily Telegraph*.[4] I wanted it to be absolutely clear that I was not going to allow UNPROFOR to be used to enforce a political settlement on the Serbs; not because I thought the plan unworkable, but because this was a war mission that would need at least 100,000 fighting troops to implement. I would not allow the UN to be used as a surrogate war-fighting force for NATO. It would be better to leave Bosnia with our heads held high, having stayed in the ring for two and a half years, rather than suffer a military defeat because we had undertaken a task beyond the capability of any peacekeeper. I didn't actually think it would come to this, but it was important the Contact Group, which had hitherto failed to consult with UNPROFOR, retained no illusions about the possibility of using peacekeepers to impose their plan on the Bosnian Serbs through a greater use of force.

The Serbs, believing that their position had strengthened as a result of contradictions in the Contact Group approach, and also in riposte to continuing attacks against their positions by the Bosnian Army, decided on 26 July to close the airport to commercial convoys using the route down Mt Igman. The Serbs had been threatening to do this for some time, and it had taken all the diplomatic efforts of Sergio de Mello, who had obtained the original agreement on 17 March 1994, to stop the Serbs doing so any earlier. This time Karadzic was adamant, citing the smuggling of weapons into Sarajevo in the commercial traffic, the failure of the Bosnians to sign up to an "anti-sniper" agreement and prisoner-exchange programme, and finally the sabotaging of the ceasefire agreement signed in Geneva. The sight of consumer goods being delivered to the citizens of Sarajevo from all over Europe, while the Bosnian Serbs were suffering from the effects of economic sanctions, was too much for him.

The Serb snipers in Grbavica also resumed their attacks on the trams, which had to be suspended from service. This was a major blow to the people of Sarajevo, who consequently had to walk long distances, often in range of the snipers. During August, newspapers around the world were once again filled with pictures of men, women and children killed or injured by snipers. This played into the hands of those people in whose interest it was to perpetuate the war, and it was accordingly much harder for us to refute the tide of criticism and propaganda unleashed in the media against the UN.

On 1 August, an Oxford don, Mark Almond, wrote a scathing article in the *Daily Mail* stating that the humanitarian aid mission in Bosnia had merely "spun out the agony of the war without contributing to its resolution".[5] From where he was sitting in his comfortable book-lined study, it must have seemed easy to advocate such a policy of non-intervention. Mark Almond did not have to face up to the consequences of this policy. It was the millions of people in Bosnia who were dependent on UN aid and the presence of UN soldiers for their survival during the war who would have had to do so.

The return of Sarajevo to conditions of virtual siege not only gave ammunition to the detractors of the UN abroad, it also caused a major row between the Bosnian Government and the UN. I was summoned by the President to an emergency meeting at 1800 hours on 26 July, in which Silajdzic launched into an angry attack on the UN, saying that we should not allow ourselves to be blackmailed by the Serbs. In his view, the closure of the airport route to commercial traffic was an attempt to sabotage the peace process and create "a pretext to resume fighting around Sarajevo".

Ganic then made what was probably the most extraordinary proposal of the entire conflict. In order to guarantee the continuing passage of commercial vehicles across the airport into Sarajevo, he demanded that I should place UN soldiers in two lines across the airfield so that commercial traffic could pass between them. If the Serbs fired at the convoys and killed the soldiers, the UN would then have a legitimate right to fire back in self-defence.

This crazy scheme confirmed my deepening suspicion that Ganic had fallen prey to his own propaganda and was now living in a world far removed from reality. For the past four months the Sarajevans had benefited from a UN-brokered agreement that was perhaps unique in war, in which a besieging force had allowed utilities to be restored and commercial goods to enter a city. For the past four months up to 100 lorries a day had been arriving in the city, and the people of Sarajevo had begun to live in relatively normal conditions. There had even been a limited movement of people across the battle lines. It was clear that Ganic had completely erased from his memory this extraordinary achievement by the UN and I was in no doubt that he was responsible for returning his people to war by sabotaging the Geneva talks.

Refusing to speak to him again, I turned to Izetbegovic. His only contribution to the debate so far had been to ask his favourite question: "What to do?" I explained that it was his own strategy of attacking the Serbs on all fronts that had undermined the fragile ceasefire in Sarajevo. In doing so, his forces had won no additional territory, but the renewed fighting had brought misery to the people of Bosnia. I quoted the Bosnian Army offensive in the Ozren mountains as the most recent example of this flawed strategy. Finally, I told Izetbegovic that the UN could not go on forever allowing its presence as peacekeepers to be used by his army to prosecute a war. He simply could not expect either the UN or the international community to fight his war for him. De Lapresle, the Force Commander, was about to issue a contingency plan for the withdrawal of the UN from Bosnia, indicating that what I had told Izetbegovic was not a vague threat. Izetbegovic looked increasingly downcast as I spoke, but made no reply. When I left, Silajdzic unexpectedly came up to me and said that he privately agreed with me. He could never understand why Delic continually launched offensives that always ended in defeat. I replied that Delic had not had the privilege of training at the British Staff College. He was, however, always welcome.

That evening Kurt Schork, the Sarajevo Reuters correspondent, came to the Residency for dinner. After a long and fiery discussion, he finally agreed with Viktor that the UN was following the only course of action possible, although he still believed the West had a moral duty to act in support of Bosnia. However, he didn't think it had the moral courage or commitment to do so. Kurt was one of the most experienced journalists working in Sarajevo at that time, and he had the cynical and enquiring mind of all members of his profession. His instincts were rarely wrong, and it was encouraging to hear him backing the UN in its efforts to find peace.

The UN took great risks in doing so, and this was sadly demonstrated the next day when a British Army logistics convoy entering Sarajevo took a route down Mt Igman used by the Bosnians instead of using the French-controlled route. As they approached Sarajevo, the Serbs, who were determined not to allow any traffic through, opened fire on the convoy, killing Cpl Bottomley. He was the seventh British soldier to die in Bosnia. The French, in whose sector the action took place, immediately sent an armoured column up Mt Igman to recover the remaining vehicles and lead the British personnel to safety. On my way to the Presidency that evening I was stopped by a television camera on the steps of the building and asked what was happening on Mt Igman.

Although I did not yet know the full details of the incident, I repeated the initial French reports I had just received. I told the reporter that it looked as though the Serbs had mistaken the convoy for a Bosnian one. When asked why the convoy was travelling along this unusual route and why the Serbs had fired upon it, I replied it was just "one of those things". It was the worst possible response I could have made. Shortly afterwards a television broadcast reported that a British soldier had been killed by the Serbs and General Rose had said that it was just "one of those things". I immediately responded by strongly condemning the Serb action, declaring that no soldier who was serving the cause of peace and the people of Bosnia should be attacked in this way. By then I knew that the Serbs had also fired on the French recovery team, who had been forced to respond with a 90mm cannon. The Serb excuse, given to me the next day, that they had mistaken the convoy for a Bosnian one was an evident lie.

The next day Sergio and I delivered an even stronger warning to the Serbs in Pale. Although Mladic was not present, his aide Brig.-Gen. Tolimir expressed regret at the attack. I always found it very difficult to remain impartial as a mediator when I was obliged to deal with the people I knew had been responsible for the deaths of my soldiers, but as Viktor said, the peace process was more important than our feelings.

Nevertheless I needed to be able to justify such tragic loss of life among the peace-keepers in terms of the success of the mission.

Meanwhile de Lapresle had sent a signal to New York outlining the initial reinforcement that would be required to safeguard the withdrawal of the UN from Bosnia, if a decision were taken by the international community to enforce the Contact Group plan. The list included 10 infantry battalions, four engineer battalions, two logistic battalions and an aviation regiment of light and heavy helicopters. It was evident from the list that de Lapresle intended such a force to be able to fight its way out of Bosnia if the need arose.

At the third ministerial Contact Group meeting on 30 July its members considered the way ahead in the light of the Serb rejection of their plan. In the end, in the words of Lord Owen, all the ministers could agree upon was to keep the Contact Group in a state of "perpetual motion".[6] It was shortly after this that the Contact Group first came to UNPROFOR for help. They finally appeared to understand the inadvisability of separating political action from the peacekeeping and humanitarian aspects of the mission in Bosnia.

At a national level, Angela's appeal in England for funds, following the Serb assault on Gorazde, had produced an enormous response around the country. Donations had already come directly to me in Sarajevo from the York Vikings Rotary Club, a Territorial Army colonel and various individuals, and further substantial sums had been raised by army wives, which, along with generous contributions from other sources, amounted to several thousands of pounds. Angela had used these funds to buy incubators for the hospitals in Pale and Gorazde and had sought the help of the British Red Cross in doing so. She had agreed with Geoffrey Dennis, the then International Director of the British Red Cross, to deliver the incubators in person, as this would increase publicity and give a boost to the Red Cross appeal for the victims of the war in the former Yugoslavia. Before leaving England, Angela had said in an article to publicise the appeal that the presentation of incubators was "symbolic of new life. The people of Bosnia want normality in their lives again, and you start with the smallest baby."

I had always agreed with her that it would not be possible for her to visit Bosnia as my wife since it was an operational theatre, which I commanded. However, she was determined to see for herself what was happening in the country and as she was entitled to visit as a representative of the British Red Cross, I found myself in the happy position of being asked by the UNHCR to assist the visit. While Angela was in Bosnia, it was planned that she would deliver the incubators to hospitals in Pale and Gorazde.

I met Angela with Goose in Kiseljak and we drove with her to Sarajevo. The road passes by Mt Igman and we could see smoke still rising from the slopes of the mountain where Cpl Bottomley's convoy had been ambushed earlier that day. This brought home to Angela the harsh reality of peacekeeping in a war zone. As we passed the smashed buildings and the twisted wreckage of battle, she asked how people who lived in a country as beautiful as Bosnia could do such things. I had no reply. That evening Viktor Andreev, who welcomed Angela like a long-lost friend, took us to dinner in a traditional Bosnian inn called a *han*, in the Muslim part of the city. All was quiet and as we sat in the courtyard watching the light slowly fading from the sky we might have been anywhere in Europe.

The next morning we made an early start, and flew in a Sea King helicopter with Kurt Schork and a cameraman to Pale, to deliver the first of the incubators. When we arrived we were met by Karadzic's black armoured Mercedes. His wife was the head of the Serbian Red Cross in Bosnia and she had sent a representative to meet us. The hospital was a converted wooden ski hotel with primitive facilities. The director of the hospital, who had worked in Sarajevo's Kosevo hospital before the war, told us that the sterilisers he used were First World War vintage and heated by wood. He proudly explained that the equipment worked well and that he had never yet had a case of secondary infection in the hospital. Upstairs was the maternity ward where rows of tiny babies lay wrapped in swaddling clothes. We were told that each mother was allowed only 24 hours in the ward after delivery and was then discharged. The gift of an incubator was particularly welcome. Because of sanctions, it was impossible to get spare parts for the ones they had and many babies had died. I wondered if the sanctions committee in New York knew about these deaths, or even cared.

We then flew on to Gorazde, to be met by David Santa Ollala, the Commanding Officer of the Duke of Wellington's Regiment, on a position above Gorazde between the two opposing lines of trenches. He looked fit and sun-tanned and clearly enjoyed bringing peace back to a town that had been so devastated in the past two years. From where we stood, we could see the entire town of Gorazde below, and David took the opportunity to brief Kurt Schork on what had happened in the town since the end of the fighting in April. Afterwards we drove down to the hospital where the director was waiting for us. A large crowd had assembled outside in the courtyard and the road. As we arrived they clapped and cheered, shouting "Rouzy! Bobby Charlton! Thatcher!" Goose remarked that they had got their priorities wrong and should have started with Bobby Charlton.

Responding to the obvious delight of the crowd, Angela and I went to shake their hands in the manner of visiting politicians. David Santa Ollala explained that the people of Gorazde had heard that I was coming with my wife to fulfil the promise that I had made to Dr Begovic, the hospital director, three months before. Many people had tears in their eyes, and even Dr Begovic looked moved as he made a speech of welcome. We trooped into the hospital where Angela handed over the incubator. The director then showed us a gruesome video of a baby that had been killed in the fighting, its intestines hanging out. This was followed by a tour of the maternity wards, where Angela spoke to the mothers. Once again the babies were swaddled in the traditional Balkan manner, and Angela commented how dreadful it was that these Muslim babies and the identical ones we had seen in Pale would almost certainly end up trying to kill each other.

We made the return trip by road, as Angela wanted to see the bridge over the Drina at Visegrad, made famous in the second book of Ivo Andric's Nobel Prize-winning trilogy. In Visegrad the military commander of the area, Col. Masal, whom I had last seen sitting under an apple tree in Gorazde at the end of the fighting in April, was waiting to receive us. He and his young officers took us to a café beside the river, where we sat drinking coffee. The river was a strange blue-green colour and, even though it was summer, it was flowing strongly. Everyone said that they were sick of the war, but they did not think that the Muslims wanted to end it. They had reconciled themselves to fighting for an all-out Serb victory.

On the way back to Sarajevo, we stopped in a town called Rogatica where all convoys travelling to Gorazde had to pass through a Serb checkpoint. Here we met Capt. Zoran who was well known to the UN soldiers because he would spend hours minutely examining the cargo manifest lists of convoys in an attempt to find an excuse for turning them back. On a previous visit he had made the mistake of accusing me of being pro-Muslim, citing the air strikes that I had ordered in Gorazde. For nearly two hours I refused to move on, while I explained to him the articles of the UN Charter, the basic principles of peacekeeping and the nature of our mission. By standing in the middle of the road and addressing not only Capt. Zoran but the soldiers manning the roadblock (as well as some Duke of Wellington's Regiment soldiers waiting patiently to pass), I was giving him a taste of his own medicine. Each time he tried to wave me on, I would tell him that I didn't think he had properly understood my point and would repeat it at even greater length. In the end, he walked away to the jeers of British soldiers and we all drove on. Today he had obviously been told to be on his best behaviour and took us to his HQ to meet his boss. He turned out to be a grim-looking man with a villainous moustache, who rather charmingly thanked Angela for having made the visit.

In Sarajevo a message was waiting for me from Izetbegovic, complaining that the UN had diverted a large number of its cargo-carrying aircraft from the Sarajevo airlift to Rwanda to help the refugees from the recent outbreak of fighting in which a million people were thought to have been killed. The diversion of aircraft had resulted in a reduced flow of aid. I told Izetbegovic that the limited human-itarian problems facing Bosnia could not compare with the scale of the disaster in Rwanda, where a far greater genocide was taking place, and that the focus of UN aid had rightly been shifted there. It was inevitable that at some point the inter-national community would tire of endlessly pouring resources into the civil war in Bosnia, where it had been made clear by all sides that no one was interested in peace.

Izetbegovic was unable to argue with me, and was reduced to pleading with us to use our influence to return the planes to Bosnia as soon as possible. This was Simon Shadbolt's last meeting in the Presidency and he could not conceal his delight at Izetbegovic's predicament. As we left the building, he said he was surprised I hadn't pointed out to Izetbegovic that his government had had the opportunity to build-up stocks of strategic supplies during the four months that commercial traffic had been flowing into Sarajevo. The Bosnian Government had not done this and the moment the roads had been closed it had started asking the UN for aid. I told Simon that I would never have received the true answer: there was a profit to be made from commercial traffic, but not from aid.

Simon had been the person on whom I had most depended since arriving in Bosnia. Kurt Schork once told me that the Sarajevan press regarded me as Simon's spokesman. Certainly his sharp, analytical mind and his ability to deal with a mass of conflicting problems had made my job much easier. He had the essential quality of guile, and had also developed a network of informants in many different camps, so that we were rarely caught out by an unexpected turn of events. He also had a great sense of fun and got on particularly well with George Waters, with whom he composed scurrilous letters that they sent to their friends in England. I was very sad to see him go, but his wife, Jan, had just had a baby called Flora, immediately dubbed Unproflora, and he was needed back home. His replacement was a Greenjacket, Lt-Col. Jamie Daniell, who had also worked in John Wilsey's HQ in England, where he had taken over the operations desk from Simon Shadbolt. He quickly picked up where Simon had left off.

Nick Costello and George Waters also left Bosnia that week. It was a pity to see the original team who had been with me for six months breaking up, but as young officers they had careers to make in the army. Before they departed they handed over to the new team an operation we had been secretly running moving displaced people across the battle lines.

This operation had started early in the tour when a woman approached me in Sarajevo and told me her parents had been killed because they were wealthy Serbs and that she was separated from the rest of her family who lived abroad. She had no means of support and was living in terrible conditions. I asked Nick Costello to see what he could do for her. When it became clear the Bosnian Government would not give her a permit to leave, he and Goose simply put her in the back of the Range Rover and drove her across the battle line. By the time Nick left Sarajevo in July, many people, both Serbs and Muslims, had been transported in this way.

At the outset I had laid down the ground rules for these mercy missions. I told Nick that we would move only helpless, displaced people separated from their families. We would never do it on official demand from either side, or for money. On another occasion I spoke with an elderly Serb in Grbavica, the Serb part of Sarajevo. Because their mother was a Muslim, his two sons had fought on the Muslim side against the Serbs. Both had been wounded, one in the head, the other had lost a leg. Although neither could fight again, the Bosnian Government refused to allow them to seek medical treatment abroad. Once again, I asked Nick and Goose if they could do something about this. Two weeks later, passing through the same part of Grbavica, the old man came up to me bearing a cake that his wife had baked for me. He told me his two sons were now in a clinic in Italy and doing well. I gave the cake to Nick and Goose but never asked them how they had got them out.

We didn't just move people. A Serb had once approached us in a park in Ilidza, a suburb of Sarajevo, and told me that he owned a flat in Sarajevo in which a Muslim friend, who had been driven out of a Serb-held suburb of Sarajevo, was now living.

He had heard that his friend had no money, and that he and his family were starving. Since the Serb had hidden a substantial sum of money in the basement of the block of flats, he asked me if I would recover the money and give it to his Muslim friend. He gave me a hand-drawn plan, showing where the money was concealed. That night, Goose went to the flats and found a parcel containing nearly 10,000 DM behind some central-heating pipes. He took the money to the Muslim, who, though grateful, showed no surprise when told where the money had come from. Small acts of kindness were commonplace between the two communities, even in the terrible circumstances of the civil war. I did not tell either the UN or the British Government about these operations, as I wasn't sure whether such activities lay within my mandate, nor did I feel it necessary to justify our actions to anyone.

Nick Costello's successor was Maj. Mike Stanley, a well-regarded officer in the Parachute Regiment. Like Nick, he was of Serb origin and had served the year before as a battalion liaison officer in Bosnia. His dark, brooding looks concealed a volatile temperament and he could be extremely touchy, especially if someone insulted the Serbs. The Bosnian Government knew of his Serb royalist origins and greatly distrusted him. Although he spoke Serbo-Croat fluently, he found it difficult to act as an interpreter during meetings, and I therefore decided to employ a separate interpreter, Dr Darko Mocibob, an orthopaedic surgeon from the main hospital in Sarajevo, who spoke good English. He had been expelled from the hospital early in the war, in spite of the shortage of qualified surgeons, because he was a Croat. He longed to join his fiancée in Paris where she was working as a doctor. He worked in the UN pool of interpreters and was detached to join my staff. This relieved much of the pressure on Mike, who was able to play an important liaison function during the many difficult meetings with the Serbs that were to follow in the coming months.

Meanwhile, at the international level, as the spectre of full-scale war stalked the Balkans, midsummer madness was breaking out in the capitals of the West. Malcolm Rifkind unexpectedly sided with those supporting the lifting of the arms embargo, declaring that there was now an "international consensus that the arms embargo should be lifted . . . and that we would respect the views of the majority". In what I felt to be a breathtaking piece of moral evasion, he then added that the UK itself would not supply arms to Bosnia. In Geneva, Lord Owen had joined the Secretary-General of the UN in calling for a withdrawal of UNPROFOR.[7] In Yugoslavia, Serb attacked Serb, as President Milosevic announced he was breaking off relations with the Bosnian Serbs following their rejection of the Contact Group plan. In Bosnia, Muslim attacked Muslim in Bihac and the Bosnian Serbs were becoming increasingly paranoid as their isolation increased.

At the start of August, the Bosnian Serbs threatened to take their weapons from the UN collecting sites around Sarajevo, and the French Sector Commander, Soubirou, had consequently reinforced the guards on all the sites, telling the Serbs that they would have to fight to get them. At 2000 hours on 2 August, I received intelligence that the Serbs were about to seize weapons from two specific sites guarded by the French and the Ukrainians. I made a public statement saying that I would use force against them if they did so, and immediately put NATO air power on standby. Since it was unlikely the guards on the weapon sites would be able to resist the Serbs for long, my plan was to hit the vehicles and weapons with air strikes as they left the weapons collection points. Later that night, a Serb commander visited two of the sites to say that the Serbs would not be coming for their weapons that night. However, two days later they did seize weapons from a site guarded by the Ukrainians, who put up no resistance. The Serbs had learned by then that it was no good trying to get weapons from any of the sites guarded by the French or the British.

The news of the weapon seizure reached me while I was in Bihac trying to stitch together a peace deal between Abdic and Dudakovic. I telephoned de Lapresle who told me that he was under great pressure from Adm. Leighton Smith to authorise NATO to attack Gulf War-style targets, including Serb ammunition bunkers and communications sites. I asked de Lapresle to delay the decision and flew immediately to Zagreb to discuss the situation with him. This was the first occasion that the Serbs had directly flouted the UN and NATO ultimatum regarding the TEZ around Sarajevo, and de Lapresle was rightly adamant that we should respond with force. I believed, however, that the UN should adopt an escalatory approach, and start by destroying individual weapons systems before moving on to wide-scale air strikes. He agreed and I departed for Sarajevo.

Although the Serbs had closed Sarajevo airport by firing at approaching aircraft, a gallant Ukrainian pilot agreed to fly us there. I believed it was essential for me to be in my own HQ if we were going to war with the Serbs. As we approached Sarajevo airport, the aircrew donned helmets and flak vests, and Goose somewhat mysteriously tucked a flak vest under my seat. Fortunately we landed without being hit.

Chaos reigned back in the Residency. Aircraft were circling, looking for targets while their pilots waited for final authorisation to strike. Going immediately to the NATO air cell I found Wg Cdr Tim Hewlett, the commander of the NATO air cell, unconcernedly watching television and drinking coffee. I asked him why no air strikes had yet taken place, and was told that Naples was still waiting for an official request from the UN in Zagreb. Calling Zagreb, I was told that I was now out of the decision-making loop, having given my consent to air strikes, and that I could play no further part in either selecting targets or bringing the NATO action to a halt. This was unacceptable and illogical.

If I had the authority to turn my half of the dual key, I replied, then I could surely turn it off. It was idiotic to separate the air and ground components of a mission in this way. It was imperative that I remained involved in the process of target selection. The situation on the ground was changing all the time and NATO had to respond to these changes. I pointed out that the main reason for the presence of NATO was to support the UN peacekeeping mission. Just as the argument was getting really heated, Brig. Roy Rattazi, the new British Chief of Staff of the UN HQ in Zagreb, intervened and immediately agreed that I could not sensibly be excluded from the decision-making process. All this had wasted valuable time.

I telephoned the NATO Air Commander in Italy, US Gen. Bear Chambers, to discuss the situation with him. He told me that he did have authorisation to strike, but that his pilots were finding it hard to identify suitable targets. The weather was closing in and it was getting dark. There was a Serb tank still within the TEZ, moving along a road to the west of Sarajevo, so I asked him if he could destroy it. He said that there was too much danger of causing collateral damage or hitting the wrong target. On his pilots' radar screens a tank on the road looked like any other vehicle.

In the end we decided to play safe: we destroyed a Serb armoured vehicle located on the edge of the TEZ on Mt Igman. I told Bear Chambers that we should now select a second target in order to show the Serbs we meant business. Reluctantly, he told me that the weather conditions over Bosnia made any further air strikes impossible and that we should wait until daylight before resuming the attacks. Within hours of the NATO air strike, I received a message in the Residency from Milovanovic saying that the Serbs were returning all their weapons back to the collecting sites and he asked me to suspend NATO air strikes while this was being done. Although we were subsequently accused of carrying out a "pin-prick" action, this air strike by NATO proved a textbook example of the precise use of force in a peacekeeping mission. The purpose of the air strike had been achieved with minimum force, and the UN was able to continue its aid convoys in Serb-held territory. Those who claimed that the UN had not used sufficient force were using war-fighting criteria as the basis for their criticism. Our mandate was to keep the peace.

Serbian tanks were not alone in violating the NATO ultimatum. On 10 August a Bosnian Army T55 tank was spotted leaving a tunnel behind the Residency. Although the Bosnian Army often fired 120mm mortars at the Serbs in the Jewish Cemetery from the grounds of the Kosevo hospital, this was the first time that we had seen one of their tanks. I therefore asked for a US AC130 aircraft that was circling Sarajevo at the time to look for it. Although the aircraft carried a sophisticated weapon system capable of putting a 105mm shell down a rabbit hole from 5,000 feet, it was unable to identify the Bosnian tank that was moving around amid the traffic and clutter of buildings in Sarajevo. Even if the aircraft had identified the target, I suspected that NATO would not have been prepared to carry out an air strike against the Bosnians, although they were in breach of their own ultimatum. Nevertheless, the sighting of the tank helped redress the perception in NATO that it was only the Serbs who violated ceasefires.

The notion that the deterioration of the military situation in Bosnia had been caused by the Serbs had recently been repeated to the press by Gen. Shalikashvili, who had until now always remained firmly on the side of common sense. He had once given me a Washington number to call if ever I needed to contact him, so I duly did so. The operator told me to wait, then I was put through to Shalikashvili's aide. He and the general were at that moment travelling in a helicopter about to land at Entebbe airport. If I was prepared to wait for five minutes the line might improve. When I called back, I told Shalikashvili I was worried by his widely reported statement that he believed there were now too many violations of the Sarajevo and Gorazde TEZs for the UN to remain credible. I told him that in the past 24 hours there had been six reported violations in each location, half by the Serbs and half by the Bosnians. None was threatening the security of either enclave. He replied that he had been misquoted and thanked me for bringing him up to date. He also asked me to try and find easy targets for NATO the next time we called for air strikes. He told me the targets that we had chosen so far could only be successfully engaged by US aircraft and this made it look as though the US was the only country prepared to carry out such actions. I agreed. The next time I called an air strike, I chose a tank in an orchard. In the event, an ageing RAF Jaguar attacked the tank – and missed.

Although the US military firmly supported the position of the UN, our State Department friends in the US Embassy next door had still not changed their position, which remained firmly against UN policy. In an attempt to repair relations, we invited them all to dinner. Things did not go well, and midway through dinner, Col. Gordon Rudd, an American Marine who worked on my staff, walked out in disgust at the propaganda being stated against the UN by his own country's official representatives in Bosnia.

Col. Rudd was one of the many people who kept me sane during the difficult times in Bosnia. He had a doctorate in international affairs, but concealed his erudition behind a direct, no-nonsense military approach. I never quite knew what he did in my HQ, but I knew he believed passionately that we were doing the right thing. He sent a stream of strongly worded signals back to the Pentagon in an effort to correct the flawed reporting from the US Embassy next door. One day, in a dusty back street in Zenica, we had overtaken him driving a stripped-down British Army Land Rover. Unfazed, he reached into an icebox as we drew alongside, and handed us a chilled can of Coca-Cola before disappearing down a side street. When I later asked him why he had been driving a British Army Land Rover, he obliquely replied that it was easier to cross the conflict line if he looked like a Brit. I still have no idea how he acquired the vehicle or where he kept it hidden.

The long hot days of August drifted slowly by in a haze of diplomatic action by the international community, and military action by the warring parties in Bosnia. On 14 August, after an 11-year-old girl had been killed by a Serb sniper in Sarajevo, Viktor Andreev managed to get both sides to sign an "anti-sniper" agreement which would be effective throughout Sarajevo. This relieved the tension in the city, and allowed the trams to run once more. We also reopened talks on the demilitarisation of Sarajevo, and this time, to my surprise, Ganic agreed that it was something he could support. I also tackled him about the firing against UN aircraft landing at Sarajevo airport, which we knew was partly coming from the Bosnians. The French battalion guarding the airport had managed to pin down one of the firing points that was in the Bosnian-held town of Butmir, close to the confrontation line. On one occasion, a French soldier had actually seen a mortar fired from Butmir, across the airfield, at aircraft waiting to unload on the dispersal apron. The Bosnian forces were evidently doing this to sustain the image of a city under siege. Ganic agreed he would stop these attacks, but he never did. He was even less co-operative when it came to stopping the fighting in Bihac. There, Fikret Abdic, having been defeated militarily, was suing for peace. Although Abdic accepted all the conditions of the Bosnian Government, Ganic refused to allow Dudakovic to sign the peace deal, as he was determined to eliminate Abdic from the political and military scene. As a result, Abdic's forces regrouped and resumed fighting.

In mid-August, the Bosnian Army shelled the Serb town of Ilijas on the outskirts of Sarajevo. Ilijas was well within the 20-kilometre exclusion zone around Sarajevo, and once again the Bosnians were in breach of the NATO ultimatum. In the attack, a school was hit and women and children killed. I told Ganic that I would have no alternative but to call in NATO air strikes if his forces carried out such an action again. He looked extremely nervous, but this, I suspect, was more the result of two bursts of heavy machine-gun fire in the street outside, rather than fear of NATO air strikes, which he probably knew would never happen. Nevertheless, the Bosnian Army stopped shelling immediately, demonstrating to me once again that the trail of blood in Bosnia always leads to the top.

Not everything was working against the peace process. On 17 August Viktor Andreev and the International Committee of the Red Cross managed to complete a massive prisoner exchange between the Serbs and the Bosnians. The negotiations, which had dragged on for months, always seemed to founder on the issue of those Bosnians who had mysteriously disappeared after being captured by the Serbs in Hadzici. Karadzic always maintained they had been killed in fighting at the start of the war, but would not produce lists until the Bosnians released their Serb prisoners of war, who were being held in inhuman conditions in a grain silo in Tarcin. On this occasion neither side allowed the issue of the missing people to interfere with the exchange and that night several busloads of tired, undernourished men crossed the Bridge of Brotherhood and Unity in both directions. It was a moving experience to see men being reunited with their families, who only hours before had few hopes of their release. When the buses carrying Muslim prisoners stopped on the Serb side of the bridge, French soldiers had to carry the wounded from the buses. Such was their hatred of the Muslims, the Serbs refused to help them.

After nearly seven months, I was beginning to find it hard living in a country which, despite its beauty and the natural good manners and hospitality of its people, was so full of hatred and inhumanity. I was becoming increasingly impatient with the protagonists in the war and with the journalists, whom I saw, for the most part, as a pack of jackals circling the decaying corpse of Bosnia.

Our meetings with the Serbs had become especially ill-tempered. Normally our meetings started at about midday when the Serb leadership had sufficiently recovered from their drinking binge of the night before. They usually looked ghastly, with bloodshot eyes and groggy heads. After about six hours of discussion, Karadzic would call for lunch. This was always the same and served while the talks continued: vegetable soup followed by lumps of lamb swimming in greasy gravy. At the end of the meal, glasses of local brandy or slivovitz were passed round. Meat was speared on knives and soup drunk directly from the bowl, giving the meal the atmosphere of a peasant feast. One particularly hot day in August, in the middle of lunch, Gvero, feeling the heat, unbuttoned his shirt and wiped his armpits with his napkin. He then proceeded to wipe his face before continuing with the meal. Only the UN party thought this unusual.

The Serbs constantly protested about their hostile treatment at the hands of the international community and demanded air strikes against the Bosnian Army for violating the NATO ultimatum. In return we demanded that they respect the Geneva agreement regarding the freedom of movement for UN convoys and stopped their attacks on civilians. Although Mladic was interested in the demilitarisation of Sarajevo – as this would release thousands of troops from the trenches around the city for deployment elsewhere – he demanded that the Bosnians would also have to demilitarise as well. We told them that the Bosnian Government would never accept this as Sarajevo was their capital city, but the Serbs persisted with this precondition. I never understood why they did so, as it would have been in their interest for the Bosnian troops to remain in Sarajevo rather than reinforce their units elsewhere.

Mladic was also making it increasingly difficult for me to move around Bosnia. Returning from a visit to a Canadian position near Visoko on 17 August, we were ambushed by a Serb paramilitary force, armed with anti-tank weapons and machine guns. I told Goose to stop, and got out of the Range Rover to demand an explanation from the Serb commander. He told us that we were illegally on Bosnian Serb territory and were under arrest. I replied that as UNPROFOR Commander I was entitled to go anywhere I wanted. Pointing at Mike Stanley, he claimed that one of his soldiers had recognised him as being a Muslim taxi driver from Visoko and that he was a spy. Mike in translating this looked furious at being called a Muslim and replied that he was as good a Serb as anyone. He then produced a photograph of his grandfather dressed in Royalist Serb uniform to prove it. While this was going on, I noticed Goose and the rest of the escort slowly moving into fire positions, and actually heard Col. Gordon Rudd, who was out for the day with us, cock his gun. The Serbs responded by taking up positions in the ditches on each side of the road. Ignoring this, I told the Serb commander that I would shortly be seeing Mladic and that I would report him for his discourtesy. The UN was in Bosnia by invitation of both sides to bring about peace. Saying this, I then launched into my well-rehearsed lecture on the principles of peacekeeping.

The commander was a sinister man with hard eyes and a scarred face who looked uneasy at the mention of Mladic. After some time, when I demanded to know if he understood what I was saying, he said rather lamely that he was not authorised to make a statement. I told him in that case, he should make a personal comment. By then his soldiers had left their positions and were listening to the debate. In the end their commander, much to their disappointment, cut the discussion short and slunk off down the road mumbling to himself. On our return to Sarajevo, Gordon Rudd turned to me and said, "Next time I come out with you, General, I am going to cock my gun *before* I leave the Residency." When I asked Goose what he would have done had it come to a fight, he replied cheerily, "Well, I was going to chuck you my rifle and call on you to lead the attack!"

At the end of the month, I took Gen. Wesley Clark, head of operations in the Pentagon, to see Mladic in Banja Luka. I was told before his arrival that he had great influence in Washington, being, like President Clinton, from Little Rock, Arkansas, and he had also been at Oxford with the President. He was clever, sharp and extremely confident. He told me that, while he understood the UN arguments against the "lift and strike" policy, he wished to deliver a message to Mladic that would leave him in no doubt what his fate would be if the Bosnian Serbs did not sign up to the Contact Group plan: he would be confronted by the military might of the US.

Before we left for Banja Luka, I warned Wes that Mladic was highly manipulative, as was generally known, and that he should not be underestimated. I told him to avoid smiling in Mladic's presence, as it did no one good to be seen fraternising with him. I told Wes that at some point a reporter would probably ambush him, and that he should have a statement prepared which he should stick to, whatever the circumstances.

Sadly for Wes, Bosnia was not the Gulf War. The rules of the game were subtler, and he turned out to be ill-equipped to deal with the brutal cunning of a man like Mladic. He started off by lecturing Mladic on the superpower status of the US, telling him that in the near future, the US would start arming the Bosnian Army. He asked what the Bosnian Serbs' reaction would be to this.

Mladic reacted angrily, launching into a violent tirade. He told Wes that if the US entered the war on behalf of the Muslims, Bosnia would cease to exist. The Serbs were a fighting nation who had never been subdued, no matter how great the enemy. Under Tito they had prepared themselves well for war against a foreign aggressor. They believed in their nation and would expend the last drop of blood fighting for it. His father and grandfather had died in war, and he had lost his only daughter to the civil war in Bosnia. The Americans were backing a fascist, fundamentalist regime. The US was militarily strong, but didn't have the stomach for war. That had been demonstrated in Vietnam. There would be war, the clock was already ticking, and the Serbs would be the victors. In the end the US would have to resort to nuclear weapons. It was naïve of Wes to think that the Serbs would surrender their lands, on which so much Serb blood had been spilled, just to save Clinton's skin. Soon, everyone would be the enemy of the Serbs and Mladic would destroy them all, from Gen. Rose to the last man.

While Mladic was hurling these statements across the table, his face became mottled and distorted with rage. His brow darkened, his eyes flashed with fury and spittle flew from his lips. He repeatedly struck the table with his fist and menacingly stabbed the air with his podgy fingers. Behind him, burly bodyguards carrying machine pistols increased the atmosphere of intimidation.

Wes seemed devastated that his carefully crafted opening statement had produced such a violent reaction and several times during the onslaught he put his head in his hands and looked down at the table. When he did this, Mladic, without stopping his tirade, would grin cheerfully at me and once slowly wound a forefinger around the little finger of his other hand in a gesture of total contempt. It was horrible to watch.

In an effort to calm him down, and showing less confidence than before, Wes said that he certainly respected the Serbs as fighting soldiers. He had closely studied the achievements of the Bosnian Serb Army, and he agreed that Mladic had not been exaggerating when he described the consequences of waging war against the Serbs. He had come to prevent war, and to remind Mladic how important it was that a path to peace be found. Time was short, and the Bosnian Serb leaders needed to come forward with proposals. The international community needed a gesture from the Serbs.

Responding to Wes's new approach, Mladic altered his own demeanour, lowering his voice. A sensible discussion then took place about the reaction of the Serbs to the proposals made by the Contact Group. As the meeting came to a close, Mladic, without obviously doing so, changed the subject and began discussing US military uniform. He said it was evident to him that the arms embargo was already being ignored by America, as he had captured some Bosnian soldiers wearing uniforms made in the US. He expressed a liking for US Army battle fatigues and particularly admired Wes's cap with its three silver stars. As he said this, he took off his own hat and gave it to Wes, who was clearly delighted to be offered some sort of olive branch. Taking Mladic's hat, he put it on. Mladic in turn put on the American's hat. Mladic announced lunch and walked with Wes to the door. As they emerged from the room, television cameras appeared. The trap had been sprung.

Wes appeared not to notice that he was being filmed and continued to laugh and joke with Mladic as we went into lunch. At the end of lunch, Mladic, who was by now in bubbling good humour, said: "Look, I have no fear of you. I disarm myself in front of you. You can have my pistol." So saying, he took his pistol from its holster and presented it to Wes. On it were engraved the words, *From General Mladic.* We were appalled.

As we left Banja Luka, one of Wes Clark's aides asked Col. Gordon Rudd, who had been present at the meeting, "Did the General do wrong?"

"Yup," replied Gordon, a man of few words, "he did wrong!"

CHAPTER SEVEN

A Return to War

For three years now, civilians have been bargaining chips in what is known as the conflict in the former Yugoslavia.

Cornelio Sommaruga,
President of the International Committee of the Red Cross, 1994

SARAJEVO HAD REMAINED RELATIVELY PEACEFUL DURING JULY AND August and throughout large areas of Bosnia the prospects for the coming harvest were good. Freedom of movement steadily improved in the Bosnian Government-held areas and that summer UN humanitarian aid convoys now represented only a small proportion of the volume of traffic moving through central Bosnia. Wheat flour could be purchased in Zenica for 1 DM per kilo, and in Sarajevo prices had dropped to almost peacetime levels. A UNHCR officer who had not been in Sarajevo since before the war, wrote of Vase Miskina street, where a terrible massacre had occurred in 1993: "Now there are open-air cafés, where one can cool off from Sarajevo's summer heat with iced soft drinks, and have an excellent pizza, followed by a banana split with fresh strawberries, all for 10 DMs."[1]

As the fighting in Bosnia died away or became limited to the odd skirmish between the warring parties, so confidence in the UN peacekeeping mission returned. The continuing success of UN measures in central Bosnia in implementing the Washington Accord, and the possibility of demilitarising Sarajevo, reflected well against the lack of any progress being achieved by the Contact Group. Not only had the Serbs rejected their plan, the Contact Group had failed to come up with any feasible "disincentives" that could be used against the Serbs.[2]

On 4 September, Assistant Secretary of State Richard Holbrooke had visited Bosnia and seen for himself the progress being made by the UN. Holbrooke was a man in a hurry. He told Andrew Ridgeway that he did not like briefings, and proceeded to question him closely on the situation in central Bosnia and on the consequences of lifting the arms embargo on the newly formed Federation. Andrew explained that the Bosnian Army was responsible for most of the ceasefire violations in south-west Bosnia, and that the lifting of the arms embargo would result in a return to war and a break-up of the Federation. At this point, one official in the US embassy in Sarajevo was overheard saying to the ambassador, Victor Jackovitch: "This is awful. It's not what we want him to hear at all!" This encouraged Andrew to continue in his current vein, as he realised that the US embassy reports being sent back to Washington were probably painting a very different picture from the one he was now describing to Holbrooke.

Holbrooke received the same message from Soubirou, who told him that despite the halting of commercial traffic into the city, the underlying trends were not all bad. The reduced incidents of violence had improved freedom of movement in many areas and had permitted the restoration of utilities in Sarajevo. The Bosnian Federation, though fragile, was working. However a new political initiative was needed, designed to bring the third party in the war, the Bosnian Serbs, back to the negotiating table. He warned Holbrooke that the increasing isolation of the Serbs was likely to result in them adopting a strategy of war. The lifting of the arms embargo, Soubirou told him, would be an unmitigated disaster for the people of Bosnia. The Serbs would launch an all-out assault on the Bosnian Army, which was not militarily capable of defending itself. If this happened there was a strong probability that the Croats might side with the Serbs, and they would divide Bosnia between themselves. In any case, the UN would be compelled to withdraw its mission and NATO, including US troops, would have to become involved in the war to defend the State of Bosnia.

Soubirou told Holbrooke that the UN undoubtedly had the ability to succeed in its peacekeeping mission if the efforts of individual members of the international community to find peace were coordinated with those of the UN. The Contact Group had not consulted with the UN before producing its plan, and this had caused a negative reaction from the Serbs. Yet it was the UN that had been forced to deal with the ensuing problems on the ground. He pointed out that even hosting Holbrooke's visit undermined the impartiality of the UN, since he had refused to visit the Serbs. Soubirou went on to explain that, in the event of the lifting of the arms embargo, the withdrawal of UNPROFOR from Bosnia would be difficult to accomplish because both sides would oppose it militarily.

Soubirou looked every inch the tough French legionnaire and when talking, his steely blue eyes would fix you with an unwavering gaze. Holbrooke was obviously impressed by his direct style of diplomacy and by the end of their meeting, he had accepted the arguments against "lift and strike". His main remit now was to find a way to get the US President off the hook on which he had been impaled by his own State Department, without losing face.

Soon afterwards, Andrei Kozyrev, the Russian Foreign Minister, confirmed that the Russians would do all that they could do to prevent the lifting of the arms embargo. He told Viktor Andreev that the Russians were delighted with the refusal of the UN to allow its mission to be hijacked by either the Bosnians or the Americans. Viktor replied that it was remarkable that, only four years after the end of the cold war, the offices of the Russians were being used to save the political reputation of an American president.

Even Jackovitch, presumably on instructions from Holbrooke, had adopted a more conciliatory tone in his dealings with the UN, although to me he still had the look of a mongoose about to attack a snake. He told me that Holbrooke had been impressed by the force of the UN argument against the lifting of the arms embargo, and that he had been particularly pleased to see the work the UN was doing on the ground in central Bosnia. Jackovitch also admitted that, on his return from Bosnia, Holbrooke had sacked most of the office in the State Department responsible for the Balkans. I wondered to myself how long it would be before Jackovitch himself departed, as he had been one of the chief architects of a flawed US policy in Bosnia that could well have resulted in America being dragged into a Vietnam-style war.

Towards the end of the discussion, he surprised me by asking if I could smuggle US Government furniture into Bosnia for the embassy. Although the building had been officially opened, it still had no furniture and he was sleeping on a camp bed. The Serbs routinely checked all cargoes arriving at Sarajevo airport to ensure that only UN humanitarian goods entered the city. I doubted if US equipment would fit into this category and told him I couldn't help.

Richard Holbrooke's visit brought great encouragement to Viktor and me as it revealed to us a new mood in Washington. Presidential elections were less than two years away, and Bill Clinton was evidently under pressure to come up with substantial results in Bosnia. He had to find alternatives to his "lift and strike" policy and had decided to compromise. The continued presence of the UN in Bosnia was now central to his thinking.

Britain, unfortunately, had not appreciated the extent of the change in US policy, and civil servants were still pushing the old US line on "lift and strike". A paper circulating at the time suggested there was a growing perception in the US that Britain was behind UNPROFOR's cautious tactics, and was the "brake on effective action to counter Bosnian Serb violations". The paper went on to say that "the slide was attributed (however unfairly) in part to the attitudes and actions of British officers who are so determined to be even-handed in theory as to be partial, i.e. to favour the Bosnian Serbs. These policies are attributed to Rose, not de Lapresle."

The insertion of parentheses suggested I was being targetted by my own side, whose logic was not hard to follow. Clinton had just invited Izetbegovic and President Tudjman to Washington to see if a way could be devised to allow the US to abandon the policy of "lift and strike" and replace it with a policy that involved a greater use of force by the UN and NATO. This would prevent any loss of face for the US as it would bring the Serbs to the negotiating table. The main obstacle to achieving this was deemed to be the present Commander of UNPROFOR. If my position could somehow be changed, then a more forceful approach to peacekeeping could be pursued. To me it was understandable that the Americans might have this perspective, but it was unacceptable that people in Britain, a country with peacekeepers on the ground, should be supporting it.

At a meeting at Chequers, soon after the distribution of this paper, John Wilsey was fortunately able to argue against allowing the UN to be pushed by either NATO or the US into following a strategy that would develop into a war with the Bosnian Serbs. Wilsey told me that the Prime Minister had revealed an instinctive understanding of the issues, and had taken a categorical stand both against a withdrawal of British troops and against the greater use of force by UNPROFOR.

Meanwhile, Akashi, de Lapresle and I were doing the rounds in Brussels and Naples to try to establish a better working relationship between UNPROFOR and NATO. On 11 September, Adm. Leighton Smith wrote a letter to de Lapresle stating that the ceasefire violations of the Bosnian Serbs were undermining the collective credibility of NATO and the UN, and suggesting that NATO should attack significant targets within the next 48 hours. In a revealing line in the letter, he told de Lapresle that "his instructions were clear". The Admiral's letter provoked surprise and shock in Zagreb and Brussels, given the low level of military activity in Bosnia that summer, as well as the apparent decision of the international community to give peace another chance. Until then, Adm. Leighton Smith had seemed to understand the careful balance that had to be maintained between the occasional need to use force and the requirements of the humanitarian mission. There were, after all, more than a million people still wholly dependent for their survival on UN aid in Bosnia, and UNHCR had warned that the coming winter would significantly increase this number. Dropping bombs on the Serbs would not help the dire humanitarian situation.

It seemed probable to de Lapresle and me that the letter had been drafted higher up the US chain of command, possibly by Joulwan, whose prime interest seemed to be the "credibility" of NATO, and that Smith had sent it against his better judgement. In a tough reply, de Lapresle restated that force should be used only in relation to a confirmed violation and that it should be proportional to the event. This accorded with his "conscience as an officer", as the troops under his command had been sent to Bosnia as peacekeepers, not combatants. He insisted that he fully supported the policies being pursued by the Commander in Bosnia, Gen. Rose. On a visit to Brussels shortly afterwards, we were consequently subjected to a charm offensive by Joulwan. I heard later that his less than sensitive handling of the UN had been noted in Washington, and he had been obliged to adopt a more conciliatory approach in what was supposed to be a supporting role.

At the meeting, I dismissed the idea that UNPROFOR had gone soft on the Serbs or was allowing a reimposition of the siege of Sarajevo as nonsense. The Serbs had not halted the delivery of aid into Sarajevo, although the recent offensives by the Bosnian Army *had* caused the Serbs to deny the passage of commercial traffic into the city. The utilities had been restored and the trams were running once again, although there were still occasional exchanges of fire. The anti-sniping agreement was generally being respected, and the prices of goods in the shops in Sarajevo were still falling. Restaurants and cafés were reopening, and life for the citizens, if not pleasant, was survivable.

Because of the success of UN mediation, people tended to forget there was still a war being fought between the two sides. To achieve this, the UN had pushed peace enforcement to the limits, despite its marginalisation by the Contact Group. Many of the NATO nations who had troops in Bosnia had warned me not to use any greater levels of force. These countries had sent peacekeepers, not combat units, to Bosnia. I ended by quoting President J. F. Kennedy: "the road to peace is a slow and painful one. You proceed step by step. There are no immediate solutions."

On 18 September, all our efforts to restore confidence in the peace process in Brussels were shattered. The Bosnian Army launched a major infantry assault and mortar bombardment against Serb positions in the eastern part of the city of Sarajevo. I had returned from Brussels two days previously, and Viktor and I had spent the earlier part of that day in Pale. There we had attempted to persuade Karadzic that the position taken by the Contact Group was not tantamount to a declaration of war against the Bosnian Serbs by the international community. We explained to him that it was unlikely the arms embargo would be lifted and that the Bosnian Serbs should persevere with the peace process. He was looking ill, his arms covered in sores. Gen. Mladic was not present, and towards the end of the meeting, Karadzic said he would like us to pass a private message to the Contact Group, which still refused to see him. Indicating a map on the wall, he told us that, although he strongly disagreed with the Contact Group map, he would be prepared to accept less than 50% of Bosnia in any territorial division of the country. Exactly where the boundaries between the two parts of the country lay would have to be the subject of further negotiation butthe Serbs would be prepared to give up claims to Sarajevo. The lines on his map showing the proposed territorial division of Bosnia looked remarkably like the original Vance–Owen proposal. He ended on an optimistic note: he was going to build a new capital city of the Republika Srpska on the other side of the Sarajevo airfield. It would be a European Hong Kong. I told him that I would pass his message on to the British Foreign Office, and duly did. He never received a reply.

We returned to Sarajevo that afternoon believing that some sort of compromise between the Serbs and the Bosnians would be possible. I was further encouraged to see a copy of an order that had been sent that morning by Milovanovic telling his forces around Sarajevo to withdraw all heavy weapons remaining in the TEZ to a distance of at least 20 kilometres from Sarajevo. I was in my office at 1730 reading this order, when an immense artillery barrage erupted in the hills nearby, to the immediate east of the Residency. The Residency building began to shake and dust drifted down from the ceiling. From the window I could see people, who seconds before had been enjoying a peaceful Sunday afternoon, seize their children and run for cover in a way they had not had to do for many months. Jamie Daniell and I jumped into the Range Rover, and with Goose driving we tore through the rapidly emptying streets to the scene of the battle. People were sheltering in doorways, looking utterly shocked by the cruel resumption of war in what, until then, had seemed to be a city gradually returning to normality. One woman holding a tiny baby was crouching behind a wall, crying helplessly, and as we passed she turned towards us, her face frozen with fear. Her eyes were devoid of hope. It seemed as though her world had come to an end.

We made for the old Turkish fort at the eastern end of Sarajevo to find out what had caused this outbreak of fighting and which side had brought the ceasefire to an end. As we approached the scene of the fighting, we saw bullets and shrapnel striking the walls of buildings and the embankment of the river.

Shortly after the signing of the Sarajevo Airport Agreement on 9 February, I had deployed a number of British Cymbeline mortar-locating radars, capable of tracking shells from the moment of firing to the point of impact. I told the Bosnians and the Serbs that this equipment allowed me to accurately identify who was responsible for breaking the ceasefire. In reality the equipment was outdated and much time had to be spent in maintenance. It was only possible to keep the radars switched on for very limited periods of time and even then the arc of observation was extremely narrow. Only when the sound of a mortar was heard could the radar equipment be switched on. A single shell could not be identified. After 45 years of the cold war, this was the best that was available from the British military inventory. Although the Jordanians and Pakistanis had better radars they could not be deployed outside central Bosnia as the Serbs would not allow UN contingents from Muslim countries to transit their territory.

When we got to the fort, we found that the British radar operators had positioned themselves in the thick of the battle. They had switched on the radars when they heard the first salvo of mortars and the traces of the shell trajectories that they had obtained so far made it clear that the Bosnian Government forces had fired the first salvos. Behind us on a hill, we could see the Bosnian infantry in the midst of a large-scale attack against the Serbs. The Serbs were responding with heavy machine-guns and rocket launchers. The noise was deafening, and the British position was being hit by fire from both sides. Fortunately, the radars were installed in two old APCs, and the operators had also taken the precaution of sandbagging their position. As I got out of the Range Rover and walked rather rapidly behind the sandbags, Jamie Daniell wandered over to the edge of the fort, supposing that the plastic sheets that had been put up to provide cover from view were in fact sandbags. He was fortunate not to be killed by a heavy burst of machine-gun fire that hit the wall of the fort just below where he was standing. He rapidly joined us in the sandbagged compound looking rather sheepish.

Inside the radar vehicles, the operators, under command of a highly experienced Royal Artillery sergeant, were calmly plotting the shells as they passed overhead. We watched the battle for about two hours, after which the fighting began to die down. The Serbs, whom we could clearly see in their trenches in the pine-covered forest behind us, had beaten off the Bosnian Army attack. By then, they were using their own artillery and mortars to fire at the Bosnian mortars, one of which had been established in the grounds of Kosevo hospital; a tactic already observed and pro-tested about my predecessor, Gen. Francis Briquemont. The Bosnians had evidently chosen this location with the intention of attracting Serb fire, in the hope that the resulting carnage would further tilt international support in their favour.

History is likely to pass judgement on the Bosnian leaders for using these inhuman tactics. "History will judge us accordingly," as Winston Churchill once said, "but do not forget that I will be one of the historians." On this occasion it was the Cymbeline mortar-locating radar troop who were the historians.

We returned to the Residency, and I immediately sent letters of protest to the military commanders of both sides threatening them with NATO air strikes if the fighting continued the next day. The next morning I received a reply from Gvero, Mladic's Deputy Army Commander, in which he stated that the Muslim forces had attacked across the line of confrontation in two places in the area of Trebevic and in the region of the villages of Faletici and Lapisnica. His estimation was that the Bosnian Army had intended to cut the two main Serb routes that ran north and south of Sarajevo. Gvero ended his signal by pointing out that the Serbs had not attempted to recover their weapons from the UN weapon-collecting sites, although they had suffered a number of casualties. In an ironic note, Gvero had ended by wondering "whether the attacks were accidental". The Bosnians did not answer my letter.

The next day limited fighting was still going on, so Viktor and I summoned a meeting with Izetbegovic, with Gen. Delic in attendance. I presented Izetbegovic with the evidence produced by the Cymbeline mortar-locating troop showing that the Bosnian Army had plainly started the fighting and had deliberately fired from positions around the hospital, the Presidency, and even close to my own HQ.

Probably for the first time in the war, the Bosnians had been caught red-handed. The evidence was incontrovertible and their actions probably constituted a war crime as well as a violation of the NATO ultimatum, as it is against the Geneva Protocol deliberately to involve civil populations in war. I reminded Izetbegovic that while the UN had to remain neutral as a mediator, it was not indifferent to the plight of the people in Bosnia who had suffered so greatly. Nevertheless, the UN could not overlook such actions by the Bosnian Army. I had to know whether it was the Bosnian Government's policy to return to war. If this were so, the UN would have no alternative but to withdraw from Bosnia. I had already been in touch with NATO regarding the use of air strikes against the Bosnian mortars and tanks. I explained to him how tragic it had been the day before to see a mother with her children desperately fleeing for cover. I showed him the Cymbeline mortar traces superimposed on a map. I would release them to the media unless he called a halt to the fighting.

Izetbegovic, who had been looking reasonably calm when I began, went white in the face. Releasing the mortar traces to the press would erode any political or moral support that he might be expecting to obtain when he went to Washington the following week. He pored over the map, asking where the Kosevo hospital was in relation to the mortar positions, while Delic sat snorting and blowing like an old walrus washed up on the beach. By the end of the meeting, Izetbegovic had been reduced to saying that his army had been responding to an increasing number of sniper attacks on their positions and that the mortars had been fired "by a drunken mortar crew". When he saw the look of incredulity that greeted this explanation, he added that he did indeed wish the UN to remain in Bosnia and that he respected our impartiality. He agreed to issue orders for an immediate cessation of fighting. Viktor Andreev then introduced the subject of the demilitarisation of Sarajevo. Clearly on the defensive, Izetbegovic said that he supported the idea in principle, but he doubted the Serbs would agree. Viktor said that he was confident they would support such a plan and added that future prospects for peace would be improved by restraint being shown by both sides. It was impossible for the UN to carry out its mission when both sides were determined on war.

There was a limit to the hard line that we could take with the Bosnian Government. They knew that the Americans were unlikely to allow NATO air power to be used against the Bosnian Army, even though it was in breach of a NATO ultimatum, nor was it likely that economic sanctions would be imposed on the Bosnians for breaking UN Security Council resolutions. In this context, UNPROFOR was not able to sustain the principle of impartiality that is so essential to any peacekeeping mission.

As a result, relations between the UN and the Bosnian Serbs became lastingly and immeasurably more difficult after the Bosnian Army offensive. On 20 September, at a meeting in Pale held to prevent the Serbs from cutting off the electricity, gas and water to Sarajevo in response to the Bosnian attack, Karadzic subjected Viktor and me to an angry diatribe. "How can you talk about the restoration of utilities to the Muslims in Sarajevo when they have just attacked us with heavy weapons in breach of the Airport Agreement and the NATO ultimatum? How can you raise such issues when they have systematically refused to talk about a cessation of hostilities, and the international community have subjected us to economic sanctions which are causing our people to live far worse than the citizens of Sarajevo? How dare you complain on behalf of a leadership that cares so little for its own people!"

Viktor, who was generally treated with a certain deference by the Bosnian Serbs, was visibly shaken by Karadzic's anger. We reiterated the fact that we had publicly condemned the actions of the Bosnian Government and that to respond to the Bosnian attack would merely strengthen the image of a city under siege and that would not help the Serbs. Karadzic eventually calmed down and said he would reconnect the Sarajevo utilities if, in return, the Bosnian Government allowed the electricity lines that passed through Bosnian territory to Banja Luka to be repaired. This seemed a reasonable trade-off. A civilian sub-committee of the UN normally dealt with the restoration of utilities in Bosnia, but their negotiations had remained, until then, in a state of deadlock.

When we presented this new proposal to Izetbegovic the next day, his attitude had changed and he seemed warm and friendly. I think he had begun to appreciate that by stopping the fighting before there were any serious civilian casualties, he had managed to contain a situation that could potentially cause great damage to the Bosnian image abroad; and that he had the UN to thank for this. He told Viktor that he wanted to develop closer relationships with the UN, and he agreed to allow the repair of the Serb electricity lines where they ran through Bosnian-controlled territory. All this promised well and Viktor and I left the meeting in happier mood. In retrospect, it was probably naive of us to think that Izetbegovic's friendly attitude towards the UN was anything other than a short-term measure designed to recover a potentially damaging situation prior to his visit to Washington. He mistakenly thought that launching the attack in Sarajevo on 18 September would produce images of war helpful to his cause. Now, faced with our evidence, he was forced to make a dramatic U-turn. The Bosnians, above all, understood the relationship between military and political action.

On 20 September, NATO unexpectedly declared it was satisfied that the TEZ around Sarajevo was clear of all heavy weapons. Although this was useful, the sudden appearance of weapons in the recent outbreak of fighting had exposed the absurdity of NATO's obsession with heavy weapon violations in the Sarajevo and Gorazde TEZs. Properly to control all the weapons in and around the TEZs would require an army of occupation in Bosnia and take years to achieve. The UN strategy had been to deter both sides from using their weapons, and the fact that the recent outbreak of fighting had been stopped so quickly by the action of the UN provided some indication that our strategy worked.

So that he could see for himself what was happening on the ground, I took Adm. Leighton Smith on a tour of the Serb part of Sarajevo on 21 September. First we stopped at a UNCHR distribution warehouse in Rajlovac, close to the conflict line, where Smith lectured the bemused Serb employees of UNHCR who were busy loading sacks of grain onto trucks. "You shoot at my aircraft," he told them, "I will stop the aid flights. If an aircraft goes down, the aid stops. My concern is for the safety of the pilots." They had not the faintest idea what he was talking about. Their job was to distribute the food to those who needed it and, being close to the confrontation line, they were often shot at while they were carrying out this task. They could not see why the pilots should be making such a big thing about being shot at.

We then moved on to a weapon-collecting site in Ilidza. It was a large abandoned factory packed with armoured vehicles, artillery guns and mortars, guarded by Ukrainian peacekeepers. The factory was close to the confrontation line and in the vicinity was stationed a Serb armoured brigade. The UN were not permitted to disable the weapons or lay mines in order to prevent weapons leaving the site, as such actions would have constituted acts of war. If the Serbs decided to take their weapons back, there was little military resistance that the UN could offer. A young Ukrainian platoon commander in charge of the site explained all this to Adm. Leighton Smith. As we departed, a number of heavily armed Serbs tried to prevent us from leaving the weapon-collecting site. The news had clearly just reached the Serb command HQ that a top NATO officer was in their midst. I told Goose to smash through the barrier that had been lowered to stop us leaving. Mercifully, no one opened fire, but Smith's expression was not a happy one as he realised he was at the mercy of Serb gunmen. It was a useful demonstration to him that in Bosnia, operating on the ground was a lot more dangerous than flying a jet in conditions of air superiority. Peacekeepers had to deal with potentially uncontrollable situations every day of their lives.

At the airport, as Smith left, a *New York Times* journalist called Roger Cohen confronted me. His reports from Sarajevo had been systematically hostile to the UN. On this occasion, with a CNN camera team filming us, he demanded to know why I had not kept my promise to keep the trams running in Sarajevo and the electricity and gas connected. Irritated by his sneering manner, I snapped back at him, "If you haven't got a sensible question to ask, please don't ask it!" He repeated his question. I angrily asked him where he had been all summer when the citizens of Sarajevo had been able to live in conditions of near normality. This was made possible by the efforts and sacrifices of thousands of UN men and women working in Bosnia for peace and I found his inference that they had achieved nothing offensive. It was not the first time I had lost my temper with a journalist, but I had never done so publicly. I was tired. I had been in Bosnia for eight months and much of what we had achieved in Sarajevo during the first months of the year had been undermined in the past few weeks. Fortunately, I was due to return to England the next day for a break that included a meeting with Douglas Hurd, the Foreign Secretary.

Before departing I went to see Izetbegovic with Sergio de Mello and Soubirou to explain our latest plans for the demilitarisation of Sarajevo. To our surprise, Izetbegovic agreed with our proposals: a greater UNPROFOR presence on the conflict line, a regrouping of the two opposing forces and a subsequent withdrawal by both armies into barracks. It was probable the US Administration had put pressure on Izetbegovic to come up with some concrete proposals, following the débâcle of the Bosnian Serb rejection of the Contact Group's plan. Only two months earlier, the Bosnian Government had refused to consider the demilitarisation of Sarajevo on the grounds that this was incompatible with their sovereign rights. This was also to be Soubirou's last meeting with Izetbegovic, who made a pretty speech thanking him for all he had done in Sarajevo during his time there. He presented Soubirou with a replica of a fourteenth-century Bosnian manuscript in a beautiful mahogany case.

As the next most senior officer in Bosnia, Soubirou assumed command of UNPROFOR in my absence. It had been Soubirou who had so crucially briefed Holbrooke when I had been away previously and I had absolute confidence in him. Before leaving for England, we had discussed the plan to increase UNPROFOR's presence on the line of conflict around Sarajevo. It had already been agreed with Milovanovic that a new observation post should be established north-west of Kosevo hospital where the fighting on 18 September had been most intense. The Bosnian Army had attempted to seize a vital hill feature from the Serbs, and Soubirou was anxious to establish the UN on this feature in order to prevent a reoccurrence of the fighting. All this seemed very straightforward and, having agreed the plan, I departed for England in an optimistic frame of mind.

As we landed at Boscombe Down in Wiltshire, Jamie Daniell's bleeper went off, and a call was put through to my new Chief of Staff in Sarajevo, Brig. Brinkman, who told us an incident had occurred between a French unit and the Bosnian Serbs. The Serbs had opened fire on the French unit as it moved on to the hill feature north-west of Kosevo hospital and a soldier had been injured. De Lapresle's son commanded the unit involved, and the Force Commander was naturally taking a close interest in what was happening! He had already decided that UNPROFOR would have to respond with air strikes. I drove at high speed the few miles from the airfield to my home in Tidworth and, rushing past Angela with only a brief explanation, immediately telephoned Sarajevo.

Again, chaos had erupted in the HQ. Soubirou agreed with de Lapresle that NATO should attack ammunition bunkers near Pale. These bunkers had always been on the NATO target list, but de Lapresle and I had, until now, agreed that any attack on

(*Left to right*) Me, Sergio Vieiro de Mello, UN Political Adviser to UNPROFOR, and Lt-Col. Simon Shadbolt, my Military Assistant, at the Geneva Peace Conference (6 June 1994). I am typing the peace deal on my laptop. Three days after the deal was signed by Gen. Ganic, the Bosnian Army launched an attack against the Serbs in the Ozren mountains.

(*Left to right*) Yasushi Akashi, Lord Owen and Thorvald Stoltenberg, co-chairmen of the International Conference for the former Yugoslavia, discussing the way ahead at the Geneva Peace Conference on 7 June 1994.

The entire Bosnian Serb leadership with the UN negotiating team at the Geneva Peace Conference, 8 June 1994. (*Left to right*) Nikola Koljevic, Ratko Mladic, Momcilo Krajisnik, Radovan Karadzic (*seated*), Aleksa Buha, Yasushi Akashi (*seated*), Sergio de Mello and me.

President Izetbegovic at a performance of Mozart's *Requiem* conducted by Zubin Mehta in the ruins of the National Library in the old part of Sarajevo on 19 June 1994.

When Croatian President Franjo Tudjman (*left*) visited Mostar in July 1994, he was booed by the Muslims and accused of being a war criminal. They held him responsible for the destruction of their city.

A temporary bridge at Mostar. Croat forces had destroyed the original bridge, which had been one of the finest architectural monuments in the former Yugoslavia (July 1994).

Lt-Col David Santa Olalla, Commanding Officer of the Duke of Wellington's Regiment, being interviewed outside Gorazde by Kurt Schork of Reuters. From the minute they arrived, the Dukes made it clear they were not going to be obstructed in the course of their mission to help the people of Gorazde and thereby advance the cause of peace (July 1994).

Lt-Col. Jamie Daniell took over from Simon Shadbolt as my Military Assistant. Jamie acted as Jimmy Carter's aide when the former US President arrived in Sarajevo.

Angela and me near the bridge across the river Drina at Visegrad, made famous by Ivo Andric's *The Bridge on the Drina*. Angela had come to Bosnia under the auspices of the UNHCR to deliver incubators to the hospitals at Pale and Gorazde (July 1994).

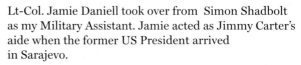

Whenever there was sniping at the trams, we always rode with the people as a demonstration of solidarity. On 14 August, after an 11-year-old girl was killed by a Serb sniper in Sarajevo, Viktor Andreev and I managed to negotiate an anti-sniper agreement between the Serbs and the Bosnians for Sarajevo. This allowed the trams to run again and the atmosphere in the city immediately improved.

Here I am being reassured by Nicholas Soames that I had the full support of the British Government in trying to prevent the UN from being dragged into a war in Bosnia (28 September 1994).

Brig.-Gen. André Soubirou, the French commander of Sector Sarajevo, was a tough uncompromising legionnaire who did much to bring peace to Sarajevo. He returned in 1995 to command the UN Rapid Reaction Force. (*S. Gubelic*)

Gen. Wes Clark (*right*), then Head of Operations in the Pentagon, with Gen. Ratko Mladic during a visit to the Serb HQ in Banja Luka on 27 August 1994. He was taken in by Mladic's false bonhomie and committed the public relations error of swapping hats with him. The *Washington Post* subsequently quoted one US official as saying, "It's like cavorting with Hermann Goering".

Goose and Capt. Jeremy Bagshaw, my aide-de-camp, relax at the back of a Russian Antonov *en route* to Sarajevo. The moment of relaxation was short-lived as, on approaching the airport, the plane's undercarriage failed to operate.

Adm. Leighton-Smith (*second from left*), Commander-in-Chief Allied Forces Southern Europe, who succeeded Adm. Mike Boorda, is greeted by myself, Gen. de Lapresle and Brig.-Gen. Hervé Gobillard, French Commander of Sector Sarajevo, who had recently taken over from Soubirou.

I visit Brig.-Gen. Ridderstadt, Commander Sector North West, at Tuzla. Ridderstadt was a Swedish part-time officer who, in civilian life, was chairman of a newspapers group in Sweden. (*ffotoworks*)

Former US President Jimmy Carter being briefed over breakfast by Viktor Andreev. Carter managed to persuade Karadzic to accept an immediate ceasefire, which lasted four months, as well as to restart peace negotiations on the basis of the Contact Group plan. His arrival undoubtedly gave new momentum to the peace process (20 December 1994).

Bosnian Army troops crossing the Mt Igman demilitarised zone (DMZ) on 8 October, 1994, in violation of the NATO ultimatum of August 1993. (*French Army*)

The Malay Battalion near Konjic was well-equipped and their soldiers did their best to cope with the winter conditions.

I look on as Yasushi Akashi attempts to persuade President Izetbegovic to agree to a four-month cessation of hostilities. On this occasion, the UN argument prevailed (23 December 1994).

Boutros Boutros-Ghali, Secretary-General of the UN (1992-6). His refusal to allow war-fighting goals to be pursued by NATO in Bosnia did not endear him to the Americans. *(AP by Enric F. Marti Slug)*

UN patrol halted by a makeshift barricade on the roadside above the Jewish Cemetery in Sarajevo (late Winter 1994).

(*Left to right*) Mrs Karadzic, Radovan Karadzic, me, Yasushi Akashi, Nikola Koljevic, a Serb officer and Gen. Ratko Mladic, to mark the occasion of the 31 December 1994 ceasefire agreement.

The media is keen to know if the peace deal will hold. I reply that it will, if the warring parties want it to. (*Pete James/Royal Navy*)

In the Bihac safe area I meet Gen. Dudakovic, the Bosnian 5th Corps commander, on 28 December 1994. Dudakovic's idea of strategy was to attack on all fronts, retreat into the enclave amid harrowing scenes of suffering and then call on the UN and NATO for help.

Fikret Abdic (*centre*), the renegade Muslim commander, finally agreed to a peace deal with the Bosnians, but Ganic, who had asked me to negotiate the deal, changed his mind and the Bosnian Army continued its attacks. Here I am in talks with Abdic, with a Bangladeshi UNMO in attendance (28 December 1994).

Maj. Mike Stanley, UN liaison officer, and Maj. Indic, Mladic's liaison officer, *en route* by air from Gornji Vakuf to Tuzla on 3 January 1995. Stanley, an officer in the Parachute Regiment, was of Serb origin and had previously served in Bosnia.

On our way to a meeting of the Joint Commission in Gornji Vakuf on 3 January 1995, the Range Rover left the road and rolled down the mountainside. No one was injured and even the mouse that lived in the vehicle survived.

them would constitute a disproportionate use of force. I reached de Lapresle in Zagreb and reminded him that there was a Serb T55 tank still within the TEZ, and suggested we should go for this target before attacking the ammunition bunkers. It was the same T55 tank that Goose and I had captured shortly before the NATO ultimatum had expired in February. The French had subsequently allowed the tank to be taken out of a UN weapon-collecting site by the Serbs for servicing, but it had never been returned. It had recently been spotted by a UN patrol hidden in an orchard near the village of Dobrosevic, about five kilometres from Sarajevo. De Lapresle agreed that it would be better to engage this tank first before taking on the ammunition bunkers.

John Wilsey then called me from his HQ near Wilton asking why I had ordered the RAF Jaguar aircraft deployed in Italy to attack the ammunition bunkers. As far as he understood, no authority had yet been obtained from New York for an escalation in the use of force. I explained that I had done no such thing and that I had already designated an alternative target to NATO. It appeared NATO had not yet called off the attack on the ammunition bunkers. Using RAF communications to the Jaguar aircraft, at that time *en route* to Pale from Italy, John briefed the pilots of the aircraft to call off their attack on the bunkers and told them to await new instructions. At the same time, I received a call from Lt-Gen. Rupert Smith in the Ministry of Defence in London. He had just received a call from a highly excited Robert Fox, defence correspondent of the *Daily Telegraph*, who told him that he had just witnessed two RAF Jaguars attacking targets near Pale and that smoke was rising from the area. British Ministers wanted to know what was going on.

By now every level of command, from the tactical to the strategic, had become involved, each with a different interpretation of events and each contributing to the confusion. For centuries, armies had tried to avoid this sort of muddle, but it was clear to me that the advent of modern communications had made the problem worse rather than better. I set about re-establishing order – using a domestic telephone from Tidworth!

At this point another complication arose. Adm. Leighton Smith had ordered that no warning be given to the Serbs prior to the attack, in order to avoid giving them time to alert their air defence system, putting the NATO pilots at greater risk. I told my Chief of Staff in Sarajevo, Brinkman, to ignore the order, as the tank was close to a village and there would very possibly be people in the vicinity. In the event, the Serbs – who were given 20 minutes notice of the air strike – only just had time to rescue some children playing around the tank before the Jaguars arrived. They might have saved themselves the trouble, as the bombs missed their target, although a nearby pigsty received a direct hit. The reason given by NATO was that the sun was shining in the pilots' eyes and they had not been able to see the tank. The UN was beginning to be rather sceptical about the capabilities of NATO aircraft. They could not engage our targets in cloud, in rain, at night, or with the sun in their eyes. They were beginning to sound very like British Rail.

As I struggled to unscramble the mess from my home in England, I could see polo players practising on a field below the house. The contrast between the two worlds could scarcely have been greater. I made a mental note to send a brisk message to Robert Fox who, from Sarajevo, had probably mistaken a forest fire in Pale for a NATO bombing raid.

I was due to meet Douglas Hurd at RAF Brize Norton where he had arrived from Germany. He had summoned a team from the Foreign Office to be present in the Station Commander's office for a decisive discussion about the future role of Britain in the UN peacekeeping mission in Bosnia. Pauline Neville-Jones, the political director in the Foreign Office, would lead the discussion. She was a firm supporter of the NATO alliance and evidently believed the UN mission should use a greater level of force against the Serbs. This would get President Clinton off the hook of "lift and strike" and be good for our relations with the US. Glynne Evans, head of the UN Department in the Foreign Office, fiercely opposed her view, but as Pauline Neville-Jones was her boss, I was fearful Pauline's voice would prevail. By good fortune, Kofi Annan, head of the UN peacekeeping department in New York, was on a visit to England and he also planned to be present at the meeting, which might help the balance of the debate.

At RAF Brize Norton, Douglas Hurd and Kofi Annan were waiting for me and Glynne Evans, who had accompanied me on the journey, but Pauline Neville-Jones was apparently stuck in heavy, Friday evening traffic coming out of London. The Foreign Secretary was in cheerful mood as he was looking forward to a rare weekend at home in Oxfordshire. As we waited for Pauline Neville-Jones to arrive, he strode purposefully up and down the room flicking the keys of his red dispatch box up into the air behind his back and catching them in front. He appeared to be practising some new bowling technique for his next appearance in his village cricket team. His young private secretary, an extremely bright young man on loan from the Overseas Development Agency, looked on mesmerised.

After waiting nearly half an hour, Douglas Hurd announced with an impatient wave of his hand that the meeting would have to start without Pauline Neville-Jones. He opened the discussion by asking Glynne Evans to brief him on the current prospects for peace in Bosnia and what she thought the UN could do to put pressure on the Serbs to agree to the Contact Group plan and thereby help our relations with the US. Glynne Evans was entirely at ease as she carefully explained the strategy of the UN and the limitations of peacekeeping. He listened intently, tossing his keys into the air as if to emphasise some point in his own mind.

When he asked me about the current situation and what the future held for the UN, I told him that much of the bad news concerning the situation in Bosnia was Bosnian Government propaganda, and that this was often being repeated by the US State Department. Richard Holbrooke, I told him, had now become aware of the progress being made by the UN, as well as of the danger for the US and ultimately for the Alliance of continuing to support the war option. I then informed the Foreign Secretary that Izetbegovic no longer intended to demand an immediate lifting of the arms embargo at his forthcoming meeting in Washington, although he would continue to use the issue to maintain support in the US Congress. A major obstacle to bringing US policy into line with that of the Europeans had now been removed.

Douglas Hurd was already aware of much of what we told him, although he had not heard that the Bosnians had changed their position on lifting the arms embargo. His advice had been that it *would* be lifted and that we would have to live with the consequences. I told him that the logic against the lifting of the embargo was too strong for this to happen, once again rehearsing the argument I had successfully used with Izetbegovic and Redman. Both now accepted that if the arms embargo were lifted, and the UN departed, Bosnia would be overrun by the Serbs. The Bosnian Army was too weak to defend itself. In addition, withdrawing the UN would be exceptionally difficult as either the Bosnians or Serbs might try to prevent them leaving. The country would unquestionably be plunged into war again and the Bosnians would lose, unless US troops were deployed on the ground to bolster the Bosnian Army. Nor was it feasible to adopt what the UN had begun to call the "lift, stay and pray" option. Several times Kofi Annan intervened, quietly and authoritatively, to reinforce the point that the UN would certainly withdraw from Bosnia if the arms embargo was lifted. He also confirmed that the UN could not use higher levels of force than it was currently using. To do so would be to make the mistakes of the previous year when a peacekeeping force in Somalia had become disastrously involved in a war.

Although Douglas Hurd restated the case for a greater use of force by the UN in its mission, I think he did so in order to hear our counter-arguments rather than because he believed in it. After an hour, it was evident that the arguements of Kofi Annan, Glynne Evans and myself had prevailed. Britain would continue to support the UN's approach to the peacekeeping mission in Bosnia. This might create further difficulties for the Foreign Secretary in his relationship with the US, but I knew from past experience that Douglas Hurd had the moral courage and the intellectual ability to face up to the Americans. "Well," he said, throwing his keys into the air for the last time, "we will just have to muddle on!" We had heard nothing from Pauline Neville-Jones.

Douglas Hurd went home by car, allowing us to use his ministerial jet to go to RAF Northolt on the outskirts of London. Glynne Evans had invited us all to dinner in Pimlico that evening, and this seemed the best way of getting to the restaurant on time. As we boarded the aircraft, a car roared up with a screech of tyres and an angry Pauline Neville-Jones got out. "Welcome!" I said cheerily. "In 10 minutes time you'll be back where you were four hours ago!" She was not amused. I still believe that if Pauline had attended the meeting, she may well have swung the argument the other way. As it was, the UN was able to buy more time for its peacekeeping mission in Bosnia.

In Bosnia, the air strikes had stirred up a hornets' nest and the Serb reaction was predictable. Mladic had issued a threat to all UN aircraft using Sarajevo airport, saying that incoming traffic would be treated as hostile. He had also sent a long, rambling letter to de Lapresle accusing him of having destroyed, by his "insensible actions, everything that both the inhabitants and their ancestors in the village of Dobrosevici created during their lives" – namely one pigsty! He ended the letter by charging de Lapresle with being responsible for the sort of reprisals that the Germans had carried out in the Balkans in 1941, in which the Nazis and Croats had murdered hundreds of thousands of Serbs.

On 22 September Karadzic had told Sergio de Mello that the partiality of the UN was no longer tolerable, and he claimed, with some justification, that it was only UNPROFOR's presence in Sarajevo that had prevented the capture of the city by his troops. He did agree that the demilitarisation of Sarajevo was an attractive idea that should be pursued, although this was dependent upon the Muslims agreeing to a total cessation of hostilities in Bosnia. He had also agreed to the restoration of the gas supply to Sarajevo, but linked this to a release of Serb "ethnic hostages" held by the Muslims.

By the end of the month the gas supply had been restored to its normal pressure and repairs had been carried out to a number of electricity lines destroyed in the recent fighting. The UNHCR programme of aid delivery had been restarted and, once again, it seemed as if peace was being given a chance. By using force in a proportionate way, and by not attacking the targets proposed by Adm. Leighton Smith, the route to a peaceful resolution of the war in Bosnia still lay open. As if to emphasise a return to the routine of the peace process, the Security Council in New York extended the UN mandate in Bosnia for another six months.

Relations with the Bosnian Government during this time had deteriorated, and Izetbegovic appeared more distant and hostile than ever before, even during the Gorazde crisis. In retrospect it was clear that the start of this decline dated from my threat to use force against him on 18 September. On 20 September, a friendly journalist in Sarajevo had privately warned me that the Bosnian Government was directing a concerted campaign of disinformation against me, and that one of the mainsprings of this campaign was a senior British UN press spokesman in Zagreb. Subsequently Robert Fox and Patrick Bishop, writing in the *Daily Telegraph*, commented on the carping that was coming from within the UN organisation by UNPROFOR officials, who regularly but anonymously let journalists know their misgivings about my style and approach. More dangerous, they added, was the bad-mouthing from across the Atlantic, because of the encouragement that it gave to the Bosnian Muslims to believe they could win on the battlefield given the support of NATO bombing.

Although much of the criticism came from the absurd logic that I was being so impartial as a peacekeeper that I was being partial to the Serbs, *any* accusation of being one-sided was dangerous to me as UNPROFOR Commander. It was my job as a peacekeeper to create the conditions necessary for peace, and this meant I had to publicly identify whoever was working against peace, even if, as in this instance, it meant denouncing the Bosnian Government.

At one point, the *Daily Telegraph* published an article by Robert Fox saying that I was about to be relieved of my command early and replaced by Lt-Gen. Rupert

Smith. As Robert is a good friend, I tracked him down to a hotel in Zagreb and telephoned him at 0200 hours demanding to know why he had published this article which simply was not true. He nervously told me that such a move was being openly talked about in the MOD. I replied to him that I had told the people of Bosnia the day after my arrival that I would be with them for a year, and that was what would happen.

The *New York Times* had also published an article on 25 September stating that I was about to be sacked, presumably in the hope that the statement would become a self-fulfilling prophecy. Two days later, John Wilsey told me that concerns were being expressed in high places in the MOD that I was looking extremely tired, the implica- tion presumably being that I was cracking under the pressure of the job. Actually I had never felt better. I had returned on 7 September from a week's leave in Fitzroy MacLean's house in Korcula on the Dalmatian coast. As far as I was concerned, the peace process was still alive and events on the ground would prove once again that the UN approach was correct.

As if to give the lie to my critics, Izetbegovic finally stated on 27 September that he would defer his request for a lifting of the arms embargo. Douglas Hurd had replied in a speech to the UN that he welcomed this decision, "as now was not the moment to lift the embargo". He did not add, "I also owe Michael Rose a fiver!" The fighting throughout Bosnia had subsided. There was still some movement around Bihac, but this seemed more the result of the aftermath of the destruction of Abdic's renegade Muslim forces than the unwinding of the peace process. Even more encouraging was the news that the requirement for UNHCR aid in Bosnia had fallen from 45,000 metric tons in January 1994 to 25,000 metric tons, almost all of which was reaching its destination.

During a visit, the Minister for the Armed Forces, Nicholas Soames, expressed concern that I might be affected by the adverse comment about me in the media. He went out of his way to tell me I had the full support of the British Government. He did warn me to watch my back, however, saying that there were people at home who were jealous of my position on the international stage. I told him that John Wilsey was keeping me up to date with what was being said in the corridors of the MOD. I quoted a statement made recently by a British admiral, who had said that I had become "too proprietorial regarding the peace process", and that I had "gone soft on the Serbs". I sent a message back saying that Mladic, whose positions I had repeatedly bombed, did not agree.

On our tour of Sarajevo, Soames, once a soldier himself, proved to be a star attraction. He spent much of his time talking and laughing with the local people in the streets and saw for himself how far the UN's faith in the peace process was justi- fied by the improved situation in Bosnia. At one point, as we walked in the sunshine, I told him that he was only a couple of hundred yards from the nearest Serb position on the hillside above and that a sniper would almost certainly have him in his sights. "Oh what fun," he exclaimed. Climbing on to a low wall, he began taking photographs of them. I kept my fingers crossed that the anti-sniper agreement would hold.

There were, however, more important things to do than act as tour guide. On

3 October, a crucially important meeting with William Perry, the US Defence Secretary, had taken place in Split, at which the UN finally convinced him that it could not be used for war-fighting purposes. Following the air strike against the Serb T55 tank, William Perry was quoted as saying: "When we go in, I want to go in with compelling force. Force not just necessary, or proportionate to the act at stake, but enough to make it clear that there is a heavy price to pay for violating the rules that NATO has established."

From this statement it sounded as though the US Administration was drifting back into the philosophy of bombing the Serbs into submission. Watching the diminutive Akashi standing in front of the giant US Air Force One, greeting the many staff officers and advisers who had accompanied Perry, I was reminded of David before Goliath. On the UN side, a small team had been assembled to support Akashi. I brought with me Col. Clifton Shroeder, a US Marines officer who had taken over from Col. Gordon Rudd as US liaison officer in Sarajevo the previous month. He had been travelling down to Split *en route* to America and I felt it only right that he should meet his Secretary of State for Defence.

Perry opened the meeting by acknowledging that there was significant disagreement between NATO and UNPROFOR and that the purpose of his visit was to improve communications between the two organisations. He reminded us that NATO was not acting as an independent force but was there to help the UN. He had not been in favour of the lifting of the arms embargo and had "fought against it in the US Government". Joulwan sat sullenly beside him, glowering at the UN team opposite. He said nothing throughout the meeting.

Perry asked Akashi for UNPROFOR's tactical assessment of the situation on the ground and also for some idea of the UN's endgame plan in achieving a political solution. Akashi replied that the sense of isolation of the Bosnian Serbs, following their rejection of the Contact Group plan, made them extremely difficult to deal with. They no longer distinguished between NATO and UNPROFOR, and this compromised the UN's work on the ground. However, he was hopeful that a combination of firmness and diplomatic flexibility would allow progress by spring of the following year. He cautioned Perry that too rigid an enforcement of the exclusion zones around Gorazde and Sarajevo would have the same effect as the lifting of the arms embargo: the UN would be seen by the Serbs as combatants rather than peacekeepers.

De Lapresle followed this by insisting that setbacks in Bosnia should not obscure the very real progress achieved. The exclusion zones had transformed the tactical situations in Sarajevo and Gorazde, but it had to be recognised that the Bosnian Serbs controlled all the approaches to Sarajevo and that they could block convoys or cut off the utilities at will. There was little that the UN could do in these circumstances. They could not change their military posture and enforce their will on the Serbs. It was important that military action by NATO did not wreck the humanitarian and political effort that UNPROFOR was here to support. He spoke confidently in English, and I marvelled at how his English had improved since his arrival in Zagreb seven months before.

Nicholas Morris, head of UNHCR in the former Yugoslavia, then laid out for Perry the humanitarian requirements of the UN mission. As this was something that NATO had clearly not considered in their readiness to bomb the Serbs, Perry listened intently. Without pulling any punches, but speaking softly and courteously, Morris told him that the two key determinants in the humanitarian programme, on which over a million people depended for their daily survival, were consent of the warring parties and the security of UN personnel. Neither would be obtained by a bombing campaign. He cited as an example the consequences of the halting of the airlift into Sarajevo. Either a military force would have to open up and maintain a corridor into Sarajevo, requiring a major military deployment, or the 380,000 people of Sarajevo would have to be sustained by airdrop. At present UNHCR had only minor security concerns and were able to fulfil their mission.

For my part, I explained that my primary mission in Bosnia was to support UNHCR and that the use of force to compel the Serbs to accept the Contact Group's plan was not part of the UN mandate. Any force used had to be within UN rules of engagement. After rehearsing, once again, the arguments for continuing with the UN peacekeeping mission, I told Perry that one of the US officers working in my HQ in Sarajevo, Col. Clifton Schroeder, was with me. He had not been warned that I might call on him to speak, but the Secretary of State for Defence might like to hear an assessment of the situation in Bosnia from one of his own officers. Schroeder calmly got up and walked over to the table, as if he had been expecting such an invitation. Joulwan glared at Schroeder, as though warning him not to say anything that might be contrary to US policy. Ignoring him, Schroeder spoke brilliantly and with great passion for about five minutes, describing what the UN had achieved in Bosnia and supporting our view about how to bring peace to Bosnia. Perry listened closely, while Joulwan fidgeted in his seat.

What Joulwan did not know, perhaps, was that Schroeder was a reservist and in civilian life was a highly successful real estate developer from Denver, Colorado. When he had volunteered to join the regular forces for a year, the US Marines had sensibly decided to send him to Bosnia. During the lunch break that followed the meeting, I introduced Schroeder to Perry who, on finding that Schroeder was a civilian, discovered they had mutual friends in Washington. The consequences of the meeting in Split were significant, for I never heard Perry again ask the UN to do more than it was legitimately able to accomplish.

On the drive back to Sarajevo from Split, I saw a mouse run across the floor of the Range Rover and asked Goose whether he had ever seen it. He replied that he had seen it some weeks before but had decided to leave it alone. He left biscuits and water for it in the vehicle from time to time. In many ways, his response to that mouse was symbolic for me of the humane character of the UN mission in Bosnia. The UN provided shelter and sustenance for displaced beings but didn't attempt to influence their ultimate destination. I later heard that after the meeting in Split, Joulwan invited Sergio to give a briefing to his NATO colleagues in his HQ in Mons, at which Sergio reinforced the UN message concerning the difficulties of mixing the objectives of a humanitarian mission with those of war-fighting.

On our return to Sarajevo, we warmly welcomed Glynne Evans. We looked forward to her visits as she invariably introduced a breath of fresh air into the debate about Bosnia. She never accepted that serious damage would be done to US–UK relations through differences of opinion over Bosnia. Indeed, she felt that if we allowed the UN to cross the "Mogadishu Line" – the line that separates peacekeeping from war-fighting – then a much greater strain would be put upon the Alliance, as it would then become embroiled in a war, which would create far greater divisions.

After each visit, she always wrote an amusing report, full of common sense and insight. Her latest was entitled "Strangulation of Sarajevo?" and it began with the words: "Well no, not really". She went on to say:

> Sarajevo is now more at peace than I have ever known it. Late at night, the only sound is dogs barking. The city is filled with flickering lights. Electricity is back. Seven out of the nine water pumps have been repaired. I went out to dinner in Sarajevo; tomato salad with cream cheese followed by knuckle of veal with potatoes accompanied by wine and a lot of bread. The restaurants and cafés are thriving. After a packed Mass at the Cathedral which I attended with Gen. Rose on Sunday, we strolled through the centre of the city thronged with people. Flower-packed stalls selling eggs, vegetables, running shoes, Ray bans and Levi jeans. The trams, which rushed past, were full. A shiny new white Mercedes with a Sarajevo number plate drove past us. The Sarajevan soul is alive and kicking.

This was certainly not what the warmongers in Bosnia and elsewhere wished to hear. Nor did the press write about this resurgence of life in Sarajevo. It was more interesting to talk about the continuing strangulation of the city, or focus on outbreaks of fighting between the armies elsewhere in Bosnia. Peace has no news value and the Bosnian Government would soon give the press what they wanted.

A demilitarised zone had been established on Mt Igman in August 1993, when Bosnian Government forces were in full retreat from the Bosnian Serbs. At that time they had recently captured the summit of Mt Igman and were about to achieve the complete encirclement of Sarajevo. The potential consequences of this were extremely serious, as the fall of Sarajevo would have almost certainly resulted in the end of the Bosnian State. In desperation, Izetbegovic appealed to the world for help and, following an ultimatum from NATO to the Serbs to withdraw their forces from Mt Igman, an agreement between Mladic and Delic was negotiated on 14 August 1993 by Gen. Briquemont for all forces to be withdrawn from the region. Brig. Vere Hayes, Chief of Staff to Briquemont, had then drawn up a map, showing the boundaries of this newly formed demilitarised zone. Any troops entering the zone would be deemed to be in violation of the NATO ultimatum and would be subject to air strikes.

Since the spring of 1994 the Bosnian Army had started to move into the old Serb positions on Mt Igman, despite attempts to prevent this by the French and Swedish troops who were garrisoning the zone. It was clear the Bosnian Government had begun to assume, with good reason, that the international community would turn a blind eye to any attempt to regain its lost territories by force. Natural justice and a feeling of sympathy would allow them to breach the international agreement that prevented them from doing this, even though the Bosnian Government had originally asked for that agreement. It was inconceivable that NATO could be seen bombing the "victim State".

The difficulty facing the UN was that, as a peacekeeping force, it had to act impartially. If it sided with one of the parties to the conflict, in the perceptions of the other party it became an opponent. Since the Serbs still controlled much of the territory in Bosnia through which the aid convoys had to pass, it was clear the UN mission could not succeed without their consent. Because the UN had previously called for NATO air strikes against the Bosnian Serb Army, it already regarded the UN as partisan. If the UN allowed the Bosnian Army to retake their former positions on Mt Igman without response from NATO then this perception would be reinforced and the situation in Bosnia would move closer to war.

Since the early spring I had been striving to get the Bosnian Army to withdraw from the demilitarised zone. I reinforced the French battalion stationed on Mt Igman with a British Warrior company and then, from October to May, with a Swedish unit used to fighting in the deep snow that covers the mountain. On one or two occasions, after a warning, the Swedish troops had opened fire on newly dug Bosnian trenches, forcing the Bosnian Army to withdraw. Nevertheless, encroachments had continued.

Izetbegovic denied the presence of Bosnian Army forces in the demilitarised zone, and had once even agreed that, under the terms of the NATO ultimatum, he would have no objection to air strikes being carried out against any military forces found there. He told me he had given unequivocal orders that no Bosnian troops should enter the zone. However, when a French unit, under their new Sector Commander Gen. Hervé Gobillard, attacked a Bosnian Army position well inside the zone, Izetbegovic protested. "But I thought you said there were no Bosnian soldiers in the zone!" Gobillard replied. By the beginning of October the Bosnian Army had become much subtler, infiltrating the zone at night and, using newly acquired night-vision aids, attacking Serb positions on the far side of the zone.

At a meeting in Pale on 5 October, attended by Akashi, de Lapresle and me, Karadzic protested that these attacks had resulted in an increasing number of Serb deaths. He demanded to know why the UN always used force against the Serbs when they were in violation of a NATO ultimatum, but never used force against the Bosnians? With customary drama, he said that the situation was becoming intolerable to him. What should he say to the widows and orphans of people killed in the NATO air strikes, some of whom were civilians? As he spoke, I noticed that Mladic was silently weeping. Karadzic went on to say that it would be better if the UN departed, and left the Serb Army to finish the job they had been prevented from completing by the arrival of the UN. He ended by warning us that if another NATO air strike was threatened against his forces, he would deem himself to be at war with the UN, and his army would start shelling UNPROFOR positions. At this point Mladic miraculously cheered up and launched into one of his more crazed accounts of what he would do to anyone who threatened the Serbs.

That same day, protests to the Bosnian Government brought angry denials from Ganic, who proceeded to call on Akashi to resign for allowing ethnic cleansing to continue around Banja Luka, and for allowing the Serbs to block UN convoys and close the airport. "If a Japanese aeroplane crashes," he insisted, "then the Minister of Transport in Japan resigns."

That night, as if to demonstrate the vital role performed by the UN on the ground in Bosnia, the largest prisoner exchange of the war took place in Sarajevo. It was a cheering sight to observe the long lines of buses waiting under floodlights on either side of the Bridge of Brotherhood and Unity, as small groups of prisoners were taken across in both directions. The silhouettes of French soldiers stamping their feet to keep warm, or earnest officials of the International Red Cross checking lists of prisoners, cast ghostly shadows in the mist rising from the river. As each group of released prisoners arrived on their side of the line, people who had been waiting patiently for nearly 24 hours surged forward to see if members of their own family were among them.

On the following night (6 October), having successfully achieved the return of its missing prisoners, a Bosnian Army patrol crossed the demilitarised zone and killed 20 Serb soldiers and nurses in a medical aid and command post. Passing through the zone, the patrol caught the Serbs unawares and most of the victims had been killed in their sleeping bags. A French doctor summoned to the scene found that eight of the Serbs had been killed with knives and most of them had been finished off with a single bullet in the back of the head. Some of the bodies had been badly burned. Four of the victims were female nurses. The next afternoon an open lorry passed us in Sarajevo with a group of black-suited soldiers with black handkerchiefs knotted round their heads waving weapons in the air and shouting "Allah Akbar!" We were told they were a specially trained unit that had just had a glorious victory on Mt Igman.

Based on the evidence presented so far, this action constituted a war crime, and Akashi courageously denounced the killings as an atrocity. The Bosnian Government countered this by claiming that the action was a legitimate military operation. "Our guys just wiped them out," bragged Ganic, while Izetbegovic accused Akashi of slandering his army.

On 8 October Milovanovic predictably sent a furious signal to Brinkman and me about the raid, accusing UNPROFOR of complicity. "By mistake or merit, 37 of my soldiers unfortunately have been killed and 34 of them wounded so far . . . You did not do anything except that you meanly killed my troops. They are not guilty, you, the generals who lead them, are, and if a revenge occurs, it is clear against whom it will be taken. You promised yesterday that you would strike the Muslims on Igman by NATO aircraft today. And what happened? As usually, you . . . are not programmed for the Muslims." True indeed. The wretched man had a point, but this did not prevent me from writing a letter of protest to Karadzic that day about a sniping incident that had occurred in Sarajevo, calling on him to prosecute the perpetrators. As peacekeepers we were not the moral guardians of either side in the war. Although we could collect evidence of war crimes, the UN had not been deployed in Bosnia to act as investigating officer or judge. It is only the victorious side in a war that can do that.

At a meeting with Ganic, also on 8 October, I once again threatened him with NATO air strikes if I found his troops in the demilitarised zone. When he denied that they had been in the zone and that they had infiltrated from another direction, I showed him a photograph taken that day of a Bosnian patrol crossing through the zone. At this, he became agitated, and started waving his hands about, saying that his soldiers were in the demilitarised zone because of the incompetence of the UN. At one point Ganic said to David Harland, a highly amusing New Zealand lawyer working in Sarajevo for the UN: "You clearly have not read the August 1993 demilitarised zone agreement and do not understand it."

David replied drily: "You forget, Mr Ganic, that I was the person who drafted it and had to explain it to you in the first place!" I often wondered who, at MIT, had been responsible for giving such an incredibly inept man a doctorate in thermodynamics.

As we left Ganic's office, news came in of a shooting at a tram in Sarajevo in which one person had been killed and 12 injured. It was all very depressing and as I went to the scene of the incident, I said to the interpreter, Darko, that I felt there was really no hope for a country that was so full of barbarism and hatred. He agreed with me.

It was clear that no side wanted peace in Bosnia, and whatever we did in the UN to try and bring about a halt to the slaughter, the leaders of the warring parties, who were revealing themselves to be no better than their snipers, always undermined our efforts. I hoped that, in the end, they would pay for their crimes, but for the time being it was the UN that had to live with the consequences.

I spoke on the telephone that evening to Gen. Corvault, Chief of Staff to Adm. Leighton Smith, to clarify NATO's position regarding the use of air strikes against the Bosnian Army, which was in permanent violation of the NATO ultimatum covering the demilitarised zone on Mt Igman. All my attempts to get the Bosnian forces to leave the zone using diplomatic means had failed and although we had tried some military action against the Bosnian Army, it was impossible for the UN to control such a vast area without air support. If we did not react to the incursions by the Bosnian forces, then not only was the impartiality of the UN undermined, but also the credibility of NATO.

Corvault replied that, if the Bosnian Army fired on the UN, NATO would only be prepared to help the French soldiers defend themselves. NATO was not prepared to carry out air strikes against the Bosnian Army merely because they were in the demilitarised zone in violation of the NATO ultimatum. For the first time I was being officially told that NATO had taken sides in the war. My concern was how to prevent UNPROFOR being dragged along with it. Sadly, this failure by NATO to act impartially was to prove terminal to the UN peacekeeping mission in Bosnia.

The UN still had some teeth, and Gobillard, the French Sector Commander in Sarajevo, relished the idea of trying once again to use his ground forces to drive the

Bosnians from the zone. He was a short, fiery individual who had already earned himself the nickname "the French bulldog" among the UN soldiers. He came from a long line of soldiers who had served France since the seventeenth century, most of whom had died in combat. Gobillard seemed very willing to follow in their footsteps. Knowing this, his Canadian military assistant, David Fraser, had persuaded him to drive an armoured Toyota Land Cruiser rather than the battered French jeep in which he used to travel about Sarajevo. This proved to be a wise move. Shortly afterwards two bullets, fired by a Bosnian sniper, struck the bulletproof window of the Toyota close to Gobillard's head as he left a meeting with Fikret Prljevljak, the Muslim brigade commander of the Mt Igman region. Gobillard had been trying to persuade him to withdraw his soldiers from the demilitarised zone, and this was probably his way of rejecting this request.

Control of Mt Igman was vital to the Bosnians because it provided the only access into Sarajevo that was not controlled by the Serbs. Goods could be ferried down the mountain to the entrance of the tunnel that ran from Butmir on one side of the airport to Dobrinja on the other. A pipeline had even been built through the tunnel and both petrol and consumer goods passed through the tunnel.

Control of the tunnel was Fikret Prljevljak's responsibility and the preservation of the tunnel and its access route over Mt Igman had not only strategic importance for the State of Bosnia, it was also a source of revenue to those who controlled it. It cost a normal citizen 5,000 DM to use the tunnel and a sizeable levy was exercised on all goods. Fikret Prljevljak and his masters in the Bosnian Government would not permit the only access route down Mt Igman to be blocked by the Serbs without a fight.

The official response of the UN, whenever it was asked about the existence of the tunnel, was that it had no knowledge of it. In 1993, the UN had arranged for the opening of the airport for the passage of humanitarian goods under an agreement between the Bosnians and the Serbs. It controlled the movement of goods by air and on the surface of the airport but it had no responsibility for what happened underground. This narrow interpretation of the UN's responsibilities allowed at least one route for the passage of goods into Sarajevo to continue without interruption throughout the war.

I had wondered many times about the extent of Izetbegovic's complicity in the profiteering that arose through his army's control of the tunnel. My initial view of him was that he was a decent man, honourably pursuing the goal of creating a multi-cultural, multi-ethnic State in Bosnia. If terrible things happened within the jurisdiction of the Bosnian Government, either it was a consequence of the confusion of war or it was because he had been deliberately kept in the dark by his army and police. In retrospect, I believe he knew exactly what was going on in Bosnia, and was personally responsible for the decision to keep his forces inside the demilitarised zone on Mt Igman.

On 15 October, I had a surprisingly friendly interview with Haris Silajdzic, the Prime Minister, who told me he thought the position of the UN was becoming impossible because the Bosnians had been persuaded it was not doing its job. When I argued that this perception had been the result of the Bosnian Government's campaign against the UN, he agreed. He said that a sad consequence of the war had been the polarising of attitudes and that the country was now in the hands of fundamentalists and extremists. This was not my fault, and he did not blame me personally for adhering strictly to the UN mandate. Nevertheless, he said that he thought Akashi was finished and that neither he nor Izetbegovic would ever see him again. I told him he was mistaken and that we should all work together for a just peace. I was not against the ultimate objectives of restoring a multi-ethnic State of Bosnia, but I deplored the short-term tactics of the Bosnian Army that were under-mining peace. If the peace process finally failed, and NATO sent troops to fight a war to impose a just peace in Bosnia, I told him that I would be the first to volunteer for the mission. War was a lot easier than peacekeeping. Silajdzic smiled at this, and said that he would try and calm things down. He did not think that there would be much military movement in the coming winter months anyway. In spite of his assurance, the number of ceasefire violations around Sarajevo increased. Every night, I slept with ear defenders to block out the sounds of shelling and firing.

In the middle of the month we had a visit from a man called Treverton, a high-level member of the National Intelligence Council in Washington. Because the airport was closed he had been forced to come through the tunnel and on his arrival in my office still smelt faintly of diesel fuel. During the discussion he admitted that the US now accepted the impossibility of Bosnia ever being more than a loose federation in which the Croats and the Serbs would have some form of separate identity. He also said that Silajdzic had privately acknowledged this view. At last, it seemed, sense was prevailing in Washington, and I hoped soon to see the results of this new realism displayed by the Bosnian Government.

Meanwhile I still had to do battle with Ganic. On one occasion, he became so insulting at a meeting that I walked out, saying to him pompously that if he had any complaints about the way UNPROFOR was being run, he should put them in writing to the Secretary-General of the UN. Catching at my coat, he tried to prevent me leaving his office, but I swept past him. Out of the corner of my eye I saw one of his military advisers grinning. No soldier really likes a politician.

Fed up with all the lies and obstruction in Sarajevo, I departed for a long visit to Gorazde. After leaving Pale we drove across a high plateau on which wild horses were roaming, before plunging down through the beech forests bathed in autumn colours into the valley of the river Drina. Above us the sky was blue and farmers, oblivious to the war, were ploughing their fields with oxen, ready for the winter planting. For centuries these people had survived invasion and war by following the laws of nature. They seemed untroubled and content with their life.

Gorazde had been transformed by four months of virtual peace. The Royal Gloucestershire, Berkshire and Wiltshire Regiment had by now replaced the Duke of Wellington's Regiment. In September, the incoming Regiment had suffered a terrible blow when four soldiers were killed and five injured in two separate road accidents in which their Saxon APCs had rolled down the mountainside near Gorazde. However, they had not alowed this terrible tragedy to affect their commitment to the task of helping the people in the enclave return to a better life.

I had a long talk with Rasic, Izetbegovic's political agent, who accepted that there had to be some compromise if the war were to stop. He said it would be catastrophic for Gorazde if the UN withdrew that year, because the enclave would be taken by the Serbs. He looked a very different person from the one I had met six months before. Then he had been undernourished and trembled with exhaustion and cold. Today he was fuller in the face and spoke with calm authority.

Two days before, the Serbs across the Drina had fired on a UNHCR lorry driven by a local man, and killed him. The Serbs claimed the lorry had been carrying military supplies but it was impossible to know. The first priority of both sides was to feed their soldiers in the trenches, and we often found that UN supplies had been diverted to the front line. Unconcerned by this, a British Royal Electrical and Mechanical Engineers (REME) team was working in the middle of the road repairing the vehicle, under the same Serb guns that had attempted to destroy it only 48 hours before. A Saxon APC with a small machine-gun was their only protection, but typically the soldiers showed no concern for their own safety. They were young men daily risking their lives so that others could live, and they were apparently glad to do so. Talking to them all my frustrations and gloom immediately dispersed. When I returned that evening to their camp, situated on what was once the football field in Gorazde, I met the young battalion Chaplain who had rowed for Brasenose College, Oxford. As the next Adjutant General, I was delighted to see that the Chaplain's Department was still recruiting such fine young men.

The next day we drove to Zepa, located in a narrow valley surrounded by 6,000ft mountains. To reach it we had to drive along winding tracks through miles of oak and beech forests. At one place we passed, some foresters were roasting a sheep on a spit. They gave us some mutton in return for a British Army ration pack. They were friendly and wanted to know about the war. Their way of life in that remote place must have remained unchanged for centuries.

The Zepa enclave was garrisoned by a Ukrainian company that manned nine static checkpoints, but seemed to do little else. They had little contact with the local people and the company commander did not even know the name of the mayor. The atmosphere in the town was one of misery and the people were full of bitterness against their own government and the UN. A woman shouted out to us that she had had no milk for her baby for weeks, and the local military commander, who would barely talk to us, made no attempt to hide his hostility. Our reception in Zepa was very different to that in Gorazde, and I determined to talk to Gobillard on my return and arrange for some JCOs to be sent in to Zepa to try and improve the condition of the people living there.

On our way back through Rogatica we called in at the HQ of the infamous Capt. Zoran, whom I had met before. He was at his most tiresome and started off by trying to arrest us for taking photographs on the way to Zepa in what he described as a security zone. I ridiculed his accusation, saying that as the UNPROFOR Commander and a non-combatant, I could take any photograph I wanted. He ordered me to hand over the film, but I refused, saying that he could complain to Pale if he wished. He suddenly changed tack and said that I was no longer welcome in his HQ. I told him I had come to talk about his continual harassment of UN convoys in Rogatica, but that if he was not prepared to discuss the subject, I would raise the matter in Pale myself. Shaking him cheerily by the hand, I said that he would always be welcome in the UNPROFOR HQ in Sarajevo, and drove away.

On my return, there was a Foreign Office telegram waiting for me telling me that Mohammed Sacirbey, the Bosnian representative in the UN in New York, had delivered a protest against my demand that the Bosnian Army should withdraw from the demilitarised zone on Mt Igman. He claimed that this demand was inconsistent with UN Security Council Resolution 836, which permitted the Bosnians to retain their forces within safe areas. He had been instructed by the Vice-President Ejup Ganic to make this point, and also to explain that the Bosnians had never officially agreed to the demilitarised zone on Mt Igman. What he said was complete nonsense, and I sent a signal to Kofi Annan in New York telling him that the August 1993 agreement had in fact been signed by *both* sides. The demilitarised zone was not a safe area, and was covered by a different NATO ultimatum. Nonetheless, in Sarajevo Ganic continued to repeat these statements, presumably using the old propaganda principle that if you repeat something often enough it becomes true.

One evening we invited a friend in the Bosnian Army, Maj. Sisak, to dine with us. An intelligent man, he had previously been military assistant to Delic, and he always seemed to understand what the UN was doing for the people of Bosnia. He had recently completed a military staff course in America and was now working as a liaison officer in the US embassy next door where we rarely saw him. He regretfully declined the invitation on the grounds that he would not be able to attend unless accompanied by a US embassy official. He was no longer a free agent. Jamie Daniell commented how sad it was that the embassy of such a great country as America, founded on the principles of freedom of speech and the rights of the individual, should act in such a repressive manner.

That night, Gobillard decided to clear all the Bosnian Army troops from the demilitarised zone on Mt Igman and led the assault himself. French troops moved on to Bosnian Army positions at last light with armoured bulldozers capable of physically destroying the Bosnian trenches. The Bosnians hurled grenades down the slopes at the French and fired rockets at their vehicles, fortunately without causing serious injury. By dawn Gobillard had driven the Bosnians out of the demilitarised zone with the exception of one small, isolated position.

The next day, Gobillard calmly sat in the President's office and explained to Izetbegovic, as well as to his army commander, the details of the operation. Delic looked furious. Izetbegovic said nothing. Gobillard always led from the front and was a wonderful example to his soldiers. He was always full of fun, and I had heard that he had taken to doing parachute rolls from his desk.

The Bosnians reacted to the actions of UNPROFOR by passing a motion in their parliament calling for my dismissal and replacement by someone who was more impartial. Akashi was incensed, and when I told him that I would frame a copy of the edict and hang it on the wall of my lavatory, he gave me an inscrutable stare through his glasses and said: "No, Michael. Far too good for it. Use it first, then flush it down the loo!"

The next day, Maj. Indic, the Bosnian Serb liaison officer and one of Mladic's chief intelligence officers, asked Mike Stanley what would happen if I was assassinated by the Muslims. When I told this to Goose, for the first time during my tour he looked slightly thoughtful.

CHAPTER EIGHT

Bihac

What we are facing today in Bihac is a sad illustration of the trials inherent in trying to run a humanitarian assistance operation in the middle of a conflict.

UNHCR official, November 1994

ON 25 OCTOBER, A BRITISH LIAISON TEAM CONSISTING OF AN RAF officer, three Royal Marines and a female Muslim interpreter who had driven across the battle line on the Kupres plateau in central Bosnia had been arrested by the Serbs as spies. The liaison team had been established by Brig. Andrew Ridgeway, the Sector Commander of south-west Bosnia, to back-up the work of the UNMOs. He had asked them to make contact with the Bosnian Serbs in Kupres and, ignoring the intensive fighting taking place at the time in the area, they had unwisely decided to drive across the conflict line. Efforts by Ridgeway to secure their release had failed and Mladic, with a look of pure pleasure, announced at our next meeting in Pale that they would be tried as spies and sentenced in accordance with Serb law. As concern mounted in England about their whereabouts and ultimate fate, I asked Viktor Andreev to use his contacts to get the British prisoners released.

With the proviso that he could not use this route often, he telephoned an old friend in Moscow. It was clearly someone of considerable influence because within 24 hours the liaison team was released unharmed. Nevertheless, Ridgeway still had to sign for his team in front of the local Serb commander at a handover ceremony on the conflict line. Mladic was very angry at Viktor's intervention. The next time he caught a British spy, he said, he would shoot him without further ado. Unfortunately this incident merely added to the worsening relations between the UN and the Bosnian Serbs.

On 30 October Koljevic warned me by phone that the Muslims had launched a major attack across the demilitarised zone on Mt Igman and were advancing with a brigade-sized force on the town of Trvono. With a rising note of hysteria in his voice, he threatened that he would order a massive artillery bombardment of Sarajevo if the Bosnian Army did not halt its advance in the next two hours. Long used to the childish histrionics of each side, I was beginning to feel that a resumption of total war in Bosnia might be simpler to deal with than the confused situation the conflict had become. Nevertheless his excitement was understandable, as the loss of the town would result in all the southern parts of Serb-held territory in

Bosnia being cut off from Pale. I reassured Koljevic that I would pass his message to the Bosnian Government.

That evening I dined with Gobillard, in the PTT building, hoping that we would be able to finish our meal before the war started and Serb shells began raining down on Sarajevo. Nothing happened, however, so after dinner we sang French legionnaire songs in the bar.

It was past midnight when I returned to the Residency. Koljevic was on the telephone again. This time he had lost all control of himself and screamed at the top of his squeaky voice that as the UN had failed to halt the Muslim offensive and they were still attacking across the Trvono-Pale road, he had just given orders for the shelling of Sarajevo. "Oh, to hell with all of you," I thought to myself and slammed down the receiver. It was not the job of the UN to intervene between the two sides unless civilians were directly threatened. All we could do was try our best to persuade the leaders of the warring factions that there was a better way to resolve their differences than killing each other. Before I went to sleep I put in my earplugs, just in case Koljevic was serious. It was an unusually quiet night in Sarajevo.

The next day Viktor Andreev and I drove to Pale for a routine discussion about the provision of UN fuel to the Serbs for the winter. By the winter of 1994 the effects of UN economic sanctions against Belgrade and Pale had created a situation in which the UNHCR was having to provide the Serbs with limited amounts of fuel to enable them to keep the roads used by the UN clear of snow. The UNHCR had also been forced to supply food and medical supplies to the Serbs because of the desperate conditions brought about by sanctions. Koljevic had no memory of our conversations the night before and was seemingly suffering from an almighty hangover. I was quite used to the swings in mood of Koljevic and his colleagues in Pale, though I was never able to fathom whether they were genuinely unbalanced or merely good actors.

As their political and military reverses mounted and they became more isolated politically, the Serbs grew steadily more irrational. In spite of all the clear evidence to the contrary, they still clung grimly to the belief that they could achieve a decisive military victory against the Muslims. For the first time in the war they had lost territory which they planned to trade for peace on their terms, yet still they failed to respond to these reverses by agreeing to a political settlement. Apart from the losses they had suffered around Trvono, they were also under pressure on the Kupres plateau. Here the Croats and the Muslims, under the auspices of the Bosnian Federation, had combined forces to create an army superior in firepower to that of the Serb forces in the region.

Further to the west, following his victory over Fikret Abdic, Dudakovic had launched an offensive southward out of the Bihac enclave with the apparent objective of joining the Muslim–Croat forces on the Kupres plateau. This advance by the 5th Corps exposed a long left flank, which in the past would have been immediately exploited by the Serbs. So far, either because of shortage of fuel or ammunition, the Serbs had not been able to concentrate their armour and artillery for a counter-attack. I was certain that a Serb response would come at some point but it was already becoming evident that the Serbs could not maintain their hold forever on the large swathes of territory they had seized in 1992.

At the meeting in Pale on 31 October, Karadzic appeared to be suffering from acute depression. The sores on his face were far worse and his fingers were bleeding where he had chewed away the remnants of his fingernails. He had recently appointed himself Commander-in-Chief and had taken to making doom-laden speeches on TV, dressed bizarrely in a baggy camouflage suit. He looked out of control. Koljevic, who was to commit suicide within two years, had already been transformed from the genial Shakespearean scholar who had greeted me on my arrival in Bosnia into something of a madman. He went red in the face at the slightest provocation and shouted obscenities at us in a high-pitched voice. Jovan Zametica, Karadzic's political adviser, had taken to showing Mike Stanley the collection of pistols and machine-guns that he kept under his bed. In saner times he had taught at Marlborough College in England and had once written a perceptive paper on the history of the Balkans for the International Institute for Strategic Studies in London. More ominously, Mladic, who was in rude good health, had not been seen in Pale for some time and this usually presaged a major offensive against the Muslims.

Early in November I joined Akashi and de Lapresle for a meeting with the Contact Group. This was the first time that UNPROFOR had met them formally since they had presented their ill fated "take it or leave it" map to the warring parties. They were an odd bunch. The US ambassador Charlie Thomas looked like an elderly character out of a Tennessee Williams play, with piercing blue eyes, greying ginger hair and a mouth permanently set in a half grimace, making it difficult to see whether he was snarling or smiling. I later found out that it was the latter and that he was actually extremely amusing and utterly charming. The German ambassador Michael Steiner seemed to be torn between his conviction that NATO should bomb the Bosnian Serbs into negotiation and a desire not to upset the French. As the most experienced of the group, he had considerable influence over the others.

Zotov, the Russian member of the Contact Group, was an old-style Soviet diplomat. He said little about the situation in Bosnia, but continually stressed the importance of not upsetting his constituents in the new democratic State of Russia by allowing NATO to bomb the Serbs. Because I was receiving so much hostile attention in the American and the Bosnian press as a result of my determination that NATO should act within the constraints of peacekeeping, he kept smiling encouragingly at me as if I were some kind of fellow traveller. The position of the French and British ambassadors lay somewhere between the Russian and American positions. They understood the need to support the UN mission, yet also wanted to maintain the cohesion of the Contact Group by not alienating the Americans. By then the Contact Group had realised that its failure to consult with Akashi over its plan and map had caused irritation in UNPROFOR and the atmosphere in the room at the start of the meeting was decidedly icy.

Akashi opened by stating politely that he had been "disappointed" not to have been consulted by the Contact Group in the course of the year, most especially before they had presented their "take it or leave it" approach to the Serbs. The existence of another international body in the negotiating process that had kept the UN wholly ignorant of its plans, had made things immeasurably more difficult for the UN's negotiators during the past six months. Neither the UN nor the Contact Group had made progress and as a result both the warring parties seemed to have decided on the war option.

I was less diplomatic when Akashi invited me to rehearse the situation in Bosnia. I told the Contact Group that its policy of isolating the Serbs should not have been regarded as an end in itself. Its purpose should have been to place psychological pressure on the Serbs through a number of specific stratagems which could only work if contact were maintained. The consequence of the Contact Group's tactic of doing no more than isolate the Serbs had been to make them more intransigent than ever. Peacekeepers could not succeed in a political vacuum, since the combatants, in the absence of any progress in peace talks, resorted to arms.

I explained that the many political and military agreements that had been obtained by the UN between the Serbs and the Bosnians – which had significantly improved the well-being of the civilian population – were being widely ignored and that the Bosnian Government in particular was openly advocating war. If the military situation deteriorated any further, I would recommend to the troop-contributing nations that they should withdraw their forces from Bosnia. There was no point in them continuing to risk their lives when there was no hope of peace. Inevitably the withdrawal of the UN mission from Bosnia would bring military defeat to the Bosnian Army and an end to the State of Bosnia itself, unless NATO deployed combat troops. My statement was received in total silence. I had long since discovered that those who were critical of the UN's peacekeeping approach in Bosnia could never themselves accept that the only alternative to peace was war.

On 9 November the UN came under further attack from an unexpected quarter. At a dinner in New York, George Soros, the financier and philanthropist, was reported as having accused the peacekeepers in Bosnia of being akin to the *Kapos* or guards of a Nazi concentration camp. He accused me of being soft on the Serbs. This was altogether too much for me to accept, so – having first discounted the possibility of suing him for defamation, on the grounds that he could certainly afford better lawyers than me – I telephoned him in New York.

He was travelling in his car at the time and was somewhat embarrassed by my call. "Is that *the* General Rose from Sarajevo?" he asked.

"It is indeed, Mr Soros," I replied, "and I am telephoning to tell you that you should not be talking about the UN as you did at the journalists' dinner last night. We are both in our different ways helping the people of Bosnia and it would be better if we worked together."

In an attempt to justify his statement, he began repeating the sort of propaganda against the UN that I had heard so often put about by the Bosnian Government. I corrected some of the more absurd assertions, one of which was that UNPROFOR was giving fuel to the Bosnian Serbs in breach of the UN sanctions. I explained that we were required to do this so that the roads used by UNHCR could be cleared by the Serbs. I then asked him for the source of this information. He assured me that he was being fully briefed on the situation in Bosnia. I told Soros that he ought to come to Bosnia to see for himself what good work the UN was actually doing for the people there and that he should stop listening to propagandists. Although as peacekeepers we were unable to stop the fighting everywhere or to deliver aid successfully to every part of the country, nevertheless the aid programme during the war had sustained millions of people. The UN had saved the lives of many people and the country from destruction. The military situation was now turning against the Serbs, and in the end they would have to sue for peace. Meanwhile it was essential to the people of Bosnia that the UN mission continued to do its present job. By the end of the discussion, his tone had softened and we agreed to meet, which we duly did.

In Bosnia, the military situation itself remained relatively stable, although in Sarajevo the number of reported ceasefire violations had risen to over 3,000 a day. This figure had started to cause comment in NATO, encouraged by the media who were reporting from the Holiday Inn that the situation in Sarajevo was spiralling out of control.

The statistics for ceasefire violations were produced daily by the French Sector HQ in Sarajevo and were something of a joke. Every UN position around Sarajevo was supposed to record the number of shots and at the end of each day their individual records were added up and the total briefed to the press, with every separate round fired representing one violation. In this way, a machine-gun fired at a wedding celebration assumed all kinds of sinister overtones by the time the statistic reached NATO or the Security Council in New York. Many of the heavy explosions heard in Sarajevo were in fact digging operations by the Bosnian Army in the area of the Jewish Cemetery. My staff also suspected that the Bosnian Army deliberately fired into the air on occasion to increase the tension in and around Sarajevo and to re-establish in the minds of the people around the world the images of war which had proved so politically expedient in the past.

More serious were reports we started to receive from the French in the city that the Bosnian forces were sometimes firing on their own citizens. In one such incident a tram had been fired on from a building on the Bosnian side of the conflict line normally occupied by paramilitary police. In another incident, following a mortar attack near the Residency that killed two children, two more shells had been fired at the same location while a French Army team was investigating the first incident. These secondary shots could only have come from the Bosnian side of the firing line. On the other side of the city, on several occasions, UN and NATO aircraft at Sarajevo airport had been fired at from the Muslim-held suburb of Butmir.

The Bosnian Government always denied that their forces had ever fired on their own people or on the UN. Nor, in the circumstances of civil war in Bosnia, was it always possible for the UN to prove conclusively who had fired any particular shot, though it was sometimes possible to identify the firing point. It is also possible that the Bosnian Government never gave orders for such attacks. Nonetheless, in my view the moral distinction between Bosnian forces firing at the Serbs with the intention of provoking retaliation against civilians and the Bosnians themselves firing on their own people is a fine one. Although the largest responsibility for the slaughter of civilians during the war in Bosnia must lie overwhelmingly with the Serbs, the Croats and Bosnians are not without blame. In a civilised judicial system a one-time murderer is not acquitted because he stands in the dock beside a serial murderer.

Despite the very high level of reported violations, civilian casualties were not increasing and life in Sarajevo was able to continue in much the same way as earlier in the summer. In response to the growing international concern caused by the escalating number of violations, I simply put a stop to the daily reports of them, although we continued to brief the press on incidents that resulted in any civilian casualties. I took this decision to reduce the political pressure growing in NATO for punitive action to be taken against the Serbs. Many times I explained the rationale for this decision, but I was still accused of protecting the Serbs by hiding the truth about the military situation around Sarajevo. I had entered a world in which the truth was deemed to be a lie. There were, however, more urgent things to worry about as a serious situation was developing elsewhere in Bosnia.

The Serbs had finally halted the Bosnian Army advance on the town of Trvono to the south-east of Sarajevo. Their success in eastern Bosnia had allowed them to regroup their armoured forces in the west, where the Croat–Muslim breakout on the Kupres plateau had fizzled out. This offensive halted because the Croats, having retaken their traditional lands – from which they had been driven two years before – had suddenly withdrawn their guns and tanks, leaving the Bosnian infantry to face the Serb tanks and artillery without support. It was clearly impossible for the Bosnians without armour and artillery to capture the town of Dorni Vakuf, which was their next objective.

By the middle of November the Serbs had managed to stabilise two out of the three fronts on which they had been fighting and were consequently able to launch the long-awaited counter offensive south of Bihac at the exposed left flank of Dudakovic's 5th Corps. The Bosnian Army immediately collapsed and Dudakovic retreated back into the Bihac enclave whence he had emerged less than a month before. This time, the Serbs did not halt on their old positions but pursued the remnants of the defeated Bosnian Army headlong into the Muslim enclave. The defeat of the 5th Corps did not surprise me. It was a repeat of what had happened in Gorazde in April. Most of the officers in the former Yugoslav Army had been Serbs and they had been well educated by their Soviet masters in the art of manoeuvre, the mass application of fire and how to concentrate their forces for a decisive attack. The Bosnian Serb Army also had the means to carry this out. The Bosnians, on the other hand, had received no military training and their army was capable only of mounting limited raids against the Serbs. Delic, no military strategist, had at one point launched attacks on five different fronts at a time when his army lacked the firepower and logistics to fight properly even on one front.

Time, however, was not on the Serbian side. Despite the arms embargo, arms had been flowing into Bosnia and President Clinton's sudden decision to stop enforcing the embargo had given a new sense of urgency to the Serbs. Knowing that this decision would accelerate the rate of change in the balance of forces that had already turned against them, they were provoked into furious military action. Viktor and I had gone to Pale to try and prevent a repetition of what had happened at Gorazde, but an angry Karadzic had warned us that the Serbs would not repeat the mistake that they had made then when they had halted their advance because of NATO air strikes. This time they intended to occupy the entire enclave and destroy all remaining elements of the Bosnian Army 5th Corps, which by now probably numbered no more than a few hundred men.

Meanwhile Silajdzic, who only days before had declared that the Bosnian Army was now capable of defeating the aggressor Serb, had begun once again to call for NATO air strikes against the Serbs around Bihac. To the north of the enclave, Fikret Abdic had retaken the town of Velika Kladusa, thereby putting yet more pressure on the 5th Corps, which was in obvious danger of collapse. Only international pressure on the Serbs and action by the UN could prevent the enclave from being overrun. If this occurred, 180,000 mainly Muslim people living in Bihac were in great danger of being driven out or killed. Whatever the limitations might be in terms of the tiny UN peacekeeping force in Bihac, the Bosnians would ensure that UNPROFOR would be blamed for such a catastrophe. They would never admit that the loss of Bihac was a direct consequence of their own policies and the failure of their army.

The UN Bangladeshi troops garrisoning the enclave were hopelessly ill-equipped to deal with the situation. Only recently arrived in Bosnia, much of their equipment had not reached them from Zagreb before they had been cut off by the fighting. During the night the temperature dropped to below freezing and it had already snowed. Because they were Muslims, Mladic considered them to be as much enemies of the Serbs as the Bosnians. On more than one occasion he protested to me that the Bangladeshi observation posts were directing Muslim artillery fire against his forces.

To reinforce the Bangladeshis I had strengthened the UN command structure in the enclave by establishing a small sector HQ in Bihac drawn from my own HQ under command of a Canadian, Col. "Chuck" Lemieux. I had also dispatched a team of JCOs to the enclave. This reinforcement allowed their commanding officer, Col. Salim, to concentrate on his principal task of commanding his battalion, rather than having to deal with a situation that was becoming increasingly mired by propaganda, much of it directed against the Bangladeshis.

The Bangladeshis were cheerful soldiers from the Bay of Bengal. They never complained about the conditions, which were probably worse than elsewhere in Bosnia. By the end of November they had been reduced to draining the oil from their vehicles in order to provide fuel for their stoves. What concerned them more than physical hardship were the rumours circulating in the press about their state of preparedness for such a mission, suggesting that the Bangladeshis had only one sleeping bag and one rifle for every two soldiers. Many times Salim had explained that they had brought with them rifles and sleeping bags for those who were likely to be deployed in the field. The remainder of the Bangladeshi troops slept in their own beds in base camps using sheets, pillows and blankets. The soldiers who did not have rifles manned machine-guns, carried pistols or were equipped with other kinds of personal weapon. I doubt if the weapon-holding statistics for a British battalion would have been very different.

It was not just the outbreak of fighting in Bihac that caused me concern. In the autumn, the Serbs had begun to deploy medium and high-level air defence systems in Bosnia, something that threatened to alter radically the balance of forces between NATO and the Serbs . Until then the Serbs had relied on SA7 low-level ground-to-air missiles for their air defence (indeed it was one of these that had shot down the Sea Harrier over Gorazde in April). However on 4 November the Serbs fired two SA2 high-level missiles from mobile launchers into the enclave of Bihac. They did not cause much damage, but revealed an ability to attack NATO aircraft patrolling the skies of Bosnia at high altitude.

Hitherto, NATO had been willing to carry out combat air patrols using only a pair of aircraft at a time, thereby allowing a round-the-clock presence over Bosnia. The appearance of SA6 medium-altitude and SA2 high-altitude missiles, backed by sophisticated target-acquisition radars, now made it too dangerous for aircraft to fly in pairs.

NATO therefore decided that combat air patrols would now consist of larger formations of aircraft, so as to provide the necessary electronic suppression and air-to-ground defence measures against the Serb threat. Given the increased cost of flying these bigger formations and the limited resources available to NATO, from November 1994 it was no longer possible for NATO to provide continuous air support for the UN.

Another consequence of the new Serb equipment was a demand from Adm. Leighton Smith in Naples to allow strategic strikes aimed at destroying the entire Serb air defence system. This would have required a lengthy air campaign similar to the one carried out in the Gulf War against Iraq, prior to the launching of the ground offensive. This operation had necessitated thousands of sorties of heavy bombers and lasted for weeks. This sort of air campaign was wholly incompatible with a UN peacekeeping mission. When strategic air strikes did finally take place in August 1995, the UN mission had effectively been brought to an end already.

Mladic was quick to take advantage of the reduction in NATO air cover over Bosnia. On 19 November Serb aircraft, operating from Udbina in the Serb-held part of Croatia, bombed targets near Cazin in the Bihac enclave. The flying time from Udbina to Cazin was only a few minutes and Mladic knew it would be impossible for NATO aircraft flying from bases in Italy to intercept the Serb planes. He also knew that the current rules of engagement prevented NATO from taking on targets in Croatia.

The concept of technological asymmetry – the use of low-tech equipment in a politically constrained battlefield to defeat a technologically superior enemy – had long ago been demonstrated successfully by the Vietnamese and the Afghans against the world's superpowers, but no one in NATO seemed to have noticed. It all seemed a very long way from the NATO war games that I had played at the Staff College where computer algorithms always ensured that NATO was the winner in every air campaign.

The Serb attack on Cazin, which killed many civilians, brought immediate calls for action from the Bosnian Government and the international community. When this happened I phoned de Lapresle who told me he was already under great pressure to respond with air strikes against the entire Bosnian Serb air defence system. Even Brig. Roy Ratazzi, his British Chief of Staff, told me that he felt it would now be difficult to resist this pressure. War seemed imminent. I decided to fly to Zagreb where de Lapresle met me with the words, "So, we have finally crossed the Mogadishu Line", meaning that the UN and the Bosnian Serbs were about to go to war with each other. I suggested that if the air strikes were limited to attacks against Udbina airfield in Croatia, then there was a possibility that we might not actually cross the "Mogadishu Line" but could remain standing upon it. It was a very fine line, however.

De Lapresle told me he had been extremely unhappy with the decisions being taken and had only given authority for NATO to bomb Udbina when he heard that the Russians had supported NATO air strikes during the debate in the UN, and that Boutros-Ghali and Akashi had accepted the inevitability of such action. For once at least the UN and NATO were in agreement.

I told him I believed this change of position by the UN in New York meant that we were at a decisive moment, for it would be impossible for UNPROFOR to remain in Bosnia in the middle of a war in which the West was involved. Since the Contact Group had presented its ill-fated plan in July there had been a total absence of any political movement by the international community, and the actions of the Bosnian Government in continually undermining the peace process had already rendered the prospect of peace uncertain. If war was to be the chosen option, the UN would have to leave. I agreed to put these ideas to de Lapresle on paper. This was the first time he had asked me to do so and I guessed that he shared my view of the deteriorating situation.

As the air strikes were planned for that day, I thought it important to return to Sarajevo. Once NATO started its bombing campaign, the Serbs would undoubtedly respond by shelling the UN. If that happened, I had to be in my HQ. The Serbs had already closed Sarajevo airport, but once again the superb Ukrainian pilots who flew the UN aircraft in Bosnia agreed to take up the gauntlet and deliver me back to my HQ.

On the way we nearly met with disaster, as the undercarriage of the ancient Antonov aircraft failed to operate. We were obliged to spend some time circling Sarajevo trying to get the wheels down. After being violently shaken while the pilot attempted to unlock the undercarriage, I began to feel it might be better to crash on the runway rather than continue in this manner. Finally a scruffy flight engineer wielding a pair of pliers emerged from his sleeping place. He moved to where the pilot was working and pulled out a bundle of wires. He carefully examined them, scratching his head thoughtfully, then suddenly cut one in half and the undercarriage lowered at once.

Safely back on the ground we soon discovered that low cloud over Udbina had prevented NATO aircraft from bombing the airfield and they had returned to Italy. Viktor was especially pleased to see me back. He had forcefully argued that an attack on Udbina would be a *retrospective* punitive action which was inappropriate for a peacekeeping mission, but Akashi had returned from New York convinced that, for political reasons, the UN had to back the NATO action.

Viktor and I went to see the Bosnian Prime Minister, Haris Silajdzic, who was just back from a meeting in Washington with Warren Christopher, the US Secretary of State. During our discussion about the way ahead for UNPROFOR in Bosnia, I explained that for the UN to withdraw at that particular moment – which was bound to happen if the intensity of the fighting increased – was military and political nonsense. I explained that the fighting power of an army derived as much from its command structures and its logistics base as it did from the size of its arsenal. The Bosnian Army still had a long way to go before it could successfully sustain a strategic-level offensive against the Serbs. The newly created command structure of the Bosnian Army had yet to acquire the necessary skills for command at the strategic level and it was also short of weapons and combat supplies. If the UN mission left, the Bosnian Army would be defeated and the State of Bosnia would cease to exist.

I told him that the solution lay in the hands of the Bosnian Government. Most of the fighting had been the result of unsuccessful attacks launched by them and, much as one might applaud their brave attempts to recover lost territories, by such actions they were, militarily, cutting their own throats. The Bosnian Government should follow a longer-term strategy and wait until their people were no longer reliant on UN aid and the new Federation had built sufficient military strength before aiming at all-out victory. Silajdzic said that he agreed with our analysis, but admitted that there were enormous internal political pressures working against this logic. Politically he could not afford to be seen to be distancing himself from the war lobby.

At the end of our discussion, I said that I had something confidential to tell him and that, as his office was probably as well-bugged as my own, we should talk outside. We walked along the corridors of the Presidency and I told him about the NATO plans for air strikes against Udbina airfield. From his reaction it was clear that he knew already.

The next day (21 November) Mike Stanley was having a working lunch with Maj. Indic, Mladic's intelligence officer in the Lukavica barracks, when I called him to warn him that air strikes against Udbina airfield were underway and he ought to return to the Bosnian side of the line. This message was sent to all UN officers working on the Serb side. Indic, however, reassured Mike that, since the air strikes were against the Croatian Serbs, he had nothing to worry about from the Bosnian Serbs. This view reflected that of the Pale leadership, for the next day the UN airlifts into Sarajevo restarted and aid convoys resumed throughout Bosnia. Because the air strikes had been restricted to the bombing of Udbina airfield and steps had been taken to avoid civilian casualties, we did not cross the "Mogadishu Line" after all.

But the war between NATO and the Serbs continued. The next day, two SA2 missiles were unsuccessfully fired at two British Sea Harriers patrolling the skies in the north of Bosnia. At 1120 hours I received a call from de Lapresle to say that he and Smith had agreed to carry out air strikes in reprisal against other Serb targets, as it had not been possible for NATO aircraft to identify the firing point of the SA2 missiles. I told him I had a large number of UN convoys in Serb-held territory at present, and that, as no NATO aircraft had actually been hit, it would be wiser to wait until another occasion. NATO should only fire in self-defence at the specific air defence units that open fire on them.

While I was talking to de Lapresle, Viktor Andreev, Brinkman and most of my staff had crowded into my room to listen anxiously to our conversation. We all firmly believed that NATO should not act outside the principles of peacekeeping. If NATO was only able to respond to such incidents in a way that risked collapsing the entire UN mission, then it would be better not to respond at all. We were all relieved to hear that shortly after this conversation, Akashi and de Lapresle called off the air strikes, mainly because of the need to protect the UN convoys, and I went running with Goose and Capt. Jeremy Bagshaw, my aide-de-camp. That afternoon all was quiet in Sarajevo, but as we ran out of the city towards Vogosca, it occurred to me that, if things had gone the other way that morning, the people of Sarajevo would be back in their shelters by now.

The next day I was telephoned by Gen. Peter Inge, the new Chief of Defence Staff, who told me that my letter to de Lapresle, laying out the options facing the UN if the military situation worsened in Bosnia, should not be too widely circulated. I had sent a copy of the letter to John Wilsey, who had sent it to the Ministry of Defence and from there a copy had apparently reached Downing Street. The clear message of my letter was that the West could not continue to support two conflicting strategies in Bosnia. It was impossible for the UN to operate effectively amid the confusion caused by policies that on the one hand supported the peacekeeping strategy of the UN mission, and on the other pursued the war-fighting strategy of NATO. These contradictory policies had already undermined the political position, credibility and effectiveness of the UN. In the letter I repeated my belief that a withdrawal of the UN could only be accomplished safely if NATO troops were deployed on the ground to guarantee the safe departure of the peacekeepers and to prevent Bosnia from being overrun by the Serbs.

I was not surprised that Inge sounded nervous on the telephone, as even he had been unable to reconcile these two opposing policies during his six months in office. He questioned me closely about the background to the paper and our conversation abruptly ended with his assurance that I still had the confidence of everyone back in London. This in turn made *me* nervous, as I began to feel that I was viewed in London in much the same light as Gen. Gordon had been when he was besieged in his Residency in Khartoum: "We have to rescue him – but not too quickly."

That night (22 November) an excited Col. Lemieux called me from Bihac to say that the Bosnian Serb Army had entered the enclave and was heading towards the town, where most of Dudakovic's troops had now withdrawn. Lemieux's main source of information in the southern sector of Bihac was Dudakovic; as the resident JCO team in Bihac was still observing the fighting between Dudakovic and Abdic's forces near the town of Coralici further north. I immediately ordered them to move south and report on what they found.

Moments later a hysterical Zametica, Karadzic's staff officer, telephoned from Pale demanding to speak to Mike Stanley. He was obviously drunk and threatened the total destruction of UNPROFOR if NATO tried to prevent the Bosnian Serb Army from hunting down and killing every member of the Bosnian Army 5th Corps.

"Don't fuck around!" he screamed. "If you hit us, that means all-out war. Pass this message on to your General: if you want to blow this, it's the end of everything here. The end of UNPROFOR. It's an all-out war. If something called the 'international community' wants it, then so be it. But you must take this very, very, very seriously."

First Mike, then I, tried to calm him down. At one point I told Zametica that the Bosnian Serb Army had apparently crossed the line into the safe area, and I asked him to ensure that they left, "otherwise the consequences would be out of our hands". This had no effect and Zametica was still threatening the UN when the call suddenly ended.

This conversation was once again intercepted by the Bosnian intelligence services and made public. I began to feel that I ought to demand royalties from them. It elicited considerable adverse comment in the US media because during my discussion with Zametica I had used the phrase "Please ensure . . . ", which was interpreted as kowtowing to the Serbs. It was fruitless to explain that negotiations are more likely to be successful if the negotiator remains polite in his dealings with people, especially when they are drunk.

The next day dawned bright and clear in Sarajevo but Bihac remained under low cloud and mist, making it impossible for me to call in air strikes against the advancing Serb tanks. Assessing the reports I received from the JCOs and Lemieux, it began to look as though Bihac would be overrun. Despite bad weather later in the day, NATO aircraft flying high-level over Bosnia fired several anti-radar missiles at Serb target-acquisition radars that had pinpointed them. When I phoned Adm. Leighton Smith to find out what was going on, he told me he intended to clear all the Serb missile systems from Bosnia before responding to any further calls from the UN for close air support. I questioned the wisdom of this approach and he replied that it was no good asking him to provide air cover for the UN and then trying to stop him from doing his job. NATO would respond to every hostile action by the Serbs with a greater use of force. There seemed to be nothing I could do to prevent this escalation. Responsibility for what was happening in Bosnia was slowly but surely drifting out of the hands of UNPROFOR.

I reported my conversation with Adm. Leighton Smith to de Lapresle, who replied that there was little he could do to prevent the NATO air campaign from moving us towards war. Even the Russians in New York had unexpectedly supported the use of

NATO air power to halt the war. It looked as though we were on our own.

Rather than do nothing, I decided to send Mike Stanley to Pale in one last attempt to get Karadzic to call a halt to the fighting in Bihac. I proposed that Karadzic should accept a local ceasefire between Dudakovic and Milovanovic, who was now in command of all Serb forces in north-western Bosnia. In Bihac, Lemieux had already got Dudakovic, now under pressure on all sides, to accept the idea. Initially Karadzic seemed to accept the plan, but just as he was about to agree to it, he received news of yet another air strike by NATO in Pale. Far from having the desired effect of causing Karadzic to halt his advance on Bihac, the air strike sent him into a rage.

"From now on," he shouted, "I will give orders to the Serbs only to halt their advance when we have destroyed the Muslim Army 5th Corps! NATO can do nothing to stop us! As far as I am concerned the UN is now an agent of NATO!"

There was another sad irony in the fact that it was doubtful whether these repeated air strikes even marginally improved the security of aircraft flying over Bosnia. They certainly did nothing for the security of the peacekeepers. In response to the NATO action, the Serbs took hostage the French, Canadian and Ukrainian soldiers in the weapon collecting sites around Sarajevo, as well as a British convoy *en route* to Gorazde. Once again the young men and women, many of them volunteers, who had come to help the people of Bosnia, had loaded weapons pointed at them by angry Serb gunmen. The NATO pilots themselves had flown back to the security of their bases in Italy, leaving UNPROFOR to pick up the pieces yet again. I was tempted to send a sardonic message of congratulations to Adm. Leighton Smith asking him what more he could do to help the UN. I should probably have sent the same message to Malcolm Rifkind, the British Defence Secretary, who following the latest air strike was reported as saying that the raids "had improved the security of UNPROFOR soldiers deployed on the ground". The hostage peacekeepers were understandably disillusioned with these efforts to "improve" their security, now that they were looking down the barrels of Serb guns.

The following day (November 24) I had two months remaining of my tour of duty in Bosnia. Despite the present difficulties, I was determined that by the time I left the guns would have fallen silent and the path to peace would have been kept open. We still had a long way to go. After breakfast, Viktor and I had a meeting with Silajdzic. He was in a conciliatory mood, no doubt elated by the continuing NATO air strikes. Viktor explained that Akashi, who was in Belgrade talking to President Milosevic, was at last making progress in his attempt to obtain a ceasefire in Bihac. The Serbs proposed a total cessation of hostilities along the entire line of conflict in return for halting their attack on Bihac. They even agreed to withdraw from some of the territory they had captured at the start of the war. This suggested they were willing to accept the Contact Group map, at least as a basis for negotiation. Silajdzic agreed in principle that there should be a total cessation of hostilities in Bosnia, but he would have to clear this with the Contact Group and with Washington. If the fighting around Bihac were halted immediately, he would be prepared to meet one of the Pale leaders. Mike Stanley arranged a meeting with Karadzic without delay.

The meeting we had that day with the Serbs proved extremely difficult. Karadzic was in a truculent mood, as he still believed the Serbs could achieve a decisive military victory over the Bosnian Army, in spite of the continuing NATO air strikes. He told us that by repeatedly launching attacks against his forces, the Muslims had challenged the Serbs to all-out war and now they were going to be taught a lesson. The UN had not consulted with the Serbs about the establishment of an exclusion zone around Bihac, which at any rate was contrary to the Geneva Convention. His army would never withdraw from territory that it had won at the cost of Serb lives. He would only meet the Bosnian leadership if it agreed to a total cessation of hostilities as a precondition to halting the fighting around Bihac. During this tirade his eyes were glazed and his entire frame was tense with fury. Koljevic tried hard to look intimidating but managed only to look ridiculous. Zametica, his face sweating profusely, beamed at us in delight at what Karadzic was saying. Tolimir, Mladic's Chief of Staff, looked exhausted and said nothing.

Karadzic had begun our meeting by saying that he could give us only 10 minutes of his time, as he had to attend a meeting of the Serb Assembly. He harangued us for almost three hours. Several times Viktor reminded him that the Serbs could not afford to go to war with the West. The UN was trying to bring about a peaceful end to the conflict, but if that proved impossible, the UN would leave and NATO ground troops would be engaged on the side of the Bosnians. In these circumstances he had no chance of winning the war. Every time Viktor intervened, Karadzic would yell at him and thump his fists on the table to emphasise his rejection of what Viktor had said. In spite of the potentially tragic outcome, it was amusing to watch these two titans of the Communist system trying to outdo each other in their exercise of old-style Soviet diplomacy. By the end of the meeting we had achieved nothing, but as we drove back to Sarajevo Viktor said to me, "Michael, I think we are getting somewhere." Obviously in the midst of these heated exchanges, I had missed something.

On our return to the Residency, I learned that the situation in Bihac had deteriorated. Though the Serbs had not actually entered Bihac they had dug themselves in on the high ground to the south and occasional shells were beginning to fall among the buildings. I had publicly committed myself to taking action against the Serbs if they started shelling Bihac and the credibility of the UN was now at stake. As the weather was improving, I telephoned de Lapresle and recommended that we prepare for air strikes against Serb artillery positions and tanks around Bihac. He didn't think NATO would respond to such a request. NATO had said it would only attack strategic targets such as command and control HQs, communications sites or ammunition bunkers. Such a measure would require a decision by the Secretary-General in New York, but in the present circumstances he didn't think this would be forthcoming. Nevertheless, he offered to pass on my suggestion to Akashi.

I went to the Presidency and told Silajdzic that the Serbs were prepared to meet him, but only on the same precondition as before: a total cessation of hostilities. He looked tired and had probably just been fed more rubbish by Delic about what was happening in Bihac. Without the calm, accurate reporting of the JCOs from Bihac it would have been impossible for me to maintain any control over the situation. They had courageously advanced on to the high ground to the south of Bihac and on several occasions were in danger of being overrun. Silajdzic was relieved when I told him that the Serbs had not entered the town and that a wholesale slaughter of the population was not taking place. It appeared that the Serbs were trying to engage with Dudakovic's forces, now in Bihac. Silajdzic listened to what I had to say, then told me that in view of the seriousness of the situation, he would be prepared to talk to Koljevic as long as a ceasefire came into being first. I passed this message to Stanley who in turn passed it on to Karadzic, but by then the Serb leadership was drinking heavily and we received no response.

At 1630 hours, Victor Jackovitch, the US ambassador to Bosnia, visited my office to enquire about the latest developments in Bihac. There was about to be an emergency debate on Bihac in the Security Council that evening and he needed to brief Madeleine Albright. During our conversation a UN watchkeeper poked his head round the door of my office and reported that shells were falling in the centre of Bihac, whereupon Jackovitch quickly left. He must have passed this undigested piece of information on to Madeleine Albright, as she went at once to see Kofi Annan to insist that NATO start bombing the Serbs. Within five minutes of Jackovitch leaving my office, Annan, in a state of anxiety, had called me to ask whether what Madeleine Albright had said was true.

Fortunately I could talk to the JCOs directly from my HQ. They were able to provide me with a more detailed report from Bihac. Although four shells had fallen near the Bosnian Army HQ, the town was not under general bombardment and the situation had not deteriorated in the past few hours. When I repeated this to Annan in New York, he had replied in his soft voice, "Oh, Michael, I'm so glad you've just told me that . . . this will make things much easier for us in the debate." He also told me how grateful the Secretary-General was for what the UN contingent in Bihac was doing and he was particularly impressed by the accuracy of our reports from there. He assured me that our refusal to be drawn into a war was the only rational approach and that the international community had to learn to use facts not propaganda as the basis for decisions.

Later that evening Viktor and I were due to attend a routine meeting with Silajdzic to brief him on the situation in Bihac, and thereby to clear up some of the confusion about what was going on in the enclave. We were shown into an empty reception room in the Presidency by a tense-looking member of the protocol staff. This was unusual, as Silajdzic normally liked to talk informally in his office. As we waited, we heard scuffling noises from the room next door. Suddenly the door burst open and Silajdzic came in amid a blaze of television camera lights followed by an entourage of about 50 journalists. We had been ambushed.

Without a word of greeting, he launched into an angry tirade against the UN. Stabbing the air with a pencil, his face white and twisted with fury, he accused me of being responsible for the deaths of 70,000 defenceless people in the UN safe area of Bihac. NATO had been ready to launch massive air strikes against the Serbs to halt the slaughter, but it had been prevented from doing so, he said, because I had refused to give the necessary authority. The situation in Bihac was far worse than the one that followed the Serb attacks on Gorazde. Even the hospital in Bihac, which held 1,500 people, was being shelled and still, he ranted, I did nothing. It was clear that the UN was now on the side of the Serbs.

As quickly as Silajdzic had begun, he finished, and departed through a side door, leaving Viktor and me behind with the journalists and cameramen, some of whom joined in the verbal assault. With difficulty we followed him into the next room where he was shaking like a leaf. For some time he could not speak, but finally he managed to say, "I will not talk to you again," and left. The whole episode had lasted less than five minutes. It was obvious that this charade had been entirely for the benefit of the media. Viktor looked stunned and made as if to leave, but this did not seem to me to be the moment to quit. Forcing a smile, I said to him cheerily, "Come on, let's go and see Silajdzic and ask him what that was all about."

His secretary tried to prevent us from entering Silajdzic's office, but he quickly emerged to repeat that he had nothing further to say to us. This time, I gave him no option. Taking him firmly by the elbow, I steered him into the corridor.

"Well?" I demanded. "What was all that about?"

For some time he said nothing, then, with a little smile, he replied, "It was nothing personal. I need to be seen to be tough on the UN."

I took this opportunity to say what I had originally come to say. I explained that I intended to call for air strikes the next day if the Serbs started shelling the civilian population of Bihac. Just an hour before, the JCOs in Bihac had reported to me that, although there was some shelling in the town, it was still being directed against Dudakovic's troops. So far, there were few reports of civilian casualties. I advised him to instruct Dudakovic to move his mortars and a tank from the grounds of the hospital if he wanted to avoid the hospital being treated as a military target by the Serbs. I explained to him that whatever happened in Bihac, under present rules NATO could not attack strategic targets as authority had yet to be given by the Security Council. Meanwhile there was some hope the Serbs would respect the TEZ around the town and that the talks in Belgrade would bring an end to the fighting.

Silajdzic tried to interrupt me, but it was now my turn and I refused to let him speak. I was furious that he had used the media to blame the UN for what was happening in Bihac. It had been Dudakovic's foolhardy attack out of the enclave that had put the people of Bihac at risk. The UN had killed no one. It had saved many lives, and soldiers under my command as well as civilians in the UNHCR were risking their own lives to bring peace to the region. It was intolerable that they should be held responsible. Only the Serbs and the Bosnians could be blamed for the disaster. Having said this, I felt much better.

At heart Silajdzic was too intelligent to believe the propaganda being put out by his own side. I always felt that his tortured appearance was a reflection of the intense and unbearable guilt that he was suffering because of the horrors that were being needlessly visited on his people, much of it attributable to the policies of his government. If Izetbegovic had accepted the Vance–Owen peace plan the country would by now have been at peace.[1] By trying to achieve a just solution, the Bosnian Government was unjustly punishing its own people, who only wanted the war to end. He calmed down and unexpectedly thanked me for having come to see him. He then said that Izetbegovic, too, wanted to see me.

I repeated the same arguments to Izetbegovic for an hour. He was friendly enough, though he must have known about the public attack mounted against me by Silajdzic. Before we left the building I warned Goose, who had seen most of what had happened, to expect a mob of press outside the building. "No problems," he said cheerfully and we hit the front ranks of the journalists with the momentum of an express train. As we crashed through their scattering ranks, I heard a voice call out, "Are you going to resign?"

I did not bother to reply.

Nevertheless, it was reasonable to assume that the UN would be blamed if Bihac fell. Accordingly, on the evening of 24 November, I sent a request to NATO to strike at all Serb tanks and artillery firing into the town. I sent my usual message of warning to Milovanovic, the Serb area commander, but received no reply. The weather around Bihac was poor but improving.

Standing in the NATO air cell, on the ground floor of the Portakabin opposite my office, I told the American air commander in Italy, Gen. Mike Ryan, that my soldiers in Bihac were now in danger of being overrun by the Serbs. I needed immediate close air support in self-defence. By couching my request in these terms I prevented him from rejecting it outright on the grounds that NATO would accede only to requests for strategic air strikes. It was obvious he could not allow UN soldiers to be put at risk without responding, particularly as many of the soldiers serving in UNPROFOR came from NATO nations.

Ryan agreed to launch a wave of bombers against the Serbs and undertook to attack any artillery or tanks found to be firing on Bihac. Regrettably, after two hours the aircraft returned to their bases in Italy, without having located any targets. "It was much easier in Iraq," complained one RAF officer in the NATO cell in my HQ. In Iraq, the Iraqi tanks and artillery had been laid out in the desert as if on a chessboard. In Bosnia, the Serb air defence systems were better concealed and highly mobile. Furthermore, their air defence radar system was controlled from an HQ outside Bosnia and could not be attacked.

Late that night Wes Clark telephoned from the Pentagon. He sounded agitated and kept repeating "what the Serbs must understand is that if they attack the Bangladeshis the consequences will be out of UNPROFOR's hands." He went on to explain that the US Administration now regarded UNPROFOR as a hostage group, unable to take decisions for itself. He added that the dual key – the system by which both the UN and NATO had to assent to air strikes – had effectively been taken out of my hands. I told him that UNPROFOR could not operate without the dual key and that I would instantly recommend the withdrawal of the UN mission if air strikes took place in Bosnia without my permission.

I was simply not prepared to allow an air campaign to be mounted by NATO. Not only did its objectives have little to do with a peacekeeping mission, but it would also hazard the lives of my peacekeepers. The result would be the same blood bath as had occurred in Somalia. I said that if NATO did override the dual key system, the Americans had better prepare a much larger invasion force than the 6,000 Marines President Clinton had recently put on standby in the Adriatic. I heard no more from him.

The next day Adm. Leighton Smith called to say that he was no longer prepared to allow the Serbs to fire missiles "up the arses of his pilots" without response, and that he was going to teach them a lesson. Speaking angrily, he told me he thought that UNPROFOR was becoming myopic and that the situation around Sarajevo was in danger of unravelling. I had the uncanny feeling I was in the same ambush that I had found myself in with Silajdzic the day before. On his visits to Sarajevo Smith had shown a fine understanding of the limits of peacekeeping and the importance of sustaining the UN mission in Bosnia. I suspected he had been ordered by Joulwan to put pressure on me in order to get me to allow NATO to do something which neither he, nor I, believed in. He did not look to me like a man who slept well at night. In the end, no strategic air campaign was mounted against the Serbs and once again the UN was able to return to the business of saving lives and trying to halt the fighting around Bihac by negotiation.

Col. Chuck Lemieux, commanding the forward UNPROFOR tactical HQ in Bihac, reassured me that the Serbs were not deliberately targeting the civilian population, although they had captured the villages of Sokolac and Privilica on the outskirts. In a footnote to his report he mentioned that he had witnessed Dudakovic interrogating a Bosnian Serb prisoner. The soldier was no more than 19 years old and had been recruited only a few days before. He had become lost in the fog and was captured driving around Bosnian-held territory in a truck. Questioning the prisoner in front of Lemieux, Dudakovic had reassured him the young man would be treated correctly as a POW; but when Lemieux left the room, a member of his staff had seen the Bosnian Serb being severely beaten outside the 5th Corps building, allegedly for killing three children in Sokolac.

Despite Karadzic's dire threats against the UN and the Bosnian Army, the Bosnian Serb Army was clearly under orders not to antagonise the international community by pursuing their assault too far into Bihac. They halted their advance on a key hill feature called Debeljaca, just outside the three-kilometre perimeter. Shortly afterwards Milovanovic issued an appeal to the 5th Corps to surrender, couching it in terms unlikely to bring the desired result: "I have already called on you to surrender. You failed to obey and were punished. If you fail to obey this time, I will not be able to guarantee your lives, since many of you have committed horrible crimes against the Serb people."

The UNHCR was finding it difficult to look after the increasing number of refugees arriving in Bihac. Food stocks were running short and there had been no aid convoys in the town for some weeks. Among the civilians there had inevitably been some casualties during the fighting, but in a report from Bihac, Ed Joseph, the UN civil affairs officer, wrote: "the citizens of Bihac are still on the streets . . . and seem to sort of stoically accept their fate." In an impassioned plea to the international community, the mayor of Bihac, Mr Kabiljagic, said that he believed more than 300,000 refugees had now flooded into the enclave, though the UNHCR estimate was closer to 180,000. People were living on 80 grams of food a day, but their situation was better than that of the UN Bangladeshi battalion, which, according to Col. Salim, was about to consume its last remaining day's rations.

Perhaps Karadzic sensed that his military successes around Bihac might afford him an opportunity for political gain. By the end of November he wrote to Boutros-Ghali proposing an immediate end to the war, without prejudice to the final territorial settlement which should be concluded within 10 days. He explained in the letter that this offer demonstrated that the Serbs were not interested in freezing the current lines of conflict. He also pointed out that the proposal emerging from the Bosnian Government was a mere three months cessation of hostilities, which he feared they would use to rearm and regroup following their military defeat.

From time to time, to add urgency to his message, the Bosnian Serb Army lobbed shells into Bihac and fired wire-guided missiles at Bosnian Government buildings in Sarajevo. I also received a letter from Karadzic telling me that NATO aircraft had carried out a massive strike against his forces in the vicinity of Bihac. It was later discovered that there had indeed been a missile attack in the area: having failed to reach their target, a salvo of Serb SA2 missiles had fallen back to earth on to his own troops!

Although freedom of movement for the UN was restricted, we continued to deliver aid and negotiate for peace throughout November. Several peacekeepers had been taken hostage after the initial air strikes, but they were soon released unharmed; though there had been one incident in which two British soldiers were physically assaulted. Meetings at all levels had continued with the Bosnian Serb Army. A number of humanitarian aid flights had arrived in Sarajevo, and the quantity of aid delivered by the UNHCR in November only narrowly missed its target. In Sarajevo, the passage of civilians still continued across the conflict line. Electricity, gas and water remained connected and the trams still operated on the main streets, although there were interruptions to the service after every sniper attack. None of this would have been possible if the UN had given way to NATO.

On the last day of November the UN Secretary-General made a fact-finding visit to Bosnia, which inevitably turned out to be another grand Balkan affair. I knew what sort of day it was going to be as soon as Viktor turned up for work crammed into a shiny, blue suit with his collar done up behind his tie. Then 40 officers from the Egyptian battalion arrived two hours early for lunch at the Residency.

At the airport Akashi, de Lapresle and I explained to Boutros-Ghali that currently the UN mission was stalled. Any progress made in the spring had been undermined by the resurgence of fighting in Bosnia, much of it instigated by the Bosnian forces. The strategic situation had recently deteriorated, following the deployment of Serb air defences. By demanding that it be allowed to carry out pre-emptive strikes on the Serb air defence system, NATO had effectively priced itself out of the peace-keeping market.

The UN Secretary-General was accompanied by Marrack Goulding, his Under-Secretary of State. They brought with them a group of elegant female secretaries who looked completely out of place amid the devastated buildings and burnt-out vehicles. Akashi was relaxed and seemed on good form.

Boutros-Ghali had originally planned to meet Karadzic at the Lukavica barracks, but he had changed his mind and refused to set foot on Serb-occupied territory. He would only meet the Pale leadership at the airport. This infuriated Karadzic, who refused to go to the airport, saying that he would not be treated like a rebel. Things did not improve when we got to the Presidency, where Izetbegovic deliberately kept the Secretary-General waiting. This was probably in retaliation for a remark Boutros-Ghali had made when last in Sarajevo. He had said that the standard of living of the people of Sarajevo, even though it was supposedly under siege, was better than that of many people in the Third World.

When the meeting eventually began, Boutros-Ghali launched a strong condem-nation of the Bosnian Government, saying that the UN would not be in Bosnia for ever. He had already withdrawn the Somalia mission and would soon be doing the same with UNPROFOR. No nation in the world was willing to fight for Bosnia, nor could the Bosnian Government expect UN peacekeepers to remain in Bosnia if it showed no interest in making peace. When Ganic intervened and berated the inter-national community for failing to come to his country's assistance, Boutros-Ghali remained unimpressed. He repeated that the UN was prepared to remain in a peace-keeping role, but that it needed the support of both sides in the conflict. I felt like cheering from the sidelines.

Outside the Presidency a well-drilled crowd chanted slogans against Boutros-Ghali. It reminded me of the half-hearted pro-Saddam demonstrations in Baghdad during the Gulf War. Muratovic had once told me he had been responsible for build-ing an artillery factory under the Iraqi desert and I wondered if the demonstration had been his idea.

The small dining room in the Residency was already filled with Egyptian officers waiting to lunch with Boutros-Ghali, who took the trouble to talk to each of them. After lunch every officer insisted on being photographed with the great man in the garden while the young staff officers in the HQ seemed more interested in the New York secretaries. Before he left the Residency, Boutros-Ghali agreed to send a letter to the Secretary-General of NATO asking him to stop NATO aircraft from flying over Bosnia in a provocative manner. He also gave a press conference that evening in which he delivered a tough message to the Bosnians and the Serbs, saying that the UN had come to Bosnia at the request of both sides in the war. If they wanted to bring the conflict to an end, they had to show a readiness to negotiate and work in good faith to find common ground. They also had to co-operate with UNPROFOR and the UNHCR. Unless they did this, the Security Council would not be persuaded to keep the UN in Bosnia. If UNPROFOR were withdrawn, UNHCR would also leave. Boutros-Ghali was a man who spoke the truth. His refusal to allow war-fighting goals to be pursued by NATO in Bosnia did not endear him to the Americans and almost certainly contributed to his final downfall.

The international press behaved disgracefully throughout the crisis in Bihac. At the start of the month, it had been cheering on the 5th Corps as it advanced south from Bihac. Now it was accusing the UN of failing to stop the fighting. The Sarajevo newspaper *Oslobodjenje*, the mouthpiece of the Bosnian Government, published a cartoon labelling Britain, France and Russia as the aggressors alongside the Bosnian Serbs. Among the many column inches devoted to criticism of the UN, one colum-nist, William Safire, referred to me in the *New York Times* as the "reincarnation of Neville Chamberlain". This was a physical impossibility as I was born before Neville Chamberlain died. Writing in the same paper, Anthony Lewis said of my dealings with the Serbs: "Not even Neville Chamberlain went this far in his supplications to Hitler." [2] It was sad to see these eminent men succumbing so easily to the logic of war.

Defence Secretary William Perry had come down firmly against the use of NATO air power to enforce a political solution in Bosnia, while the efforts of the UN mission were still primarily directed at humanitarian support. He even conceded that NATO was powerless to stop the Serb offensive in Bihac with air strikes and that only a huge deployment of troops would be decisive.

"Air strikes," he said, "can punish the Serbs, but they cannot determine the outcome of ground combat. It would take 100,000 troops with heavy weapons even to enforce the peace. To affect the outcome of the war – to win the war – would take several hundred thousands troops with heavy weapons involving significant casualties." [3] In Sarajevo, we hoped that this statement was a signal that President Clinton and NATO were beginning to accept the argument in favour of the peace process.

On 29 November Senator Robert Dole had criticised the UN for failing to take tough action against the Serbs. I was able to publicly respond to him on *News Hour*, a US television programme. During the interview, which was transmitted from the Sarajevo Residency, I was asked what my answer would be to Senator Dole and other American politicians who had said that the UN was not serving any useful purpose in Bosnia and should leave. I replied that the best answer would come from the people of Gorazde, Zepa and Srebrenica, whose lives depended on the presence of the UN peacekeepers. There was a war going on in the country and the UN had been able to sustain the aid delivery programme and give people hope for the future. It was not our job to stop the war. This could only be done by a war-fighting force, not by peacekeepers. More than 300 people working for the UN and other aid organisations had been killed in Yugoslavia, but no one involved in the programmes had ever doubted the value of the mission. It was a cruel deception to suggest that peacekeepers were equipped or mandated to defend territory or offer full protection to civilians caught up in fighting. A UN safe area was a designated area in which a civilian population could shelter from the fighting. It could only be maintained with the support of both sides. If one or both combatants breached the haven of the safe area, UN peace-keepers were not capable of fighting military actions to defend it. All they could do was use a limited amount of force to deter combatants from entering the area. What air power could do in these circumstances was also limited.

I was next asked whether I had ever contemplated resigning in the face of the criticism I had received, particularly in the last month. When I arrived in Bosnia, I replied, I had promised the people of Sarajevo I would be with them for a year, and that during that time it was my intention that the UN would advance the cause of peace. We had taken serious steps in that direction and I would not abandon the people of Bosnia now. At the end of the interview I was asked how it felt as a professional soldier to find myself the target of political attacks from around the world.

"Sir," I said, "I believe that the United Nations Protection Force in Bosnia-Hercegovina is making history. These criticisms will end up in the rubbish dump."

In a paper addressed to Akashi analysing the strategic situation in Bosnia, de Lapresle wrote that as there was no military solution to the civil war in Bosnia, there could only be negotiated solutions. Unfortunately public opinion, manipulated by the media, was probably in favour of military action. As overall mission commander, de Lapresle's priorities were to meet the peacekeeping objectives of the UN and to ensure the security and protection of his troops and aid workers. He would always respond favourably to any request that he received from me for air strikes in defence of UN soldiers, but he would oppose any request from NATO to carry out massive air strikes against the Bosnian Serbs. He ended his paper by calling for international *political* action to bring the warring parties to the conference table.

His call was duly answered. By the end of the month, the US Administration had fallen into line with the UN and abandoned the "take it or leave it" approach of the Contact Group towards the Serbs. In a speech on 30 November, Anthony Lake, the US National Security Adviser, hinted that a compromise deal would have to be struck with Pale and that some sort of confederate structure for Bosnia might be necessary. In this confederation the Bosnian Serbs would be allowed to maintain the sort of relationship with Belgrade as the one envisaged between the Bosnian Croats and Zagreb. Chuck Redman, who had returned to the scene from Bonn where he was now US ambassador, reinforced this message. It was evident that his job was to put pressure on the Bosnian Government to accept some form of compromise. He had now been authorised to negotiate with the Serbs in Pale, thus ending the policy of isolation that the Contact Group had insisted upon. John Major, speaking earlier in the month at the British Army Staff College in Camberley, had called on President Clinton to join the European governments in searching for a negotiated settlement to the war. At last the long months of argument and discussion with the Americans had paid off.

The arrival of winter, the increase in ethnic cleansing of the Muslim and Croat minority populations in Serb-held parts of Bosnia and the renewed outbreak of fighting in Bihac, placed an enormous burden on the UNHCR to provide food and shelter to displaced and war-affected people. All discussion of a possible withdrawal of the UN vanished from the agendas of political leaders in the West as they focussed on the possible consequences of abandoning the UN peace mission and the need to alleviate suffering. The international community was at last about to get its act together.

Throughout December, the Serbs continued to harass the Bosnian Army and Muslim population, but this did little to change the strategic balance. The UN pursued its purpose of sustaining the aid programme and trying to bring about peace. By then, I had over 24,000 peacekeepers from 16 nations deployed in Bosnia. UN military engineers rebuilt roads, bridges, schools, hospitals and old people's homes. They reconnected the water and electricity supply not only to Sarajevo, but also to many other villages and towns throughout Bosnia. French and Belgian military engineers helped operate the coal mine and power station in Kakanj, west of Sarajevo, which supplied most of the power for the city. In the first month following its arrival in central Bosnia, a Pakistani field hospital had carried out more than 3,000 medical interventions among the civilian population. They also rebuilt a school and a Catholic church for the Croat minority population living in their area of responsibility. British soldiers had been involved in over 200 civil reconstruction programmes. These included the building of a 50-mile dual carriageway from Tomislavgrad to the Laskva Valley, along which all the aid into central Bosnia had flowed, until a new route from Mostar was opened up by Royal Engineers. British soldiers also cleared minefields and built bridges, such as a replacement for the historic Turkish bridge in Mostar.

Daily life for the peacekeepers was a perpetual round of escorting convoys, guarding bases and UN weapons collection points and checkpoints. They were on permanent standby to deploy at short notice to rescue convoys and stop local outbreaks of fighting. They arranged medical evacuation for the sick and wounded, transport for refugees and supervised the exchanges of POWs and other bodies. In everything, they had to deal with local military and civilian authorities who were always looking to turn any humanitarian action to their own advantage. The job of the peacekeepers was not just to bring about conditions of peace, but to assist in the reconstruction of the country when peace arrived. Most tours of duty for the soldiers lasted for six months, during which period there was little spare time and no place for recreation in Bosnia. However all national contingents maintained rest-and-recreation centres on the Dalmatian coast for the peacekeepers where they normally spent one week in the middle of the tour. The New Zealand company attached to the British battalion had, however, found time to beat the Muslims at rugby 60–nil.

The peacekeepers were almost always welcomed by local people, but often treated contemptuously by the warlords and their political masters. Sometimes they were physically attacked or shot at. One young British liaison officer was leaving a hospital in Zenica when he was brutally attacked by mujahedin, who pistol-whipped him and tried to take his weapon. He was on a mission to obtain clearance for the evacuation of some Muslim casualties. It was only the intervention of the hospital staff that prevented him from coming to further harm. He returned the next day and completed the casualty evacuation.

At the start of December, the Serbs took hostage a British convoy of the Royal

Gloucestershire, Berkshire and Wiltshire Regiment, including their commanding officer, Lt-Col. Patrick Davidson-Houston, on its way to Gorazde. The Serbs had offered to allow the commanding officer to continue, but he had refused. After five days the embarrassed Serbs released the British soldiers, but not before they had been taught to sing regimental songs and Christmas carols.

The story of the young peacekeepers in UNPROFOR is a story of heroism and commitment to the people of Bosnia. While the headlines in the newspapers screamed about bloodshed, the peacekeepers and aid workers quietly went about saving lives.

Taking advantage of a change of mood in the Contact Group, Akashi embarked on a new round of shuttle diplomacy between Belgrade, Pale and Sarajevo. Neither side would budge, though the continued prosecution of the war only prolonged the suffering of the civilian population. Ganic demanded a local ceasefire in Bihac as a precondition for a cessation of hostilities. Karadzic went on insisting that a ceasefire in Bihac could only be negotiated within the context of a total peace plan. I noticed that Akashi's eloquence had lost some of its magic and he began to sound like a lawyer fighting a case he had little hope of winning. After every meeting at the Presidency, he received a trouncing from Ganic in front of the television cameras; but somehow Akashi never resisted a chance to take him on in public debate. On one occasion, unable to watch him suffer any more, I simply walked him away from the television cameras in mid-sentence.

De Lapresle was also beginning to look depressed at the lack of progress. My own frustration and tiredness manifested itself in the venomous way I treated anyone I thought was obstructing the peace process. On one occasion I accused the head of the UN information service in Zagreb not only of being incapable of doing his job, but also of actively undermining the work of UNPROFOR by repeating Bosnian propaganda. The only people I felt at ease with were my own team and particularly Viktor Andreev, whose familiar cure of iced vodka and caviar always seemed to make me feel better.

On 3 December I received a call from John Major. I had always been unwilling to accept calls from the Prime Minister, or indeed from President Clinton, who once tried to call me. To do so would have been to short-circuit the chain of command and would have been particularly discourteous to John Wilsey, as well as to the command structure in the UK. On this occasion, I felt it was time the Prime Minister heard directly from me about the difficulties faced by UNPROFOR.

I gave him roughly the same message contained in my paper to de Lapresle and brought him up to date with what was happening in the chief trouble spots in Bosnia. I told him that there was a gradual deterioration in the military position throughout the country. The Serbs were now using wire-guided missiles against Government targets in Sarajevo and the UN was returning fire with heavy weapons. Though the Serbs did not appear to want to overrun the town of Bihac, fighting was still continuing in the area where the condition of the population was giving most cause for alarm, since it had been impossible for the UN to deliver aid into the enclave.

The Bosnian troops were firing at the French on Mt Igman where they remained, in violation of the 1993 NATO ultimatum. Although 20 British troops had been released, the Serbs were still holding 250 UN peacekeepers hostage. The risks to the UN troops and aid workers were becoming unacceptable, and in the absence of any real desire to find a way to peace among the warring parties and without a new, substantial political initiative by the international community, there would be no point in the UN staying in Bosnia after the winter.

The Prime Minister told me that contingency plans to withdraw the UN were currently being made. Obviously he had no wish for this to happen, but I believe he wanted to concentrate the minds of Americans like Senator Dole, as well as the Bosnian Government, on the consequences of the war option. Concerned by the extent and possible effect of the propaganda against the UN, he urged me not to let it get me down for it had clearly originated with the Bosnian Government. He asked for a paper with which to brief the Cabinet. I said I would prepare one, but that I would pass it up the chain of command. He agreed to this, but asked me nevertheless to send him a private copy. No doubt he had long experience of papers being so watered down by officials that the original message was lost by the time it reached him.

His intervention was carefully timed and was probably the result of a personal desire to see a peaceful and successful outcome of the British involvement in Bosnia. I never felt that he was a politician trying to use a situation to enhance his reputation. His compassion for the ordinary people of Bosnia was genuine and he was determined to help them.

The next day, the Chief of Defence Staff and Malcolm Rifkind flew out to Split to discuss the Prime Minister's paper with me. I suggested that they read it before we spoke. I had pulled no punches about the military situation or the consequences of a UN withdrawal, although I had recommended that, on balance, UNPROFOR should remain in Bosnia at least until the spring. They were naturally concerned about the potential political damage NATO would suffer after a UN withdrawal, but Rifkind's attendant civil servant seemed more alarmed to learn that I had been asked to send my paper directly to the Prime Minister. I gave her one copy and sent another direct to Downing Street, just in case.

John Menzies, the new US ambassador in Sarajevo, appreciated the problems facing the UN and had obviously been told by Holbrooke to try and keep the peacekeepers *in situ* until a deal could be struck between the Bosnians and the Serbs. He was a more approachable person than his predecessor, Jackovitch, and seemed keen to work with the UN HQ in Sarajevo towards a negotiated settlement of the war. He had been at school in England for a number of years, and played cricket. I included him in every discussion that we had at my HQ about the way ahead, and I also gave him full accounts of all meetings we had between the UN and the warring parties. He was especially useful in persuading Ganic to face up to the facts of the situation, although he could never stop him from talking drivel.

Menzies went out of his way to maintain good relations with all of my staff, and he almost became part of the UN team, often eating with us and debating late into the night as to how we could bring the Bosnians and the Serbs together. At one point he told me that he believed UNPROFOR had made history by developing a "third way" in conflict resolution, something that lay between traditional peace-keeping and war-fighting. If Menzies had been in the post at the start of 1994, I believe the war in Bosnia might well have been ended that year, following the 9 February Airport Agreement and the Washington Accord. He could have dissuaded the Bosnian Government from launching their unsuccessful offensives, which had finally derailed the burgeoning peace process. He would also, I think, have been prepared to maintain sufficient contact with the Serbs to bring them to the negotiating table, something the Contact Group had refused to do.

On 6 December Menzies was in and out of my office every few hours because the Serbs had, that day, forcibly removed a number of weapons from the UN weapon-collecting sites around Sarajevo. They told the UN soldiers guarding the sites that they were being threatened by NATO air strikes and needed their air defence weapons back. This was too much. It was a repetition of what had happened in April.

I sent a signal to Mladic saying that if the weapons were not returned I would retaliate by calling on NATO to hit strategic-level targets that had already been selected. Although UN soldiers were still being held hostage, I felt that the UN had to enforce the return of these weapons or any credibility still attached to the mission would be gone. That night I went to bed not knowing whether the next day would see an end to the UN mission. When I awoke, a relieved Jamie Daniell told me that all the weapons had been returned during the night.

On 7 December, Karadzic made a public statement on Serb television saying that he was willing to negotiate on the basis of the Contact Group map. John Menzies came round to the Residency straightaway and told me that Redman would return to Pale as rapidly as possible to continue negotiations. Even as events appeared to be irreversibly moving towards catastrophe, everyone seemed to have realised what the consequences of their policies might be and had stepped back. Nobody wanted a Third World War.

At a meeting of the 52-nation conference in Budapest on Security and Co-operation in Europe, John Major unequivocally declared that the British Government believed that UNPROFOR should continue its valuable mission, but that it was threatened by continued fighting on the ground. He also pointed out that the "tactics of the Bosnian Serbs are preventing the peacekeepers and aid workers from doing their jobs". President Clinton was also there and he appealed to the Bosnian Serbs to put a halt to their aggression and agree to a ceasefire. Significantly he did not mention the lifting of the arms embargo. He additionally offered to commit 25,000 troops as part of a NATO force to cover the UN's withdrawal from Bosnia, in the event that this happened.[4]

The only discordant note came from Izetbegovic. He blamed the UN and NATO for not helping the Bosnians put a stop to the war, "due to a mixture of incapability, hesitation and sometimes ill will". However, when the Canadian troops in Visoko had once again tried to leave their camp later that week because of heavy shelling in the area, it was the Bosnian Army that blocked their route with mines. Whatever negative propaganda Izetbegovic put out against the UN peacekeepers, his soldiers knew that they could not survive their departure.

Meanwhile in Belgrade, President Milosevic had told Douglas Hurd and Alain Juppé that he would try to get the Bosnian Serbs to accept the modified Contact Group plan, allowing them to hold 49% of the State of Bosnia. In Washington, William Perry, the US Secretary of State for Defence, suggested that, far from withdrawing its troops, France and Britain should reinforce the UN peacekeeping mission. Suddenly peace was back on the agenda and Christmas looked like being a time of celebration after all.

CHAPTER NINE

A Cessation of Hostilities

*I came here to convey to both sides a simple message . . . First, they must
show a readiness to negotiate in good faith to find common ground.
Secondly, they must cooperate with UNPROFOR and the UNHCR.*
Boutros Boutros-Ghali, Secretary-General of the UN, 1994

THE SEASON OF GOODWILL TO ALL MEN PASSED WITH A FANFARE OF machine-gun and rifle fire from the mountains, as the jubilant troops in the trenches celebrated their own personal survival in the war. This was their way of communicating the Christmas spirit. From time to time it was possible to distinguish carols in the bursts of gunfire. Their favourite tune was "Jingle Bells".

Meanwhile, Akashi and de Lapresle, after weeks of shuttling between Belgrade, Sarajevo and Pale, had finally obtained a ceasefire. In this drawn-out process, they had received the unexpected help of former US President Jimmy Carter, following a telephone call made to him by Karadzic appealing for help.

Jimmy Carter had flown to Bosnia with his wife on 18 December, and after meetings with the Bosnian Serb leadership he had managed to persuade Karadzic to agree to an immediate ceasefire, as well as to restart peace negotiations "on the basis of the Contact Group plan". For their part, the Bosnian Government had said that they were prepared to accept a complete cessation of hostilities in Bosnia for a period of three months, but that the Contact Group plan could not be renegotiated. During the week that Jimmy Carter and his wife stayed in Sarajevo, they virtually became part of the UN, sharing the over-crowded, often unheated accommodation with other members of the staff. At this time living conditions in the UN HQ were particularly difficult as the Serbs had halted all UN flights into the city for the past month. The shortage of heating, electricity or food did not seem to trouble Carter in the slightest. As I was away from Bosnia during their visit the Carters used my office and bedroom as their base, and Jamie Daniell, who acted as their military assistant, looked after them. Once he found the former President wandering about in his pyjamas in the main kitchen at six in the morning, making his wife a cup of tea. Jimmy Carter seemed to enjoy being treated as a working member of the UN staff and politely refused all offers of preferential treatment.

Many journalists accused him of naivety in his dealings with the Serbs, particularly after he had praised the Bosnian Serbs for their "commitment to peace". My own view now is that Carter's arrival before Christmas in Sarajevo gave new momentum to the peace process, although Noel Malcolm in the *Daily Telegraph* called his attempt to break the deadlock ham-fisted and predicted that the Carter-brokered ceasefire would be a short one.[1] It lasted for more than four months.

Far from being weak or naïve, Carter had put enormous pressure on both sides by telling them that if they failed to agree with his proposals, he would ensure they were condemned as warmongers for rejecting his plan and perpetuating the war. Although others, including myself, had used this tactic many times, coming from a former US President, both sides took the threat seriously. The Bosnians could not afford to risk losing support in the US, while Karadzic regarded Carter as being the only person of influence in the US who would listen to the Serbs. Carter's intervention had given peace one more chance.

When I returned to Bosnia on 22 December from a holiday with my family, Sarajevo was covered in snow and the weather was overcast. As we drove into town, people trudged through the snow, muffled against the cold, pulling sledges behind them. Gen. Hervé Gobillard, who had been in command of UNPROFOR during my absence, told me that he had become thoroughly exasperated by the endless lies and shifts of position of the Bosnian Government, whose forces still remained in the zone. That day he had at last persuaded Gen. Karavelic, who commanded the Bosnian forces on the mountain, to clear all his troops from the demilitarised zone. But, just before he met me at the airport, Gobillard had been told that Karavelic, after speaking to Izetbegovic, had reneged on the agreement. As a result, Gobillard felt he should now cancel a Christmas holiday in France with his family. I told him he should do no such thing, as the problem would certainly still be there when he returned.

The presence of Bosnian troops in the demilitarised zone remained the most significant obstacle to getting the Serbs back into the peace process, and Gobillard had been working tirelessly during the past three months to resolve the Mt Igman crisis. This last reversal was a blow, above all to Gobillard, who saw each new obstacle put in his path as a challenge to the French nation as well as a potential catastrophe for the people of Bosnia.

I drove back to the Residency thoroughly depressed. As we passed the Holiday Inn, I saw French Army medics attending to a man lying on the ground. Either he had been hit by a sniper or had slipped on the frozen ground. It didn't seem to matter much any more. From what Gobillard had told me it appeared the country was heading for war.

At the Residency I was cheered up when Jamie gave me a more encouraging account of the progress that had been made in my absence. However bad the news, Jamie always remained bright and cheerful. He told me that Akashi now believed a full cessation of hostilities agreement could be obtained before the end of the year, although Ganic was still trying to find ways of preventing this. On 23 December, the Zagreb Flying Circus arrived in Sarajevo to get signatures for the Carter ceasefire, which proved to be more troublesome than expected.

In Pale, after some tough negotiation, Karadzic and Mladic had signed a document agreeing to a ceasefire throughout Bosnia which would hopefully lead to an agreement to cease hostilities for a four-month period. We returned in a confident mood to Sarajevo, believing that an important step had been achieved. On our arrival at the Presidency, Akashi, to my astonishment, instead of handing an unsigned copy of the ceasefire agreement to Ganic, gave him the copy signed by the Serbs. Although Ganic had previously agreed to the substance of the agreement, Akashi had made some changes to the wording to meet International Red Cross requirements concerning the exchange of prisoners. In Ganic's eyes, this change of wording, accompanied by the signatures of Karadzic and Mladic, made it a Serb document. He flew into a rage, shouting at Akashi that he had been presented with a Serb *fait accompli*, and that there would be no ceasefire. I urged Akashi to go to Izetbegovic and take the unsigned copy of the agreement to him for signature. Meanwhile I would go to the US Embassy and persuade John Menzies, the new ambassador, to get Washington to put pressure on the Bosnian Government to accept the reworded agreement. We could not allow Ganic's tantrums to derail the peace process.

In order to get Izetbegovic to sign the ceasefire agreement, Akashi agreed to eliminate the disputed paragraph from the document, despite the fact that before leaving Pale, he and Karadzic had publicly hailed it as "the beginning of the end of the war". As a result the UN now had two different peace documents, each bearing different signatures and neither of which accorded with each other. I told de Lapresle I was glad that it was his countersignature on the documents, not mine. He responded with a wry smile.

Akashi seemed strangely unconcerned by the potential loss of credibility that would face the UN when it became known there were two peace agreements. After another press conference in Sarajevo, at which he triumphantly waved both pieces of paper in the air, he departed for the airport. Before he left, he told Viktor and me to let Karadzic know that a paragraph had been removed from the Serb version of the ceasefire agreement. He agreed with us that it was unsatisfactory having two different peace documents, but removing the offending paragraph had been the only way that he could get Izetbegovic's signature on the agreement. He believed that what he had achieved was better than nothing. He then wished us all a happy Christmas, and departed for the airport, leaving Viktor and me, for a moment, speechless on the pavement outside the Presidency. After a moment's pause, Viktor muttered, "I tried to stop him, I tried to stop him." I said nothing. We had just witnessed a piece of stage management that would be difficult enough to pull off on Broadway, and we awaited the consequences with foreboding.

But we had not read the minds of the Bosnian Serb leadership as well as Akashi had done. To our astonishment, Karadzic accepted the deletion of the paragraph without demur, and the next day the guns fell silent throughout Bosnia for the first time since 1992. Well, almost all of the guns. Fighting still continued in Bihac between the Bosnian Army and the renegade forces of Abdic, who had not been part of the ceasefire agreement.

The next day all the senior UN officers in Sarajevo were invited to a Christmas Eve party at the Presidency where Izetbegovic welcomed us with his ministers. No one offered so much as a toast to peace, or even discussed the war. That night I attended a Mass in Sarajevo Cathedral. Archbishop Pulic began the service by welcoming people of all religions and denominations – except for "those who celebrate Christmas on a different day". The congregation muttered in agreement. The Serbs, though they were Christians, were not welcome. Later the Archbishop, in his sermon, called on the leaders of all sides to put a stop to the terrible war. To end the service, the choir softly sang the old German carol "Stille Nacht, heilige Nacht". As we left the cathedral and I looked up at the snow-covered mountains in the moonlight above the city, it struck me that for the first time in two years, the words in the carol had been answered.

We went to bed at 0200 hours, having drunk champagne with practically everyone in the Residency. Goose stuck to his army issue tin mug, on the grounds, I suppose, that it held more champagne. Jamie Daniell rather ill-advisedly shared a bottle of vodka with Viktor Andreev. Each time he slugged back another glass he would stamp his foot and declare, "Good Lord, is that the time?"

On Christmas Day, armed with a crate of whisky, I visited the French positions around Sarajevo. There had been a heavy snowfall in the night, so much of the route had to be covered on foot. We were following hard on the heels of a French Army padre who was giving Mass to the soldiers in their isolated outposts on the confrontation line. At one point we caught up with him climbing a path, carrying the sacrament in his rucksack. Goose insisted on sharing the best part of a bottle of whisky with him before we parted company. We last saw him wandering uncertainly in the direction of a forward observation post. The French soldiers in Bosnia were mostly conscripts who had volunteered to serve abroad, though this meant they had to extend their period of military service by an extra year. Many did this because of the high unemployment in France, the double pay that they received when on operations, and also because of the additional help they were given by the French Government in finding civilian employment when they left military service.

Many of the French soldiers were waiting to go to university and it was extremely useful for me to discuss UN strategy with them and hear their views on the war. Many of them had previously served in Bosnia and they had few illusions about the willingness of the warring parties to respect a ceasefire. Nevertheless, they felt that a real opportunity for peace had been opened up, and they were generally hopeful Bosnia would remain quiet until the New Year.

The main topic of conversation was an Ilyushin 76 cargo plane that had crashed at Sarajevo airport the day before. It had been carrying 30,000 bottles of wine presented by the French Government. Surprisingly, none of the wine had been damaged in the crash, but it had been necessary to individually unload each bottle from the wrecked aircraft. The French soldiers proudly told me that this task had been accomplished with the loss of only one bottle.

On the afternoon of Christmas Day, the UN staff of the Residency held the inaugural race of the Sarajevo Hash House Harriers. The race was first run in the jungle of pre-war Malaya and is akin to orienteering. As we ran through the empty streets of Sarajevo following the ritual cries of "On! On!", we attracted swarms of children. The race was held up because the UN competitors, their pockets filled with sweets, stopped to distribute them. No one seemed concerned that no winner was declared at the end of the day. It was a pleasant interlude from peacekeeping.

That evening I faxed to the Serb leadership in Pale and to the Bosnian Presidency a draft agreement for a four-month cessation of hostilities. I had been discussing a draft of the document with Zagreb for a number of days, and each time that Viktor and I had reduced it in length the staff in Zagreb had reinstated the words we had removed. In the end, we sent our own shortened version to the warring parties. The cessation of hostilities was to come into effect after the ceasefire had been in existence for seven days. This was the next necessary step towards a permanent peace.

Viktor and I set off to Pale on Boxing Day to discover that the reaction of Karadzic and Mladic to the draft was surprisingly positive. Rather than link the proposed cessation of hostilities to a global peace plan, as they had always done hitherto, they now wished to exploit the new position that they believed had emerged from the visit by Jimmy Carter. As long as the Contact Group plan could be regarded as the "basis of negotiation", rather than an imposed measure, they were prepared to agree to a cessation of hostilities. Karadzic also said that the Serbs believed that certain qualitative factors should be taken into account when any division of Bosnia was discussed, which in his opinion the Contact Group had manifestly failed to do. The Serbs were in a mood to compromise at last. They had probably begun to realise that it was better to negotiate while they were still in a militarily superior position, rather than wait until the tide turned against them. The military build-up of forces in the Croat–Muslim Federation, the difficulties caused by sanctions and disillusionment with the war among the Serb people, would make this inevitable. It would be the Serb Orthodox Christmas Day in a few days, and it seemed to us as we returned to Sarajevo that the notion of peace and goodwill had made an early appearance in Pale.

Sadly, this same spirit was not apparent on the other side of the conflict line. Crossing the Bridge of Brotherhood and Unity we were ambushed by a group of Bosnian soldiers. One soldier stood directly in front of my Range Rover and aimed his AK47 rifle directly at me, while others tried to force open the doors of the vehicle from the sides. They were either drunk or acting on the orders of the Bosnian Government. Either way, Goose was taking no chances, and with a roar of the 4-litre engine we leapt forward. The soldier in front of the vehicle disappeared from sight. As we sped off, I thought I heard the sound of firing coming from behind, but as the vehicle weighed several tons and its armour was more than an inch thick, it was difficult to tell. I never discovered whether any Bosnians were injured, but no mention of the incident was ever made by Ganic.

We arrived at the Residency just in time for the staff Christmas lunch party, at which the UN officers acted as waiters for the Bosnian staff and their families. Each child had a present and a hat. Many of them had never seen paper hats or crackers before, and had never eaten turkey or jelly. One boy was so worried about losing his teddy bear that he clutched it to his chest throughout the meal. Every time his waiter, a burly RAF officer, tried to serve him, the little boy kicked him sharply on the shins, causing the officer's cheery smile to become somewhat fixed by the end of the meal. After the party the war was forgotten and a snowball fight took place in the garden of the Residency between the staff and the UN. It was plainly a highlight in many of the children's lives, though I suspect we enjoyed the occasion as much as they did. The UN officers had been away from their own families for a long time, and Christmas 1994 was a sad time for them too.

A week later the Residency manager, who had been a member of staff since the building had been the Delegates' Club in Tito's time, was savagely beaten up in the street by the Bosnian secret police and his life was threatened. After the UN Christmas party in the Residency, he had told Bosnian intelligence he would no longer work for them. This had been their reply. We smuggled him out of Sarajevo the next day, and he is now living abroad.

On 28 December I flew with Kurt Schork, the Reuters reporter, and the photographer Robert Adams, to the Bihac enclave in an attempt to bring about a ceasefire between Abdic and Dudakovic. Ganic had said that he would not negotiate a cessation of hostilities between the Serbs and the Bosnians until Abdic halted his advance on Bihac from the north. Since the fight with Abdic was the result of an internecine struggle between two opposing Muslim factions, this condition was plainly a spoiling action designed to prevent the peace negotiations between the Serbs and the Muslims from advancing. Ganic was obviously worried that Karadzic was about to agree to the new Bosnian Government proposals regarding the cessation of hostilities, and this might permanently freeze the line of conflict in its present position. It was a legitimate concern of the Bosnian Government, but their policy of sabotaging the UN peace mission to prevent such a situation occurring only prolonged the suffering of their people.

We flew in a French Puma helicopter from Split to Bihac, having obtained clearances for the flight from the Serbs, over whose territory the route lay. As we passed Knin, a message to the French pilot was received from the Serbs ordering us to turn back. If we did not, they threatened, we would be shot down. The pilot asked me what he should do. I told him to spiral down from the high altitude route that we were following and continue the flight to Bihac at low level using the mountainous terrain for cover. The pilot shrugged his shoulders and grinned. Suddenly we fell like a stone from the sky, and I shouted across the helicopter above the noise of the engine to explain what was happening. Kurt looked unconcerned, but I noticed that his photographer was rapidly loading his camera, presumably to film any Serb attack. How he expected his film to be recovered from the wreckage of the helicopter if it was shot down, I don't know. Like me, I expect he was just taking one problem at a time. For a minute we held our breath until we reached the relative security of the valley below where we levelled out. Keeping close to the ground, we made our way without further excitement to Coralici, the location of the Bangladeshi battalion HQ. The next day, Mladic, who personally monitored all incidents in Bosnia, told me that my decision to ignore the Serb instruction to turn back had been very stupid, as he had only just managed to prevent a missile being fired at us.

Col. Salim, who had attended the British Army Staff College at Camberley, met us in Coralici. He was highly intelligent, and looked and spoke like a pre-war Indian Army officer. He had recently been the senior instructor in the Bangladeshi Staff College and had worked closely with a British Army training team, where he had clearly acquired a good understanding of British peacekeeping doctrine. I always had total confidence that his soldiers, who were mainly Muslims, would remain impartial and not overreact to the difficulties facing them.

I had not yet had an opportunity to visit the Bangladeshi battalion, whose soldiers that winter were facing some of the worst conditions experienced by any UN peace-keepers in Bosnia. Despite the difficulties facing them, the Bangladeshis proved to be excellent soldiers who retained many British military characteristics.

Driving through the enclave, it became obvious that the real conditions in Bihac were quite different from the picture being painted by the propaganda machine of the Bosnian Government and the media. Far from there being no fuel in the enclave, our convoy was held up by heavy traffic on the ten-mile drive between Coralici and Bihac, and at one point we passed a bulldozer clearing snow. There were horse-drawn wagons on the road, a common sight in this predominately rural region, and it was, of course, pictures of these wagons that dominated the television screens of the world.

I spent an hour with the Bosnian commander of 5th Corps, Gen. Dudakovic, who looked surprisingly well and certainly did not have the appearance of a commander who had been fighting for survival in some Stalingrad-style situation. He flatly refused to accept any ceasefire deal with Abdic, and spent most of the meeting railing against the renegade Muslim leader. I told him curtly that I was in Bihac at the express wish of Ganic to arrange a ceasefire between him and Abdic, and that in civilised countries the military obeyed the instructions of their political masters. After further acrimonious discussion, Dudakovic agreed that if I persuaded Abdic to stop fighting, he would accept the ruling of the Bosnian Government on this matter.

After another drive across the enclave inside a cramped Soviet APC, we reached the town of Velika Kladusa, the HQ of Abdic. On the way Salim had insisted that the armoured vehicles should be closed down in order to cross the battle line, and we had all arrived feeling rather sick. In Velika Kladusa, we were met by one of Abdic's men driving a stolen Bosnian police car. With some relief I climbed into it with Kurt Schork, as I wanted to show him as much of Bihac as possible, and we departed at high speed for Abdic's secret hideout, leaving Salim and the remainder of the UN team floundering along behind. We drew up outside a large villa on the outskirts of Velika Kladusa, where Abdic and a UN military observer awaited us.

The intervening months of war had not appeared to cause Abdic any more stress than they had Dudakovic, for he had put on weight since we last met. Nevertheless he proceeded to subject me to a long and disjointed catalogue of the misfortunes that had befallen him, which made even Candide's adventures seem rather tame. There was no time for commiseration, however, so I demanded that he stopped fighting and joined the peace process. I explained that Ganic had asked me specifically to negotiate with him to stop the fighting in Bihac. It was in his interests to do so. Now that the Croats were allies of the Muslims in the new Bosnian Federation, they would no longer support him against Dudakovic and as his other allies, the Krajina Serbs, came under pressure from the increasingly strong Croatian Army, they would not be in a position to help him either. He should accept the conditions set out by Ganic while he still had time.

Abdic withdrew to consult with his advisers (one of whom, curiously, was the brother of one of Dudakovic's officers), and shortly afterwards he returned to say that he would agree to a ceasefire. Carrying a piece of paper bearing Abdic's signature I flew to Sarajevo and went directly to the Presidency. By the time I had arrived, however, Ganic had changed his mind. He refused to sign the peace deal and forbade Dudakovic to do so. We had all expended a great deal of time and energy obtaining precisely what he had asked for, and had been lucky not to have a helicopter and ourselves shot down in the process. Nothing, it seemed, would satisfy Ganic. Whenever we were close to a peace deal, he found an excuse for derailing the process.

Later I found out that, shortly before we had arrived in Bihac, a tank belonging to Dudakovic had fired a single round through the door of a fortified house somewhere along the battle line in Bihac, killing Abdic's best military commander. While this had forced Abdic to sue for peace, the effect of the news on Ganic had been the reverse. He now felt that the Bosnians were in a position to inflict a military defeat on Abdic, and they no longer needed the UN to save Dudakovic from annihilation.

The next day, 29 December, I became even more disenchanted with my role as mediator when I had to sit across a table from Mladic during a lengthy meeting, watching him trying to burst a large boil on his already pustulous nose. He kept squinting into a small vanity mirror, which he held in front of his face, while trying to trap the boil between his podgy fingers. This made sensible conversation rather difficult, and we all became as obsessed with the boil as Mladic. Suddenly, to a sigh of relief round the room, there was a burst of pus and blood from the end of his nose and Mladic mopped up the mess on the table in front of him with a grimy handkerchief. The effect on Mladic was obviously cathartic. Without further argument, he agreed all the proposals contained in the agreement. We were then invited to lunch, but this we politely declined.

At the Bosnian Presidency, Ganic and Muratovic, the minister responsible for liaison with the UN, were still trying to prevent the ceasefire from developing into a full-blown cessation of hostilities. This time the sheer venality and lack of humanity of the Bosnian Muslims took my breath away. Muratovic stated that a precondition for holding any further peace talks was that the Serbs should allow the free passage of commercial goods into the city. The delivery of humanitarian aid alone was no longer acceptable. This was tantamount to saying that the Bosnian Government was prepared to keep the people of Sarajevo starving and without fuel until its businesses could start trading again.

The Serbs had always allowed some movement of commercial goods across the battle lines surrounding Sarajevo, although they reportedly charged a heavy tariff on goods entering the city. It now seemed that Muratovic had decided not to pay the tariff and he was prepared to continue the war to achieve his end. Muratovic refused to accept the UN argument that it would be more logical to view the restoration of commercial traffic as a product of peace, and not to try and make it part of a continuing war.

Fortunately the UN negotiating team in Sarajevo had been joined by a Miami lawyer, Matt Hodes. He had a reputation for toughness in prosecuting international drug barons and would accept no nonsense from either side. In the face of his aggressive, argumentative approach, neither Ganic nor Muratovic were able to sustain their barbaric position for long.

I was, anyway, also keeping John Menzies briefed, and he could see the US Government could not support these extreme demands of the Bosnian Government. I told John that the supply of utilities to the city had in fact been reconnected, that the delivery of aid was at an historic high and that the number of civilian deaths by shooting was lower in Sarajevo than in many US cities.

The State Department in Washington was by now firmly supporting the UN peace mission, and through them, John was able to bring considerable pressure to bear on the Bosnians to take the UN proposals seriously. By 30 December it looked as if both sides would sign up to a cessation of hostilities in Bosnia, so I invited Akashi and de Lapresle to return to Sarajevo to witness the deal.

When they saw how close to peace we were getting, both the Serbs and the Bosnians sought to make last-minute gains, which caused further complications. Karadzic wanted to remove from the final document the words "according to the UN Security Council Resolution" on the grounds that, as the Republika Srpska was not recognised by the UN, he could hardly put his signature to the document. On the other side, Ganic insisted that these words be included, confident that the Serbs would continue to accept the document.

At 1330 hours on 31 December, Akashi arrived at the Bosnian Presidency bearing a message from Pale that Karadzic was still refusing to sign any accord that mentioned the UN. This suggestion invited a stream of abuse from Ganic and Muratovic, who accused Akashi of always siding with the Serbs. They, for there part, refused to sign any document that did not make specific mention of the UN in the precise words they had proposed. Tapping his long, thin fingers on the table, Ganic stood up and announced that there would be no agreement to cease hostilities. He would now brief the press that the collapse of the peace talks was the fault of the UN, who had done no more than offer a "hollow document".

All this would have been a cheap, irrelevant little charade, were not so much at stake. Before he left the room, and in some desperation, I passed a note to Akashi saying that he should insist on going to see Izetbegovic. We were too close to a solution to be thwarted by Ganic. Akashi told Ganic that he would not accept the talks had ended, and that he insisted on seeing the President. Ganic replied with a dismissive wave of his hand that he would not permit this. He had been fully authorised by the President to conduct the peace negotiations. Izetbegovic was attending a

New Year reception elsewhere, and was unavailable. In the middle of the furious argument that followed, a note was passed to me from the Bosnian Government side of the table. It read: "Please keep trying ... *demand* a meeting with Izetbegovic." I did not look at the person I suspected of being the author of the note on the opposite side of the table. Akashi continued to insist on seeing Izetbegovic, and the meeting finally broke up with Ganic agreeing to delay his press conference in order to give the UN one last chance to get Karadzic to change *his* mind.

Meanwhile Mike Stanley had been in Pale for the past three days where he was involved in intense and at times almost violent debate with the Serb leadership. Mike told me that there was a deep division between them about whether they should accept a political settlement short of what they hoped to achieve, in order to end the war now, or whether they should fight on for an all-out victory. His advice was that the Pale leadership could be pushed a little further into accepting the latest demands of the Bosnian Government, but that if we pushed them too far, we would be playing into the hands of the war camp in Pale.

Through Mike, I relayed a message to Karadzic with a new form of words that Akashi had devised with the help of John Menzies and David Harland. Mike took the modified document to Karadzic, who was by now in permanent session with his colleagues in Pale. Mladic and Koljevic were in favour of pursuing peace, while Karadzic and Tolimir, Mladic's military assistant, wanted to continue the war. In order to stop an argument about what sinister motive was behind the latest proposal, Mike arranged for Akashi and Karadzic to speak together directly on the US tactical satellite system; but before doing so, he had to teach Karadzic how to operate the American equipment. Hearing Mike explain the UN radio procedure to Karadzic lightened the atmosphere in the room, and under the combined pressure of Akashi and Mike, Karadzic finally gave way, and agreed to the new form of words.

Our next problem was how to ensure that Ganic did not wreck the negotiations at the last moment. The UN had recently appointed a softly-spoken Irishman, Colm Murphy, as its new press spokesman in Sarajevo. He had not been involved in our previous acrimonious disputes with Ganic and he seemed to get on with him. He used his immense Gaelic charm to avoid confrontation, without compromising on his strong determination to obtain peace through peaceful means. He once told me that he thought the use of NATO bombs in Gorazde had been an insult to the UN Charter. Akashi dispatched him to the Presidency with instructions to nail Ganic to the floor and to return with an agreement. Colm subsequently reported that Ganic had been considerably shaken and annoyed by the news that the Serbs had accepted the Bosnian Government's demands, and he said that he would have to talk to the President before accepting the new proposals.

In the President's office, however, he found John Menzies already briefing Izetbegovic on the deal, which now had the complete support of Washington. For once, Ganic was outflanked by the UN. In a last ditch attempt to prevent peace, he asked to speak to the President alone. Later John told me that, outside Izetbegovic's office, he could hear Ganic shouting at the President, who had replied calmly but firmly. Izetbegovic then returned to his office and told John that he would accept a four-month cessation of hostilities in Bosnia. The ceasefire was to start at midnight on 31 December 1994. It was the thousandth day since the beginning of the siege of Sarajevo and the start of war.

Although pleased by the news, I was not confident that during the next four months the international community would be able to take advantage of this hard-won opportunity to bring the war to an end. Nor, I suspected, would the ordinary people of Bosnia have many illusions about the long-term prospects of peace. They had seen too many ceasefires broken. For my part, I had spent nearly a year of my life pursuing the goal of silencing the guns in Bosnia, and that task was, for the moment, completed.

I felt strangely unelated. The sight of Ganic in front of the cameras, smiling and smirking as he claimed credit for the deal, destroyed any possible sense of joy or satis-faction. Only two hours earlier he had been behaving in an arrogant and insulting way to Akashi, doing his best to wreck the deal. As the conference ended, he had even asked Akashi if he could have a seat on his UN aircraft when he left Sarajevo, so that he could holiday in Turkey. Akashi flatly refused. I was delighted to think that Ganic, as a consequence, would have to crawl through the tunnel under the airport and then walk up Mt Igman within range of the Serb guns. Perhaps for the first time in his life he would be hoping that peace prevailed, at least for as long as it took him to get out of range of the guns.

For a while I walked about the streets stopping occasionally to talk to people about the peace deal. The news of the successful outcome of the talks in the Presidency had already reached them, but their reaction was muted. It was always difficult to discover behind their tired, worn faces what the ordinary people really thought about any political event. For most of their lives they had not been allowed true freedom of expression and I doubted if they would ever have the courage to rid themselves of their leadership and create a true state of democracy, freedom and justice. It was easier for them to continue to live in a political system in which they were absolved from making decisions or taking on any moral responsibility for their fellow human beings.

Although I had lived among the Bosnians for nearly a year, I had been in a separate world. Nevertheless, in my own way, I had experienced the same emotions of elation, betrayal and despair. I was becoming as physically drained as they were, and every time I saw my face on television or in newspapers, I recognised a certain grimness that was a reflection of the faces of the people of Bosnia.

At the first meeting of the Joint Commission to supervise the implementation of the cessation of hostilities agreement, I began to feel I might have been wrong to suspect the warring parties' true intentions with regard to peace. Although Mladic and Delic did not attend, their representatives, Tolimir and Karavelic, appeared keen to keep up the momentum of the deal at the military level. It was quickly agreed that liaison officers representing both HQs would attend the regional meetings of the Joint Commission throughout Bosnia, and that they would be authorised to take decisions without reference to their superior commanders.

It was also decided that UNPROFOR positions would be established between the opposing forces, that the line of conflict would be defined, and that troops on each side would withdraw out of range of each other. Full freedom of movement for all UNPROFOR convoys was also agreed, as was the opening of the Sarajevo airport for all humanitarian and UN missions. The demilitarised zone on Mt Igman would be cleared of combatants and each side would be able to inspect the area under the auspices of the UN. Finally, the exchange of prisoners would immediately recommence.

Fighting was still going on in Bihac between Abdic and Dudakovic, but because it did not directly involve the Serbs, it was not a matter that could be resolved by the Joint Commission. It was suggested, however, that arrangements for bringing an end to the war in Bihac should take place in the margins of the main meetings. As I left with Viktor Andreev, we agreed that it had been the most productive and successful meeting that had taken place between the two sides since the 9 February Airport Agreement that had so transformed the situation around Sarajevo the previous year.

Sadly, the goodwill shown at the first meeting of the Joint Commission was not repeated, and the peace process was stalled again as both sides became obstructive and bureaucratic in their attempts to slow down the pace that the UN had set. On the one hand, the Bosnian Serbs refused to allow the routes across Sarajevo airport to be opened until they had verified there were no remaining Bosnian forces within the Mt Igman demilitarised zone. On the other, the Bosnian Government refused to accept the presence of Serb liaison officers on their territory, even though the agreement specified that liaison officers should be placed in the relevant UN HQ. Since all of the UN sector HQs were on Bosnian territory, the refusal made it impossible for the UN to hold regional meetings.

In order to break the impasse, I decided to escort the Serb liaison officer, Maj. Indic, to the first meetings of the regional Joint Commissions. Two meetings were to be held on the same day in Gornji Vakuf and Tuzla, both in central Bosnia. My intention had been to fly to each of the locations, but a blizzard prevented all movement by helicopter, and I was forced to drive Indic in a convoy of UN vehicles across Bosnian territory. Indic, who worked directly for Mladic, was highly nervous lest he be identified by the Bosnians at their checkpoints; we all knew that if he was taken, he would be interrogated and killed. Fortunately his nervousness was overcome by his curiosity. He had not been able to travel in central Bosnia for nearly four years, and he agreed to make the journey by road despite the extreme personal danger.

We encountered our first problem on the drive out of the mountains into Gornji Vakuf. The Range Rover that I was travelling in and Goose was driving, skidded on the ice and rolled down the mountainside. Mercifully, the fall of the heavy armoured vehicle was cushioned by deep snow and there was only a small slope before the ground levelled out. The main risk to my life had come from Goose, who kept falling on me as the vehicle rolled for more than 100 metres down the slope. No one was badly damaged and we were able to continue in the remaining vehicles.

In Gornji Vakuf, Brig. Robert Gordon, who commanded the UN forces in south-western Bosnia, ran the first meeting of the regional Joint Commission with all the clarity and efficiency of a meeting of the Chiefs of Staff Committee, of which he had recently been the Secretary. He began by introducing Maj. Indic to the local Bosnian and Croat commanders, who were astonished to find him in their midst. Robert outlined the agenda and listed the tasks that had to be achieved. He also laid down precise rules of procedure for future meetings. We were all very impressed. The atmosphere at this first meeting was surprisingly good, and we left Gornji Vakuf feeling that progress was being made.

By then, the weather in central Bosnia had cleared sufficiently for us to fly to Tuzla, so avoiding the roadblocks that the Bosnian Army would undoubtedly throw across the country, now that they knew Indic was in their midst. In Tuzla, Gen. Delic – no relation to the Bosnian Army commander – greeted Indic warmly, but the meeting soon deteriorated when the Bosnians would not accept the presence of a Serb "aggressor" in Tuzla. Brig. Ridderstadt, the Swedish commander of the north-west UN sector of Bosnia, pointed out that the establishment of liaison officers in each of the UN HQs had been prescribed in the cessation of hostilities agreement. He had already been given the name of the Serb liaison officer who was to work in his HQ and he intended to stick to the letter of the agreement signed in Sarajevo. In spite of this, the meeting hardly progressed beyond this issue, and since the weather was deteriorating again, I left the meeting early, taking Indic with me.

After one attempt to cross the mountain range by helicopter, we were forced to return to Tuzla and travel to Sarajevo by road. Given the state of the roads, this would take about six hours. When I explained this to Indic, he became extremely agitated. He knew that by now the Bosnian Army would have sealed off all the roads between Tuzla and Sarajevo, and he was not at all reassured by the fact he would be travelling under UN protection. In 1993, a Serb soldier had shot and killed a Bosnian Vice-Prime Minister in the back of a French armoured vehicle at a check-point, even though he had an escort of armed guards. It might have been regarded as poetic justice that Indic was now in danger of suffering the same fate. However, we knew the area well and made our way back along a network of mountain roads that were unlikely to be patrolled or blocked by the Bosnian Army. We arrived back in Sarajevo after midnight. As Maj. Indic and I parted at a Serb checkpoint, I said to him: "You have just experienced a typical day in the life of a UN peacekeeper. For nearly 18 hours, while working for peace, you have been messed about by obstructive Serbs, hostile Bosnians, the Balkan weather and the dreadful condition of your roads. Congratulations!" He was too relieved to be back home to appreciate my brand of humour.

Within a day, to prevent any further meetings of the regional Joint Commission, the Bosnian Army had established permanent blocks around Gornji Vakuf and Tuzla and threatened to shoot down UN helicopters transporting British liaison officers to the Serb-held town of Banja Luka. Nor was it possible for the UN to find alternative locations for these meetings, as the Serbs insisted that the 31 December agreement (stating that meetings of the regional Joint Commissions would be held in UN HQs) was strictly adhered to. Peacekeeping was never going to be easy, but it becomes impossible when those who have asked for help threaten to kill those who come to their aid.

Very occasionally, moments of humour and humanity relieved the tedium of the lengthy meetings of the Central Joint Commission, which now occupied most of my time. Once, Tolimir began to read out a list of Croatian regular army units that he claimed had entered Bosnia in violation of UN resolutions. The list was so long that everyone started to get up and walk around the room, beginning conversations of their own, and ignoring Tolimir, who ploughed on relentlessly. When he finished, a silence descended on the room, and he said: "I thank you all for listening to me so carefully." Muratovic, with an unexpected flash of wit, replied, "Tolimir, I would be a happy man if only half of what you said were true!"

On another occasion, Mladic asked me if I was religious and whether I prayed every day. When I replied yes to the first question and no to the second, he launched forth on a strange, rambling statement of his own religious beliefs. He prayed every day for his soldiers, and always before going into battle. He assured me that chaplains had a very important place in the Bosnian Serb Army and were even allowed to influence decisions on the battlefield. He also wanted to know whether I was allowed to take part in politics. He found it extraordinary that the British Army had not been involved in politics since our own civil war around 350 years ago. He told me that he believed the Gulf War was a Western attempt to defeat Muslim fundamentalism, and in the next breath asserted that the war in Bosnia was an attack on the Serb Orthodox religion. On another occasion, in a break between the formal sessions of a meeting, he had given a rendition of a Croat folk song to demonstrate a point he was making to Blaskic, the Bosnian Croatian general. It turned out that Mladic could sing.

The most intractable problem that had to be resolved at the top-level meetings of the Joint Commission involved the withdrawal of all forces from the Mt Igman demilitarised zone. This zone had been established in 1993 to prevent the encirclement of Sarajevo by the Bosnian Serb Army. Since then, there had been repeated incursions into the zone by the Bosnian Army from where they attacked the Serbs. During one meeting, Koljevic told me that Mladic had never forgiven himself for allowing Mt Igman to be given up. It had taken the lives of many young Serb soldiers to capture the mountain, and their old positions were now being used to inflict further casualties on his men. On 11 January, after many hours of bitter argument, the UN finally got the Bosnian Government to agree to withdraw its forces from the demilitarised zone and to accept an inspection of the zone by the Serbs. At a signing ceremony at the airport, in which each side formally agreed to implement all elements contained in the cessation of hostilities agreement, Delic publicly shook hands with Mladic. This had not happened before, and it was not to happen again. Viktor and I left the meeting just after midnight. "Victor," I said, "that is the very last time I shall ever chair a meeting of those crooks and hoodlums. Now that we have agreed the military requirement, the Joint Commission is all yours!" He cunningly pointed out that as he had always attended the *military* sessions of the Joint Commission, he would expect me to attend the *political* discussions that he chaired.

The efforts of the UN to bring peace to Bosnia were accompanied by a flurry of international activity aimed at achieving a political settlement that would end the war. Richard Holbrooke arrived with a strong team of negotiators and spoke highly of the UN mission to the BBC. He was insistent that the Serbs should not be permitted to use the Contact Group plan "as a basis for further negotiation", and made little progress in achieving an agreement. The Contact Group also visited Sarajevo to see what it could do. Perhaps it was conscious that as yet, in the words of Lord Owen, there had been "no peacemaking to match the UN peacekeeping". Unable to get the Serbs to accept their proposals either, the Contact Group rapidly lost sight of their principal strategic objective and became bogged down in arguments about the opening of routes into Sarajevo.

Although the Serbs were prepared to allow humanitarian aid into Sarajevo they still objected to the passage of commercial traffic into the city. The international media unhelpfully reported this as the "re-strangulation" of Sarajevo. We spent a great deal of time explaining to the Contact Group that it was not the Serbs who were preventing the movement of humanitarian aid into Sarajevo but the Bosnian Government, which had made the free movement of commercial traffic into the city a precondition to the delivery of aid. On one occasion Muratovic had personally stopped a UN convoy of firewood, donated by the Austrian people, from crossing the airport into Sarajevo. He made it quite clear that he would rather see his people freeze than give up a chance of personal gain by the restoration of commercial traffic.

During these difficult negotiations to restore the flow of aid, NATO proceeded to undermine the UN effort, by inexplicably flying bombers very low and aggressively over Pale. The purpose of this manoeuvre was not clear, but the effect was to make the Serbs extremely nervous, for there were ammunition bunkers in Pale, and an important communication site located not far away at Jahorina. I had previously urged Adm. Leighton Smith to cease flying in this hostile way, and asked him to put the same faith in the peace process as the UN had.

My plea went ignored. Exasperated, I told Wg-Cdr Tim Hewlett, the RAF officer commanding the NATO air cell in Sarajevo, that I would brief CNN on the negative effect the NATO air action was having on the peace process. Within seconds of making this threat, all communications between Naples and Sarajevo were cut off. Adm. Leighton Smith's liaison officer, a US Marines colonel, had overheard me and immediately reported my words to Smith, who had taken them literally. I wrote a letter of apology to Smith, regretting what I had said and explaining that this had not been a reflection of my true intentions. A week later I received a charming reply saying that we had never allowed our professional disagreements to spill over into personal animosity. This was true, but only just.

Earlier in the month John Simpson of the BBC had been sent to Bosnia to report on my year-long UNPROFOR command. He had an open mind about the contribution made by the UN during the past year, and appeared to be coming round to the view that the reporting of the war in Bosnia by the international media had been less than even-handed. He was accompanied by a large South African cameraman called Nigel, who managed to squeeze himself alongside John in the back of the Range Rover to film Goose as we drove round Sarajevo. I wanted him to meet as many Bosnians as possible. They would tell him a very different story to the official Bosnian Government version. I took him on the Sarajevo trams, walked with him in the streets, and finally flew with him to Gorazde, where he met the director of the hospital, Dr Begovic, and the mayor Mr Ohranovic, both of whom spoke highly of the UN.

It was a breath of fresh air for me to spend time with a journalist who had such an objective approach to the war. Simpson was also surprisingly tough for a reporter. After a visit to a British position in the mountains above Gorazde, I suggested we walk in the snow down through the woods and across the battle lines back to town. He agreed that this would give Nigel a chance to take some good background shots for his report. The route ran down a steep, icy path through the trees, and because John was only wearing leather shoes and a blue city overcoat, he arrived back at base soaking wet and bruised, having fallen over many times. However, he didn't worry about his own safety, or appear to notice his bedraggled state. He was only interested in finding out from the local people what had truly happened in Gorazde.

When he first arrived in Sarajevo, I explained to him that in 1994 the majority of breakdowns of the UN-brokered ceasefires had been the result of offensives launched by the Bosnian forces, notably the shelling of the Serb positions around Sarajevo on 18 September. He asked me what was happening in Bihac, and I explained that most of the fighting there was between the two Muslim armies belonging to Abdic and Dudakovic. Equipped with these facts, he challenged the Prime Minister, Haris Silajdzic, to substantiate his claim that thousands of civilians had been killed during the Serb attacks on Gorazde and Bihac. At the time, Silajdzic had publicly accused me of being responsible for these casualties by not calling for a greater use of NATO air strikes. Now he could not produce any evidence for these claims, and he showed considerable irritation at being exposed as a liar on camera.

I said farewell to Izetbegovic on 20 January. He looked old and tired, and was about to leave Sarajevo for Cairo on one of his many visits abroad to ensure continued support for the Muslim cause in Bosnia. After the usual complaints about the inability of the UN to force the Serbs to allow commercial traffic into Sarajevo, we discussed the long-term prospects for peace in Bosnia. I told him that I thought that Karadzic would be prepared to make compromises and accept less than 50% of the country and I repeated Karadzic's assertion that the Serbs were more interested in quality rather than quantity in any territorial exchange.

Izetbegovic thought this was unlikely, and told me that if I had used more force at the time of Gorazde, then peace would have returned to Bosnia by now. I reminded him that I had used more force than any peacekeeper on similar missions in the UN, and that peacekeepers could not be expected to fight other people's wars. My primary responsibility was to the countries that had contributed peacekeeping troops to the mission and I could not allow them to become combatants, hostages or casualties in a war. A peacekeeping force would never compel the Serbs to sign up to a political solution they had so persistently rejected. A war-fighting force might have had more success.

He fell silent. After a while he said that, although I was a good general, I was not a good politician. He thanked me for all the good things I had done in my time in Bosnia. Shaking me by the hand, he said sadly, "We all have to do what we think is best." They were the last words that he spoke to me. He was a courageous man caught up in a web of deceit, corruption and religious extremism within his party, the SDA, from which he could not escape. The history of the Balkans was too powerful and bloody for one man to change the way things were done in Bosnia. Nevertheless, as the President of Bosnia, he was one of many responsible for the unnecessary prolongation of the war.

As I left the building Mrs Kapitanovic, Izetbegovic's interpreter, followed me into the street. She was and had always been supportive of our efforts to find a peaceful way to end the war, and she had often tried to calm Ganic down during his more insane outbursts. Her eyes misting over, she shook my hand and thanked me for all I had done to bring peace to Bosnia.

The farewell from the Serbs was very different. The entire leadership, dressed in their best suits, had assembled to greet me. After a formal exchange of speeches I was taken to lunch with Mladic in a nearby hotel. There was not a hint of threat or hostility in his manner; he was at his most charming. At the end of lunch, he presented me with an extraordinary surrealist watercolour painting depicting many of the events that had taken place during my time in Bosnia. It was full of a very Serbian foreboding, symbolising religion and war. Several bullet holes had been painted in a haphazard pattern across the picture, apparently representing the NATO bombs I had dropped on the Bosnian Serb Army. Late in the day, as we crossed the Bridge of Brotherhood and Unity to the Bosnian part of Sarajevo, we observed a routine prisoner exchange. Another 100 people were at last going home, and so was I.

That night Muratovic gave a dinner party for me. He was in a very cheerful mood, presumably because I was departing the next day. Throughout dinner I teased him about some of the more absurd accusations he had made against me personally and the UN in general. He had a comedian's face, able to rapidly change expression. Even at his most serious, his face would suddenly crinkle into a smile when he saw the funny side of something. At one point, he told me that now the fuel pipeline through the tunnel into Sarajevo had been completed, he was prepared to undercut the price the UN was paying for fuel. This was only fair, he explained, as he and the other citizens of Sarajevo had survived during the war by stealing fuel from the UN. At the end of the meal, Muratovic reverted to his old form and asked if I would give him a seat on my aircraft flying out of Bosnia the next day.

On my last day in Bosnia (23 January 1995) I wandered about my own HQ, thanking people for all they had done to support the UN mission. After lunch, before leaving for the airport, I sat alone in my empty office thinking of all that had happened in the past year. I wrote a note to Lt-Gen. Rupert Smith, my successor, tied it with a ribbon to a bottle of champagne and placed it on the empty desk. It simply said: "Good luck. Your life will never be the same again."

On the way to the airport, we drove past streets full of people going about their business. It was a bright sunny afternoon and there was an air of normality about the city. Sarajevo was a very different place from the city I had come to live in exactly one year and one day before. At the airport my only sad moment came when I had to say goodbye to Viktor Andreev. I gave him an enormous bear-hug. We had been through momentous times together and he had been a marvellous colleague and friend. We would never work together again. After expressing a few words to the waiting press about my hopes for peace and a better future for the people of Bosnia, I climbed up the steps of the Yak 40 aircraft and, without a backward glance, I left Bosnia for ever.

EPILOGUE

The result in war is never absolute.
Karl von Clausewitz

THERE ARE MANY QUESTIONS THAT MUST BE ANSWERED CONCERNING my time in command of UNPROFOR, but none is more important than why I refused to allow NATO to mount a strategic air campaign against the Serbs. If it was possible to force the Serbs to the negotiating table and thereby end the war by bombing them in September 1995, why could this not have been done the previous year?

The answer is simple. The two-week campaign against the Bosnian Serbs, in which 3,500 aircraft sorties were flown, nearly 100 cruise missiles fired and almost 400 different Serb targets engaged, did not alone end the war in Bosnia. The NATO air campaign in Bosnia in August and September 1995 formed part of a series of strategic actions taking place at that time. These included the use of artillery and mortar by the UN Rapid Reaction Force to neutralise the Bosnian Serb heavy weapons around Sarajevo, the Croat–Muslim Federation ground offensive in the west of Bosnia, and most important of all, the emergence of a political settlement acceptable to all sides. The NATO air campaign was no more than a useful signal to the Serbs that the peacekeeping option had been suspended and that the West was now prepared to use a greater level of enforcement than before. It also helped assuage US domestic opinion.

In 1994, on the other hand, all the necessary conditions for an end to the war were not yet in place. Most of the population of Bosnia was still heavily dependent on UN aid for its survival. Peacekeepers and aid workers were scattered across the country in a way that made them extremely vulnerable to being taken hostage by the Serbs. Even in May 1995, when Lt-Gen. Rupert Smith, my successor, attempted to use NATO air strikes to stop Serbs attacking Sarajevo and get them to return their heavy weapons to UN collecting sites, he was forced to call off the action because Mladic took over 350 of his peacekeepers hostage.[1] This occurred despite the fact that by then UNPROFOR had been reinforced with a multi-national brigade equipped with attack helicopters, artillery and heavy mortars.

After Srebrenica had been overrun by the Serbs in mid-July 1995 – when 7,000 people were massacred – a decision was taken at the London conference later that month to withdraw all UN personnel from Serb-occupied territory and to temporarily suspend the peacekeeping mission. The Muslim enclave of Gorazde and all UN weapon collecting sites were abandoned by UN peacekeeping forces. Only then did it finally become possible for NATO to launch strategic air strikes against targets that included Serb HQs, communications, air defence systems and logistic bases.

By mid-1995 the political climate had radically changed, creating the conditions in which military force at a strategic level had some political relevance and purpose. (1) Belgrade had withdrawn its support from Pale, reducing the risk of Serbia entering the war if the West attacked the Bosnian Serbs. (2) The Bosnian Serb Army had ceased to be militarily superior to the armies of the Croat–Muslim Federation and it could no longer respond to NATO air strikes by overwhelming the Bosnian Army. (3) The Americans had finally accepted the fact that a "just" political settlement was not obtainable and that territorial concessions would have to be made to the Bosnian Serbs. (4) The Bosnian Government had been persuaded by the Americans that the ideal of a multi-cultural, multi-ethnic State within a single political structure could not be achieved and that some recognition would have to be given to a Republika Srpska within a Bosnian federal structure. (5) A secret peace deal had almost certainly been struck between President Tudjman and President Milosevic to allow the Croats to reoccupy the Serb-held parts of the Krajinas, in return for preventing the Muslims from achieving total victory over the Serbs. A resurgent Muslim nation situated in their midst was something neither the Croats nor the Serbs were prepared to accept. Although the evidence for such a deal is circumstantial, it is known that well before the Croat Army attacked into the Krajinas, all regular Yugoslav units were ordered to withdraw from this historic Serb region to a line later enshrined in the Dayton Agreement. President Milosevic had realised that there could never be peace in the Balkans until he did so. By doing this he obtained peace, the lifting of sanctions, the recognition of the Republika Srpska, a territorial division of Bosnia not far short of what the Bosnian Serbs wanted, and he successfully curtailed the political aspirations of Izetbegovic.

The economic and social conditions in Bosnia were also different in 1995 from those in 1994. By the time the Croat ground offensive had been launched in western Bosnia during the summer of 1995, the requirement for aid had fallen dramatically. As a result of the work of the UNHCR and UNPROFOR during the previous three years, most people in Bosnia were able to fend for themselves. The Washington Accord had opened up central Bosnia to commercial traffic and the civil infrastructure in many regions had been restored. Farmers were less dependent on the UNHCR for their tractor fuel and seeds (28,000 tonnes of seed had been distributed in 1994). Roads had been rebuilt, power stations reopened and water pumping stations repaired. Hospitals were working efficiently and children were returning to school. The humanitarian aspects of the UN mission were no longer of primary importance. (*See diagram on the next page*)

There is another more interesting question we might ask: what would have happened if NATO had deployed to Bosnia not in 1995 but in 1992 when President Izetbegovic appealed to the West to send troops to prevent the war from starting?

Targets and deliveries from January 1994 to December 1994

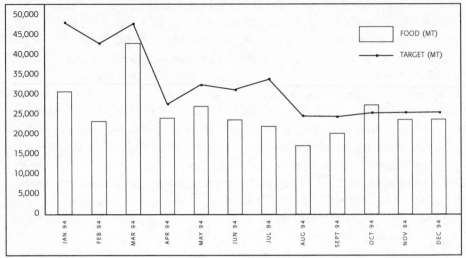

UNHCR analysis of aid delivery. The aid delivered to Bosnia was so effective that, by the end of 1994, the number of people dependent on aid had fallen by half.

Assuming that the Americans would have refused to deploy troops in Bosnia before a peace deal had been struck, it is arguable that it would still have been possible for the European members of NATO to deploy, leaving the Americans to support the mission from the air. It proved to be disastrous for the people of Bosnia that the political and military thinking in the Alliance at that time made a preventative NATO deployment to Bosnia politically impossible.

NATO was still trapped in the logic of the cold war and saw its role as being the defence of Western Europe against some ill-defined threat from its flanks. Nor did NATO political and military planners at that time foresee that in the future peace-keeping would be its most important role or that it would be engaged in operations outside the boundaries of Western Europe. For "historic reasons" the Germans did not feel able to deploy troops outside Germany and the French were suspicious of any military involvement with NATO. After the UN mission in Bosnia, NATO has come to revise its strategic thinking and has learned lessons that will ensure its continued relevance as a military organisation well into the next century.

But it took over three years of sacrifice and heroism on the part of the UN peace-keepers, aid workers and non-governmental organisations (NGOs) working in the midst of a bloody civil war for the world to learn these lessons. During this time UNPROFOR had to develop new concepts of peacekeeping, which combined a humanitarian programme with high levels of military enforcement. It had to adapt to a hostile environment in which its efforts were continually being thwarted by the warring parties and its peacekeepers were killed. It had to defend itself against accusations of genocide, of being soft on the Serbs and of failing to live up to its mandate. None of this diminished the commitment to the peace process of the 23,500 young men and women serving in UNPROFOR. Neither the Washington

Accord nor the Dayton Agreement, which brought peace to Bosnia, could have happened without them.

Another question that needs to be answered is whether the political settlement obtained by the Dayton Agreement could have been achieved in 1994. In my view, it probably could have been, had the Americans understood earlier the political realities of the situation in Bosnia. While it was morally laudable for the US Administration to declare in 1994 that "the aggressor must be punished", it did not provide a basis for political settlement, only military action. If no country is prepared to go to war against the aggressor then, to obtain a political settlement, the participation of that aggressor must be sought in some sort of negotiating process. The opportunities for peace created by the Vance–Owen Peace Plan in 1993 and by UNPROFOR in 1994 were repeatedly destroyed by unenforceable demands being made by the Bosnian Government, backed by the US and wedded to the Contact Group's "take it or leave it" approach towards the Serbs. When this approach was finally abandoned in 1995, the exchanges of territory agreed at Dayton on 21 November did not differ significantly from those proposed by Karadzic and broadly accepted by the Bosnians in the summer of 1994.

The refusal by the Bosnian Government and the US to accept anything less than a "just" solution undoubtedly caused the collapse of the talks between Mladic and Delic in April 1994. The demand by the Bosnian Government that the Serbs withdraw from Gorazde before any talks could take place was wholly unrealistic given the overwhelming defeat they had just suffered. Even after UNPROFOR had managed to obtain the withdrawal of the Bosnian Serbs to the three-kilometre line, Ganic still refused to accept the proposal of a ceasefire longer than one month, although Karadzic had agreed to a four-month cessation of hostilities. Had the talks not been undermined in this way, the resulting four-month deal could well have led to the same compromises that finally ended the conflict a year and a half later. These missed opportunities for peace prolonged the war and added to the suffering of the Bosnian people.

It is also a fair question to ask whether strategic air strikes rather than tactical level strikes might not have halted the Bosnian Serb Army attacks against Gorazde and Bihac, particularly as the Security Council resolution authorised the UN to use all possible means.[2] To this question there is no simple answer as it is impossible to drawn a clear line between the permissible use of force in a peacekeeping mission and an act of war. The limit that I termed the "Mogadishu Line" is defined by the goals being pursued, the levels of force, the strategic imperatives facing the combatants and the political circumstances existing at the time. (*See diagram on next page*)

In determining the goals to be pursued and the level of force, I could not, as a commander, ignore the primary humanitarian aspects of the mission, or ever forget that 2.7 million people were still dependent on UN aid for their survival. Every time I called for NATO air strikes the movement of aid across Serb-held territory was halted and people died. In the next century peacekeepers will not be able to afford to be pacifists in the hostile situations they are likely to face, and in Bosnia

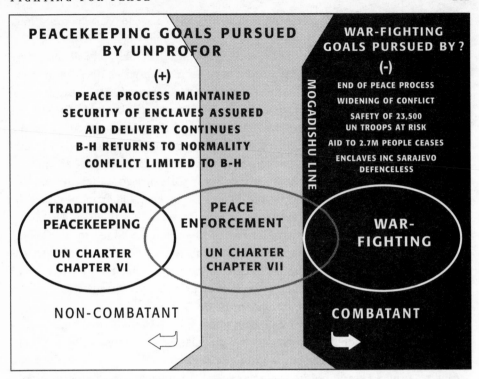

PEACEKEEPING GOALS PURSUED BY UNPROFOR

(+)

PEACE PROCESS MAINTAINED
SECURITY OF ENCLAVES ASSURED
AID DELIVERY CONTINUES
B-H RETURNS TO NORMALITY
CONFLICT LIMITED TO B-H

WAR-FIGHTING GOALS PURSUED BY?

(-)

END OF PEACE PROCESS
WIDENING OF CONFLICT
SAFETY OF 23,500
UN TROOPS AT RISK
AID TO 2.7M PEOPLE CEASES
ENCLAVES INC SARAJEVO
DEFENCELESS

MOGADISHU LINE

TRADITIONAL PEACEKEEPING

UN CHARTER CHAPTER VI

PEACE ENFORCEMENT

UN CHARTER CHAPTER VII

WAR-FIGHTING

NON-COMBATANT

COMBATANT

Diagram showing differences between peacekeeping and war-fighting. The principles of peace-keeping require that 1) the minimum level of force necessary should be used to achieve a particular objective; 2) force should be used only after due warning has been given; and 3) any force must be applied impartially. Not to follow these rules is to cross the "Mogadishu line", as happened with disastrous consequences in Somalia in 1993.

UNPROFOR used a level of force never before seen in any humanitarian-based peacekeeping mission. Had it used too much force or confused peacekeeping with war-fighting, UNPROFOR would have been regarded as a combatant by the Serbs, who at that time controlled 70% of the territory in Bosnia. In these circumstances it would have been impossible to continue the mission.

There was also a clear limit set to the UN's use of force by the troop-contributing nations who were rightly concerned that their soldiers were not caught up in a war. The potentially disastrous consequences of this were still fresh in people's minds following the UN's experiences in Somalia. The plea most frequently made to me by visiting heads of states, foreign secretaries, defence ministers and military chiefs of the troop-contributing nations, was not that the UN should use more force but that it should use less. They were conscious of their responsibility to get their young volunteer peacekeepers home alive. This consideration will always greatly inhibit the use of force in any peacekeeping mission, but it is one that is rarely mentioned by politicians in countries that do not have peacekeeping troops at risk.

Nor were the limitations on the use of NATO air power in the context of the Bosnian civil war sufficiently recognised by critics of the UN. NATO aircraft were originally designed for general war-fighting, not for attacking individual targets usually concealed among civilian buildings. Because NATO commanders were uncomfortable with these tactical targets, there was always pressure to allow NATO pilots to attack the sort of targets for which their aircraft had been designed. There were also requests to allow NATO to destroy the Serb air defence systems. These actions would have taken the use of force to an unacceptable level for a peacekeeping mission, but for refusing to allow attacks to take place against strategic level targets the UN was accused of being weak or soft on the Serbs.

Despite the high levels of force used by UNPROFOR on the ground and in the air, the Serbs continued to believe that it was in their strategic interests to retain the presence of the UN in Bosnia. Until July 1995 none of the safe areas designated in UN Security Council Resolution 824 was actually overrun by the Bosnian Serbs. Many lessons will undoubtedly emerge from the massacre that took place when Srebrenica was finally overrun, but none will be more obvious than that peacekeepers cannot defend territory or keep the peace forever in a political vacuum.

The greatest weakness of the UN mission in Bosnia was the inability of the UN to win the information battle. The war in Bosnia has been described as a war of information and misinformation, a battle for the sympathy of the world in which all too often the media was manipulated by the propaganda machines of the protagonists. In situations of chaos and confusion, the influence of the media on a peacekeeping mission can be critical. What is reported and seen on television directly affects policies being developed abroad, as well as the attitudes of people within the theatre of operations, including the peacekeepers.

In 1994, UNPROFOR radically changed its approach to the media and started treating journalists as part of the process of peacekeeping rather than as a threat to that process. Military spokesmen rather than civilians were used to give the daily briefings, to analyse what was happening on the ground and to explain the tactics being followed by UNPROFOR. Journalists were invited to accompany UN teams wherever possible on visits to the front line or to areas where peacekeepers and aid workers were rebuilding the damaged civil infrastructure of Bosnia. The open door policy in the HQ in Sarajevo allowed journalists for the first time to take part in debates on future UN strategy and also to see first-hand how problems were dealt with.

Despite this, the UN was never able to persuade some powerful members of the international media of its case, or to overcome the powerful propaganda being put out by those determined to undermine its efforts. The continual dissemination of images of war sent a strong message to the world that the UN was failing in its mission and exaggerated reports of fighting in Gorazde, Bihac and Sarajevo were calculated to put pressure on the UN to raise the level of force used.[3] The emotions of people around the world were cynically and cleverly manipulated and the carefully compiled, more accurate reports from UNPROFOR or the UNHCR never received the same coverage.

My own fury at this misrepresentation of the truth did little to stem the tide of propaganda. The perception of many US East Coast commentators is that during the fighting in Gorazde the UN deliberately misled the world about what happened, underestimated the scale of the disaster and was economical with the truth. I explained that most of the damaged houses in Gorazde revealed by US air recon-naissance had not been destroyed in the fighting that took place in the town in April 1994. They had been destroyed in 1992 when the Muslims drove the Serbs from the town and surrounding area. These former Serb homes had no roofs, window frames or doors and had been stripped of all furniture and fittings. Many of them had been torched. They were demonstrably not buildings recently subjected to shelling. Today the UN still stands condemned for having underplayed the damage done by the Serbs in Gorazde.

The allegation that UNPROFOR was soft on the Serbs originated with the Bosnian Presidency, which felt that the UN should not be impartial in its approach to media-tion. If the UN was not *with* the Bosnians, then it must be *against* them and therefore with the Serbs. UNPROFOR was never indifferent to the plight of Bosnia (itself a member of the UN), but it had to mediate impartially between the two sides if it was successfully to bring them together in a negotiated settlement. When, in 1994, NATO enforced its ultimatums against the Serbs but not against the Bosnians in the Sarajevo TEZ and the Mount Igman demilitarised zone, the Serbs became convinced that the UN had taken sides, making a UN-negotiated settlement impossible. This erosion of UNPROFOR's perceived impartiality – a vital element in any peacekeeping mission – was one of the major causes of difficulty in finding peace in Bosnia.

Yet if UNPROFOR had allowed its response at the time to be influenced by propa-ganda, a dangerous muddle would have ensued and the international community would ultimately have found it harder to develop a strategy for ending the war. In civil wars it is the attitudes and beliefs of people that count more than the defeat of armies or the occupying of terrain. People who have the confidence that peace is returning and that law and order have been permanently restored are less likely to turn against their neighbours than when they can hear the sound of guns and see smoke rising from villages in the next valley.

Had the UN been able to appeal directly to the people of Bosnia (who always said that it was not their war), then public pressure could have been put on the political and military leaders to end the war earlier. However, it would have been enormously difficult to get the three communities in Bosnia to form themselves into a party jointly determined to end the war through peaceful means, for the manipulation of public opinion through fear and hatred did not just happen among the Serbs, but among the Croats and Muslims as well.

These failures to project the necessary images of success greatly undermined the credibility of UNPROFOR and sapped the international will to support the peacekeeping mission. Well aware that UNPROFOR was losing the information battle, Akashi had tried to establish a UN broadcasting service in Bosnia, but the UN Secretariat in New York was unable to provide the necessary funds. A lesson for the future must be that any peacekeeping force should be supported by an effective mass communications strategy capable of winning the information battle internationally and able to appeal over the heads of the warlords to the people themselves.[4]

The UN has often been criticised for failing to stop the terrible ethnic cleansing which occurred during the war. This barbarous practice was condemned in numerous Security Council resolutions, and yet UNPROFOR appeared to do little to prevent it. However it is not the peacekeepers but the international community as a whole that should be held to greater account. It decided not to deploy its armies to Bosnia in 1992, thus allowing the scourge of ethnic cleansing to take place. Policing every town and village and monitoring the running of the State to stop the sort of psychological, judicial and terrorist acts that occurred in Bosnia, would have required an army of occupation, not a peacekeeping force. Most of the ethnic cleansing of Muslims and Croats happened in the west and east of Bosnia, in Serb-held areas where there were no UN garrisons.

UNPROFOR had originally been deployed in Bosnia to help the beleaguered Muslims of Sarajevo, and subsequently those in central Bosnia and the enclaves. Where the UN was deployed on the ground, peacekeepers were able to prevent many incidents of ethnic cleansing, as in the Laskva Valley. By reporting incidents, UN observers and EC monitors were able to reduce the levels of ethnic cleansing, but by the end of 1994 it was probably too late to stop the mass exodus of the minority populations – 40,000 Muslims and 30,000 Croats – still living in Bosnian Serb areas who were desperate to leave their homes.

In November 1994, because of threats and harassment, 800 Croats had left Banja Luka in a privately organised movement. Akashi and Nicholas Morris, head of the UNHCR in the former Yugoslavia, continually confronted Karadzic with the crimes committed by his police or soldiers, but the ethnic cleansing did not stop. There was little they could do. Nor was it just the Serbs who were involved in ethnic cleansing. It was happening on a lesser scale in all the communities. It must also be remembered that in 1996, as a result of the Dayton Agreement, 250,000 Serbs left the Krajina part of Croatia and western Bosnia. Ethnic violence does not recognise political boundaries.

Perhaps the greatest public relations disaster for UNPROFOR during its mission concerned the safe area policy. In the words of de Lapresle, this was a "military and humanitarian disaster-in-waiting". From the outset, Security Council Resolutions 824 and 836 gave the impression that the territory and populations of the designated safe areas would be guaranteed by the UN. Yet they expressly use the phrase "*deter* attacks against the safe areas", and the words "*defend*" or "*protect*" were specifically avoided. In the clamour of international protest against what was happening in the enclaves it was invariably overlooked that deterrence in a peacekeeping mission is a long way from defending or protecting. Defence or protection are war-fighting operations which the peacekeepers were never instructed or equipped to pursue.

The concept of a safe area, a designated sanctuary for civilians endangered by battle, is as old as war itself, but it can only work if all the parties to a conflict respect the agreement. When Bosnian forces used a safe area as a base from which to attack the enemy and the Serbs responded by attacking that safe area, there was little that UNPROFOR could do to protect the civilian population. In May 1994, UNPROFOR had submitted a document to the Secretary-General of the UN describing our mis-givings about UNSCR 836, stating that the resolution could not be satisfactorily implemented. The Security Council had chosen to take no action. Had the UN been able to deploy an adequate number of troops into Gorazde, Srebrenica and Zepa prior to the Serb offensive, the Serbs might have desisted.[5]

The UN Security Council resolutions concerning safe areas also failed to suffi-ciently define the extent of those areas. This made it impossible for UNPROFOR to draw a line on the ground which, if crossed by the Serbs, would result in air strikes. Following the experience of Gorazde, I attempted to get New York to define the boundary of the safe area of Bihac, which they were prepared to do.[6] In the event, they were prevented from doing so by Mohammed Sacirbey, the Bosnian Government Representative to the UN. He apparently thought that UNPROFOR should regard the whole of Bosnia as a safe area. In the absence of any geographical definition, the town of Bihac into which the civilians had withdrawn was designated a safe area. This decision resulted in further accusations that UNPROFOR was not acting forcibly enough each time the conflict line was breached by the Serbs. As the tragedy of Srebrenica in 1995 demonstrated, if an army is determined to overrun a safe area, peacekeepers cannot oppose it.

The muddle over the safe areas gave the Bosnian Government and its sympathis-ers abroad enormous scope for propaganda against the UN mission. Yet for nearly three years of bloody civil war, all the safe areas including Sarajevo survived without being overrun by the Serbs. This was due to the presence of the peacekeepers rather than the Bosnian Army. If the Serbs had captured the safe areas, then the State of Bosnia would have ceased to exist. NATO air power could not have saved them.

Another weakness in the mission that I was unable to correct during my time in command in Bosnia was the limitation placed on the movement of UNPROFOR. In November 1993 the warring parties signed an agreement in Geneva which reaffirmed the right of the peacekeepers to move freely throughout Bosnia, but they had failed to observe this agreement. Early in 1994, I set about restoring the right to free movement by encouraging a more robust approach to peacekeeping. At first the strategy succeeded, but as time went by the warring parties became subtler in the ways in which they prevented UN and UNHCR convoys from moving about Bosnia. The Serbs in particular wished to retain control of humanitarian goods, because the delivery of aid to Sarajevo or to the enclaves worked against their strategic interests. However, the Serbs never blocked convoys in such a systematic manner that a mili-tary response from UNPROFOR became inevitable. Even during 1994, at a time when the Serbs were accused of the "strangulation of Sarajevo", stocks of food in the city were never completely exhausted, gas and water remained connected and so, for much of the time, did electricity. Rather, the Serbs played a cat-and-mouse game, giving in to the UN whenever the pressure on them grew too much, then becoming obstructive when the UN began to concern itself with other things.

The unsung heroes in my HQ in Sarajevo were the Belgian staff officers who manned the UN convoy operations centre. Day after day they had to deal with the frustration caused by requests for convoys being rejected or convoys being turned back or halted on the road, sometimes for days. Although safe passage of unarmed aid convoys cannot be guaranteed without an army to secure the routes, the Serbs could have been compelled to give greater freedom of movement if national contingents had adopted a universally robust approach on the ground. While some contingents risked their own lives to enforce the passage of a convoy, others too often allowed their vehicles to be hijacked with little response. (One particular nation always managed to get its convoys through by selling petrol to the Serbs.) A peace-keeping force, composed of voluntarily contributed contingents, lacks the discipline and command authority of an army or even an integrated alliance such as NATO. In the final analysis, it is the character and tradition of the national contingent involved that determines the outcome of an armed confrontation at a roadblock deep in hostile territory. Nevertheless, through dogged determination, moral persuasion and the occasional use of force, most UN convoys eventually reached their destinations. The success of the work of the peacekeepers and aid workers in the UNHCR was measured by the tonnages moved and the lives saved, but an important lesson for the future must be that freedom of movement is an essential precondition of any peacekeeping mission. If the warring parties do not grant that right, the mission should be suspended and possibly withdrawn.

The UN had arrived in Bosnia prepared for a role of traditional peacekeeping in accordance with Chapter VI of the UN Charter, but it was actually required to operate in the more demanding Chapter VII role. Under Chapter VI, the combatants agree to end their conflict and invite the UN to become a mediator to help negotiate and implement the elements of a peace deal. Under Chapter VII, however, it is likely that there will be no prior agreement to end the war and the mission of the UN will be to deliver humanitarian aid and to help create the conditions in which the conflict can be brought to an end. If there is little consent for the presence of the peace-keepers, as in Bosnia, a great deal of enforcement may be necessary.

Despite its many weaknesses the UNPROFOR mission succeeded to a surprising degree when measured against its mandate. Through the heroic work of the aid workers and the UN peacekeepers, 2.7 million people were sustained during the three and half years of the conflict. On average some 2,000 metric tonnes of s tores were delivered each day to the most remote parts of Bosnia, along roads built by the UN and to and from airfields operated by the UN. The fact that the opportunities for peace created by the UN were frequently ignored by the political leaders and warlords of the Balkans (and their external supporters) cannot be blamed on UNPROFOR. Nor should the young volunteer peacekeepers of UNPROFOR be criticised for failing to impose a "just" political settlement in Bosnia or for failing to prevent the atrocities committed by all sides during the war. To have accomplished this would have required an army of occupation of at least 100,000 men, and the world in 1992 was not prepared to pay the necessary human and financial cost of deploying such a force to Bosnia.

The second element of the UN mission in Bosnia, to create the necessary conditions for a peaceful settlement of the war, was also largely obtained through the pacifying presence of UN peacekeepers on the ground. Following the deployment of the UN into Bosnia in 1992, the civilian casualty rate from the war dropped from 130,000 killed that year to around 3,000 killed in the next. By 1994, according to one American source, the death toll was 3,000, mostly soldiers killed in combat. Far from presiding over genocide, as some propagandists declared, the effect of UNPROFOR's presence on the ground was to halt genocide in its tracks. It was also UNPROFOR that helped bring about an end to the fighting between the Muslims and Croats by implementing the Washington Accord. By doing this, the UN created the necessary preconditions for the Dayton Peace Agreement that finally brought an end to the war in Bosnia.

Thirdly, the conflict was almost entirely contained within Bosnia, with minimal spill over into other parts of the Balkans.

During its three and half years in Bosnia, UNPROFOR succeeded in breaking the traditional moulds of peacekeeping that were no longer relevant to the circumstances of the post-cold war world. It demonstrated that it was possible for a peacekeeping force to be effective in circumstances in which the warring parties showed no sign of wanting to end the fighting and on the ground gave only patchy consent to the presence of the peacekeepers. A new international way of responding to civil wars and international disorder that lay somewhere between traditional peacekeeping and war-fighting, was developed. UNPROFOR instigated an evolution in peacekeeping that will ensure the relevance of the concept well into the next century.

The specific lessons from Bosnia are clear. Peacekeepers must have an unequivocal mandate backed by adequate resources and the unflinching political will of the international community. A mandate has to spell out not just the aspirations of the Security Council but also the military and political limitations of the mission. Within the mandate, there also needs to be unequivocal direction regarding the extent to which military force can be used to achieve the objectives of the mission. The UN is not a pacifist organisation and in conditions similar to those prevailing in Bosnia a peacekeeping force will need to be extremely robust in its use of force; its contingents must be prepared and equipped to use force. Nevertheless it is vital that war-fighting goals are not pursued and that the principles which also apply to the use of air power, regarding the minimum use of force, are clearly understood. Whenever force is used, commanders must accept that there will be an adverse effect on the humanitarian aspects of the mission. Those against whom force is being directed will react by blocking relief convoys and halting the flow of aid. As a result, the plight of people dependent on UN assistance will worsen and some will die.

Despite the difficulties encountered, an indispensable role was played by NATO air power in Bosnia and many lessons were learned about bringing a regional military alliance to support a UN peacekeeping mission under Chapter VIII of the UN

Charter, by which regional agencies can be uused for enforcement. The presence of NATO aircraft in the skies above Bosnia gave UN peacekeepers and aid workers the confidence they needed to deploy to many dispersed and remote places. It was NATO air power that helped deter attacks by the Bosnian Serbs against the safe areas, and that preserved the TEZ for heavy weapons around Sarajevo and Gorazde. Where two organisations with different mandates are involved in a single theatre of operations it will be essential to have a "dual key" arrangement similar to the one that operated in Bosnia.

In humanitarian-based peacekeeping operations there is always going to be a need for close coordination of the aid delivery programme, the security operation and political action. An agreed campaign plan based on a common strategy is central to the achievement of proper coordination among the many different agencies that will be found in areas where disasters have occurred. Coordination between UNPRO-FOR and the UNHCR was achieved in Bosnia by the co-location of operational cells and HQs at all levels of command. At the start of the war, some NGOs refused to work with UNPROFOR on the grounds that they did not want to compromise their neutral status by associating with UN peacekeepers. By 1994 most NGOs came to see the need to operate closely with the UN in order to guarantee the security of their workers, and the arrangement in which UNHCR became the lead agency coordinating the work of others is likely to remain the model for future humanitarian aid missions in this type of enviroment.

The coordination of political activity with the humanitarian and security elements of the mission in Bosnia was never properly achieved and made it more difficult for the UN to help bring about peace. Difficulties were caused by the lack of any agreed political strategy in the international community about how to bring the war to an end and also by the failure of the Contact Group to consult sufficiently with the UN. The clear lesson for the future is that it is simply not possible for a peacekeeping mission to succeed for long in a political vacuum. Unless some hopes of a politically inspired peace are kept alive, the warring factions will violate their ceasefire agreements and revert to war.

No military force can operate properly without a responsive command structure and UN peacekeeping missions are no exception. Since the end of the cold war the UN has made many improvements to its HQ structure in New York to ensure that it can run efficiently many operations simultaneously around the world. A 24-hour-a-day operational staff has been established in New York, a contingency planning capability had been developed and a new post of Under-Secretary-General for Humanitarian Affairs has been created, in particular to coordinate the peacekeeping and humanitarian aspects of a mission. The ability of the UN to deploy troops and HQs into the field more rapidly than it was able to in Bosnia or Rwanda has been improved by the creation of a High Readiness Standby Brigade drawn from a consortium of countries led by Denmark.[7] This will allow the UN to react immediately to developing situations, rather than after the conflict has intensified and opportunities for an early peace have been lost.

In a war zone such as Bosnia had become, a UN peacekeeping mission needs to be equipped with the force structure, command disciplines and military technology of war if it is to survive. The greatest military weakness of UNPROFOR in 1994 was perhaps its lack of airmobile reserve, which could have been deployed to potential trouble spots. UNPROFOR also lacked the necessary military hardware and effective command structures to enable it to contend with the dangerous and chaotic circumstances in which it had to operate. It lacked firepower, protection from mines, mortars, shoulder-controlled weapons and mobility. It lacked secure communications and an intelligence-gathering capability, especially surveillance systems able to work in all weather conditions. Had UNPROFOR possessed such systems in 1994, it is certain that the people who fired a mortar bomb into the Markele market in February of that year, killing 68 people, would not have done so for fear of being identified as the culprits. A mission also needs to be less dependent on the warring parties for its logistics than UNPROFOR was in Bosnia. If the UN is reliant on the goodwill of the warlords for its own survival, then it will become liable to pressure being placed upon it to act in a partisan way. The lesson for the future is that, even though it is not itself engaged in a war, a peacekeeping force must have a strong military capability if it is to be effective in the circumstances of civil war.

UNPROFOR was fortunate in that many of the countries contributing troops also belonged to NATO and this enabled common NATO doctrine and staff procedures to be adopted at the start of the mission. Those countries joining the mission later on, such as the Russian contingent, had to conform to the already established procedures. This had the unexpected benefit of helping advance the Partnership for Peace arrangements between NATO and the former countries of the Warsaw Pact. Nevertheless peacekeeping doctrine needs to be further refined, incorporating the lessons of Somalia, Rwanda and the former Yugoslavia.

Soon after arriving in Bosnia in 1996, Gen. Nash, who commanded the US Armoured Division in the NATO Implementation Force, observed: "I have trained 30 years to read a battlefield ... now you are asking me to read a peace field. It doesn't come easy. It ain't natural. It ain't intuitive. They don't teach this stuff at Leavenworth." Since that time many countries have contributed to new thinking on peacekeeping and the UN and NATO have rewritten their peacekeeping handbooks.

Because of the challenges of a peacekeeping mission in situations of disorder and violence, where the peacekeepers themselves are likely to be under physical attack and subject to hostile propaganda, extraordinary demands will be placed on leadership at all levels. If the peacekeepers lose faith in the mission and come to believe the propaganda message that they are making the situation worse by their presence, their willingness to continue risking their lives will be diminished. In the conditions that prevailed in Bosnia, the UN mission simply could not have continued without the outstanding leadership shown by junior levels of command. It is a testament to the quality of this leadership that, during my year in Bosnia, I never heard anyone question the value of the mission, although I frequently heard those outside it do so. If commanders are to exercise effective leadership during future peacekeeping missions, military training colleges will need to study the many lessons in leadership that have emerged from the UN's recent peacekeeping experiences.

The UN mission in Bosnia had been deployed in the worst possible circumstances, without adequate political direction or resources. In 1992, the Secretary-General of the UN had said, "I do not believe that in its present phase this conflict is susceptible to UN peacekeeping treatment." UNPROFOR first went to the former Yugoslavia to resolve the conflict in Croatia, and later to help provide aid for the victims of a civil war. As the world became sickened by the slaughter and the ethnic cleansing, the UN's mission radically changed into one of bringing peace to Bosnia. The means of doing so were never provided. Nevertheless for three and a half years UNPROFOR sustained the people of Bosnia, by its presence reduced the slaughter and helped create the conditions for a political dialogue that was necessary to end the war. Through force of argument and by demonstrating the realities on the ground in Bosnia, UNPROFOR was able to reverse policies designed to involve it and NATO in the war. UNPROFOR was able to demonstrate to the US that the lifting of the arms embargo would result in the defeat of the Bosnian Army and the probable deployment of US troops to preserve the State.

Lady Thatcher, a strong proponent of the "lift and strike" argument, once declared that when Britain had called on America to send it arms to fight against Nazi Germany, America had sent arms. Now that the Bosnians were calling on the West to send it arms to fight the Serbs, the West refused.

William Perry replied: "Yes, Margaret, America did send Great Britain arms. We also sent you millions of soldiers to help you in that fight, many of whom never returned."

Looking back, the cautious response by the international community to the war in Bosnia is understandable. It had attempted to prevent war by keeping the former Yugoslavia together. When that policy failed, it sought to limit the conflict by imposing an arms embargo, and it tried to alleviate suffering by sending humanitarian relief. Through UNPROFOR it ensured that the State as well as the people of Bosnia survived. By its presence, UNPROFOR also helped create the necessary conditions for a political settlement that included the implementation of the peace deal between the Croats and the Muslims. When it was certain that the people and State of Bosnia would survive, the peace process was suspended for a brief period and the Serbs were compelled by force of arms to accept a negotiated settlement that ended the war. Once the final peace treaty had been secured, it was possible to revert to peacekeeping with NATO troops.

The irony in all of this was that NATO did not deploy in 1992, instead of the UN, when the Alliance's superior military power would have enabled it to operate more effectively than the UN in a peace-enforcement role. This would have allowed the UN to assume its more traditional task after the Dayton Peace Agreement, when the requirement to use force was less likely.

It is important for the future of world security that neither the hard lessons learned by UNPROFOR nor the sacrifices of the young peacekeepers are forgotten. More than 300 peacekeepers died during the course of the UNPROFOR mission in Bosnia, a casualty rate higher than those killed in combat during the Gulf War.

Today, the West can afford to be less cautious about becoming involved in similar situations in the future. The difference between war-fighting and peacekeeping is clearer. The danger of a peacekeeping force being drawn into the conflict is more obvious. The ethnic cleansing of the Muslim Albanians from Kosovo has aroused the same strong emotions as the atrocities that occurred in Bosnia. The West has not yet taken military action, nor without clear political objectives can it do so. Whether future political objectives are limited to containment or involve direct intervention to halt the brutal injustices that are being perpetrated, any peacekeeping mission will be an expensive and dangerous undertaking. But as President Harry S Truman once said, "If you are not prepared to pay the price of peace, you had better be prepared to pay the price of war."

In Bosnia the scars of war remain, but its people are at peace. They do not live in a free or a just society or in a country that measures up to the ideal of a multi-cultural, multi-ethnic State within a single political structure. There is too great a sense of loss and bitterness for that. Yet the country will not return to war as long as NATO remains *in situ*. The curse of the Balkans is its history, and it will take many generations before memories fade and the political leaders, whose war it was, are replaced by a new generation with a faith in humanity and compassion. Yet it is just possible that the strong desire of the people of the Balkans to be part of the European community will persuade them to say "never again".

The establishment of the international War Crimes Tribunal in The Hague is an important step for future peacekeeping missions, and it may also help the healing process.[8] But the Tribunal remains only a substitute for national justice, and one day, when true democracy and freedom of expression flourish in the former Yugoslavia, as surely they must, then the people themselves will prosecute those who created, perpetuated and profited from a war that cost so many lives. The desire to see justice does exist. The democratic structures through which justice is delivered do not – yet.

As my own memories of the brutality and destruction of the war in Bosnia fade, I recall the beauty of the countryside and the welcome of the ordinary people. But most of all I remember the heroism, humour and courage of the thousands of young men and women of UNPROFOR who came from all over the world and risked their lives so willingly that others might live.

NOTES

INTRODUCTION

1. Tito, adopted name of Josip Broz (1892–1980). Yugoslav Communist politician. In the Second World War he organised the National Liberation Army to carry out guerrilla warfare against the invading Germans. He was created Marshal in 1943. He was Prime Minister 1946–53 and then President from 1953.

2. Rebecca West, *Black Lamb and Grey Falcon* (London, 1941).

3. Ezer Weizman, President of Israel, opened the United States Holocaust Memorial Museum in Washington, DC in 1993.

4. The United Nations Protection Force was established in February 1992 to "create the conditions of peace and security required for the negotiation of an overall settlement of the Yugoslav crisis within the framework of the European Community's Conference on Yugoslavia." Quoted in Anthony Parsons, *From Cold War to Hot Peace: UN Interventions 1947–1994* (London, 1995), p. 226.

5. Dag Hammarskjold (1905–61): Swedish statesman and UN official. He was UN Secretary-General 1953–61 and was awarded the Nobel Prize for Peace in 1961.

6. Boutros Boutros-Ghali to the President of the Security Council, 24 July 1994: "UNPROFOR is deployed to work with the parties in a transparent and impartial mode; it is not a combat force and is not equipped or deployed to take offensive action against any of the parties."

CHAPTER ONE: *A Collapsing Mission*

1. France had about 6,000 men on the ground.

2. Francis Briquemont, *Le Point*, 5 January 1994.

3. *Spectator*, 29 January 1994: "So eager has the UN force in Sarajevo become to avoid antagonising the Serbs that it now acts as a sort of hired gaoler – a Balkan Group Four Security – on the Serbs' behalf, actively enforcing rules invented by them about who and what may be allowed to enter or leave the city."

4. UNHCR Field Report, February 1994.

5. *Spectator*, 5 February 1994.

CHAPTER TWO: *The Bombing of the Market Place*

1. Letter from the UN Secretary-General to the NATO Secretary-General, 6 February 1994.

2. Noel Malcolm, *Sunday Telegraph*, 13 February 1994.

3. UN Secretary-General's report, 9 May 1994: "On 10 February 1994, the North

Atlantic Council declared that non-compliance with the withdrawal of heavy weapons from a 20-kilometre radius from the centre of Sarajevo would result in the initiation of air strikes 10 days from that date."

4. Gen. Bertrand de Lapresle, *Le Monde*, 25 October 1994: "There is a difference in culture between the UN and NATO. NATO likes to identify an enemy, demonstrate its military effectiveness and win victories. UNPROFOR has a peacekeeping mission."

5. *Daily Telegraph*, 10 February 1994: "Ambassadors from the 16 countries gave the Serbs 10 days to withdraw their estimated 500 heavy guns at least 13 miles from Sarajevo or face air strikes."

6. *The Times*, 22 February 1994.

7. John Major, Douglas Hurd and Malcolm Rifkind met with Warren Christopher and Raymond Seitz (US Ambassador to the United Kingdom) at Chevening on 2 May. The British were "dumbfounded" at how far the White House was prepared to go. "They fired back at Christopher a series of questions – about what would happen if British troops were attacked; what would happen if the Croats blocked the supply of weapons; what exactly would provoke an air strike on the Serbs – which he was unable to answer." Anthony Seldon, *Major: A Political Life* (London, 1997), p. 374.

8. David Owen, *Balkan Odyssey* (London, 1995), pp. 235–36.

9. Mark Almond, *Daily Mail*, 21 February 1994: "Have no doubt. The very idea of Russian troops so close to Western Europe sends shivers down the spines of NATO strategists. They are beginning to ask what will be the long-term strategic price of welcoming Russia to pacify the Balkans."

CHAPTER THREE: *A New Direction*

1. Washington Accord, March 1994: "The immediate justification for the Accords was that they stopped the Croat-Muslim war, which is indubitable. Unfortunately the accords were perceived by the Bosnian Serbs and Croatian Serbs as an anti-Serb alliance." David Owen, *Balkan Odyssey*, p. 384.

2. UN Security Council Resolution 900 (4 March 1994): "welcoming the agreement (. . .) on the ceasefire and measures related to heavy weapons in and around Sarajevo, reached on 9 February 1994."

3. David Owen, *Balkan Odyssey*, p. 232.

4. UN Security Council Resolution 908 (31 March 1994): "Demands that the Bosnian Serb party cease forthwith all military operations against the town of Maglaj and remove all obstacles to free access to it; *condemns* all such obstacles; and *calls upon* all parties to show restraint."

CHAPTER FOUR: *Gorazde*

1. Emma Daly, *Independent*, 23 March 1994. A United Nations Ilyushin 76 landed at Tuzla on 22 March, opening an air bridge to more than a million people in the Muslim heartland of central Bosnia. Yasushi Akashi was quoted: "This is a very

happy day for all of us. There's a new positive momentum for a ceasefire, disengagement, the establishment of a durable peace and the improvement of the life of the people in Bosnia and Hercegovina. I think the dark days are almost over."

2. UN Secretary-General's report, 1 December 1994: "The intention of the safe-area concept is to protect the civilian populations and to ensure unimpeded access for humanitarian assistance. For the reasons explained below, this is not compatible with the use of the safe areas for military activities. This problem has become particularly acute with the recent offensive of the Government Army from within the Bihac pocket, which in turn triggered a major counter-offensive by the Bosnian-Serb forces and the involvement of the Krajina Serb forces in the conflict. (. . .) When a safe area has strategic importance in ongoing military operations launched or provoked by the forces defending the area, it would be unrealistic to expect the other party to avoid attacking that area, even with full knowledge of the likely consequences of violating the relevant Security Council resolutions. (. . .) In such circumstances the impartiality of UNPROFOR becomes difficult to maintain and there is a risk of the force being seen as a party to the conflict."

3. An agreement on a settlement in Bosnia was initialled on 21 November 1995 at the US air base in Dayton, Ohio. Present were Presidents Izetbegovic (Bosnia-Hercegovina), Milosevic (Serbia) and Tudjman (Croatia) as well as representatives of the Contact Group.

4. UN Security Council Resolution 836 (4 June 1993), paragraph 9: "Authorizes UNPROFOR (. . .) in carrying out the mandate defined in paragraph 5 above, acting in self-defence, to take the necessary measures, including the use of force, in reply to bombardments against the safe areas by any of the parties or to armed incursion into them".

CHAPTER FIVE: *A Phoney Peace*

1. *Daily Express*, "TROOPS OUT", 18 April 1994. (The *Daily Mail* ran a similar headline, "BRING TROOPS HOME", on the same day.)

CHAPTER SIX: *The Day the General Smiled*

1. The Sarajevo airlift began on 2 July 1992.

2. UNHCR Information Report, July 1994.

3. Noel Malcolm, *Daily Telegraph*, 14 July 1994: "This is the kind of international diplomacy in which it becomes hard to see the difference between a firefighter and an arsonist. None of this would have happened if, from the first moment, we had all stood back and said: 'We shall not get involved; we shall let the Bosnians defend themselves'."

4. Tim Butcher, *Daily Telegraph*, 19 July 1994, quoting General Rose: "'There is a limit to how much enforcement a peacekeeping force can undertake. (. . .) There will come a time when I will have to say, as commander in Bosnia-Hercegovina of a peacekeeping force, that I really do have to hand over to somebody else such as NATO if we are going to go further down the route of enforcement'."

5. Mark Almond, *Daily Mail*, 1 August 1994: "Since the West was not prepared to take sides, it should never have interfered. As it happens, our combination of a one-sided arms embargo and corrupt and half-hearted regime of sanctions and humanitarian aid has helped the wrong side, the Serbs."

6. David Owen, *Balkan Odyssey*, p. 319.

7. David Owen, *Balkan Odyssey*, pp. 316-17.

CHAPTER SEVEN: *A Return to War*

1. UNHCR Information Report, July 1994.

2. First meeting of the Contact Group, 26 April 1994. Second meeting, 5 July 1994. Third meeting, 30 July 1994. The map presented by the Contact Group was accepted by the Muslims but rejected by the Bosnian Serbs.

CHAPTER EIGHT: *Bihac*

1. The Vance–Owen Peace Plan was first introduced 2 January 1993 to five delegations of the Bosnian parties. A three-part package comprising 10 constitutional principles, a detailed cessation of hostilities and a map, the plan eventually fell foul of the US Administration in May 1993.

2. *New York Times*, 28 November 1994, William Safire: "Sir Michael Rose, the reincarnation of Neville Chamberlain, has just admitted that his UN force of 23,000 Europeans is unable to 'deter' Bosnian Serbs from destroying cities the Security Council has established as safe havens."

3. William Perry, US Defense Secretary, quoted in *Daily Telegraph*, 29 November 1994.

4. The Conference on Security and Co-operation in Europe (CSCE) in Budapest (November–December 1994). On 6 December Russia vetoed a statement condemning Serbian aggression in Bosnia. On 1 January 1995, the CSCE became the Organisation for Security and Co-operation in Europe (OSCE).

CHAPTER NINE: *A Cessation of Hostilities*

1. Noel Malcolm, *Daily Telegraph*, 22 December 1994: "After what was diplomatically called 'Negotiation', Mr Carter emerged with a ceasefire agreement. Or rather with two, one for the Bosnian Government, the other, on slightly more advantageous terms, for the Serbs."

EPILOGUE

1. David Owen, *Balkan Odyssey*, p. 348: "On 25 May NATO aircraft launched air strikes against the Serb ammunition dumps near Pale. (. . .) The US wanted further air strikes. The Serbs shelled a café area in Tuzla, killing seventy-five people. On 26 May NATO air strikes took place again, followed by wholesale hostage-taking. In retrospect, Akashi believed that this second round of air strikes tipped the Bosnian Serbs over the brink into seeing the UN as the enemy."

2. Security Council Resolution 836 (4 June 1993), paragraph 10: "Member States (...) may take, under the authority of the Security Council and subject to close coordination with the Secretary-General and UNPROFOR, all necessary measures, through the use of air power, in and around the safe areas."

3. Lt-Col. J. C. McColl, Commander's Report, Operation Grapple 4, 29 October 1994: "We took every opportunity to brief the international media on the relative success being achieved in Central Bosnia and UNPROFOR's role in the region. However, there was very little guidance about lines to take or points of emphasis. (...) It is important that whenever [the media] speak to UNPROFOR commanders they receive the same message, particularly about key issues. The appointment of SO1 Public Information on General Rose's staff will hopefully help in this respect."

4. Alan Makee: "Most of the media is in the business of 'Infotainment'. An amalgamation of fact and drama. To sell papers or air time, journalists must describe news in sensational terms, even when the situation is plainly bland. The danger is that decision-makers react to this 'Infotainment' prior to the collection of more accurate information."

5. UN Secretary-General's report, 1 December 1994: "I had pointed out that UNPROFOR would require some 34,000 troops in order to effectively deter attacks upon the safe areas. The Council, however, decided in its resolution 844 (1993) of 18 June to authorize a 'light option' of 7,600 additional troops."

6. *Ibid.*: "The boundaries of the safe areas need to be clearly defined. Such delineation will be necessary whether or not an agreement between the parties on the demilitarization of the safe areas is obtained. (...) UNPROFOR remains ready to issue its own delineation if authorized to do so by the Security Council."

7. See Anthony Parsons, *From Cold War to Hot Peace*: "if a potential aggressor or warlord knew that his forces would be met by a UN force armed, equipped and mandated to fight with Great Power air or naval support available as relevant, this would constitute a powerful disincentive."

8. The International Criminal Tribunal for the Former Yugoslavia established by Security Council Resolution 827.

GLOSSARY OF NAMES

ABDIC, Fikret Leader of the Independent Muslim faction in Bihac

AKASHI, Yasushi UN Secretary-General's Special Representative to the former Yugoslavia, December 1993–October 1995

ALAGIC, Major-General Mehmet (Bosnian Army) Commander 3rd Corps

ALBRIGHT, Madeleine US Permanent Representative to the UN, 1993–96; US Secretary of State since 1997

AMMANPOUR, Christiane Foreign Correspondent, CNN

ANDREEV, Viktor Russian UN Civil Adviser, Sarajevo; later Head of Civil Affairs for Bosnia-Hercegovina

ANNAN, Kofi Head of UN Peacekeeping Department; UN Secretary-General since 1997

ASHY, General Joe (US Air Force) Air Commander, Allied Forces South, Naples, 1994.

BAGSHAW, Captain Jeremy (Coldstream Guards) aide-de-camp to General Rose

BALANZINO, Ambassador Acting NATO Secretary-General

BOORDA, late Admiral Mike (US Navy) Commander Allied Forces South, Naples, 1992–94

BOUTROS-GHALI, Boutros UN Secretary-General, 1992–96

BRINKMAN, Brigadier (Dutch Army) Chief of Staff to General Rose

BRIQUEMONT, General Francis (Belgian Army) UNPROFOR Commander for Bosnia-Hercegovina, 1993

BUHA, Aleksa Bosnian Serb Foreign Minister

CARTER, Jimmy President of the United States, 1977–81

CHALKER, Baroness Linda UK Minister for Overseas Development, 1989–97

CHAMBERS, General Bear (US Air Force) Air Commander, Allied Forces South, Naples

CHRISTOPHER, Warren US Secretary of State, 1993–97

CHURKIN, Vitaly Russian Special Envoy to former Yugoslavia, 1993–94

CLINTON, Bill President of the United States since 1993

CORVAULT, Lt-General (US Army) Chief of Staff to Admiral Leighton Smith

COSTELLO, Captain Nick (British Army) Interpreter and Liaison Officer to General Rose

COT, General Jean (French Army) UNPROFOR Commander in former Yugoslavia, 1993–94

CUNY, Fred Head of the International Rescue Committee, based in Texas; missing Chechnya, 1995

DALY, Lance Sergeant Mick (Coldstream Guards) orderly to General Rose

DANIELL, Lieutenant-Colonel James Military Assistant to General Rose

DAVIDSON-HOUSTON, Lieutenant-Colonel Patrick, Officer Commanding Royal Gloucestershire, Berkshire and Wiltshire Regiment

DELIC, General Rasim Commander of Bosnian Army

DEZONIE, Wing Commander Des (Royal Air Force) Officer Commanding NATO Air Cell, Sarajevo

DIVJAK, Major-General Deputy Commander of Bosnian Army

DOLE, Senator Bob   US Senator for Kansas, 1969–96

DUDAKOVIC, Major-General   Commander of 5th Corps, Bosnian Army, Bihac

EVANS, Glynne   Head of UN Department, UK Foreign and Commonwealth Office

FRASER, Major David   (Canadian Army) Military Assistant to French Commander, Sector Sarajevo

GALVIN, General John   Supreme Allied Commander Europe, 1987–92

GANIC, Ejup   Vice-President of Bosnia-Hercegovina, 1992–96; Vice-President Federation of Bosnia-Hercegovina, 1994–96

GOBILLARD, Brigadier-General Hervé   French Commander, Sector Sarajevo, 1994–95

GOOSE   (Parachute Regiment, British Army) Driver and bodyguard to General Rose

GORDON, Brigadier Robert   Commander of UN South-West Sector, Bosnia-Hercegovina

GVERO, Major-General Milan   Deputy Army Commander, Bosnian Serb Army

HANNAY, Sir David   UK Permanent Representative to the UN, New York, 1990–95

HAJRULAHOVIC, Brigadier   (Bosnian Army) Chief of Operations, Sarajevo

HEWLETT, Wing-Commander Tim   (Royal Air Force) Officer Commanding NATO Air Cell, Sarajevo

HOLBROOKE, Richard   US Assistant Secretary of State 1994–

HOLLINGWORTH, Larry   Head of UNHCR, central Bosnia

HURD, Rt Hon. Douglas   UK Secretary of State for Foreign and Commonwealth Affairs, 1989–95

INDIC, Major   (Bosnian Serb Army) Intelligence Officer to General Mladic

INGE, General Sir Peter   Chief of General Staff and later Chief of Defence Staff, 1994–97

IZETBEGOVIC, Alija   President of Bosnia-Hercegovina, 1990–96; co-President of Federation of Bosnia-Hercegovina since 1996

JACKOVITCH, Victor   US Ambassador, Sarajevo, 1994

JOULWAN, General George   Supreme Allied Commander Europe, 1993–97

JUPPÉ, Alain   Foreign Minister of France 1994–95; Prime Minister, 1995–97

KARADZIC, Dr Radovan   President of self-declared Republika Srpska, resigned 1996; international arrest warrant issued July 1996 for alleged war crimes

KARAVELIC, Major-General   Commander of Bosnian forces on Mount Igman

KOLJEVIC, Nikola   Bosnian Serb leader, committed suicide 1996

KOZYREV, Andrei   Foreign Minister of Russian Federation

KRAJISNIK, Momcilo   Bosnian Serb leader; former President of the Assembly of Bosnia-Hercegovina

KRESEVLJAKOVIC, Mohammed   Mayor of Sarajevo, 1994

LANXADE, Admiral   Jacques Chief of Defence of French Armed Forces, 1991–95

LAPRESLE, Bertrand de   (French Army) UNPROFOR Commander in Former Yugoslavia 1994–95

LEGRIER, Colonel   Commander of French battalion "Frebat 3", Bihac

LEMIEUX, Colonel Charles ("Chuck")   (Canadian Army) Commander UNPROFOR Forward HQ, Bihac

LEVAK, Major William ("Willie")   (British Army) Intelligence Officer to General Rose

MACLEAN, Sir Fitzroy   Founder member of the Special Air Service; Winston Churchill's personal representative and commander of the British military mission to the partisans in German-occupied Yugoslavia; Under-Secretary of State for War.

MAJOR, Rt. Hon. John,   Prime Minister of the United Kingdom, 1990–97

MARGESSON, Major The Hon. Richard   No. 3 Company Commander, Coldstream Guards

MELLO, Sergio Vieira de   UN Head of Civil Affairs, Bosnia-Hercegovina and former Yugoslavia (on loan from UNHCR)

MENZIES, John   US Ambassador, Sarajevo, 1994–95

MILOSEVIC, Slobodan   President of Serbia, 1990–97; President of Yugoslavia, since 1997

MILOVANOVIC, Major-General Manojlo   (Bosnian Serb Army) Chief of Staff to General Mladic

MITTERRAND, François   President of France, 1981–1995

MLADIC, General Ratko   Commander of the Bosnian Serb Army; international arrest warrant issued July 1996 for alleged war crimes

MORRILLON, Lt-General Philippe   (French Army) Commander UNPROFOR in Bosnia, 1993

MORRIS, Nicholas   Head of UNHCR mission to former Yugoslavia

MURATOVIC, Hassan Minister for Co-operation with UNPROFOR

MURPHY, Colm   UN Press Spokesman, Sarajevo

NEVILLE-JONES, Pauline   Political Director, Foreign and Commonwealth Office

OGATA, Sadako   UN High Commissioner for Refugees since 1991

OWEN, David The Lord   Co-Chairman of the Steering Committee of the International Conference on the Former Yugoslavia, 1992–95

PANIC, Milan   Prime Minister of the former Republic of Yugoslavia (Serbia and Montenegro), 1992

PEARCE, Colour Sergeant "Percy"   (Coldstream Guards) Member of General Rose's Staff

PERRY, Dr William   US Defense Secretary, 1994–97

PRICHARD, Lieutenant-Colonel Rupert   (British Army) Deputy Chief UNMO, Zagreb

PRLJEVLJAK, Fikret   Muslim Brigade Commander of the Mount Igman region

RATAZZI, Brigadier Roy   (British Army) British Chief of Staff to UN HQ, Zagreb

REDMAN, Charles   US Special Envoy to the former Yugoslavia, 1993–94

REITH, Brigadier John   Commander South-West Sector, Bosnia-Hercegovina, December 1993–May 1994

RIDGEWAY, Brigadier Andrew   Commander South-West Sector, Bosnia-Hercegovina, May 1994–November 1994

RIDDERSTADT, Brigadier   (Swedish Army) Commander North-West Sector, Bosnia-Hercegovina

RIFKIND, Rt. Hon. Malcolm   UK Defence Secretary, 1992–95; Foreign Secretary, 1995–97

ROSO, Lt-General Anto   Bosnian Croat Army Commander, 1996

ROUS, Lieutenant-General The Hon. Sir William   (Coldstream Guards); Military Secretary, Ministry of Defence, 1991–94

RUDD, Colonel Gordon   (US Marines) Liaison Officer, Sarajevo

SACIRBEY, Mohammed   Bosnian Government Representative to the UN 1992–95

SADIC, Major-General Hazim   Commander of 2nd Bosnian Army

SALIM, Colonel   Commander of UN Bangladeshi battalion, Bihac

SANTA OLLALA, Lieutenant-Colonel David   Officer Commanding Duke of Wellington's Regiment

SCHORK, Kurt   Foreign Correspondent, Reuters

SCHROEDER, Colonel Clifton   (US Marines) Liaison Officer, Sarajevo

SHADBOLT, Lieutenant-Colonel Simon   (Royal Marines) Military Assistant to General Rose

SHALIKASHVILI, General John   Supreme Allied Commander Europe, 1992–93; Chairman, Joint Chiefs of Staff, USA, 1993–97

SILAJDZIC, Haris   Prime Minister of Bosnia-Hercegovina, 1993–96; Co-Chairman newly formed Government of Bosnia and Hercegovina, since 1996

SIMPSON, John   Editor, World Affairs Unit, BBC

SISAK, Major   (Bosnian Army) Liaison Officer to US Embassy, Sarajevo

SOAMES, Nicholas   UK Minister for the Armed Forces

SMITH, Admiral Leighton (US Navy)   Commander in Chief Allied Forces South, Naples

SMITH, Lieutenant-General Rupert   (British Army) UNPROFOR Commander in Bosnia-Hercegovina, 1995

SOUBIROU, Brigadier-General André   French Commander, Sector Sarajevo

STANLEY, Major Mike   Interpreter and Liaison Officer to General Rose

STEINER, Michael   German member of Contact Group

STOLTENBERG, Thorvald   Special Representative of UN Secretary-General for the former Yugoslavia, 1993–94; UN peace negotiator, the former Yugoslavia, 1993–96

SWINBURN, Lieutenant-General Sir Richard   Deputy Commander-in-Chief, UK Land Forces; Commander UK Field Army, 1994–95

THAROOR, Shashi   Under Secretary, United Nations HQ, New York

THOMAS, Charles   US Envoy to the former Yugoslavia, 1994; US member of Contact Group

TOLIMIR, Brigadier-General   Staff Assistant to General Mladic

TUDJMAN, Franjo   President of Croatia since 1990

VAN BAAL, Brigadier   (Dutch Army) Chief of Staff to General Rose

VANCE, Cyrus   Co-Chairman of the Steering Committee of the International Conference on the former Yugoslavia, 1991–92

VERE HAYES, Brigadier   (British Army) Chief of Staff to General Briquemont

VOROBIEV, Colonel   Officer Commanding Russian UN battalion, Sarajevo

WATERS, Captain George   (Coldstream Guards) aide-de-camp to General Rose

WILLIAMS, Lt-Colonel Peter   Officer Commanding, Coldstream Guards

WILSEY, General Sir John   Joint Commander British Forces in Former Republic of Yugoslavia 1993–96

ZAMETICA, Jovan   Staff Officer to Radovan Karadzic, Pale

ZUBAK, Kresimir   Croat Head of Bosnian Federation

ZAMETICA, Joan   Staff Officer to Radovan Karadzic, Pale

INDEX